EARLIER THAN YOU THINK

Earlier than You Think

A PERSONAL VIEW OF
MAN IN AMERICA

BY

George F. Carter

TEXAS A&M UNIVERSITY PRESS

College Station

Library of Congress Cataloging in Publication Data

Carter, George Francis, 1912–
    Earlier than you think.
    Bibliography: p.
    Includes index.
    1. Paleo-Indians. 2. America—Antiquities.
3. Dating in archaeology. I. Title.
E61.C34   970.01   79-5280
ISBN 0-89096-091-7

Contents

Illustrations

TABLES

Preface

IT has long been my contention that man entered America with a Lower Paleolithic culture about 100,000 years ago. This time figure is based on the estimate of the last interglacial according to the dating that was current about 25 years ago. As will be seen, Pleistocene dating is in a state of flux, but the date still seems to be the right order of magnitude. Most of the field of American archeology has in this period clung to a 12,000-year first entry date and has attributed that entry to a people with an Upper Paleolithic hunting specialization. This difference of opinion has engendered considerable heat but not a proportionate amount of light.

After writing *Pleistocene Man at San Diego* (1957), in which I presented at considerable length the geomorphology of the San Diego area and placed the archeology in the geomorphic chronology, I withdrew for about fifteen years. We had reached the 'tis-'tain't stage, and it was clear that only new sites or dating methods were going to change the position of the majority. With H. L. Minshall's discovery of the Buchanan Canyon site in 1970 (Moriarty and Minshall, 1972; Minshall, 1974, 1975, 1976) and W. M. Childers' finds in the Imperial Valley (1974, 1977a, 1977b) as well as R. D. Simpson's important site in the Mohave Desert, the Calico site (Simpson and Schuiling, 1970), it became clear that the needed further information as to sites and lithic industries was appearing. New dating systems also have been developed: 0-18, U/Th, obsidian hydration, superhydration, thermoluminescence, fission tracking, protein racemization, fluorine penetration. All of these have the potential of identifying very high dates. far beyond that of C-14, which has been unable to date the earliest traces of man in America. Even C-14 dating may now be greatly extended by directly counting the atoms rather than their breakdown (Grootes, 1978). We are, then, in the midst of a revolution in dating.

It has often been suggested that I should again present my views on the earliest Americans, but, apart from some articles, I have resisted. Without new data, it seemed pointless to continue to fly in the face of the whole field. Now that a younger generation, better trained in lithic technology, can recognize the early lithic industries and the new dating systems are showing the proper time placement of these materials, it seems worthwhile to set out the picture of early man in America as seen from San Diego. I will not limit myself entirely to San Diego, but since that is the area I know best, that is where I can best demonstrate the cultural sequence and its chronological placement.

My interest in the archeology of the San Diego area is lengthy. Beginning in 1927, I haunted the San Diego Museum of Man, where Malcolm Rogers was then the curator. Since I was a most persistent pest, Rogers undertook to control me by allowing me to do volunteer work in the museum, and beginning in 1927 I spent many afternoons there, happily washing and drying and numbering artifacts. M. J. Rogers was to be a powerful influence in my life for the next ten years. He took me to San Nicolas Island in 1930 as his assistant on a five-week expedition to that out-of-the-way corner of the world and on many shorter field trips along the coast, into the Mohave and Colorado deserts, and into Baja California. I went off to the University of California, where I earned a B.A. degree in anthropology under such luminaries as A. L. Kroeber, Robert Lowie, E. W. Gifford, and Ronald Olson. In the depths of the depression, when jobs were incredibly scarce, Rogers hired me at the San Diego Museum of Man with the grandiloquent title of curator of anthropology and the magnificent salary of seventy-five dollars per month. I flourished at the museum until my increasingly radical thinking about early man in America made me a burr under the saddle and I was eased out of my job. Our relationship terminated when I breached the time barrier: not 4,000, but 40,000—now, 100,000 years.

Through a curious twist of events, I was drafted immediately as part-time teaching assistant in geography at San Diego State College under Alvena Suhl Storm, my first geography teacher and the wife of my old Sea Scout skipper. She and Lauren Post were soon urging me to go to Berkeley to study under Carl Sauer. Vaguely

I knew of Sauer's anthropological, archeological, and cultural-historical interests, and I hoped that in geography I could get the climatology, geomorphology, and other earth sciences that, it was becoming increasingly obvious, were the keys to the antiquity of man in America. It was an enormously enriching experience to add onto ten years of field archeology and cultural anthropology. I was deflected into southwestern agriculture for a Ph.D. thesis. Then came Pearl Harbor and a journey into the East to fight in the battle of the Potomac and to hold a position at the Johns Hopkins University.

When the war was over, I began a decade-long period of summers at San Diego, studying the geomorphology of that region in relation to the time of the arrival of man. Geomorphology includes some geology, that part that influences the surface of the earth. I concentrated on the phenomena that could be related to the changing events of the Pleistocene: sea levels, terraces, soils, and climates. It was my plan to build a time scale built on geomorphology and then to place man in that framework. I did, and man fell into the last interglacial period, around 100,000 years ago.

My approach to knowledge is to assemble as many lines of evidence as possible. It is not enough that some broken rocks look old because they are of crude workmanship. They must also show age by their degree of weathering or their geologic placement or be datable by some geophysical system such as C-14. Ideally, one would have at least three systems in use for any chronological placement. I am sometimes accused of constructing my chronology solely on typology: if a tool looks crude, it is old. No one who has read my work could ever say that.

The apology for this personal note is that it explains why a geographer dares to intrude on the sacred soil of the archeologist. I started as an archeologist, broadened into an archeologist with physical earth-science background, and added cultural-historical interests. Through it all, my interest has centered on the question of time.

What one does is to some extent an accident of history, one's personal history. What is done and not done, accepted or rejected is also strongly historically conditioned. Leonardo's notions of airplanes and tanks were ideas born out of their time. He was a Connecticut Yankee in Renaissance Italy, and in less spectacular ways this misfit phenomenon is commonplace. Acceptance and rejection of ideas often depends on idiosyncracies of individuals, the accidents of position, and such character traits as pugnacity, productivity, and perseverance. Kroeber in his great book, *Anthropology* (1948), has a marvelous chapter on the role of personality among the inventors of steamboats. The real inventors—there were several —failed, usually from personality difficulties that prevented their getting backing for their projects. My place in the early-man controversy is with these perverse creatures. I have been ahead of my time and in conflict with the established authorities, whom I have more often annoyed than convinced.

All fields of endeavor tend to stick in well-defined ruts; their paradigm becomes the sole model of how to attack the currently fashionable problem. The breakthrough discoveries often languish because they are outside the rut, and change comes like a train jumping the track. Kuhn has caught the essence of this pattern in his *Structure of Scientific Revolutions* (1970). Because such elements, although nonscholarly and unscientific in the usual sense, are actually such powerful forces in the real world of inquiry, whether in the humanities or the sciences, some of the personal factors and personality conflicts underlying my study of early man will be included throughout the book.

This means that this work will depart from the usual scientific report. I have not written it for the narrow scientist. It is meant for the educated layman. Jargon is kept to a minimum, and just enough technical detail is included to make the whole picture understandable. I have selected from several thousand articles and books in my personal collection the material that seems to illustrate best the themes dealt with. Selection implies omissions, and any man's work must be judged by the judiciousness of his choice. It is always possible to point to omissions, and I am probably guilty of some important ones.

No man is an island, for we all are in debt to others for ideas, support, and challenges that led to further thought and work and changes of direction and conclusions. When one has been at work in an area for fifty years, the list of those to whom one is indebted is embarrassingly long, and it is impossible to name everyone. At the risk of offending those who could well be included, I will mention some key people.

Malcolm Rogers of the San Diego Museum of Man started me on my way when I was a high school boy. Though we drifted tens of millenia apart, I owe him a great deal. Alvena Storm and Lauren Post of San Diego State University intervened at a critical point in my scholarly life and sent me on into graduate work in geography with Carl Sauer at Berkeley, an invaluable, immensely broadening experience. During ten long summers of fieldwork at San Diego, Carl Hubbs was a challenging friendly critic. Later Phil Orr of the Santa Barbara Museum of Natural History introduced me to work in the Lahontan area and made it possible for me to visit Santa Rosa Island. Ruth DeEtte Simpson has been a friendly critic with whom it has always been a pleasure to work. Herb Minshall, a friend from childhood and a co-worker in archeology, has proved to be a stimulating and critical thinker and a perceptive and energetic field man. More recently, W. M. Childers of El Centro has been a source of new information and a hard man to convince—a most valuable trait. Thomas Lee, courageous editor of the *Canadian Journal of Anthropology*, has been a long-term friend. Junius Bird has long been a hard-headed critic, but always with the greatest gentleness, and he now accepts some of the most controversial materials. At the San Diego Museum of Man, Spencer Rogers and Rose Tyson have been most helpful, and at the San Diego Museum of Natural History it has been Ray Gilmore who gave help when needed. The list could be greatly extended, and I apologize to the many friendly critics as well as the warm supporters not mentioned here. To these and many others I am deeply indebted.

I have worked with several men in attempts to date material. Wallace Broecker showed charcoal from the Texas Street site to be beyond the C-14 range. Jeffrey Bada of the Scripps Institution of Oceanography has used protein racemization to provide revolutionary dates for human skeletons in the region. I have worked recently with Edward Zeller of the University of Kansas on thermoluminescence dating and with Douglas MacDougle at the Scripps Institution of Oceanography on fission-trace dating—with inconclusive results from both methods so far. Soils men from the U.S.D.A.

Regional Salinity Laboratory at Riverside have aided me, and numerous geologists and geomorphologists have looked over the sites. To these and many others I am deeply grateful.

I have borrowed ideas here, there, and everywhere. After a time working with others and exchanging ideas, it becomes difficult to know just which idea is yours, which is mine, and which is some amalgam. Some of the best ideas here will probably be due to some of those named above. The bad ideas are surely mine; some of the good, surely theirs; but full responsibility is all mine.

Although I regret some of the things said and done by me and to me, my aim has always been to keep the channels of communication open. With some people such as Junius Bird and Carl Hubbs, it is possible to carry on decades of dialogue, more often in disagreement than in agreement, without a ripple of personal antagonism. This is unfortunately rare. I tend to argue vigorously, but I try to do so without anger. I expressed this goal best, perhaps, in my invocation for the Friends of the Pleistocene, when I met with them at San Diego to inspect the sites and soils of the San Diego area in the fall of 1975.

> O ye gods of ice and snow
> That make the glaciers rise and flow
> And the mighty seas to come and go,
> Heed our pleas both con and pro
> And part us friends
> And never foes.

Would that it could be so!

EARLIER THAN YOU THINK

Chapter 1

Introduction

THERE are few questions about America before Columbus that are not controversial. The only thing that everyone agrees on is that man did not originate in America, but that he came here belatedly. In comparison with the million-year history of man in Eurasia and Africa, the history of man in America is short, but how short is the question. Is it 2,000, 4,000, 10,000, 25,000, or 100,000 years? All but the highest of these dates have been defended by distinguished professional anthropologists within my scholarly lifetime. I have proposed that the real date is near 100,000 years.

Few things are so difficult to measure as time. For most of human history mankind did not worry about it. For biblical writers, a recitation of begats sufficed to indicate lineal origins, which were important to them, and to suggest time depth, the exact extent of which was unimportant to them. The inspired writers of the Bible had eternal verities not timetables on their minds. Our concern with absolute time and our concept of vast reaches of time are phenomena that mark little more than the last one hundred years. We now are asking somewhat different questions in very different ways than men did in the past, for we are greatly concerned with the processes of change, and process and change always involve time. So it is that we must deal with measures of time and the history of our concept of time, and that we will do in a later chapter.

The problem of race is almost as difficult as the problem of time. Is there an American Indian race? Or are there several races among Indians? Is the racial picture the result of the inflow of one kind of man that diverged in America in response to the environments in which men lived? Or was the incoming population already racially mixed? Perhaps there was not one migration but two, or perhaps several, maybe many. Is it possible that long after the initial wave or waves of land-bound immigrants, there were biologically significant numbers of seaborne immigrants to further complicate the situation?

Are there blonds in the cloudy areas, blacks in the sunny zones, and browns in between, as in the Old World? There are not. What is the meaning of this? Such changes in color would not be expectable in 10,000 years of environmental differences, might be expectable in 100,000 years, would be expectable in 500,000 years, and certainly would occur in 1 million years. Time is of the essence in all of these questions. And here in the New World evidence is likely to tell us something about the Old World, for we do not know when distinctive skin color appeared in the Old World, and we will never learn it from skeletons. However long man has been in the New World, the time has been insufficient to color men here as they are colored there.

Man probably entered America from Asia, but does this necessarily mean that he was a classic Mongoloid? Time is critical here, too. We have thought in short time spans, adjacent geography, and modern racial distributions: 5,000 or 10,000 years, Siberia, and Mongoloids. But if the time since man's New World arrival is 100,000 or 200,000 years, perhaps we should be considering just what men occupied east Asia at those times. Perhaps we should be looking farther afield: to southeast Asia, with side glances perhaps as far as Africa, which is now supplying the most knowledge about man's origin and greatly expanding the timetable. Even those adventurous souls of the last few decades who dared think in the 20,000- to 30,000-year time frame and especially those who looked hard at Eskimo origins found themselves pondering the intricate and detailed similarities between Eskimo hunting equipment and that of the Upper Paleolithic Europeans. The greater the time, the wider our geographic net should be cast. To stretch the simile, perhaps we have been casting our nets in the temporal shallows and catching minnows while the big game fish eluded us in the deeps.

The race problem has historical and amusing sides to it. When the Spaniards discovered America, they thought they had stumbled onto a whole new world. No one in the Mediterranean—Spaniard, Portuguese, or Italian—had any lingering knowledge of America in the fifteenth century, although their ancestors had probably been here centuries earlier, and the discovery of whole continents threw

Europe into turmoil. Not the least troublesome question concerned the people in these new lands. Who were they? Were they really men descended from Adam, Noah, et al., or were they the result of some separate creation? It is hard now for us to conceive of such questions, but they serve us well, for they measure the shock of the discovery. Perhaps if our space mariners return with news of sentient beings on other planets, we will relive the experience. But these were not "other beings." These were ordinary men and women of varied hue, though mostly some shade of dusky brown that the Europeans called red, a poor choice. Even if white, black, and yellow were preempted, why not brown? Perhaps it is as with eggs. The Mexicans call brown-shelled eggs *colorado*, red, and *colorado*, reddish brown, the American Indians were dubbed; hence, "red skins," a term much better applied to an Irishman after a long day in the sun.

The Europeans were Bible-oriented, and, while there is much good in biblical studies, unfortunate attempts were made to account for the Indians as one of the Israelite tribes, a lost one. However, Europeans had used up all the tribes long ago in folkloristic explanations of the peopling of the earth, and so these unexpected people in a New World posed problems. If the Indians could not be accounted for in biblical terms, were they then really sons of God, true men? This was referred to the Pope, who replied: They are true men and have all the rights of other men, and your duty as Christians is to bring them the message of the Gospels. The priests tried, but they were few, and the conquistadors were many. The Indians were treated shabbily: a little Christianity and a lot of slavery.

The problem then became: if these are men and they came from the same area as the rest of men, how did they get off here in these strange lands? Astonishingly early this got a remarkably astute answer. Father Acosta noted that not only were the human beings of this New World like men elsewhere, but so were many of the plants and animals. For example, quail, rabbits, ducks, and deer were much like those of Europe. He considered the possibility that men might have come to the Americas by boat and brought the animals. However, he noted that the Americas had poisonous snakes and dangerous animals such as *el tigre*, the giant cat of tropical America. Surely man would not have brought these. So, he reasoned, the

animals must have walked (crept, flown or slithered) in by some
land connection, and, if the animals did, so could man have. By
this time the Spaniards had discovered the Pacific and explored a
part of the Pacific coast. They knew that there was no land connection in the Atlantic, and Father Acosta therefore concluded that the
indicated connection must lie to the northwest, in the unknown
north Pacific region. And of course there is a connection there: the
now barely drowned land bridge at Bering Strait. We know that
through geologic time (millions of years) plants and animals have
migrated back and forth across this bridge at times when it was
not submerged. Redwoods from Asia, horses and camels from
America, moose and buffalo from Asia, mastodons early and mammoths later to America: the traffic would have been formidable if
the time had not been so long and the bridge so wide.

If plants and animals, why not man? We still think that this is
indeed the way the earliest men reached America. Perhaps it was
not the only way, and it surely was not a one-way street. Man went
back and forth over a long time period. Problems arise, however,
when one finds evidence of truly primitive, very early men in America.

Is Bering Strait a feasible route for Lower Paleolithic men,
men presumably ill equipped for life in the Arctic? Is there no
other way? If not, what is the Bering Strait like now? What was it
like in the past? Here again time and the associated cultural problems become entangled. Eskimos can cross at Bering almost any
time. How far back can we project Eskimo-like cultural equipment?
Perhaps 20,000 or 30,000 years if we look to Europe and Upper
Paleolithic cultures. If we have earlier dates in America than that,
then what do we conclude? Did earlier men live in more extreme
climates? How extreme and how early? Could men 100,000 and
200,000 years ago be candidates for arctic passages? This is a complex problem in geomorphology, physical climatology, and physiological climatology, with interesting findings.

On a short time scale, say 10,000 years, we must expect our
first entrants via the Bering Strait to have been modern Asiatics,
equipped for arctic life, largely of one group of mankind, who
spread swiftly over America and quickly generated civilization. Such
was once our view. Now we see greater antiquity, and the problems

change. What kind of man becomes what kind of men, and what culture becomes what cultures.

In the 1930's we were taught that the first immigrants entered America about 5,000 years ago, just prior to the beginning of the Neolithic, the time of revolutionary changes in life-style marked by the beginning of domestication of plants and animals. Some deny that such thoughts were ever entertained by enlightened anthropologists. One has but to consult the 1923 edition of A. L. Kroeber's *Anthropology* to see that at that time this great man considered that the earliest entrants to America brought the bow and arrow with them—an implement now thought to date in America to not much before the time of Christ. See Kroeber's figure 35, page 340, in the 1923 edition. To be fair to Kroeber, he identified the first entrants as probably early Neolithic but mentioned the possibility that they might have been Upper Paleolithic, though he obviously thought that if this were so they were late Upper Paleolithic. He was comfortable with a 5,000-year date and not opposed to a 10,000-year date. In his most extreme position, Kroeber (1973) expressed a preference for the theory of the entry of a single, pure race of men about 2,000 years ago—a position so extreme as to defy comprehension.

In the 1920's and 1930's, we were indeed thinking of early Neolithic, 5,000-year beginnings as probable and earlier dates as only possible. Only reluctantly were the Paleo-Indians, the Great Hunters, accorded 10,000- to 12,000-year age and status as representatives of an Upper Paleolithic cultural level. This change pales beside the challenge, now maintained for a quarter-century that states that the Paleo-Indians mark the beginning of the late period in America, not the real beginning of man in America. Instead, a lengthy and complex Lower Paleolithic is thought to mark American beginnings. This concept has been bitterly contested but is steadily gaining ground as physical-chemical dating methods more and more support the thesis of high antiquity for primitive lithic industries. It is this Lower Paleolithic stratum, or more correctly strata, that will be emphasized here. If it exists, then its bearers were the first Americans.

One has to defend the use of European terms such as Neolithic, Upper Paleolithic, and Lower Paleolithic. The implications of similar ages and of direct relationships and diffusion of knowledge raise hackles all too often. I will use the terms primarily to indicate similar cultural stages: domestic plants and animals mark the Neolithic; varied kinds of specialized stone tools and some indication of specialization in hunting large animals mark the Upper Paleolithic lifeway. I will present evidence suggesting that the Middle Paleolithic is marked by a turn toward a gathering specialization in hard-seeded plants. The Lower Paleolithic was a period of simple, often heavy, stone tools, usually unspecialized and apparently primarily for the working of wood—to make the spears and other wooden implements that dominated the technology. If the terms are used in this way, then the words *Neolithic* and *Paleolithic* are helpful for describing stages in man's cultural development. The ages of these stages are highly varied. Some men lingered in the Lower Paleolithic right into the seventeenth century: Tasmanians, Australians, and a few others. The stage need not imply a particular time. Indeed, as table 1 shows, a given cultural stage, with its distinctive technology, would have appeared at quite different times in Eurasia than in America. It is obvious in the table that nearly everything is later in America and that the discrepancies get much larger as time deepens. The discrepancy between the appearance of metals or the Neolithic in the Old World and the New World is only a few thousand years, but the discrepancy between the appearance of pebble tools looks more like a million years. Northeast Asia may have been an area of vast cultural lag, or our dates may be off, or pebble tools may just be one of those things that man produces when he has pebbles to work with.

Quite another set of questions arises when one finds that the people he is dealing with not only are on a particular stage but are making specific tools to the same pattern as men elsewhere in the world who are at that stage. Is this due to functionalism and limited possibilities? The La Jollan stone tools of southern California are virtual duplicates of southeast Asian tools. One set was being made right into the end of the nineteenth century, and the other had its inception in the Lower Paleolithic of Asia, a few hundred thousand years ago. They are also separated about as far as possible on this well-rounded earth of ours, with a vast ocean in between and only an arctic passage if one insists on a walking relationship. At first

TABLE 1

Man, Time, and Culture

Years B.P.	Geologic	Biological	Cultural/Technological — Eurasia	America
1,500				METALS
5,000			METALS	NEOLITHIC
7,000			NEOLITHIC	ARCHAIC
10,000	**Recent**	*Homo sapiens sapiens*	MESOLITHIC	UPPER PALEOLITHIC Folsom Clovis
12,000	**Pleistocene**			
30,000		*Homo sapiens* Cro Magnon	UPPER PALEOLITHIC fine blades	MIDDLE PALEOLITHIC heavy unifaces
60,000				
70,000				
80,000				
100,000		Neanderthal	MIDDLE PALEOLITHIC uniface flakes	LOWER PALEOLITHIC heavy bifaces heavy blades pebble tools or steep edge
500,000		*Homo erectus* Swanscombe Choukoutien	LOWER PALEOLITHIC heavy unifaces and heavy blades (Southeast Asia) heavy bifaces (Eurafrica) pebble tools	
1,000,000				

NOTE: It is most difficult to arrange a table that is both simple enough and not too misleading. This is intended as an introductory guide, and many of the terms and dates will be explained and defended in the text.

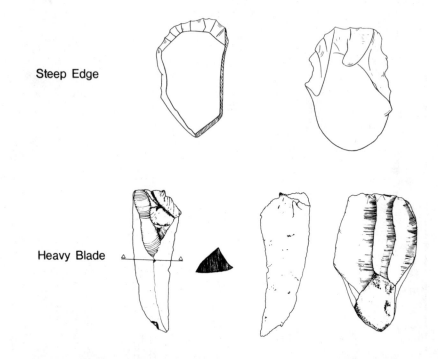

Steep Edge

Heavy Blade

FIGURE 1. The basic stages of lithic work in America are shown across these two pages. The two pieces on the top of this page represent steep edge work. Compare the short, steep flakes on the left-hand piece of this pair with the longer flakes on the younger, bifaced pieces on the top of the facing page. The right-hand steep edge piece here is a flaked cobble or pebble and hence a pebble tool. The second row on this page shows typical heavy blades, with their elongate outline and triangular cross section. The type of core from which such blades are struck is shown on the right end of the row.

glance, then, it seems most unlikely that there is any meaningful connection: not diffusion of a basic idea of how to work stone, but a case of limited possibilities and the inevitable duplication of lithic technologies. However, there are other straws in the wind. There are similar wooden tools, and there are some similarities in the areas of religion, ritual, and belief—areas of infinite possibilities for variation and, hence, of reduced probability of duplication. At this point, we can turn to highly specific comparisons, and the probability of real connections, difficult as they seem at first glance in terms of time and distance, must be reckoned with. When we

Biface

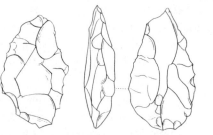

Uniface

Paleo Indian

The top row on this page illustrates bifacial flaking to produce heavy core tools. These are often called elongate or ovate bifaces in order to avoid calling them by the Old World term, hand ax. The middle row shows two typical pieces of uniface work. The bottom row's illustration is a fluted point to stand for the Paleo-Indian period, which initiated the making of finely flaked knives and spear points, around 12,000 years ago.

Scales differ for these artifacts.

reach this point in the discussion, I will become specific: particular times and peoples and opportunities for spread of men and ideas—in other words, the diffusion of a particular culture. At other times I will use such terms as Neolithic and Paleolithic in the general sense of a stage of development.

One of the thorniest problems for early-man advocates concerns the identification of stone tools. For the later tools there is no problem, but the earliest stone tools are sometimes said to be just naturally broken rocks or else preforms—that is, roughed out or unfinished tools—or just quarry debris, the discarded broken rock left by later men. If one does not expect or accept the possibility of Lower Paleolithic men in America but acknowledges only men of 10,000 years, then such views of early-type stonework are forced upon one. Suppose, however, that the time of man's entry is 100,000 years ago? Then one must consider at least Middle Paleolithic stone technologies and probably Lower Paleolithic work. This calls for hand axes and chopping tools—heavy, unrefined work typical of early man (see figure 1 for a sketch of various tool types). Expectable becomes acceptable, and conversely the unexpected is unacceptable. Our preconceptions always color our views.

But when is a broken stone an artifact, that is, made by man, and when is it a geofact, something broken by nature? Is it difficult or easy to determine this? The problem has been blown out of all proportion, but since it is part of the folklore of archeology that nature frequently breaks rocks, all kinds of rocks, in ways that simulate man's work, this topic must be dealt with. The history of our learning to recognize man's handiwork is as stormy as all the other problems. One hundred years ago in Europe, scholars refused to accept hand axes as evidence of human work partly because they were unfamiliar with such tools and partly because the axes were being found with the bones of extinct animals in ancient river gravels of obviously great age. Boucher de Perthes is described by Boule and Vallois (1957) as struggling for decades to win recognition of "these most obvious artifacts," as Haynes (1973) has dubbed them, inferring that of course archeologists would recognize the obvious. He forgot that Europeans would not or could not. The two words are closely connected. In America we are still struggling with the problem of recognizing blade and core work—obviously the work of man, once you have learned its diagnostic traits, but work that American archeologists tend to reject when it turns up in ancient river gravels that "are too old for man in America." I am more identified with this controversy than anyone else in America. If an archeologist finds a trace of man, a crude stone tool, it is an artifact. But if Carter finds it, it is a cartifact— evidence not for early man, but for Carter's folly.

The general setting then is this. In the 1900 to 1930 period, man in America was thought not only to be a recent arrival, meaning postglacial, but probably to have been here for only about 5,000 years and perhaps a good deal less. He arrived with the bow and arrow, but without agriculture and metallurgy. In the 1930 to 1960 period, a pre–bow and arrow American Indian level was grudgingly admitted, and the time was established as 12,000 years ago. It was generally admitted that this was a cultural equivalent to the Old World Upper Paleolithic, though obviously somewhat younger. By 1940 serious claims for the early peopling of America by people on a Lower Paleolithic level at a time of about 100,000 years ago—in the last interglacial—began to appear. This was greeted just as the Upper Paleolithic material had been: with incredulous anger. Nevertheless, accumulating evidence is nudging the field along: from 10 or 12 thousand certain and 15 or 20 thousand possible to probably 20 or 30 or possibly 30 or 40 thousand. The direction of movement is clear, even if the end is not.

I will deal first with some of the personalities and the conflicts that arise between strong-minded men in a controversial field and then move on to the problem of determining time, tools, cultures, and men. Throughout, personalities will be allowed to intrude, lest the details of time and glaciers and sea levels and landforms and broken rocks make a lively field seem dull. With this introduction the nature of the controversy should be clear, and we can move through personalities to problems of measuring time and recognizing artifacts, to some classic sites, and then to the related problems of such things as the Bering bridge and the men that did and did not cross it.

Chapter 2

Feet of Clay

When the antiquity of man was first proclaimed from the
discovery of the Abbeville flints by Boucher de Perthes, no
one believed it. Everybody thought him like the mad man
who swore all the world was mad; and so it seemed,
then, as if all the world had mental obliquity of vision,
which made them declare our savant of Abbeville to be
labouring under a delusion.

Mackie, 1862 (quoted in Gruber, 1948)

FAR too often results are presented in a most impersonal way, and
the conflict of personalities that underlies and often challenges the
findings being presented is blandly ignored. Reality is not at all like
that, for scientists are human beings and more often filled with
pride and ambition than most people. They defend their ideas with
the ferocity of a mother bear for her cubs. In vain has it been
pointed out over and over again that ideas once launched should be
viewed dispassionately as if they had no parentage. We simply cannot do that. Our ideas are our children, and we cling to them and
defend them, right or wrong.

First, some comments may help to explain the ferocity of the
conflict between men who are presumably of good will and all
seeking to advance knowledge. My claims concerning the antiquity
of man have been far out of step with the field—100,000 years,
not 10,000. This is shown in graph form in figure 2. If I was right,
a lot of experts were holding the wrong line: no men in America
before Recent times, the period after the Ice Age (Pleistocene
period). Or, if men arrived in the Pleistocene, they were here only
in its last gasp, say for a thousand years or so. With this claim go
bushels of assumptions. If man is so recent, he is fully modern
man when he gets to America, he has already developed tool kits,
and so forth. My claim has been that he came early, with primitive
tool kits, and perhaps was not even fully modern man. We—the

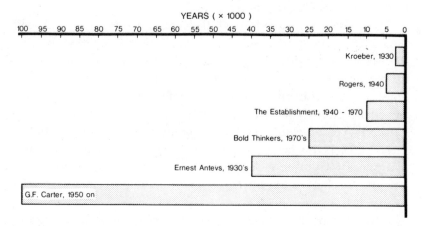

SCALES: Estimates of the Antiquity of Man in America

YEARS (× 1000)

Kroeber, 1930

Rogers, 1940

The Establishment, 1940 - 1970

Bold Thinkers, 1970's

Ernest Antevs, 1930's

G.F. Carter, 1950 on

FIGURE 2. Probably no more dramatic illustration of the conflict over the antiquity of man in America can be presented than these time scales, which show the varying estimates. Antevs is not discussed in the text; he was a student of the late Pleistocene and documented the occurrence of a warm period around 40,000 years ago, which he thought caused an ice retreat sufficient to allow men to enter America.

experts and I—did not disagree a little bit; we disagreed totally.

So, how did I get that way? Well, I read on soils, landforms, climatic changes, and sea-level changes and related these to the glacial time scale as we then understood it. The archeologists neither understood these systems nor saw any reason to delve into them, for, they assumed, such things in no way concerned man in America. For some reason, although raised on the same dogma, I came to develop these other tools, and my observations then led me to other conclusions. I found crude tools of definite patterns in deposits that reached far back into the Ice Age, the Pleistocene— not one or a few thousand years, but tens of thousands of years. The soils, the landforms, the sea levels all spoke of glacial times— not only the present time of high sea stands and dry climates and cliffs on sea fronts and drowned valley mouths, but also past times of lowered sea levels, exposed, sea-cut benches, down-cutting valleys, and much greater rainfall. These included both glacial and non-glacial phenomena and implied many tens of thousands of years.

In the deposits of these varied times, there were stone tools, or so the broken stones seemed to me to be.

The tools were crude, and their patterns at times matched those of the Old World Middle and even Lower Paleolithic. While they seemed somewhat younger than similar tools in the Old World, they were in terms of geomorphology vastly older than the archeologists' 10,000-year limit. So head-on conflict was set: was I reading the land correctly? Were the broken rocks really the work of man (artifacts) or of nature (geofacts) or of my imagination (cartifacts)? The battle rapidly became so highly personal that a name was coined for broken rocks found in ancient formations by Carter: not *artifacts* but *cartifacts*. The struggle rapidly became as much one of personalities as of facts.

So I begin this account on a personal note. Some of the actors in the drama concerning the antiquity of man in America will be introduced. There are villains and heroes and lots of just plain humans. I will briefly introduce many ideas that will be more fully developed later. An example is the relationship of the glaciers to sea levels and landforms and how this relationship can be used for dating. In this personality-slanted account, I will not try to explain at any length how such things work. This will be done in subsequent chapters, and one can readily refer to those chapters if the questions become of particular interest. I hope this lively beginning will carry laymen through some of the more technical chapters that follow. I begin with the man who started me off in the field of archeology and nearly finished me off, too: M. J. Rogers.

THE ROGERS YEARS: 1927–1938

M. J. Rogers (pictured in figure 3) was educated as a mining engineer, served in the Marine Corps in World War I, and never used profanity thereafter, for, as he expressed it, he had heard enough to last several lifetimes. His father, Frederick S. Rogers, was a pioneer in the electrical business in upstate New York and became wealthy. His father's wealth influenced Malcolm's life, for instead of working as a mining engineer he settled in the Escondido Valley just north of San Diego as an orange grower. As a member of the Orange Growers' Coop, he was virtually a gentleman farmer with little to do except watch the oranges grow, for the coop sprayed

FIGURE 3. M. J. Rogers is shown here on one of the early sites near La Jolla, the vicinity that has given its name to one of the early American cultures. He is holding a metate, a basin-shaped stone in which wild seeds were ground. The brief shorts, the pith helmet, and the deep tan are typical of the man. (Photo courtesy of the San Diego Museum of Man)

and picked and did most of the chores. Rogers began to use his spare time on archeology. He soon found that the rounded, red-earth knolls of that area had material on them that was totally different from materials used by the historic Indians: no pottery, no arrow points. The blackened earth of recent camps was long gone, as was any trace of bone, shell, or other biodegradable material. Only stonework remained, and it was mostly scrapers of one sort or another. Large, leaf-shaped knives or possible spear points were relatively rare, and little crescent-shaped flaked objects were even rarer. The sites were subject to erosion and had no depth to aid stratigraphic studies. Late sites were located completely differently: near water supplies rather than on dry knolls. Modern sites had black earth charged with ash and charcoal, while the sites on the knolls had no trace of the organic stain that must once have characterized them. Stone tools made of the same stone were fresh on the late Indian sites but oxidized and hydrated to a depth of a millimeter or more on the old, red-knoll sites. It was clear that two very different people had lived in San Diego County, and that they were separated by a wide time gap. This was contrary to A. L. Kroeber's view that there was no archeological time depth in California, and Rogers had difficulty getting a report published, but it eventually appeared in the *American Anthropologist* (Rogers, 1929).

Rogers read widely and noted that his older material had many traits in common with the Aurignacian of Europe, a culture dating to 20,000 or so years ago. He expanded his investigations to the coast, where he saw extensive shell middens (ancient garbage piles). He then began investigating the adjacent deserts, the Colorado and the Mohave. Everywhere he looked, he found evidence for the presence of man under varying conditions. The tool kits varied. The sites occupied were different. The degrees of weathering of stone tools were different. He was clearly looking at evidence for a long occupancy, with major cultural changes. Due to his unflagging efforts, great quantities of artifacts were collected, site locations were carefully recorded on maps, priceless notes were made on site situations. Skeletal material was collected. Today one could not duplicate his work, for most of his sites have been destroyed or stripped. He saved the record.

An example of his work as a salvage archeologist, as he would be described today, is the situation at La Jolla. A ridge of sand stood about twenty-five feet above sea level at La Jolla Shores, and nearby was a marsh area. In the late 1920's realtors decided to use the ridge to fill the marsh. The work was done by a steam shovel loading trucks, and the steam shovel presently started spilling human skulls and bones, which came from two or more levels. The old sand ridge had long been utilized by man as a campsite and burial ground. The engineer in charge stopped the work, a courageous act since it cost the contractor money, rushed to a phone, and got in touch with the director of the San Diego Museum, then Dr. Edgar Lee Hewett, a man noted for his work in southwestern archeology. The engineer explained that the excavation showed at least two levels of occupation which suggested considerable age, and he offered to stop the work whenever they hit significant material so that the museum could salvage it. Dr. Hewett stated that there were only Digger Indians in California, that there was no significance to layers of skeletons, and that there was no such thing as early man in America. "Throw the bones in the marsh," he said. All of this is just as told to me by Malcolm Rogers. It was a neat measure of the archeological outlook of the opening decades of this century in California. There was no "archeology" in California, so Hewett did his work in the glamorous Southwest. And, most especially, there was no early man in California or in America. The time scale of these most unbiblical scholars was close to that of Archbishop Usher, who precisely established the date of the Creation as 4004 B.C.

Rogers was still an orange grower in Escondido. When news of these finds reached him, he drove down to salvage what he could. The engineers saved bits and pieces and gave him elevations, plan, and profile for the finds. The most significant find was a human frontal in place in the cross-bedded sands of the sand ridge. It had the minimum age of the landform, while the other burials were from subsequent Indian camps on the landform. Rogers correctly read the landform as possibly a beach ridge built when the land-sea relationship was such that the sea could build this ridge twenty-five feet above the present beach. His notes indicate that he considered land movement, sea movement, and possibly great antiquity, but he reached no firm conclusion. For years the frontal was exhibited

along with material of the classic San Dieguito culture of the Encin-
itas-Escondido area: material now dated about 10,000 years, while
the frontal is now dated about 40,000.

One would expect that Rogers would have been an ardent
believer in early man in America. He had the evidence that man
was here when the sea stood higher than the present at La Jolla.
He had excavated in some of the river mouths and had found that
man's evidence extended as far below sea level as his pumps would
allow him to dig. In the Mohave Desert he found that man had
lived around lakes where today there are only dry clay flats, the
dry lakes of the Mohave. These men left no pottery or arrow points,
but they did leave dart points. Elsewhere Rogers found crude stone
tools showing evidences of great weathering age and limited to old
land surfaces. He had all these clues and many more that pointed to
differing climates, differing sea levels, and differing cultures. However, he drifted to a conclusion of 4,000 or 5,000 years for man in
America.

Rogers was an intense and very sensitive man who was insecure
in archeology because he lacked professional training and an advanced degree. He was plain Mr. Rogers adrift in a sea of doctors
of philosophy. When everyone was being introduced as Dr. this and
Dr. that, he too was often designated Dr. Rogers. He always declined
the honor, but with him and many others I have seen this leave a
scar. It takes a lot of self-confidence to override the absence of that
academic degree. Three of the brightest and most productive men
in the field today are Morlin Childers, Herb Minshall, and Tom
Lee, and there is nary a Ph.D. among them. It almost becomes a
mark of distinction not to have one.

Rogers' findings potentially were widely at variance with his
learned colleagues' views. Man in the desert during the last glacial
period, up to 40,000 years ago? Man at San Diego during the
twenty-five-foot sea stand of the last interglacial, about 100,000
years ago? Rogers lacked the self-confidence to battle the academic
establishment, so he opted for a twenty-five-foot postglacial sea stand
to account for the coastal situation, and he used postglacial rainy
periods to account for the desert situation. This placed him safely
with the majority, who also invented warm, dry periods and other
explanations as needed to avoid concluding for high antiquity.

Rogers was a Galileo of sorts: he had produced the evidence for great antiquity of man in America, but he could not withstand the archeological papacy. I suppose that none of this was conscious, but I do think that it comes pretty close to the mark in explaining this enigmatic man. American archeology will always be hugely in his debt for his tireless collecting and recording. The material that he put in the San Diego Museum collection can be interpreted and reinterpreted to eternity, but the artifacts and skeletons are the hard-core facts. Without Rogers we would not have them.

In 1930 I was taken on the museum's five-week expedition to San Nicolas Island, quite an adventure for a newly graduated high schooler. Although we concentrated on the obvious middens, we saw much more. Hearths marking temporary camps could be seen at many positions in dunes, and the sands were often strongly cemented. On the top of the island we found large, leaf-shaped spear points, quite different from any of the later material. There were strange accumulations of snail shells that Rogers thought were due to man. At depth in the sea cliffs we could see bones sticking out. Rogers correctly identified the earth in these sea cliffs covering the ancient, "uplifted" sea beaches that were now being destroyed by wave attack as Pleistocene formations, so of course we did not examine them. My notebook refers to hearths extending through these deep accumulations of earth from top to bottom. Today we know that this is Wisconsin (last glacial) material of 10,000- to 70,000-year antiquity. Rogers borrowed my notebook when making his final notes on the island, so he read what I observed, but he clearly drew back from the precipice of high antiquity.

We often had clues in hand that we did not understand but whose meaning would emerge decades later. Red abalones, for instance, were prominent in certain village levels but lacking in others. The intertidal rocks were plastered with black abalones as thick as they could stick, but there were no reds. Years later, I mentioned this to Carl Hubbs of the Scripps Institution of Oceanography, and he commented, "The red abalone is a cold-water form and not expectable in the tidal zone south of Monterey." From Phil Orr's work on Santa Rosa Island in the 1950's (Orr, 1968), we would learn that this cold-water era persisted until about 7,000 years ago. The clues to the time puzzle were there, but we either could not read them or, burdened by the certainty of our belief in the recency of man in America, we would not see them.

It was the same in the Mohave Desert. In a trip through Death Valley and Owens Valley, I looked with awe and interest at the great terraces standing high above the valley floors: "Shouldn't we look on those terraces, Mr. Rogers?" "No, George, those are Pleistocene in age," was the reply.

We did collect artifacts from lesser terraces around smaller lakes such as Silver Lake, but Rogers attributed these to a post-glacial rainy period, so he retained his good standing in the academic community. Those who disagreed—for instance, M. R. Harrington of the Southwest Museum, who ,fought for glacial-pluvial age (10,000 years plus)—were castigated unmercifully (see, for example, Meighan and Haynes, 1970). Now we know that Harrington, E. C. Campbell, and the heroic handful who dared argue for antiquity were right. The magic of C-14 has dated the lakes as Pleistocene, and the evidence of man on their latest shores is on the 10,000-year time scale. Evidence for man on older and higher shores is also there, but we missed it, for we knew that there was no point in looking there.

A note on time scales: astronomers deal with light years, geologists with tens of millions if not hundreds of millions of years, geomorphologists with hundreds of thousands of years, and American archeologists with a 10,000-year scale. The archeologic time scale has varied from the 3,000- to 5,000-year scale of my undergraduate days to the 10,000- to 12,000-year scale currently in use. We are about to move to a 100,000-year scale, as will be shown presently. Throughout this book, my tendency will be to give round numbers, for they express our real situation. When we are arguing about whether the age of man in America is 10,000 or 100,000 years, it is pretentious to carry dates to 10, 100, or even 1,000 years. We seldom if ever have precise dates, but we should know whether we are dealing with 10,000, 100,000, or several hundred thousand years.

I worked with Rogers on the coast and in the Colorado and Mohave deserts and in Baja California. His method was surface survey work, for he was convinced that there was nothing to be found by digging. He had started in the Escondido-Encinitas area

doing surface collecting on the eroding fields and had clearly distinguished his classic San Dieguito culture. On the coast, after one
extensive attempt in 1929 at excavating in the shell middens, he
virtually abandoned excavation, for the yield was small, the stratigraphy slight, burial finds rare. Surface collecting yielded endless
amounts of artifacts, and burials were more easily found as they
eroded out of gullies and sea cliffs than by digging for them. In
1976 further excavation on a site that Rogers had tested in 1929
showed that burials of 50,000, 15,000, and 5,000 years of age all
were found at one level. This dating was dictated by the shallow
surface soil underlain at a depth of about thirty inches by a hard
sandstone. Stratigraphy was nearly meaningless on these upland
sites. On the other hand, the sites in the valley floors offered deep
stratigraphy but posed problems in moving large amounts of earth
and controlling water. Rogers opted for surface surveys.

In the desert Rogers began by going to the obvious water
sources, where he found late material mostly. It was Elizabeth Crozier
Campbell (Campbell and Campbell, 1935; Campbell et al., 1937)
who made the breakthrough of finding dart-point cultures on the
terraces of the extinct lakes. Rogers furiously attacked her Pinto
Wash evidence as a confusion of a superficial mixture of dart points
and extinct animal bone. He may have been correct in this, but
part of his fury may have been pique at her having preceded him
on lake-terrace work. Thereafter, he vigorously surveyed the ancient
lakeshores, and we—for I was with him in most of this work—
found extensive evidence of man in the Mohave Desert when it
was filled with lakes. For Rogers, this was due to a postglacial cool
period only a few thousand years before the present, and it was
not evidence for man in a rainy (pluvial) period that correlated with
the last glacial period.

The working of the human mind is well illustrated by something that happened around this time. We were working in the
Mohave, going to water points as usual, and blissfully ignorant of
the possibility of finding evidence of man even on the youngest
of the shorelines around the now-dry lake beds. In the midst of
the sand waste, just before we reached the clay flat of a dry lake,
we got a flat tire. The sand was excessively loose, and we could not
get the jack to lift the car. It just sank into the sand. As the junior

member of the party, I was told to go off and scrounge around for something to put the jack on. I came back shortly with a large grinding stone or metate. I dropped it triumphantly, exclaiming: "Look what some dumb collector left out here in the desert." In later years we realized that we had had our flat tire on an ancient beach line and I had picked up a very obvious piece of evidence that man had lived there. It was pretty massive evidence, but we explained it away readily enough.

I found a clue that indicated that Rogers was wrong in his short time scale, and, in retrospect, that was the beginning of the end of our relationship. We collected on desert surfaces fairly systematically by dragging a stick as we walked in parallel. We could thus tell where we had walked and what areas we had missed. We did not, as we should have, record the location of each item; rather, we contented ourselves with recording material by sizable areas: whole sites instead of work areas, house sites, and so forth. On one of these sweeps of the lake shorelines near the overflow of ancient Silver Lake, beyond Yermo along the Mohave River drainage, I found a fluted point. I knew when I saw it that it was a Folsom-type point, and I let out a yell. A fluted point instantly told us where we were in time, for it cross-tied us to the Folsom-Clovis, Great-Hunter period of the Plains. The time would be the 10,000-year level, and the expected climate would be that of the end of the Pleistocene—rainier than now and thus accounting for this former lake in the desert.

My elation led me to propose immediate publication on this most significant find, and, when we got back to the museum, I began preparing a note. After two days Rogers demanded that I cease and desist forthwith. I was told in no uncertain terms that he was in charge. All material collected was under his care. All writing would be done by him. I acquiesced, but things were never the same thereafter.

Rogers never fully reported this very significant find. The point was finally illustrated in a plate of aberrant forms (Rogers, 1939), and few if any noted its presence or had a clue as to its significance. Campbell et al. (1937) reported finding several more fluted points. The classic San Dieguito of the Encinitas area now cross-ties via the Mohave desert and the Lake Lahontan area to the

Folsom period, and C-14 methods have confirmed the dating in the San Diego area. Rogers virtually buried a very important find.

This sounds rough on Rogers, but it is meant to be explanatory not condemnatory. We all owe Rogers a huge debt, and I especially do. He took me under his wing, taught me how to recognize crude artifacts, and was the soul of patience in all of his dealings with me. We had a decade-long association that was invaluable to me. I began to displease Rogers when my reading in the library combined with my reading of the field evidence led to the 40,000-year date while Rogers was stuck at 4,000 years. The 40,000-year position arose from combining evidence for man living on the shores of glacial-pluvial lakes in the desert with Antev's dating of the mid-Wisconsin glacial corridor, which would have allowed man to enter America from the Bering region. It was more conflict than this basically insecure man could stand, and I was eased out of the museum and landed fortuitously in geography.

ANTHROPOLOGY PLUS GEOGRAPHY
EQUALS HUMAN ECOLOGY

At San Diego State College (now University), both Alvena Storm and Lauren Post of the geography department were soon urging me to go to Berkeley to do graduate work with Carl Sauer. In a vague way, I associated Sauer with a broad interest in man in America, and I clearly needed physical earth science to attack the problems of the Pleistocene, which it was by then obvious, at least to me, was the time of man's appearance in America. At the meetings of the Pacific Coast A.A.A.S. (American Association for the Advancement of Science) that spring, I gave two papers: one for the geographers on lima bean farming and soil erosion in the Encinitas area (1938) and the other on archeological work at Point Sal near Santa Barbara (1941). I had done this work without Rogers, hence he could not object to my presentation. At that same meeting, Frank Fenenga presented a paper jointly prepared with Bob Heizer; these were names with which I was to be associated in friendship and conflict for decades to come.

At Berkeley I did work in oceanography, climatology, and meteorology, as well as taking courses in cultural geography and performing teaching-assistance work in physical, cultural, and eco-

nomic geography. I took a course with A. L. Kroeber—an interesting experience, for I appreciated what he was doing infinitely more
than I had as an undergraduate. He simply took a topic and worked
with it. He did not recite facts; he posed questions and then turned
and twisted them, pointing out various ways to think about the
problem and several possible answers, one of which he usually
indicated as more probable than the others. I recall that he did this
in my undergraduate days, too, but I winnowed out mere facts
that might appear on the multiple-choice examinations then in vogue
and bypassed the reasoning. Now I appreciated the balancing, testing, and tentative concluding. Kroeber and Sauer were among the
greatest minds I had the priceless experience of being exposed to.
I disagreed with Kroeber on the antiquity of man in America and
on the reality of transoceanic diffusion. I like to think that with the
massive evidence now available he would join me. He was seldom
doctrinaire and normally open to new evidence, and I have never
understood how some of his students became such opposites.

Twenty years later this combination of geography and anthropology gave rise to what the anthropologists called human ecology.
To a geographer, it was old-fashioned physical-environmental deter-
minism, the giving of undue weight to the physical environment in
explaining what man is, culturally as well as physically. This is an
ancient theme in geography, where it once was used to explain almost everything man did. The Berkeley school of geography led in
greatly modifying this view to consider culture as active and dominant in man's affairs and the physical environment as passive and
secondary. My work at San Diego, with its extensive studies of the
physical setting of the area, naturally had a strong environmental
slant, which a couple of years ago elicited from a young anthropologist the surprised statement that "you were using ecological archeology twenty years before the rest of the field." Properly used, it is
a powerful tool.

The geography and anthropology students at Berkeley were
traditionally close, reflecting the strong, mutually enriching interaction between Carl Sauer and Alfred Kroeber, and the ecological outlook engendered there at that time was soundly balanced. My best
friend among the anthropology graduate students was Bob Heizer.
We shared an interest in California archeology and spent many

hours discussing the evidence for cultural relationships, sequences, and antiquities. Frank Fenenga, Gordon Hewes, and others were part of this compatible group, some of whom have remained life-long friends.

BACK TO THE FIELD

The war ended academic work for a time and took me to Washington, D.C., and thence to the Johns Hopkins University. I had time during these war years to read and think about soil weathering, marine terraces, and problems of time, and I evolved a theory that would let me solve the question of the age of man in America by some rather simple observations on the coast at San Diego. When the war ended, I began returning summers to pick up my work on early man in America. Malcolm Farmer at the San Diego Museum of Man took me out to the Scripps Institution of Oceanography to meet Carl Hubbs and to see the hearth (charcoal and burned animal bone) that Hubbs had recently found at the very base of the cliff just north of the Scripps pier. This was the beginning of a long, stormy, warmly cherished friendship with Carl and Laura Hubbs. Hubbs's primary field was ichthyology (fishes), but he is best described as an ichthyologist with an itch to know everything. He was combative, assertive, enormously learned, and a very good friend. Carl was for years of two minds: half for me, half against me. He died in July, 1979, as this manuscript was in its final stages. More on Hubbs presently.

My first summer's work was disillusioning. Neither the river terraces nor the coastal terraces were simply and easily "read." The facts in the field were not as neat and simple as my armchair theories, and it took ten years of work to develop a coherent system into which the local archeology could be fitted. It indicated at least a last-interglacial age for man in America. The reaction to this evidence was extreme, quite in proportion to the changes in chronology and cultural level proposed: from 10,000 to 100,000; from Neolithic to Lower Paleolithic. But it was more than just that. I have only slowly realized that I was plunging in where I was most unwelcome. I was no longer a Californian or an archeologist, but an Easterner and a geographer. The best way to portray this situation is to describe some of the characters in action.

When I returned to California for a summer's work, the first go-round with Carl Hubbs was classic. We argued vehemently. In the period since our last association, Carl had been exposed to the full blast of the Indians-are-recent school. The Berkeley-U.C.L.A. axis had proved to him that I was mistaken, wrong-headedly, stubbornly, stupidly mistaken—blindly pressing my idiotic argument for high antiquity for man in America in the face of all higher wisdom (theirs). Carl is one of the more strong-minded men I have known, and it is a good measure of the pressure that they could brainwash him so thoroughly. But so they did.

Our sessions in Carl's office overlooking the Pacific turned as fast as I could move them into discussions of the facts that were virtually, but not quite, visible from his window. At the very base of the forty-foot high cliff to the north of the pier of the Scripps Institution of Oceanography campus, Hubbs himself had found a fireplace with abundant charcoal and small-animal bone, material unfortunately now lost. Immediately beneath the cliff lay a Pleistocene beach. Over it lay forty feet of alluvium. To build up the alluvium would require changing the land-sea relationship so that a shelf was exposed on which the alluvium could accumulate. The alluvium obviously accumulated slowly, for there were well-developed soil horizons in it, marking long periods of stability. Fire areas marked these surfaces, indicating the presence of man. I argued that that piece of campus was all one needed to prove man's presence throughout the period of the last glaciation, which lowered the sea level and allowed the alluvium to accumulate. With rumblings and grumblings, Carl would change the subject, and we would be on an argumentative but mutually respectful footing for the rest of the summer. In another year or two, I would have to do it all over again.

As C-14 dates accumulated, it became easier, for the alluvium was soon proved to be fully as old as I said it was, and several scholars accepted the fire zones as evidence of man: E. Sellards (1952, 1960), Alex Krieger (1964), Luther Cressman (1973, 1977), to name some notables. That Carl and I remained friends through the din of battle is a measure of Carl's greatness, of his intense pursuit of knowledge, and of his openness. He told me to my face what others did not, and that allowed me to answer. Carl was finally converted to the high antiquity of man in America.

In this difficult period, Hubbs, through his association with Hans Suess, began obtaining C-14 dates for sites all along the California and Baja California coast. He took me on a several-days trip into Baja California to show me the sites, plaguing me to describe in advance what the soil evidence would be.

Soils and sites with absolute dates were a rarity at that time, and it was a bit awesome to have to state in advance just what 4,000 years of weathering would look like. I considered his few-thousand-year-old dates to be insignificant for soil development, so I said that development would be slight, and it was. There was little cementation and only faint discoloration. En route we looked at a midden dated at a few thousand years. It was densely packed with shells, mostly mussel, and was still black, loose, and fluffy. Beneath it lay an old red clay–loam soil that had resulted from weathering of an underlying lava flow. In it, deeply stained by the iron of the soil, lay a bifaced cobble chopper. This, I argued, was evidence many orders of magnitude older than the midden.

During the trip I repeatedly pointed out that when we went down to the sea margin on the young terraces the soils were brown. When the road swung inland and climbed onto higher terraces, the soils became progressively redder. It was even possible to point out that this was independent of parent material. It applied to alluvium, to basalts, and to granites. Carl related some of this to others and apparently got a frosty reception.

On one occasion he took me along to a meeting at the California Institute of Technology, where he gave a paper on some of his work in Baja California. He was then making a series of measurements of the temperature of the coastal water and correlating these with changes in fish and shellfish. The Indian middens, their garbage piles, were of enormous interest to him, for the shells in the middens sometimes differed from what was available there today. Since the shellfish were temperature-sensitive, he could read the past temperatures from the ancient shell mounds. From C-14 he could obtain dates and thus construct a scale of sea-temperature changes through time. When he finished speaking, he faced a barrage of questions about soils, terraces, time, and crustal stability. He promptly excused himself, saying that such questions were more properly put to George Carter, who happened to be present. I found myself on the stand answering questions for the next fifteen minutes. My impression was that the experts were quite surprised that I could present data plus a reasoned argument as to why the soil color, terrace, and time sequence were not only clearly visible but understandable. Later the California Institute of Technology seismology group confirmed my key concept: the San Diego area constitutes a relatively stable block in an otherwise extremely unstable area (Allen, Silver, and Stehli, 1960; Allen, St. Amand, Richter, and Nordquist, 1965).

The major apparent movement has been such that terraces have been slowly uplifted and hence preserved from destruction by waves. Real movement, on the other hand, has been a continuing lowering of world sea level over the last 1 million years (Evans, 1971). Consequently, the oldest terraces are highest and have been exposed to weathering longest. Weathering tends through time to create chemical changes that include a drift toward redder and redder colors (Carter, 1956). Soil color, in a broad sense, is a measure of time if one makes all the usual provisos subsumed under the heading "all other things being equal." More on this later. Also, although in keeping with the usual geological expression the land is described as rising, worldwide data now indicate that it is the sea that is falling, while the land in such areas as San Diego has stood relatively still. More on this later, also.

My 1953 trip into Baja California with Carl Hubbs was memorable for many things. Laura Hubbs was along, of course. She was at least half of the team of Hubbs and Hubbs, and the comment has often been made that whoever coined the phrase "the better half" must have been thinking of Laura Hubbs, for her contributions to Carl's enormous achievements were huge. Carl collected everything: lizards, snakes, artifacts, shells. A run-over but still active rattlesnake was popped in a sack and tossed in back along with lizards, horned toads, and other snakes. Nothing that moved that Carl could grab escaped being thrown in a bag, and I began to feel sorry for the creatures wiggling in bags in the bumping carryall in the stifling heat and dust. A large nonpoisonous snake grabbed by the middle once turned and bit Carl on the hand, and Carl did a lively dance trying to dislodge the fangs and bag the snake. "Why don't you go help him?" Laura asked, as I stayed firmly rooted in the carryall. "I'm on the snake's side," I muttered.

We camped the second night on a bluff above a cobble ramp, with a noisy surf rolling the cobbles up and down the ramp. These ramps in Baja California are something to see. They may extend for miles. Millions of smoothly rounded cobbles form a steep beach, and the beach ramp or ridge may rise fifteen to twenty-five feet or more above high tide.

The height of the ramps in Baja California measures the force of storm waves, which can throw rocks unexpected distances. In England, for instance, lighthouses have had their lights smashed 150 feet above sea level by storm-thrown rocks. Moral: do not walk along cobble ramps at times of great storms. You might as well walk in no-man's-land in the midst of battle.

These flying stones created a situation that Hubbs could not wait to spring on me. I had argued vehemently that nature does not normally break rocks by percussive action and rarely does so by pressure, and hence that percussively broken rocks even in alluvial deposits were normally the work of man. Like the notion of crustal stability at San Diego, this thesis was viewed as eccentric, at least. In measuring the water temperature along these ramps, Carl had found that he could not wade into the surf, for the tumbling rocks surging up and down the ramp with each wave would severely bruise his legs, even in mild weather. Never one easily stopped, he rigged maximum-minimum thermometers on a surf caster's rod and reel, stood on the beach to cast his instruments upon the water, and got his readings.

The combination of shin damage and the incessant roar set up as each wave advanced and receded and tumbled the rocks about predisposes one to assume that rock breakage must be going on. However, one can examine millions of these rocks without finding a broken one. They are being rounded and smoothed, not flaked.

Most scholars would have taken their readings and gone on, but not this ichthyologist, snatcher of snakes, and battler in archeology. Hubbs looked closely at the rock ramps, and on the upper part of the ramps he saw many percussively flaked rocks. His challenge to me was: "Aren't these percussively flaked by nature? And aren't they indistinguishable from man-flaked stones?" My first look left me stunned, for the material surely resembled man's work. There were single percussive flakes, stones with multiple flakes, even one large, round flake that had edge flaking all around, making it look like a disc chopper.

There were plenty of these specimens on top of the cobble ramps where the storm waves had thrown them. Thorny bushes had caught some cobbles and held them in their thick, stiff twigs. It was all too clear that under storm conditions rocks were thrown and sometimes struck on rock and fractured. There is no difference in a percussion blow's effect whether nature is the actor or man. I had the sinking feeling that I might have to eat these geofacts (as opposed to artifacts; made by nature rather than man). However, on the bluff above the beach there were plenty of genuine artifacts made from these same beach cobbles, and the obvious thing to do before lunching on metabasalt cobble a la Hubbs was to compare two sets: flaked cobbles from the ramp, obviously nature's work, and flaked cobbles from the camps, most certainly man's work. With an armful of material from the ramp, I climbed the high bluff, walked into the middle of an occupation zone, set down my ramp rocks, and collected a like number of broken rocks from the Indian site. A very few minutes of comparison saved my teeth. The stones broken by man had fresh flake surfaces. The stones broken by the surf had at most one fresh flake surface; if there was more than one flake surface, the others showed excessive all-over wear. Wear, if visible at all on the man-broken rocks, was strictly limited to working edges. The differentiation was easy.

Hubbs had the common notion that stone could be heated and flaked by sudden cooling with water. The idea probably arose from men's seeing the Indians warm rocks to anneal them and so increase their ease of flaking. I had carried out heat experiments and had read of others, and I knew that each kind of rock has a temperature limit. Below it there is little change. Above it the unequal expansion of the varied minerals pries the rock apart, and it becomes a mass of microscopic fissures, has a sugary, grainy texture, and is useless for flaking. I stated this, but Hubbs did not believe it. So we heated rocks in the camp fire, then threw water on them or dropped them in water, and examined the results. I was right, and Carl retired growling. To my great surprise, first thing in the morning he roundly conceded the point, and I have always admired him for it.

There were interesting asides. Hubbs collected quantities of these naturifacts, as he called the rocks broken when thrown out of the surf, and at a 1953 meeting of the Great Basin Conference at the Southwest Museum he brought a washtub full, expecting to get some critical and, he hoped, constructive discussion of the materials and processes. No one looked at them. This was a memorable meeting. R. D. Simpson, then with the Southwest Museum, now at the San Bernardino County Museum, had arranged the meeting and had set aside the morning for examination of collections of early lithic materials. She had material from the Mohave Desert on display. I brought material from the controversial sites at San Diego. To our consternation none of the University of California–U.C.L.A. axis or their followers appeared. Not one. I learned a year or two later that they had held a rump meeting at U.C.L.A. that morning. They did appear at the afternoon session, but they sat in a group and discussed none of our papers. When I gave mine and there was no discussion, I looked over to where this group sat in a body and addressed myself to one of them whom I had had a small role in getting started in archeology, asking if he did not have some comment to make. He was obviously uncomfortable but replied that he "had nothing to say at this time." In an evening session I was one of a panel supposed to discuss these early lithic problems. I sat between one of the opposition archeologists and Carl Hubbs, with his tub of geofacts that never got examined or discussed. My opposition managed the near miracle of negotiating the entire evening without looking at me or speaking to me. Even professional fighters extend more courtesies.

Robert Heizer and I were graduate students together at Berkeley, he in anthropology and I in geography. We were good friends, worked, talked, and dated together. My penchant for seeing high antiquity was already obvious, and Heizer and I discussed such views freely. Once I began to publish on the matter, however, Heizer backed off from our friendship. At Berkeley about 1948 in his office, surrounded by other men with whom I had shared the vicissitudes of graduate work, he turned his back on me and refused to speak. In my succeeding visits to the Berkeley campus, not even pressure from senior professors, such as Ronald Olson, could get him to eat lunch with a faculty group that included me. This marked the beginning of a one-sided enmity that poisoned the U.C.-U.C.L.A. group and its products.

Surprisingly few archeologists are familiar with lithic technology, though this is now changing slowly and studies in this field are becoming more common. Still, the old eolith problem haunts the field. For those not haunted by eoliths, these are the broken rocks over which there is controversy concerning whether man or nature is the manufacturer. Much of the difficulty in Europe then, and in America now, stemmed from the certainty that man could not be "that old" and that he surely was not making tools "that early." Why should they look for Lower Paleolithic tools if they had been taught that there were none? If they did not look, they surely would not find them, and their having found none would then prove that there were none. One does not have to be a skilled logician to recognize some circular reasoning in this sequence.

At a lecture recently I was asked by a young archeologist how it could be that I could find so many artifacts in such ancient sites when the archeologists could not. My reply was to ask two questions: in the past five years, how many days have you spent looking in Upper Pleistocene formations in this, your own area? And would you know what parts of this immediate environment where you do your research and teach are Upper Pleistocene, pre-Pleistocene, and Recent? He was honest. His replies were: "I have not looked, and I would not know." He has many intellectual companions.

Many of these statements will seem extreme and will certainly be taken as offensive by many professional archeologists, but the list of prominent archeologists, including lithic technologists, who have flunked the course at Calico is so extensive as to be understandable only as a sort of mass hysteria. Today, Clay Singer, after advanced graduate studies at U.C.L.A. and then two years of further work in lithic analysis in France in addition to field experience in Mexico and South America, is describing the blade and core work at Calico as containing many of the tool types known in the European blade and core industry (1979). It is not only present but shows strong use-wear patterns. Calico is a highly controversial site in the Mohave Desert; it will be discussed later. A glance at the list of notables at the Calico Conference (1966), where hundreds of Calico artifacts were laid out for inspection and rejected by the assembled moguls, would suggest that a mere graduate student is outvoted. Outvoted, yes. Wrong, absolutely not. The most interesting test is to hand an archeologist a Calico tool without telling him where it is from. "Well, that is an artifact. No one will deny that. Where is it from?" was a recent exclamation. When I replied "Calico," the victim of my duplicity was astonished, for his professors who had been to Calico had told him that there were no artifacts there. Among others, Vance Haynes was so victimized at the Friends of the Pleistocene Meeting at San Diego in 1975. Items from Calico are artifacts unless you know they are from Calico.

There were and are reasons for the Americanists' difficulty with the Lower Paleolithic. They inherited a most cautious attitude toward early types of stonework. If they did study Lower Paleolithic work, it was in Europe, and even there it was more often the rich Upper Paleolithic that most intrigued them. Those who worked in Europe did not, until recently, also work in America. East is east and west is west. The fixed idea of no-great-antiquity-for-man-in-America blocked interest in traces of ancient man. Archeologists focused on pot sherds and arrowheads and, after 1930, on dart points, but they ignored the Lower Paleolithic work so generously strewn across their landscape.

At San Diego virtually nothing has been done in recent decades to collect, salvage, or record the glacial and interglacial sites to be described below, which were exposed and largely destroyed in the vast spurt of urbanization of the area. There was no lack of manpower, for there were the San Diego Museum of Man, the San Diego State College (now University), and the University of San Diego. Later there were potential collectors at the University of California at San Diego, where most of the campus itself was a vast complex of early-man sites, most of which were destroyed in the building of the campus and the last of which got belated attention through the efforts of Jeffry Bada, a geochemist at the Scripps Institution of Oceanography. If I had not alerted Bada, after some difficulty, to the presence of early-man evidence on his campus, we would have lost that last bit of evidence. James Moriarty was an exception of sorts, for, while working as the staff artist for Francis P. Shepard at the Scripps Institution of Ocean-ography, he persisted in work on the La Jollan sites. However, he pretty ruggedly ignored the glacial and interglacial sites and often underestimated the age of the sites he worked on (Moriarty, 1966, 1969). Although the evidence for interglacial and glacial man in the area was extensively reported in 1957, it was nearly twenty years before a member of the San Diego Museum of Man staff set foot on the principal site. Dr. Emma Lou Davis, now emerging as an early-man supporter, as late as 1973 had not read the only book on the local archeology and geomorphology (Carter, 1957) or any other of the fifty or more papers that I had written on the subject. This is all the more remarkable in view of the fact that she au-thored a piece in a book on the archeology of the immediate area (Davis, 1966).

As this manuscript was going through the last throes of editing a letter arrived from Emma Lou Davis in which she stated that she now recognized the blade and core work at San Diego as a very sophisticated pebble technology. Very few people have the courage to acknowledge, especially to their "adversary," evidence for a view they have been vociferously rejecting for some years. Emma Lou does not know it, but she only lived so long because Herb Minshall intervened when I was about to brain her with a Paleolithic im-plement. She was looking at hundreds of artifacts, with many ex-tremely fine examples of cores, blades, concave scrapers, chopping tools with wedge-shaped cross sections—a whole complex of tool types—and proclaiming to me as I tried to get her to see what she was looking at that they "were just naturally broken rocks." I have seldom gotten so mad at anyone. Herb sensed my reaching a boiling point and intervened before I exploded. So for Emma Lou to totally change, and to write me that she had done so is no small thing and enormously to her credit.

While other archeologists were ignoring or rejecting evidence for early man, Ruth DeEtte (Dee) Simpson (see figure 4) focused on the Mohave Desert and after extensive surveys settled down to excavate the Calico site near Yermo (Simpson, 1958; Simpson and Schuiling, 1970; Schuiling, 1979). I had a long though slight associ-ation with this site. Malcolm Rogers, sometime in the early 1930's during a trip in the Mohave Desert, took me to the site. The vast

FIGURE 4. Ruth DeEtte (Dee) Simpson has dedicated more than twenty years to developing the Calico site in the Mohave Desert into one of the finest demonstrations of early man in America.

litter of flake debris and core tools on the surface he explained as workshop debris left at a quarry. The landform he described as an old river channel. He stated that excavation was useless, for, as always in the desert, there was no depth to the archeological materials. Fortunately, Dee Simpson and her associates in the archeological survey of the Mohave were not possessed of this superior knowledge and, guided, encouraged, and supported by L. S. B. Leakey of African fame, she has carried out a classic excavation tens of feet deep into some of the most firmly cemented desert conglomerate I have ever seen.

From my initial visit to her excavation, I was convinced of the reality of the evidence for man. The early clincher for me was the presence of concave scrapers with a special technique of sharpening that involved battering the concave edge. Later I pointed out the presence of an extensive blade and core industry with a large suite of microblade implements that would be quite at home in a European Paleolithic setting. These are the materials now being studied by Clay Singer (1979). His report details the evidence not only

for human work but for use wear on them, and this means that
Calico was not just a quarry, it was a living area. As will be shown
later, the problem at Calico is the site's age. While no one yet has
a real measure of the age, it is obviously very old. My guess has
been beyond 100,000 years. Simpson, Leakey, and Clements have
guessed less than 100,000 years. Extremists have guessed 500,000
years or more. Obviously, we are all guesstimating, and no one
really knows. More on this later.

The questions one faces in the field tend to persist, like a
haunting refrain, and my observations on San Nicolas Island combined with my work on early man at San Diego soon had me cor-
responding with Phil Orr of the Santa Barbara Museum of Natural
History. He was reporting on dwarf elephants on Santa Rosa Island, a topic that had interested me for a long time. About 1950 I
had talked with Dr. Chester Stock, paleontologist at the California
Institute of Technology, about these creatures, for he had excavated
some of their remains. I was also trying to get an identification of
a bit of mammal bone that I found in the cliff at Scripps, which
proved to be a bit of a seal skull. Stock described the elephant skeletons as coming from the same geomorphic situation: a sea cliff
of alluvium standing over a "raised beach."* I queried Stock closely
concerning evidence for man at the elephant sites, pointing out that
on San Nicolas Island and at San Diego there was clear evidence
for man in just such locations. Stock stoutly denied ever having
seen any evidence for man with, at, or near his elephant sites.

When Orr began reporting on his archeological and paleontological work on Santa Rosa Island in the Pacific off Santa Barbara,
I wrote him asking if the two ever coincided: dwarf elephants for
dinner, perhaps. He replied, "No." I replied that they ought to and

---

*Raised beach is a euphemism. A sea beach now well above sea level is assumed
to have been carried up by a rise of the land. A safer assumption is that the sea
once stood higher, for we know that over the last million years the sea has risen
and fallen with the glacial retreats and advances but that overall worldwide sea
level has been falling for the last 1 million years. Whether the land has moved and
in what direction has to be proved, while movement of the sea can be assumed.
Any given beach has to be investigated to be sure it is not in an active crustal zone,
but, lacking evidence to the contrary, the safest assumption is sea-level change. We
know that such change has been rapid, relatively recent, and in the same directions
worldwide.

urged him to look harder the next time he was on the island. He did and wrote me, "No evidence for man in the elephant levels." Again I argued: "Well, there ought to be, for if man reached San Nicolas, he surely could reach Santa Rosa. If man was at San Nicolas and at San Diego at the time the alluvium was accumulating over the so-called raised beaches, then he should also have been on Santa Rosa Island at that time." Orr's reaction was: "All right, wise guy, you come and look for yourself," and he added, "at my expense." And thereby hangs a tale. Orr had various people come to the island at his expense, and he once put on a conference, inviting all his critics, some of the most vocal of whom declined to come. For this, he won from one of those too busy to come the accusation that Orr made extraordinary claims while preventing archeologists from coming and checking on him. Orr did, as required by the land-owner, maintain a monopoly on excavation, but he not only invited inspection, he even paid for it.

This led to one of the more bizarre adventures of my life. At Orr's invitation, Wallace Broecker, then a graduate student at the Lamont Laboratory at Columbia University, joined Orr and me for several days' tour of extinct Lake Lahontan's shorelines and caves near Reno, Nevada. From there we went to Santa Rosa Island. I had, for years, wanted to see those Lake Lahontan shorelines, for, if I was even half right about the antiquity of man in America, man must have lived on the shores of that lake. I had been solemnly assured by men who had carried the rod for Ernst Antevs when he was surveying some of these terraces that there was no evidence for man on them. At the time I believed them, but as my work progressed, I came to doubt their observational powers. I came to suspect a case of carry-the-rod and spoil-the-observation. The evidence had to be there, and I welcomed the opportunity to go and look for myself.

Orr had been working on cave deposits around the lake. This is a fixation that American archeologists inherited from their colleagues in the Old World, where caves have been major sources of information. Someone apparently forgot to tell the American Indians about caves, for while they used them now and then they left no such record as is found in Europe. But Orr with money from the Western Speleological Foundation dug caves, as did repeated expeditions from Berkeley. Only belatedly have the enormous open-air sites around the lake been recognized.

So it was that we looked at caves. They were impressive enough. Man had used them intermittently. Pack rats had used them, too. The accumulated dusty debris recorded all of postglacial time. In the bottom was pine pollen recording the near presence of pine trees far out in the desert. Above that came cactus, recording the oncoming drought and desert conditions. Cactus, it must be noted, is not a plant of the heart of the desert, but it is an edge-of-the-desert plant. As full modern aridity came on, the cactus disappeared to be replaced by the hardy, deep-rooted desert shrubs. The human record ran all the way through this sequence.

It is an interesting record: stonework was scarce and advanced: fine dart points, not crude choppers and scrapers. There were large amounts of cordage and wood and some skins. The dry dust retained everything: fleas, flies, lice, and mosquitoes. Bodies tucked into such dryness simply dried up, natural mummies. There the people are, one woman in her grass skirt still clutching her grass sack purse. Orr handed me a pelican skin with the feathers still intact and the skin still supple. Since these materials could date back as much as 10,000 years, I was seeing and handling material that made the Egyptian mummies youthful in comparison.

Other phenomena were equally impressive. The cliff swallows had built their mud nests in some of the caves, and, ten thousand years after the lake whose marshy edges had supplied the insects for their way of life had ceased to exist, their little cup-shaped nests still clung to the cave walls. Desert preservation of even such perishables as this is well-nigh incredible.

Outside the cave, the shoreline of the ancient lake stood so fresh and clear that it was hard to imagine that we were looking at features 10,000 years old. But this was a principal interest, and young Wally Broecker took the calcareous coating that marked some of these shorelines as his particular problem. Orr had the capricious notion that since these stony deposits had been precipitated in association with algae they might contain an organic component that could be C-14 dated. Phil Orr had neglected to pick up a Ph.D. along the road, so he was unencumbered by a lot of "it is not possibles." He is also remarkably unimpressed by authorities and pos-

sessed of an unlimited curiosity. Although geologists assured him
that tufa could not be dated, he persuaded Broecker to try. It could
be, and we could then date the final stages of Lake Lahontan and
thereby date the human remains (Broecker and Orr, 1958). In
round numbers, Lahontan dried up when the glaciers began their
final retreat 10,000 years ago. The glaciers in the north and the
lakes in the desert marched to the beat of the same climatic drum.
The glaciers and the lakes advanced and retreated synchronously,
while the seas advanced and retreated in counterpoint: lakes and
glaciers up, but seas down, and vice versa. It is like a stately minuet
with 40,000 years to the beat.

In visiting the caves along the Lake Lahontan shoreline, we
had to cross the ancient beaches. When we reached a cobble ramp,
I called a halt. "Hey, you guys! Here we are on a beach where storm
waves have pounded. There are a million rocks in sight. Find me
a single broken one, just one cartifact."

The first time this happened, Broecker and Orr rose enthusias-
tically to the challenge, but each successive failure to find even one
cracked rock soon produced such disillusionment that presently I
could not get them even to pause to look. Winds off the Sierras
have been described by Mark Twain as Washo Zephyrs, little
breezes of sixty miles per hour. The cobble ramps, wave-cut cliffs,
and great beach ridges record the strong surf engendered in this
inland sea, but the violent water action produced no pseudoartifacts.

Orr nearly created an artifact by leaning over and spilling his
glasses out of his shirt pocket and onto the cobbles. I leaped forward with an exclamation of dismay. Orr's reaction was: "They
are not broken. Cheap glasses never break." And he flipped them
up six feet in the air and let them fall again. "See. They are okay,"
and as he tucked them in his shirt pocket he chuckled, "Buy them
at the dime store."

Orr was interested, too, in some of the pack-rat nests that had
a patina on the wood. It was a dark, shellaclike coating that he called
"amber rat." "It only marks the old ones, and it is really old," he
commented. A decade or so later botanists noted that those pack
rats had gathered kinds of wood that do not occur within a hundred
miles of these sites. Such energetic pack rats. Well, not really, for
C-14 dating showed that these nests had survived in the aridity of

the desert for 20,000 years and more and had preserved the record
of the climate of the desert as expressed in vegetation during a
glacial period. Orr's observations and methods may have been un-
orthodox, but he had an unerring sense of what was important.

However, our Lahontan tour was overly oriented to cave and
tufa for my interests, and time was too short, for we hurried from
Nevada to Santa Barbara and thence out to sea, to Santa Rosa Island. But I wanted to see and learn more about Lahontan and man,
and this I accomplished in the usual academic manner. I got a sum-
mer-session job at the University of Nevada the next summer. This
gave me six weeks of afternoons and weekends to look at the evidence for man along the lakeshores at more leisure. I used some of
the time to go up into the Sierras to look at the glacial moraines—
old, middle age, and young.

The first free afternoon I loaded the family in the car, took
a last look at the topographic map, and set off. The road crossed
the lakeshore in a zone of gently sloping alluvial fans, and I drove
right over the shoreline. When it was clear that I had missed it, I
stopped on a rise and looked back. From a distance, I could make
out the dim, white line of the old sand beach, and by picking careful landmarks I managed to stop the car on it. The sharpness of
the shorelines varies. On gently sloping sandy margins, the lakeshore may be difficult to see. Along steep and rocky shorelines, it
is usually as marked as the molding around a room. But even this
can vary, for in my first visit the line was very visible, but in my
second visit only barely visible. The difference was caused by an intervening unusually wet winter, which encouraged the desert annuals
and left a fuzz of dry vegetation on even the rocky areas of the old
waterline, blurring the line.

My first stop on this trip was on a shallow, sandy beach area,
and it took careful looking to see the old beach lines. They were
there, and so was abundant evidence of man's past presence. But
I had been told that there was no evidence for man on the beaches.
True, there are steep and rocky sections of the shoreline where there
is little if any evidence for man, but there, on this sandy shore on
a large, shallow arm of the lake, the evidence for man's occupancy
extended for miles, and it was most revealing. The material being
used to make artifacts covered a wide range of fine stones quarried

FIGURE 5. The probable sequence at Lake Lahontan leading to the making of fine, bifacially flaked arrow and dart points is shown here. Heavy leaf-shaped knives, with either bifacial or unifacial flaking, appeared first, then good dart points, then fine dart points. The materials changed, too. At first, at least in this area, only dark basalts were used, but later fine, glassy rocks were quarried in the nearby mountains.

from the nearby mountains: jasper, chalcedony, chert, and some fine-grained basalts. The early people had not used these stones. All of the material was fresh as a daisy, not sandblasted, not water-worn, not weathered (oxidized, hydrated, or iron- and manganese-coated). The artifacts were principally finely made dart points with side and basal notching (see figure 5). No arrowheads and no pottery or other evidence of late occupation was present. No artifacts would have been expected here, for this area was far out in a desert basin with no water for miles and no concentration of any food resources. And yet here were lineal miles of evidence of extensive human occupation. In the caves we had seen that flaked stone made up only a small percentage of the cultural material of these people. Wooden tools, basketry, cordage, skins, feathers, and so forth made up the great bulk of their equipment. For each dart point there were at least a hundred perishable items. Here on the desert surface all of the perishable items were gone, but the flake debris was extensive, and the dart points had once been present by the thousands. This I determined by visiting and talking with the local collectors, who had searched these areas for years and had arranged the hundreds of dart points into fancy designs on boards, even Indian heads complete with feather headdresses, in which each feather was a long, leaf-shaped point. They neither knew the destruction they had wrought nor had the slightest idea of the age of the material. But the archeologists were equally guilty, for they neither harnessed this amateur energy nor did the collecting themselves. The lake was Pleistocene; ergo, there was no evidence of man expectable there. Nonetheless, the flake debris alone showed that hundreds of other people had lived here for every cave dweller.

Broecker's dates, made upon Orr's suggestion that the tufa could be dated, established that the youngest, highest beaches were 10,000 years old. The material on them was advanced dart points, not the early, leaf-shaped points and not the heavy flake and core tools of the early people. To find the older material, one had to look at the ancient desert surfaces that the lake had not touched, and then there they were: crude in form, strongly weathered, beyond the reach of the waves that had surged along the shores of the fluctuating levels of Lake Lahontan. Notice that three distinct systems indicate the pre–10,000 year age: location, weathering, and typology. One alone might leave some questions. Location could be due to some special attraction. Typological crudeness could be due to quarrying and taking away the material to be finished up, leaving only crude debris. Weathering could be due to special conditions or special rock. But the sites were not at quarries, the weathering environments were the same, and at times even the rock types were the same, for the later people occasionally used the same basalts that the earlier people had usually worked with. The 10,000-year-old basalt dart points showed no discernible weathering, but the heavy core tools showed deep weathering (see figure 6). One set of tools was several times older than the other. If the dart points

FIGURE 6. The early cultural stages at Lake Lahontan are represented in these heavy core tools, typical of the La Jollan stage, with their unifacial flaking and the cores from which long blade-type flakes were struck. Both the location of these tools in relation to the lake and their weathering indicate that these artifacts are far older than 10,000 years and that the blade cores are far older than the uniface work.

are 10,000 years old, then the core tools were x times 10,000. It was not a popular suggestion (Carter, 1958a).

The glacial moraines also attracted my attention. I had read about glacial weathering in the Midwest and in the Sierras. The glacial geologists had varied weathering scales for differentiating one glacial from another. In the upper Midwest, they wrote of the depth of calcium removal, of the depth of oxidation, and of the decay of pebbles. This was for the late glacial remains, and the measures all indicated slight weathering. They then recorded a huge break to extreme weathering that produced heavy clay soils that

they called gumbo tills, and these were interglacial soils. The difference was the leap from 10,000 to 100,000 years. In the Sierra
Nevadas Blackwelder (1931) noted that the later glacial moraines
could be dated by the degree of weathering of the granites. Young
moraines had hard, white, unweathered granite. Middle and Early
Wisconsin moraines showed progressively greater amounts of weathering, and he worked out ratios for this. In the pre-Wisconsin moraines all granites were thoroughly rotted (see table 2).

Here we meet the "difference man" and the "similarity man."
There are differences in granites, and different granites weather at
differing rates. The "difference man" bears down on this and pro-
claims that therefore there can be no significance to granite weathering and time relationships. The "similarity man" sees that, despite
differences in granites and their weathering rates, there is an overall similarity. No granite boulder survives 100,000 years of weathering. With a little care to use comparable granites, one can distinguish weathering differences on a 10,000-year scale—for example, early, middle, and late Wisconsin. Descriptively, the youngest
morainic material is fresh and retains polish and striae, while the
earlier, last-glacial material is discolored and partially rotted. The
time may be of the order of 20,000 and 60,000 years to the maxima
of the Tioga and Tahoe glaciations. The difficulty in applying the
granite-weathering method to artifacts is that it is usually difficult
to be sure that fresh granite rather than somewhat weathered granite
was used. For the Truckhaven site, to be described later, it will be
shown that when we can control this weathering problem the granite
weathering still obviously is in a Tahoe stage, or something of the
magnitude of 60,000 years of age or greater.

The younger moraines had large, leaf-shaped basalt knives on
their surfaces, indicating that these artifacts were less than 20,000
years old. One of the older morainic deposits had all the marks of
early Wisconsin weathering: much iron staining, clay formation,
granite rotting, and so forth. Its minimum age was early Wisconsin.
A mano, the hand-held stone for grinding seeds, was firmly in place
in this matrix. For those firmly convinced that seed-grinding equipment is only 10,000 years old anywhere in the world (e.g., Krieger,
1959, 1964), such finds simply do not exist or are simply ludicrous
claims, but, as will be shown later, they are not the only such finds.

Table 2
Granite Weathering

	Tioga*	Tahoe	Sherwin
Striation	usual	rare on granite; usual on quartz, aplite, quartzite	none on granite
Soils†	ashen gray	light buff	rusty or tawny
Boulder Weathering‡	90%a, 10%b, 0%c	30%a, 60%b, 10%c	0%a, 30%b, 70%c
Age (Evans' scale)	20,000	60,000	110,000
Archeological Weathering‡		Many hammer stones at Truckhaven and many manos and metates in the Yuha Desert are at stage c. This is also true of manos and metates in geomorphically old sites on the coast.	

SOURCE: Based on Blackwelder, 1931; time scale from Evans, 1971. Blackwelder's work has been repeated with careful controls by others, with the same general results. The data apply best to the arid regions west of the Sierras and Peninsular Range. Weathering rates increase on the western, humid side of the Sierra. The archeological weathering information has been added for comparisons.

*Tioga, Tahoe, and Sherwin are the names given by Blackwelder to the glacial periods along the east face of the Sierra Nevadas. Striation refers to the scratches visible on rocks that the glaciers have carried or overridden. Since they are surface phenomena, they disappear early, and earliest on the softer rocks and minerals.

†Some early archeological sites have rusty to tawny soils and rotted granite tools that should bear striations but show none. This suggests a Sherwin age for them.

‡Weathering scale

    (a)   almost unweathered

    (b)   decayed surface, solid interior

    (c)   greatly weathered, cavernous, rotten

FIGURE 7. Shown here are (*left to right*) Carl Hubbs, Phil Orr, George Carter, and Wallace Broecker, setting out from Santa Barbara for Santa Rosa Island on the expedition that led to the finding of evidence for man's cooking elephants there about 30,000 years ago. (Photo courtesy of Phil Orr and the Santa Barbara Museum of Natural History)

The gist of the Lahontan experience was that evidence of 10,000 years for man was abundant and marked relatively late times. The heavy-core tools with the accompanying flakes and manos and metates for seed grinding were orders of magnitude earlier. The evidence was there for anyone to read, but it required a background in geology and geomorphology that the archeologists lacked and felt no need for since American archeology did not extend into geologic time.

From the Lahontan, Orr, Broecker, and I went to Santa Barbara where we met Carl Hubbs aboard a Scripps Institution of Oceanography vessel (see figure 7), a little tuglike boat that shipped water in big swells in the Santa Barbara channel and rolled too much for my queasy stomach. I was glad to reach Santa Rosa Island. We tied up to the pier but only briefly, for the swells had us banging into the pilings so briskly that we decided to send the boat back to the safe anchorage of Santa Barbara while we moved ashore into the bunkhouse and ate at the ranch house.

The first afternoon we drove out to Skunk Point, an area within easy reach for a half-day's work. I had quizzed Orr about core tools, the typical cobble and flake material of the Southern California coast. "Not on Santa Rosa," was his reply. At Skunk Point I found the middens littered with just such material, and I walked up to Phil with an armload. "Where did you get those?" he demanded. "You are walking on them," I replied. Orr is fundamentally a bone man, a paleontological sort, and he concentrated his work on the opposite end of the island where the dwarf elephant material was most abundant and where there was also a great plenty of later archeological material. But at that end of the island, there was little or no hard rock for the early-lithic folk. Near Skunk Point there was an abundant supply, and there was a consequent tonnage of flakes and cores. Orr was to catch me later stomping on some of his precious elephant bones. I saw stone; he saw bone.

Another point of special interest for me at Skunk Point was a cemented sand stratum filled with flaked stone of violet-colored rhyolite. The cementation was so strong that I could not get artifacts out without breaking them, and the stratum dipped beneath the surf. The men who flaked this stone had lived when the sea was well below its present level. Nearby I found a piece of this rock showing classic marks of bipolar flaking, a very old technique of working stone. Orr does not remember it this way—stones and bones again. Carl Hubbs does not remember it at all; he was on a shell hunt for his ocean-temperature studies. Wally Broecker was a graduate student moving from geology into physical-chemical dating, brighter than a brand-new silver dollar, but not yet attuned to lithics, sea levels, and archeological evaluations. Someone sometime will have to resurrect that site when the times and interests are right.

The next three days we spent on the opposite end of the island (see figure 8). We saw house rings as perfectly preserved as if they had been abandoned last year instead of 1,000 years ago and burials in sand dunes dating to 7,000 years ago, with slight evidence of weathering or cementation of the sands. Beneath the sands lay stratified alluvium laid down over Pleistocene beach material; the sea was now chewing its way into alluvium, creating cliffs forty

Figure 8. Pictured here are the sea cliffs on the west end of Santa Rosa Island. The light material capping the cliff is dune sand and contains archeological material 2,000 to 5,000 years old. The man (indicated by the arrow) is standing on the 12,500-year level; shell middens extend to this depth. In the beds below this were the traces of man's fireplaces and, in huge pits, barbecued elephants. One of these dated to almost 30,000 years ago. (Photo courtesy of Phil Orr)

to sixty feet high. Few details differed from the cliffs at La Jolla, which will be described later. The general setting was the same; the required sequence was the same: sea down to expose a shelf for the alluvium to accumulate on; sea up to truncate the alluvium. This should be read: glacially lowered seas, followed by the recent sea-level rise. As at La Jolla, the C-14 dates in the upper part of the alluvium could be projected to the base and suggested a date for the underlying beach of about 60,000 years. As at La Jolla, there were interruptions in the deposition, marked by weathering of the exposed land surface, and, especially on these land surfaces, there were orange areas that I maintained were fireplaces that had burned the earth to a soft brick. The idea was not kindly received, for where, my friends asked, are the tools or other evidence of human activity? Where, I asked, are you going to get frequent, localized, intense fire of such duration as to burn the earth to brick?

All day we looked. At night we argued. Black material assumed to be charcoal and hence useful for dating by some was mistrusted by Hubbs. "It's too shiney and crystalline," he opined, and a Hubbs opinion is usually pretty forcefully expressed. The upshot of this argument was that Hubbs put a match to the alleged charcoal and nearly drove us out of the bunkhouse. It was ancient petroleum, and it stank. Hubbs was right, again.

I argued for my fires as evidence of man, citing literature that forest fires did not scorch the earth in this fashion. Orr later wrote an excellent article with Rainer Berger of U.C.L.A., presenting convincing data that supported this notion (Orr and Berger, 1966), but at that earlier time he was unconvinced. The dwarf elephant skeletons were found all through the alluvium except for the top layers, which represented the last 10,000 years or thereabouts. They were conspicuously present in the same levels as the fires. Plaintively, I asked if Orr had not ever found at least one burned elephant bone. I reasoned that man would have eaten an elephant now and then, even if he had to wait for one to die of old age, just as the later California Indians feasted on dead whales that drifted ashore. "No, never," and other negatives flowed from Orr, and I generally retired early, for with only the fireplaces I had too little ammunition to engage in battle.

On our last day Hubbs wanted to collect fish bone and shell from a dated village. We left him with a screen, seated on the ground, sifting away. Each screening sent up a cloud of dust in which Hubbs disappeared as if in a smoke screen. As the sea breeze blew him clear, he could be seen sitting there, Buddha-like, with his eyes closed, and covered with dust. Ah, science!

Wally Broecker wanted to take a last look at the stratigraphy of the sea cliff, and we dropped him at a convenient spot. Orr then turned to me and asked "Well, what do you want to do?" "I want to find a cooked elephant," I replied. Phil sighed at such obstinacy but said, "Well, I excavated a skeleton near here, so let's start there."

We parked the four-wheel-drive vehicle and started down a ravine toward the sea cliff. Just before we got there, I spotted one of "my" burned-earth areas and paused to look closer. My excitement was considerable when I saw sizable bones radiating from the fire like spokes from a wheel. They were burned at the

fire end and not at the other. Orr got a bit excited and started snapping pictures while also snapping at me for stomping on his bones.
When he calmed down a bit, he realized that he had no film in
his camera. The bones were elephant-rib bone. In the face of the
nearby sea cliff, I could see where Orr had excavated his nearly
complete elephant skeleton. I could also see that the skeleton had
rested in a pit whose walls were burned to a soft brick. We were
face to face with an elephant barbecue, complete with spareribs
done in a bonfire for those who could not wait. Orr's excitement
had him at the boiling point. "Come on. I took out another half
a mile down the coast." We piled in the jeep, and he drove down
a faint track with ruts that resembled crevasses, which he outma-
neuvered by straddling them, while I kept one foot on the running
board, ready to leap. Leaving the vehicle, we scrambled like human
flies along the cliff face, and once again we came face to face with
evidence for an elephant cookout. Back at the museum, I inspected
the elephant skeleton that had been assembled from such spots. The
bones were black: charred. "And you told me you never saw evidence of man and elephant," I said accusingly. "Look at all those
charred bones." "How was I to know they were charred? Bones get
black from manganese and other minerals, you know," was Phil's
defense. He was right, of course: black bones need not be charred
bones. But again, notice how the set of the mind conditions the
understanding of what one sees. Broecker capped the argument by
dating the charred bones on one of the finds at 29,650 years. For
years few were willing to consider this date as evidence for man.
But with dates for human skeletons in Southern California far beyond that, there is now no excuse for rejecting the date. But then,
there never really was. Just how would whole elephant skeletons
repeatedly get into pits and then be burned? We four had fun inventing an elephantine funeral rite in which the older elephants
used their tusks to dig pits and their trunks to collect wood to fill
the pit, thus creating a funeral pyre. Then all they had to do was
wait for a lightning strike to light the pyre, and they could make
a flaming exit from this world and bequeath an insoluble puzzle to
anthropological posterity. The weakest point in this fantasy is the
lightning. Southern California is one of the most lightning-free

FIGURE 9. Morlin Childers demonstrates here how he made a duplicate of one of the unusual artifacts found on early sites in the Yuha Desert in the Imperial Valley.

areas in the world. To which the archeological answer might be: "Oh well, elephants are long-lived. They could wait."

At a conference at the Calico site in 1970, I met Morlin Childers, keen amateur observer from the Imperial Valley (see figure 9). Lacking professional credentials, Morlin gained entrance to the conference as a reporter. He had brought along some alleged artifacts, but almost no one would look at them or even talk with him. Fortunately, he was shunted to me. Birds of a feather, you know. I needed no more than a glance to see that Morlin had artifacts, and it took about two minutes to see that they were old and belonged in the pre-projectile-point era, that is, they were clearly older than 10,000 years. That opened a whole vista of material in the Imperial Valley that Rogers and I had missed. Among the material that Morlin had was the core-and-blade and concave-scraper assemblage common to Texas Street, Buchanan Canyon, Calico, and now to the southwest corner of the Imperial Valley, an area called the Yuha Desert.

So the early lithic industry at San Diego no longer stood alone. Sites were now being found widely at San Diego and in the adjacent Colorado and Mohave deserts. No matter what kind of stone was used, characteristic tools were produced by a uniform technique. Although absolute time was uncertain, all of the sites were associated with ancient landforms and extreme degrees of weathering.

New dating methods were appearing, and old ones were being extended. At the Scripps Institution of Oceanography, Dr. Jeffrey Bada was developing a method for dating material containing protein; therefore, he could date bones and hence human skeletons. When word of this reached me and I learned that the process could reach out for a few hundred thousand years, I tried at once to interest Bada in my material. There was some delay. Bada did not reply to my letter of inquiry, and I later learned that this was because he was assured that my notion of great antiquity for man in America was not only groundless but madness. However, I knew that the San Diego Museum of Man had skeletons found under conditions suggesting high antiquity, and they afforded too good an opportunity to be passed up. A dating directly on human bones would bypass innumerable arguments. We have many skeletons found under conditions suggesting antiquity, but none that have occurred without some possibility of late intrusion or some alternative explanation. Thus Jenks's Minnesota skeleton (1936) may or may not have been in place in glacial lake sediments, and so on for a long list of finds. And none of these possible early skeletons was so primitive as to compel a conclusion that it was of great age, though some of them looked remarkably primitive to be just very recent man.

M. J. Rogers had collected skeletons from situations suggesting great age in the 1920's and 1930's and had shown me the bones and the sites. When the possibility of dating the bones directly finally arrived in 1972, I was the last person alive who knew of their potential significance. The museum had the bones and the records, but over the ensuing years the significance of the materials had been lost. Everything was preserved, except the awareness of the meaning of the material.

Bada was advised by those he consulted that I should be ignored, and the museum had long ago written me off as a wild man. Bada could see no reason to waste time on dating bones of no great age, especially at the urging of a wild man. The museum was certain that the bones dated only to about 7,000 years, and this was almost too young for Bada's system to work with. Dating material found half a century earlier was of much less interest to the museum staff than dating some of the material that they had recently uncovered.

My approach to the museum was made through Dr. Ray Gilmore of the natural history museum at San Diego. Gilmore (1942) had written a Ph.D. thesis on the stenocranius voles of the Bering Strait region. His interest was in the evolution of these mice in the Bering region, with its isolated populations on islands and its larger representation on two continents whose linkages were controlled by the rising and falling sea levels of glacial and interglacial times. We had met during my many-summers' work at San Diego. When I first published on my reading of the evidence as indicating an interglacial age for man in America, Gilmore chided me for not crediting him with preceding me with the idea. I apologized for having missed his publication and asked where I could find it. He replied, "Oh, it is in my unpublished Ph.D. thesis." When I obtained this on interlibrary loan, I found that not only had he considered the implications of the opening and closing of the linkage between America and Asia at Bering Strait for the migration of voles, but he had also expanded his discussion to include sea birds, sea mammals, and even man.

He placed man in the same framework as the animals in this gateway to America and viewed the sequence as being like a two-cycle pump. Man and animals moved up from Asia to the Bering Strait in a warm period and moved onto the emerging landmass when an oncoming cold period dropped the sea level. They survived on the Beringean landmass during a glacial period and proceeded into America as the seas rose, drowning the bridge, and the ice melted, opening up corridors into America. His assessment of the evidence was that man, along with many of the animals, had moved through this complex system by the last interglacial period. It was a most interesting analysis for a zoologist and gave us a common bond of interest.

Gilmore talked with Rose Tyson, curator of physical anthro-

pology at the San Diego Museum of Man, and she undertook a
search for the skeletal remains that I described. They were there,
but she and Dr. Spencer Rogers, the scientific director of the mu-
scum, expressed considerable surprise at any special interest in these
specimens. One finely preserved skull was a classic example of La
Jollan man—exceptable age 5,000 to 7,000 years. Another fragmentary burial has an olivella-shell bead cemented to its rib bones,
surely not what one expects in vast antiquity. Why bother to date
the obviously late material?

Bada was also reluctant, and he not only did not answer
letters, but when I phoned him when I was in California he was
too busy to see me that day. So I called on him in his office without any previous warning, introduced myself, and sat down quickly,
for I have found that it is difficult to throw someone out of your
office if he is sitting down. This gave me a chance to talk with
Bada, and he thawed rapidly as I talked of the evidence for high
antiquity for man right on his campus. I gave him a copy of my
book on the area, which was rather promptly stolen from him, and
perhaps this among other things indicated that there was something
of significance in the area. Presently he agreed to date the skeletons
if his laboratory expenses were met. I then had to convince the museum that the dating should be tried. This too was a struggle.
First they had to be assured that precious specimens would not
be destroyed. This is one of the strong points of Bada's method.
He needs only tiny amounts, while C-14 needs huge amounts of
bone. Then I had to convince them that my suggestions instead of
theirs were worth dating. We finally compromised. We would submit some of their selections and some of mine.

The skeletal materials that I wanted tested were from conditions suggesting great age; one surely was, and two probably were.
At Del Mar, on the north side of the mouth of the San Diequito
River, Malcolm Rogers had found a human skeleton eroding out
of a sea cliff (see figure 10). The body had been on the sea side
of the cliff, and most of it was lost. The skull was still in place in
the cliff, many feet below the land surface. Normal burial depth is
about two feet, so this greater depth suggested geologic deposition.
Preservation was extremely good, indicating that deep burial had
occurred relatively quickly, so that the skeleton had spent little

FIGURE 10. M. J. Rogers is shown excavating the skull that proved to be 48,000 years old. The location is at the mouth of the San Dieguito River, near the race track at Del Mar. The skull was found in 1929 and finally dated in 1974 by Jeffrey Bada, using the protein racemization method. (Photo courtesy of the San Diego Museum of Man)

time in the weathering zone. The deep placement of this skeleton was out of keeping with the cultural pattern of the region and suggested that accumulating sediments rapidly put a thick layer of sand over what had been a shallow burial. The normal way for this to happen would be in something like a valley bottom under conditions of rapid deposition, just the situation of the present valley fill, separated from the present valley fill by a period of excavation of the valley during a glacially lowered sea level. This would call for a very high age, minimally something around 40,000 years. This was one possibility, but there were others. The burial could have been covered by slope wash from the height of land behind it, or it could have been a most abnormally deep burial. This is typical of most early finds. There are too many "ifs" in the situation, and this is precisely why we have needed a system for dating skeletons directly.

When the samples were finally in Bada's hands, I dropped by his office to see how things were going. He showed me what the museum had sent and asked me what I thought. I checked them over and put them in two lots, saying that one set would date around 5,000 to 7,000 years and that the other would date at something like ten times that. The dates came out just that way (Bada, Schroeder, and Carter, 1974). The earliest ones dated 30,000 to 48,000 years; these were the ones that I had selected. The museum's selections came out in the 5,000- to 7,000-year range. The results created a great deal of excitement, and the museum was delighted. I found myself restored to good standing in that community. Bada also decided that his advisers were a little less than prophetic, and he was so generous that he not only put my name on the article reporting the early dates but never mentioned the matter of expense. When I most hesitantly raised the question, he snorted, "Oh, I was only going to charge you if you had been wasting my time with some nonsense about early man in America." Actually I embroiled him in the donnybrook over the antiquity of man in America, but he is a courageous fighter, and the facts are on his side, so there is no doubt that he will emerge triumphant.

Bada had no idea what a maelstrom he was entering. In the relatively sane and sober realm of physical chemistry one experimented, tested, checked, cross-checked, compared, and reported. But when Bada's data contradicted the passionately held opinions of the archeologists, they peremptorily rejected his findings. In a recent discussion, I asked an archeologist who refused to accept Bada's findings and consistently misrepresented Bada's work which of Bada's papers he had read. "None," was the reply. "Don't you feel a little uneasy at criticizing and rejecting a man's work without reading it?" I asked. "No, I just take the word of others," he said.

I should not leave the world of physical-chemical dating portrayed as a placid sea, across which the ship of science sails its unruffled way. It is a stormy sea in its own right. Protein racemization was tried by others before Bada and judged to be too full of possible error to be useful. Bada took it up and developed it to useful levels, but he was then furiously attacked by those who had discarded the system. This quarrel within the ranks of the geochemists has, of course, not gone unnoticed by the anti–early man people in archeology, who utilize the dissension in the ranks to attack the early dates. Archeological meetings now reach a fevered pitch when Bada and his opponents lock horns before an audience already emotionally involved in the man-and-time argument. At a recent meeting Bada and Rainer Protsch went at each other hot and heavy. Protsch presented data to support a hypothesis that fully modern man (*Homo sapiens sapiens*) was no more than 40,000 years old anywhere in the world and expectably much younger in America. Therefore, he concluded, Bada's 50,000-year dates for highly developed man (racially marked, even) in America could not possibly be correct. Rose Tyson and I were immediately on our feet attacking Protsch's statements about the skulls in the San Diego Museum of Man dated by Bada, and things became lively. The idea of no chronologically early man in America because there are no primitive men in America is an idea long promoted by Aleš Hrdlička, so I told Protsch that we would call his hypothesis the Hrdlička a-protsch. Fortunately, he thought the pun funny, so that avenue for exchange of ideas remains open. The question of the time of appearance of *Homo sapiens, Homo sapiens sapiens,* and races will be discussed later. It is no settled matter. The point of this paragraph is that few things are. Even the hard sciences such as chemistry can be pretty volcanic at times.

As an example of the role of attitudes and of varying results, consider the case of James Moriarty. Jim received an A.B. degree in anthropology from San Diego State and along with it a ferocious indoctrination against Carter's early-man theories. He then went to work for Francis Shepard at the Scripps Institution of Oceanography as an artist-draftsman, a position he held for many years. This was during the period of my active work on the geomorphology of the area, and I was in close contact with both Hubbs and Shepard. Moriarty was continuing his real interest, archeology, and collecting and excavating on his free time.

When Shepard, the marine geologist at Scripps, took his graduate students into the field with me, Moriarty passed word along through Shepard and the Hubbs (Hubbs being plural since all matters Hubbsian involved both Carl and Laura) to ask if I would allow Moriarty to accompany the group. I invited him to come along. Perhaps a day in the field would convince him, for we would be dealing with hard evidence (landforms and soils) and discussing interpretations with some very well-informed people. I was confident that I could hold my own and so could see nothing but potential good in Jim's being along.

As the day began, Jim hung back, but as the day progressed he pressed forward into the front ranks. We were friends thereafter, though it was about fifteen years before he took some of my notions seriously. We argued for decades over the age of the La Jollan and the reality of the evidence for man at Texas Street. The Buchanan Canyon site convinced Jim that there was a lithic industry at San Diego that could not be fitted into the accepted cultures and led him finally to join Minshall and me in excavation at Buchanan Canyon and Texas Street. Since then he has excavated the Charles H. Brown site, three miles west of the Texas Street site, and has confirmed my controversial cultural sequence. He remains very conservative in his dates for early man.

Not everyone is easily converted. Clement Meighan came down from U.C.L.A. and went over the Texas Street site with me and listened and nodded, I thought in understanding and agreement. When I learned that he had "bought it not," I wrote him to ask why he had not disagreed with me in the field and given me a chance to answer his objections. He replied that he was under no obligation to express his disagreement to me. True, in a way, but my ideal is a session in the field looking at the evidence or in the laboratory handling the alleged artifacts, with interpretations, ideas, and opinions laid out to be dissected, defended, or defeated. I have the apparently curious notion that this is how progress is made.

Another such episode involved soils men from Berkeley. My notions of great antiquity and a soil record of past climates was extremely distasteful to Hans Jenny, professor of soils at U.C. Berkeley. He came to the San Diego area, bringing an Australian colleague then on the Berkeley staff. Jenny knew that I was in the field that summer but stayed away from me. The Aussie, however, phoned me and explained apologetically that, while Jenny chose to remain aloof, he would like to spend a day in the field with me. We had a very interesting day together. I showed him the alluvial sequence at Scripps and then took him to the La Jolla Cove to show him a greatly decayed sandstone metate in place in the alluvial cover there. From this vantage point, we could look back and have a panoramic view of the truncated alluvial fan south of the Scripps pier, in those days not obscured by seawalls or houses except right near the pier. I pointed to the convex surface, normal to a fan, and summarized what we had seen when we were examining it close up. "My word," he said, "it is exactly as you described it." "That is an odd comment," I replied, "What leads you to say that?" "Well," he explained, "at Berkeley I was told that the feature was not at all as you described it and in fact did not exist."

The metate in place in the alluvial cover remained there for several years, and I showed it to all visitors. Eventually winter rains and the feet of the users of the nearby drinking fountain eroded it away. Twenty years later Paul Chase, then of the San Diego Museum of Man, in challenging my evidence for manos and metates in the Wisconsin-age alluvial covers asked for evidence and witnesses. Those who had come and would look saw this one. Paul Chase was born a bit late and would have to ask people like R. D. Simpson, who did come and see—though why not ask me?

I also left a mano in place in the cliff south of Scripps for three years and, before taking it out before the sea claimed it, I got two of Carl Hubbs's graduate students to come down and witness

FIGURE 11. These three cores from the 1973 exhibit at the University of San Diego all illustrate the same fundamental blade and core technology. A flat striking platform has been prepared at the top of each core, and blows have been struck on that platform in such a way as to remove long flakes (blades) that ran from end to end of the core. Core *a*, from Mexico, may be as little as 1,000 years old. Core *b*, from France, is about 10,000 years old. Core *c*, porphyritic felsite from the Tijuana River, is something less than 100,000 years.

it. The problem is that few would even look: in ten year's work, no one came from Berkeley, only Meighan from U.C.L.A., and no one from San Diego State.

In 1973 things had changed little. We excavated at Texas Street and exposed hearths, living floors, and artifacts. I wrote to numerous people that we would be doing so and visited a number of centers before we began work: U.C. Davis, U.C. Berkeley, Stanford, San Diego State, and others. Berkeley was particularly interesting. I had written that I would be visiting, bringing artifacts. I was there before the end of the school year, but everyone was "out of town," and a graduate student was detailed to talk with me, which he did, most courteously. Then when the work was well advanced at San Diego, I phoned around. No major archeological personage appeared other than R. D. Simpson. Only U.C. Riverside looked in, sending geographers, geomorphologists, and soils men. San Diego State University adamantly refused to look at work in their own backyard.

In 1973 we (Carter, Minshall, and Moriarty) laid out at the University of San Diego an immense mass of material from Buchanan Canyon and Texas Street. On one table I placed an exhibit to illustrate blade and core work (see figure 11). It began with a Mexican obsidian core fluted by flake scars as regularly spaced as the flutes in a Greek pillar. Next to it we placed a French Neolithic flint core, which had large, regular flake scars and was clearly of the same technology as the Mexican core. Then came a near-twin to the French core: same prepared platform, same edge trimming, same long flake scars running from a broad striking platform to a pointed tip. But this example came from an interglacial terrace near the mouth of the Tijuana River. Only the materials were different: felsitic porphyry instead of flint. Then we had six more—lumpier, but clearly cores with prepared platforms and long, parallel flake scars running down their sides. One visitor, Carl Hansen, a geomorphologist from the University of California at Riverside with wide experience in Africa where he had paid special attention to Lower Paleolithic work, looked at that table and then went and sat down. I approached him to ask: "What's up, aren't you going to look at the rest of the material?" "No need to," he replied. "That material is all one needs to demonstrate that you have human work, and not natural breakage of stone." Carl Hansen's background is especially interesting for this question. As a geomorphologist, he is particularly aware of problems of human versus natural breakage. As a man with experience with Old World Lower Paleolithic work he could recognize purposeful lithic work even on crude levels.

A comparable event occurred at a meeting in the spring of 1979 in west Texas. I took a sample of the highly controversial Texas Street material to the meetings. Paul Ezell, retired from San Diego State University, brought over some of M. J. Rogers' material borrowed from the San Diego Museum. Tony Andretta had early material from west Texas. Julian Hayden brought some material from the Pinacate range in Sonora, Mexico. I had not seen Julian Hayden since 1938 when we had been on an archeological dig in the San Dieguito Canyon, and we had differed a bit on archeological matters. When I handed Julian Texas Street material piece by piece, he commented on one after another: "Well, that's an artifact."

Tony Andretta looked over the material and added, "I know of sites with material like that." Tony and Julian are retired, and they never were Ph.D. professional archeologists. Both, however, have had long and wide experience in archeology. With no career or academic position to maintain, they simply exercise their observational powers. The academic like the Ph.D. professor with a position to maintain looks over his shoulder to see what his colleagues are likely to say. He avoids controversy and shuns the heretic. So, at west Texas and many another occasion, it has been the man free from fear of his academic peers that has accepted the evidence.

At a Pecos conference thirty years ago the Texas Street material was looked over and largely rejected. At a meeting of the Society for American Archeology in Chapel Hill about twenty years ago the material was again exhibited. One archeologist whose specialty was the Lower Paleolithic of India looked the material over, asking "What is this?" When I said it was the Texas Street material, the comment was: "The archeologists that have been denying that these are artifacts had better go back and redo Archeology 1-A." One archeologist who was dubious about the material at the Pecos conference accepted it outright thirty years later.

This has been a continuing saga. I have lugged my broken rocks around from place to place; I found acceptance to be zero twenty-five years ago, but it is gradually building up now. Some people simply will not look; they can be dismissed. The more interesting cases are those who will now look and, with prepared minds and with considerable courage, reverse themselves. Then there are the younger men, better trained in lithic analysis and freer of prior commitments. New evidence for the view of man's early arrival in America continues to accumulate. The conditions that I set at the time of publication of *Pleistocene Man at San Diego* have been met. By 1973 we had many sites, all with evidence of great antiquity and all having the same fundamental industry. It was time to reopen old sites and old arguments and to reassess the picture using the new dating tools. And so I returned to the archeological wars.

In 1976 while working on the preliminary draft of this book, I spent the summer in La Jolla. Bada wanted excavation done on some of the key sites in the area but could find no local archeologist interested in doing any work there. So he brought in Jason Smith, trained in arctic archeology, who had formerly taught at California State University, Northridge. Jason started work on sites that M. J. Rogers had worked on in 1929, that I had excavated skeletons from in the 1930's, and that Jim Moriarty had excavated skeletons from in the 1940's—to mention just a few of the efforts made on that site. Jason is a whiz at public relations; he managed to get the *New York Times* and the *National Geographic* to send reporters to the site. He also got R. S. "Scotty" MacNeish, Director of the Peabody Foundation, who recently had found evidence of modestly early man in South America, out to look at the site.

I did my best to help by volunteering information based on my forty-year acquaintance with the site. The *New York Times* man wrote that "no one minded very much," since I had been the key man in getting the early skeletons dated and it was that which had made possible this interest in excavation. Ah well, I will try to be less helpful in the future, and they probably will not mind at all.

Jason Smith also got B. O. K. Reeves, archeologist at the University of Calgary, Canada, to come down to look, and Reeves found the situation interesting enough to return to spend a sabbatical looking around. Herb Minshall showed him the collections of interglacial artifacts and the interglacial sites that we had found over the years, and Reeves read Minshall's book, which details the sequence of findings of Rogers, Carter, Minshall, and others in the area. Reeves filed a report with the San Diego museum in which he stated that he had set out to test Minshall's and Carter's contentions (i.e., that there was a very long pre-Clovis history at San Diego) and that his conclusion was that we were right. Headlines in the local paper, however, proclaimed that it was Reeves who had discovered the evidence and that it indicated man had been at San Diego as early as 120,000 years ago. At an anthropology meeting in the spring of 1977, Ronald Olson, emeritus professor of anthropology at the University of California and my first anthropology professor (in 1931), walked up to me and said in his loud voice, "Say, George, let's you and me go to Peru and discover Machu Pichu."

Reeves made one very pertinent observation. The oldest material is not found on the younger terraces. We know that the lower, younger, nearer-the-sea terraces were very advantageous places to live, as was shown by the great abundance of hearths, shell mounds, and stone tools left by the later men. The very early stone tools appeared only above 100 feet or so, a datable level in terms of fluctuating sea levels, and their limitation to these levels is clear evidence that the record below this was erased due to later events: here, high sea levels of late interglacial times. It is a complex argument unless you are at home with glaciers, sea levels, climatic change, and time —all of which are to be considered later. I had finally stumbled onto this fact in the summer of 1976 but had not published on it, so Reeves reached this point quite independently. It needs development by sharpening the precise cutoff point and then precise dating of that geologic event.

The Charles H. Brown site, near the controversial Texas Street site, will go far towards settling this highly charged, overly personalized argument as to how long man has lived in America, with the San Diego area as one of the principal testing grounds. It provides stratigraphic evidence of the sequence of some of the lithic stages that we have been arguing about. We have some dating, even if only geological instead of geochemical dates. Already the preliminary reports in letters from Minshall show that the site verifies most of my heretical notions, and I therefore await publication of the site report with considerable interest. We can hope that some of the shouting and name-calling will then subside and we can get on with the business of finding out just what did happen in America and when.

So it is that fifty years after I began work with M. J. Rogers and the San Diego Museum of Man and thirty years after my heretical claim for interglacial man of Lower-Paleolithic stage and 100,-000-year age, we reach a time when new sites and new technologies for dating begin to test the conclusions reached decades ago. With this personalized review behind us, we can now proceed to look more impersonally, though not totally so, at the nature of the evidence for man, his entry into America, the timing of this event, the question of single or plural entries, the questions of stage (Lower Paleolithic, Middle Paleolithic, Upper Paleolithic, Neolithic?), the problems in determining age, the kinds of men, and the rest of these interrelated problems.

Chapter 3

Groping toward a Time Scale

MUCH of the personal and emotional reaction in the early-man field stems from conflicts over time. Few things have been more difficult to deal with, and even today we are only on the threshold of understanding and measuring the time involved in human prehistory. Our knowledge has been changing so rapidly as to be shocking, and the perfectly normal reaction is to question the validity of the systems that produce the shock rather than the security of the foundation of the ideas being challenged. This might be acceptable if the scale against which the new dates or dating systems is tested had been firmly founded in the first place, but in actuality little archeological dating is even yet firmly established, and this is especially true of the earliest dates. Those of the past decades were often mere guesses. We are, in a sense, just emerging from a troglodyte period of dating into a Neolithic period, from guesswork to our first steps toward absolute time measures. Even the newest dating systems are in their infancy, in partial conflict, and the resolution of the discrepancies and the establishment of real time are still some distance down the academic road. W. B. Harland has aptly described the misplaced faith in published time scales in his charge that the scale proposed in the 1964 edition of *The Phanerozoic Time Scale* "had an effect opposite of that intended. It sealed with the authority of hard covers a work intended to pinpoint and publicize the deficiencies of the current time scale" (1971, p. 4). As the 1971 edition shows, we are still plodding toward certainty. Progress certainly, but certainty, not yet.

This is normal in science, even as in the humanities, for we deal not with absolute knowledge but only with probabilities. Our facts are scattered bits of information, which we arrange in some seemingly orderly fashion, and we then treat that arrangement as "fact," forgetting that our fact is but the momentary arrangement of bits and pieces of information on hand. Worse, these bits and pieces were often selected to fit our own particular paradigm, the way in which we see our particular scholarly world. Some American archeologists still see their world as beginning at 10,000 B.C. The geologists until very recently saw a world of fixed and motionless continents. The biologists of a hundred years ago saw a world of unchanging life forms. When the new facts showed up that challenged these views—Mendel with his peas, Wegener with his drifting continents, Darwin with his evolution—they were bitterly attacked. Yet Mendel had found the key to changing life forms, Wegener was correct on the motion of continents, and Darwin despite plenty of errors was fundamentally on the right track.

One does have to discriminate. Von Daniken is no Mendel, and the proponents of Atlantis are simply misusing evidence. I have been constantly astounded at the scientists who have read Von Daniken and have thought his work to be profound and exciting. They exemplify one of the great failings of our present educational system. We too seldom turn out educated men, but too often narrowly trained technicians, and with that goes loss of the art of judgment. This was so well expressed two millennia ago by Aristotle in his *Parts of Animals* 1, that I quote it here: "There are as it seems two ways in which a person may be competent in respect to any study or investigation . . . . He may have either what can rightly be called a scientific knowledge of the subject or he may have what is roughly described as an educated person's competence, and therefore be able to judge correctly which parts of an exposition are satisfactory and which are not. That, in fact, is the sort of person we take the man of general education to be; his 'education' consists of his ability to do this."

The study of time is filled with illustrations of the great contributions of the specialists and of the general failure of the scientists to be able to judge correctly which of the many propositions put before them are the more correct. Time is a knotty problem complicated by the fact that few people know how recently we have come to think in great time depth. We moderns, like our predecessors, tend to take the present situation as eternal. But just as we have not always had airplanes and atomic bombs, we have not always had knowledge of past times. Primitive men dealt with quite short time

spans. "In the days of our grandfathers. . . ." is about their depth
in history. Beyond that lies a dream world of indefinite time, the infinite expanse when things began. For many North American tribes,
"in the beginning, all was water," a very biblical-sounding start,
but then the beaver or some other water animal dives and brings up
mud and the earth's story begins. Just where that beaver came from
is never mentioned. There is no mention of years back to this event.
Who needed years? The account is explanatory, and adding years
would only cause confusion. Our biblical account is similar in that
it starts with water and deals most casually with time. Why bother
with years when transcendental truths are timeless? For countless
millennia men did not bother themselves with establishing such
mundane facts as the exact time of events in the earth's history.

The change came just about 150 years ago when the geologists
began systematically to deal with the data before them. Canal digging in England revealed alternate episodes when the sea covered
the land and when strange animals roamed over England. Clearly
these changes had not occurred overnight, and the geologists began
to talk of the age of the earth as perhaps a few hundred thousand
years. It slowly dawned on the geologists that many different things
had happened. There had been several marine invasions, and the
plants and animals changed from one period to the other. Time
began to loom large, and change through time loomed even larger.

Presently it was noticed that on the plains in front of the Alps
there were great piles of sand, gravel, and boulders that were exactly
like the material the Alpine glaciers piled at their melting snouts
today. But the glaciers were now tens of miles away. Had they once
been clear down here on the plain? One man concluded that the
answer was yes, and the professors went into their frenzied dance
of negation. And presently, as with the dance of the bees, busy
workers were going out to seek the nectar of truth.

It was a long dance. The first suggestions of glacial expansion
date to the eighteenth century. When the observations were repeated
in the early nineteenth century, Louis Agassiz, starting as an incredulous critic, found that the evidence was overwhelming and even
more extensive than had been stated. He became such a fervent pro-
ponent of a past time when ice was vastly more extensive on the
earth than it now is that he is generally thought to be the father of

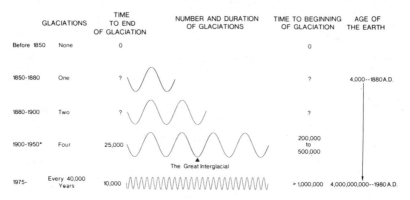

OUR CHANGING VIEW OF PAST TIME

GLACIATIONS	TIME TO END OF GLACIATION	NUMBER AND DURATION OF GLACIATIONS	TIME TO BEGINNING OF GLACIATION	AGE OF THE EARTH
Before 1850 None	0		0	
1850-1880 One	?		?	4,000--1880 A.D.
1880-1900 Two	?		?	
1900-1950* Four	25,000	The Great Interglacial	200,000 to 500,000	
1975- Every 40,000 Years	10,000		> 1,000,000	4,000,000,000--1980 A.D.

FIGURE 12. The last hundred years have seen a revolution in our thinking about time. We actually became aware of the shortness of postglacial time only after 1950, when the C-14 dates began to accumulate. The changes are so great and so rapid that science, philosophy, theology, and archeology are still floundering at the task of revising old ideas.

the ice age rather than the man who confirmed it. When Agassiz came to Harvard to 1846, he promptly found evidence of the ice age here, too. It is easy to find in New England, for many a rocky outcrop is still smoothed and shiney from its long, rasping acquaintance with the great ice sheets. Suddenly we had a time marker. There was the present time, and before that there was the ice age.

Some astute observer noted that some of the glacial deposits were vastly more weathered than others. This led to the idea of two ice ages. It was clear that little time had elapsed since the last ice age, for the rocks in its deposits were fresh, not strongly weathered. The earlier deposits were enormously weathered, and this indicated that a very long period separated the two ice ages. Presently still more ice ages were discerned, and eventually they were systematized into four, with three periods of warmth in between, and everyone settled back with a sigh of contentment to teach this new time scale and to begin to try to convert it to absolute time (see figure 12 for a representation of changing ideas about past time).

The fourfold system of glaciers became a sacred thing, strongly resistant to all challenges. But the evidence accumulating compelled alterations. Each glaciation was complex, and presently each was divided. The last glaciation, the Wisconsin, became Wisconsin I and

II. Then the interglacials became complex, and the last interglacial was divided into three parts. But if the interglacial was divided into three warm periods, there must have been two intervening cold periods, and it should have been obvious that the classification was faulty. The whole system should have been junked in its infancy, but instead it was patched and emended endlessly. Only slowly has it dawned on us that the fourfold system was just as simplistic as the twofold system.

The most interesting point is that all along there had been a rational explanation for the glacial sequences, which called for many glaciations not few, but it was brushed aside. Only with the arrival of new dating systems and the accumulation of long series of dates from ocean cores was the reality of solar control—actually the geometry of the earth's movements in relation to the sun—admitted. This leads to a system in which glacial periods occur on the average every 40,000 years, and this means that we have had twenty-five glaciations, not four, in the past 1 million years. One can no longer read any of the older literature without a correction sheet, for the old terms *Kansan glaciation*, the *Great Interglacial*, and so forth are now virtually meaningless. The whole episode is typical of thinking in science. We are forever leaping to conclusions on incomplete evidence, then solidifying our conclusions and demanding that overwhelming evidence be brought to bear to justify any change. It is both nonsensical and very human.

With the ice age as a marker, efforts quickly turned to putting some real time on these events. A natural beginning was to try to determine the time when the ice age ended. The retreat of such falls as Niagara and St. Anthony gave variable results. The figure for the Fall of St. Anthony was about right—12,000 years—but in the early days there seemed to be no way to know which date was right. Rates of erosion of cliffs, accumulation of deltas, the accumulation of peat, the precipitation of travertine, and so forth gave highly variable readings: from 2,500 to 25,000 years. In retrospect we can see that the figure of 8,000 to 11,000 years kept reappearing, but there was little way of knowing then that this was the right order of magnitude of time. The radioactivity of travertines at Yellowstone National Park, for instance, yielded a date of 11,200 years, almost exactly the date now accepted as the end of the last glacial period, but no one trusted that date either. For now unfathomable reasons, 25,000 years was selected as the date for the end of the last ice age, and for decades every freshman learned that fundamental date.

The geochemical revolution in dating, to be discussed below, has had a radical effect on our thinking about glacial-interglacial times and sequences. This is best summarized in Evans' "Towards a Pleistocene Time-Scale" (1971), and the following pages are based on his work. His title is also a fortunate one, for it expresses the idea that we are making progress but are by no means at any state of final and absolute knowledge. Our progress in dating events in the Pleistocene, the crucial period for human development, is neatly summarized in our estimates of the timing of the Mindel glaciation, the second oldest in the fourfold classification. It has been dated from 200,000 to 1,450,000 years ago. Evans' discussion suggests an age around 220,000 to 320,000 thousand years. The previous estimate varied by a factor of seven for the time to the Mindel glaciation and by a factor of twenty for the duration. We obviously were guessing.

Large changes in our knowledge of the Pleistocene came from records of polarity changes and from radiometric dating of volcanic rocks, of sediments from deep-sea cores, and of shells from high shorelines. The radiometric dates show that the evidence for a major climatic change marking the opening of the glacial Pleistocene is weak indeed. The Pliocene-Pleistocene boundary is, then, a matter of convenience, and notions of a sudden shift from equable climates to an ice age is one more cliché to be discarded.

The best evidence of time and climatic change comes from deep-sea cores. The proportions of the isotope 0-18 in foraminifera shells, the relative abundance of temperature-sensitive foraminifera, and changes in sediments taken together provide a good climatic and time record. That part of the record within reach of the 0-18 method shows a somewhat irregular alternation between warm and cold, averaging about 40,000 years. This approximates the Milankovitch calculations based on changes in insolation (rate of delivery of solar energy) received at sixty-five degrees north and south latitudes.

Evans prepared an insolation curve, compared this with the climate-time curves from the deep-sea cores, and found that cool periods followed times of low summer insolation and warm periods followed times of high summer insolation. The lag time was about 4,000 years. Radiometric data for insolation curves reach back 300,000 years, and extrapolations reach back to 1 million years—as far as the astronomical calculations extend at present. The 300,000-year period of firmest dating exceeds even the most extreme dates yet suggested for American archeology (Hueyatlaco, Mexico, 250,-000 years).

Evans proposes numbering the climatic cycles (see table 3), starting with the present relatively warm period as cycle 1W, the preceding cold as 1C, and so on through twenty-five cycles reaching back a million years, roughly the second half of the Pleistocene, as he defines it. His system deals realistically with the sequence of warm and cold periods and breaks completely with the system of four glaciers. Twenty-five names would be difficult, but a sequence of numbers is easily managed, and if further glaciers are found the system can be extended to accommodate them. The dates of high sea levels "appear to be satisfactory back to at least 200,000 years, very probably satisfactory to 500,000 years, and somewhat approximate to a million years" (Evans, 1971, p. 124). Satisfactory dates on high sea levels to 200,000 years is an enormous step forward, for the archeological record along seacoasts is tied into high and low sea-level phenomena.

Each succeeding high sea level tends to be about seven meters (twenty-five feet) below the preceding high sea level, but with much variation (see table 3). This finding means that the ocean basins of the world have been deepening over at least the last million years. It also means that this record should appear on all stable or rising coasts as a flight of sea terraces and related valley fills with the oldest, highest. Conversely, any coast showing this sequence of terraces must be stable or rising. It is Evans' conclusion that all major climatic changes in the Pleistocene fit into the astronomical cycles and are thus datable. He excludes from this such short cycles as the eleven-year sunspot cycle and a few other minor anomalies.

Evans' treatment of the problem of dating is interesting in terms of his use of multiple lines of evidence. Even when each line is tentative, if several pieces of evidence fit like the bits of a jigsaw puzzle, then this general agreement gives great strength. This type

TABLE 3
Climatic Cycles, Sea Levels, and Time

	Height		Mediter-ranean	Age (in thousands of years)	San Diego
Cycle	meters	feet	Terraces	(midpoint)	Terraces
1 W	2.5	8.25	Flandrian	5	
1 C				20	
* 2 W	3.5	12.00	Epi Monastiran	40	Coronado
2 C				60	
3 W	7.5	25.00	Late Monastiran	85	Tijuana
3 C				110	
4 W	18.0	60.00	Main Monastiran	130	Nestor
4 C				150	
* 5 W	24.0	80.00		170	
5 C				190	
6 W	32.0	100.00	Tyrrhenian	210	Chula Vista
6 C				230	
7 W	40.0	132.00		250	
7 C				270	
8 W	49.0	165.00		290	
8 C				310	
9 W	57.0	190.00		330	
9 C			Milazzean	350	
10 W	62.0	200.00		370	Avondale

SOURCE: Table compiled from Evans, 1971, with some correlations at San Diego indicated.

NOTE: The exact matching of the Mediterranean terraces with the San Diego terraces supports the correlation of terraces and times by Evans' system and is also consistent with geologic stability of the San Diego area.

*Cycles with no fully warm period.

of work in American archeology has been derided as the use of tenuous bits of evidence. It would appear that some American archeologists are trying to be more scientific than the scientists.

For archeology in general and American archeology in particular, it is the 40,000-year cycle that is of greatest interest, for it is a useful basis for dating such climatically controlled events as glacials, pluvials, desert lakes, high and low sea stands, and cuts and fills of valley mouths. An irregular 40,000-year cycle is well known for earth-sun relationships. The causes are due to changes in the tilt of the earth's axis, the shape of the earth's orbit, and the precession of the equinoxes. These respectively control solar energy receipt by latitude, relative lengths of summer and winter, and times of the year when the earth is nearest and farthest from the sun. Each of these factors has its own period, and their interaction causes the irregularities in the 40,000-year cycle.

In high latitudes, about sixty-five degrees north and south, the insolation changes have been calculated to produce warm-cold cycles varying from 30,000 to 50,000 years, averaging 40,000 years. It is this 40,000-year cycle that appears so prominently in the oceanic core data, and compels the acceptance of the tilt of the axis as the primary cause of the glaciations. It is no new idea, for it first appeared in 1842, was restated about a hunded years ago, and has more recently been advanced by Koeppen and Milankovitch. The notion had been rejected because the amount of change due to these shifts was considered too small to accomplish the glacial-interglacial shifts and because it called for too many glaciations. The whole trend of glaciology has been to find more and more glaciations, and meteorology has long insisted that it would take but little change to tip the balance from glacial to interglacial. The radiometric dates are then the final bit of evidence closing the case.

There are many points of interest. There was a peak of unusual warmth about 10,000 years ago, followed by the altithermal (warm period) about 6,000 years ago. A lag of about 4,000 years is normal. The great cold about 24,000 years ago was followed by the peak of the late Wisconsin glacial about 20,000 years ago. Between 34,000 and 63,000 years ago the major components of the insolation curves were out of phase, and this gave rise to a long period of fluctuating but mainly intermediate temperatures between Wisconsin I and Wisconsin II. Polar summers were warmer, and most temperate regions had cooler-than-average summers. As an example of how this becomes archeologically significant, consider that man was living at Old Crow in Yukon about 30,000 years ago (Harington, Bonnichsen, and Morlan, 1975; Morlan, 1978), a time of warmer than usual polar climates.

The climatic changes can be calculated from astronomical data with more accuracy than we can measure by any other system, and we can then take this solar hypothesis—with all the usual reservations that we understand it to be less than perfect and probably subject to some change—and use it for dating related systems.

Evans makes important reservations in his summary concerning the system that he is putting forward. Among these is the fact that nearly half the cool periods were not sufficiently cold to cause important glaciation and some mild periods were not warm enough to provide clear-cut separations between glaciations. As a consequence, only about half of the potential glaciations can be recognized —or at least have been recognized. Nevertheless, Evans makes clear that we have a time scale for glacial events that is tied to the geometry of earth-sun relations and that as a consequence can have dates calculated for it. The glacial sequence controls sea-level fluctuation, which in turn controls coastal landforms, and this extends this chronometric system worldwide.

There are many climatically controlled systems that can be related to the glacial-interglacial sequence and so come under the dating system put forward by Evans. Soils are recorders of climates and of time. Humid soils and arid soils differ in pH (acidity), in clay minerals, in particle-size distributions, in humic content, and so on. In areas of relatively stable landforms, such as old marine terraces with their relatively flat surfaces, truly ancient soils can be preserved. Where there are series of marine terraces, separated by approximately 40,000 years of weathering time, there should be clear sequences of weathering age, with the youngest on the lower terraces and the oldest on the highest terraces. Since the terraces are exposed by low sea stands and these are times of glacial accumulation in many areas of the world, the soils that accumulate on the terraces will do so under moist or pluvial conditions. The converse will hold for valleys. They will fill under interglacial, dry conditions, and the valley fill will reflect this in grain size and in alkalinity. The terraces in the valley will have their surface weathered similarly to those in the marine terraces, with the older terraces being the more weathered. Wherever these features can be related to a sea level, there is the possibility of deriving a date in the glacial time scale, and the landform, the soil, the sea level, and the date can all be checked against one another. Interlocking systems of this sort give us real dating opportunities.

Many of these soil measures can be done quite simply. Soil color is measured by taking a sample and comparing it with a standard color chart. This requires a little skill in using the color charts and the masks that isolate one color at a time. The result is a color with a definite designation, which can be used for comparisons. This gets around the fact that subjectively one man's pink is another man's red. The acidity of a soil is easily measured in the field with a soil-test kit and a bottle of a reagent that changes color to indicate the acidity or the alkalinity of the soil. Skilled soils men can guess the clay content of a soil with extraordinary accuracy simply by the feel of it, but ordinary mortals have to have laboratory analyses run. One has to turn to the laboratory for determination of the type of clay, for humus content, and so forth. All of these vary with the climate and age of the soil and so supply to the informed soils man a whole chapter of information about the age of the soil, the kinds of climates that it has been exposed to, the kind of vegetation that has grown on it, and so forth. A soil is a lot more than just dirt; it is often a little encyclopedia recording a lengthy history. There are no old soils within the glaciated regions, for a 10,000-year span leaves soils in a youthful stage. But many areas of the world have soils that are up to 1 million years old, and at San Diego, California, there are soils of immensely varied age—from gray, youthful ones through brown, mature ones, to bright red, ancient ones. To a surprising extent this is true elsewhere, as well.

Climatic changes not only caused soil changes but also created vegetative changes in the desert. The desert edges became humid. Vegetation zones shifted down the mountain ranges, often 2,000 feet or more. Now-barren ranges in the deserts once carried pine, pinyon pine, or juniper forests, and this is recorded in the most unlikely way: in the pack-rat nests built in rock shelters with the vegetation around them. Carbon 14 showed these nests to be more than 40,000 years old; many are 7,000 to 20,000 years old and contain a rich vegetation record. The desert is an amazing place for the preservation of records.

The other record of past climate in the desert comes from

pollen. Pollen, too, is usually preserved in pack-rat nests, supplementing the leaf, twig, and fruit record. More interesting to archeologists, pollen is preserved under the stones of ancient rock alignments in the desert, and this pollen sometimes records a full glacial-pluvial climate. We are left with the problem of which glacial, and while it is easiest to assume that it was the last one, which peaked about 20,000 years ago, this may be too simple an explanation.

The cooling and the shifts in rainfall belts also created numerous lakes in the desert, especially in the Basin-Range province, the Great Basin, the land between the Sierra Nevadas and the Rockies. Many minor basins filled with water, and two huge lakes came into existance. Lake Bonneville filled much of the interior of Utah, and Lake Lahontan filled much of the interior of Nevada. These were full of fish and clams and in winter had great numbers of waterfowl. Their shores were fringed with vegetation useful to man for food, shelter, and clothing, and a human record is expectable on the shores of these lakes every time that they formed after man's entry into America. With the glacial timetable, we can peg the expectable dates with considerable precision.

As should be clear from all of this, there are many opportunities for dating events. While the ice sheets came and went in the north, lakes formed and disappeared in the deserts and vegetation shifted, both north and south and vertically up and down mountain ranges. The animals also shifted, following their accustomed vegetational habitats. All along the seacoasts of the world, the sea fell with each glaciation and rose with each interglacial. Much of this was like an elaborate polka: glaciers up, and sea levels down. Sea levels up, and desert lakes down. Vegetation moving down the mountains as the lakes rose at their base. With so orderly and intricately related a set of systems, it is amazing to see how great the difficulty has been in discovering how the pieces fit together—and in fitting them together, putting numbers in real years on these periods, and fitting man into the system.

A habitation site, in a soil that records a past climate, in a landform relatable to sea levels, which are related to glaciers whose advances and retreats can be measured and explained and dated by earth-sun relations looks like one of those problems that would require only a little energy to solve. Many solutions were tried, but few were accepted. How could they be accepted when there was little agreement on sea-terrace correlations around the world, on soils' ages and their ability to preserve climatic records, on the number or timing of the glaciers, or even on why there were glacial episodes anyway? Change and reduction of this confusion came with the application of physical chemistry to the problem.

THE PHYSICAL-CHEMICAL REVOLUTION

It had earlier been found that the ages of rocks could be determined from study of the decay of uranium. This told the geologists when events had occurred on a million-year scale, but 1 million years came close to being their smallest number. This method, therefore, was not useful for the anthropologist, least of all for the American archeologist.

A system was needed that would measure shorter time periods, and the first useful one to emerge was the radioactive-carbon method. Carbon has two forms: normal, stable carbon, C-12, and radioactive, unstable carbon, C-14. Carbon 14 is created in the outer atmosphere when high-energy radiation coming in from outer space hits a nitrogen atom. The C-14 so created comes on down into the atmosphere and enters through photosynthesis into the food chain: from plants to animals to man. All living things have a small amount of radioactive carbon in their tissues, and this amount is generally the same everywhere for all. That there are a few exceptions, has gradually become clear. Some plants and animals under special circumstances may use old carbon and hence may appear older than they actually are. It was assumed that the rate of formation of C-14 was constant through time, but this too is proving to be less than exact. Nevertheless, if uniformity of formation and distribution is assumed, with reservations, we can proceed. Radioactive carbon decays in such a way that in approximately 5,000 years (5,568 in early estimates, 5,730 now), one-half of that present changes to C-12. If all living matter has the same amount of C-14, say ten units, then a piece of nonliving matter that has only five units has lost half of its original amount, and this we know requires 5,000-plus years. Therefore, all other things being equal, that particular piece of biological matter ceased living 5,000 years ago; that is, it ceased to take in C-14 in the process of living. It is assumed that after its death no C-14 was lost or added, and this is only partially true. In this regard, charcoal gives the most reliable reading; shell, a less reliable one; and bone, the least reliable. Hence, they vary in their value for dating.

The system was tested against wood of known age, such as Egyptian coffins. The classical archeologists could date the coffins to within a year or so, but the C-14 method could place them only within twenty or thirty years or more, and I recall the classicists' being pretty sniffy about their superiority. But for those who did not know time within a millennium or, as it presently turned out, within tens of millennia, this looked like the answer to a prayer.

The system was tried on American archeology, and the first I heard of it was in a letter from Gordon Willey of Harvard. We had argued over the time of the appearance of agriculture in the eastern United States. I said early; he said late; C-14 said early, and he hastened to write me. I was intrigued, as well as most impressed with Willey as a scholar who was more concerned with knowledge than with defending a position.

The next major finding was that the last gasp of the last ice cap in America consisted of a vigorous thrust of the ice, which buried a forest near Green Bay, Wisconsin. This dated about 11,000 years ago. I am amused to recall that I rejected that date out of hand. Impossible! I had learned, as every freshman learned, that the end of the last ice age dated to 25,000 years ago. I had passed numerous examinations using that number and had won an A.B. degree in anthropology and a Ph.D. degree in geography. It was virtually a sacred number.

The glacial period was only 10,000 years in the past, not 25,000? Then the extinction of the animals of the Pleistocene moved up in time, as did the pluvial lakes in the Great Basin, the lowered sea levels of all our coasts, and the last great climatic changes. The feeling was similar to what one experiences in an earthquake. The solid earth, your one fixed and permanent, immovable plane of reference, suddenly moves, and your equilibrium is totally upset. It is frightening. I felt threatened, and I resisted the whole C-14 revolution until overwhelmed by the evidence. It has left me with some sympathy for others whose basic reference points are threatened by change. The situation automatically engenders fear, and fear leads to anger and to emotional outbursts. It is perfectly natural, even if unpleasant at times.

Carbon-14 dating has proved to be an invaluable tool. It has straightened out conflicts over such matters as the relative ages of the Adena and Hopewell cultures in the eastern United States and has established the time for innumerable archeological sites. At first it reached only 10,000 years or so, and I then predicted that it would not solve the problem of the antiquity of man in America. Now that it reaches 30,000 to 40,000 years, it still fails to reach the age of the earliest sites. However, it has clarified the last 25,000 years and brought some order to a chaotic area. As was noted earlier, we had some correct measures of postglacial time, but they were but some of the straws among many flying in the wind, and no one could be sure which of the many was right. Carbon 14 clarified that problem, among many others.

Currently scientists are proposing to attack the C-14 problem in a new way that may very greatly extend its dating range. The present method counts the individual breakdowns of C-14 atoms to C-12. Since there is very little C-14 to start with and half of this disappears every 5,000 years, then one is shortly counting extremely rare events. It is now suggested that we can count all of the C-14 atoms present. This would give large numbers and simultaneously increase the counting ability and decrease the probability of error (Muller, 1977; Grootes, 1978; Stuiver, Heuser, and Yang, 1978). This system may make C-14 dates comparable to protein racemization, thermoluminescence, and fission tracking, and other physical-chemical systems. If they all agree, then we will have as close an approach to absolute dating as is possible. Many archeological sites offer only one datable substance, but some contain more than one, and these will be the best testing grounds.

As implied above, other dating systems are now emerging, and the gap between the 30,000- to 40,000-year C-14 limit and the million-year uranium limit is about to be closed. An interesting case was the dating of the Olduvai Gorge in Africa. L. S. B. Leakey had guessed at an age of 200,000 years. Potassium-argon (K/A) dating of the lavas suggested 1.75 million years for the base (Evernden and Curtis, 1964). This brought hoots of derision: "to be taken *cum grano salis!*" We think we are doubly devastating if we can say it in Latin. Fission tracking then verified the K/A date (Macdougal, 1976). Fission tracking involves counting the tracks left by high-energy particles released by the breakdown of radioactive minerals in a rock. The tracks are microscopic cracks in the crystals, and they can be annealed (healed) by moderate heat maintained for a few hours. This erases the record of past atomic breakdowns with their discharge of high-energy particles. The atomic breakdowns continue, however, and a new set of tracks begins to accumulate. Since the amount and kind of radioactive minerals can be determined and the rate of their breakdown is known, the time necessary to accumulate the observed number of fission tracks since the heating can be calculated.

The important point for the Olduvai Gorge site was the fact that the two systems, K/A and fission tracking, are unrelated. When they gave dates of the same order of magnitude, it was strong evidence—strong enough to compel the skeptics to revise their thinking. This was one of the great leaps back in time in the study of early man, and strong evidence was required. In America the same sort of thing is required, but up until now we have lacked the physical-chemical systems that could reach the earliest sites and skeletons. When we finally produced such a method, the results were rejected, or at least set aside to await the arrival of some other system that would test the first method.

Fission tracking at first held out great promise for the San Diego archeology, for the ideal crystal to work with is zircon and it is present there in abundance. Enthusiasm was dampened, however, by our finding that the stones in the hearths had been heated high enough but not maintained at the necessary temperature long enough to anneal the tracks. We will with some luck and a lot of persistence find fire pits that have had long-maintained heat, and we will then be able to get some fission-track dates.

We have a related system that is more likely to provide numerous dates and reach out for a few hundred thousand years. This is thermoluminescence. Most rocks contain minute amounts of uranium and thorium and potassium. These break down at known rates and are the principal sources of electrons trapped in the rock. Most rocks are spongelike to electrons. The sponge can be wrung out by heating the rock, usually to 500 degrees centigrade; the electron output can be measured as thermoluminescence. A rock or a piece of earth or clay that has been heated at some time past has been wrung out. Electrons continue to be released and to accumulate, and how much has accumulated is a measure of how much time has passed since the rock material was heated. The method was first used to date pottery, for the firing of the clays set their atomic clocks at zero, and reheating drove off the accumulation of electrons that had built up since that event. Development of the system has given increasing accuracy and increasing time depth. Any burned material can be used: pottery, burned earth, burned rocks, burned artifacts—just as long as some radioactive minerals are present. It is a method with great promise and should presently be supplying us with dates comparable to those of other systems; just the cross-checking situation that we have needed.

The system involved in the greatest controversy at the moment is protein racemization, a dating system developed by Jeff Bada, a chemist at the Scripps Institution of Oceanography (Bada, Schroeder, and Carter, 1974; Bada and Helfman, 1975). This method is rattling the skeletons in the museum closets. Protein-racemization dating is based on the fact that protein molecules can be right-handed or left-handed; the one is the mirror image of the other. The oddity is that life forms use only the left-handed molecules. After death, a slow process of reverting to a balance of left and right molecules begins, and measuring how much conversion from left to right has occurred yields a measure of time. This sounds simple, but as with all such methods there are complications. There may be exchanges with the environment, with extraneous protein molecules moving into the bone. Susceptibility to this varies with tooth, bone, coral, and shell. The biggest variable, however, is temperature. The higher the temperature, the more rapid the change, and this must be compensated for in some way. For very old material, we are quite unsure of just what temperatures they may have been subjected to, especially if they are old enough to have experienced glacial and interglacial changes. Bada calibrates his measurements against some dating system that is not temperature-sensitive. For his initial work in southern California, he used the Laguna Beach skeleton which had been dated by C-14 as about 17,000 years old. Bada determined how much shift of left- to right-protein molecules had occurred in that skeleton. That became his standard for a measure of 17,000 years for bone in the coastal zone of southern California. A nearby bone with a similar shift must be about 17,000 years old—if more, older; if less, younger. Exactly how much older or younger can be calculated using standard mathematical treatments.

Bada's dates for skeletons in southern California came out too high to agree with the accepted views of the antiquity of man in America, and his system then came under bitter attack. I was accused of jumping on Bada's bandwagon simply because the dates he obtained agreed with my own work. It never occurred to the critics, apparently, that they could equally well be accused of rejecting the system because it challenged their work. Bada has worked widely over the world: South America, North Africa, around the Mediterranean, as well as in America. In the Old World his dates check very nicely with the archeological sequences, the known geological sequences, and the paleontological data. As he humorously remarks: physical chemistry seems to change at the mid-Atlantic Ridge, so the system does not work in America.

We have often wished that we could date stone tools directly. They are the best-preserved of all the evidences of man's activities. Many systems have been tried, with varying success. The rate of penetration of water into obsidian, obsidian hydration, has been moderately successful, but there are formidable lists of variables. Temperature, moisture, and rock variation all enter into the problem. A new proposal has been to measure the rate of penetration of fluorine into the rock. There is fluorine in most groundwaters, and for most waters the range of difference is not great. Fluorine penetrates rock slowly, and even modest penetration indicates a high date. The method is in its infancy, and it is costly, but it is being pressed, for it would be invaluable to be able to date artifacts directly. It might give us the ultimate: a human skeleton clutching an artifact in its hand, with both the skeleton and the artifact being datable. We might be able to go a step or two farther by dating the fire next to which the ancient man laid his weary bones down for their last repose—until the archeologists' spade played the role of Gabriel's trumpet.

Some dating methods yield dates of mixed value. Ku and Kern

(1974) used uranium-series studies on shell and coral from Pleistocene beaches at San Diego. The shell dates gave such irregular results as to be useless. The coral dates seem reliable, and this has been the experience of other investigators also. Ku and Kern then took the date for the "raised beach" that they had dated and calculated the rate of uplift of the San Diego region (they simply assumed uplift, ignoring possible sea-level lowering). The rate came out the same as the worldwide fall of sea level reported by Evans. I assume that Evans' research was unknown to Ku and Kern. Is it just an accident that the San Diego area is rising at precisely the rate of the worldwide sea-level fall? It seems much more likely that the record is that of sea-level fall in relation to a relatively stable coast at San Diego. Ku is apparently the laboratory man, and Kern is the geologist. The laboratory man is guided in his geologic interpretations by the professional in that field. Geologists tend very strongly to assume land movement, for that, after all, is what they observe to have occurred worldwide through millions of years. It is virtually impossible to convince a California geologist that any part of the state is even modestly stable. Currently, when the Palmdale Bulge northeast of Los Angeles, an area the size of one of our smallest eastern states, is moving up and down six inches at a time, one can have some sympathy with their view. However, any study of maps of fault lines and strain maps of southern California quickly brings out the concentration of these features to the east and north of the San Diego region. San Diego itself is singularly isolated from the major fault lines, and it is to this that it owes its relative stability.

That is the general status of archeological dating at the moment. The geochemists and geophysicists have been supplying more and more methods of reading time. We now have opportunities to measure the age of stone artifacts directly from the stone or of skeletons directly from the bone. Simultaneously we can measure by either thermoluminescence or fission tracking, the age of the fireplaces that man used. There is even the possibility that we will be able to do so by measuring the shifts in the location of the magnetic pole, for heated particles line up with the pole at the time they are heated and remain frozen in that position. The pole meanwhile wanders around, and if and when we have its wanderings catalogued we may be able to use fossilized polarization as a time measure. It is already useful on sites of not-too-great age and may be extended to greater ages.

Time then has suddenly become measurable in ways that we had not dreamed of when my work began. The new measures are upsetting the notions that we had, but the old ideas were built on the quicksand of guesswork based on extrapolations from poorly understood data. We should never have treated them as sacred numbers, though that has been the tendency. We are now entering an era when physical measurements from several systems can be checked one against the other. We will then have as near to absolute dates as we are ever likely to have. It is already clear that we have made huge advances. Now all we have to do is to clear our minds of the rubbish of the past decades of guess-dating and to analyze the new dating systems. Clearing the rubbish of the past is the more difficult task.

Chapter 4

Mankind on the Rock Pile

INTRODUCTION

TOOL making marks man, and determining what man made and what nature made marks the acheologist, and at times it is virtually the mark of Cain, setting brother archeologists at each other's throats.

Somewhere near the two-million-year mark man learned to break rock and thus to create a sharp edge that turned a rounded rock into a cutting tool. This multiplied man's efficiency both as a hunter and as a gatherer. Digging roots is done with sharp sticks, and sharp stones can cut and shape sharper and harder sticks. Stone not only gave man a cutting tool that he could use as a hand-held weapon but, probably more importantly, it also gave him a tool that allowed him to improve his ancient bone and wood tools. Stone became the tool maker's principal material.

We have overemphasized the projectile points and underplayed the tools. There were woodworking tools, which shaped the shaft, the bow, the spear thrower, the curved throwing stick. There were tools that shaped the bone points and pins, made shell beads, gorgets, and sticks for snares and traps, and cut the grass for baskets and the numerous other perishable items that made life easier, surer, and safer. Stone was the nearly universal material for the tool to make the tool, and in the history of mankind this tool-making role was vastly more important than the late, brief, and dramatic use of stone to tip projectile shafts.

Raymond Dart of South Africa (1960, 1971) is probably correct in thinking that prehumans had long used bone, antler, and animal teeth for tools for cutting, and Oswald Menghin's (1931) more ambitious theme of ages of wooden tools before bone tools and bone tools before stone tools is not improbable, though it is virtually unprovable due to lack of preservation of evidence. The one bit of evidence we have is that man lacks fangs for fighting, cutting, and tearing, and even the earliest men likewise lacked them. With no fangs and with the need to cut and tear, mankind must have had tools for millions of years. This assumption is all we have at the moment, and, as with all assumptions, it may or may not be true.

At Olduvai Gorge in east Africa nearly 2 million years ago, man was carrying cobbles long distances, breaking them percussively to create sharp edges, and in the process creating sharp-edged flakes. Even with *Homo erectus* at work in such very poor flaking material as quartzite, the impress of human action is clearly evident, and this suggests that the difficulty some experience in recognizing man's handiwork in stone stems from a very limited knowledge of the characteristics of human work. As a footnote to history, when L. S. B. Leakey brought the first of the skeletal materials from Olduvai to America, the Wenner Gren foundation had a dinner meeting at their headquarters in New York. Bones and broken stones were available for examination. The broken stones were one bifaced quartzite piece and some simple flakes. They were eyed askance by most, and attention was focused on the bones. Only Junius Bird and I fastened onto the broken stone. We agreed that it was clearly human work. The others were dubious.

The belated acceptance of chimpanzee tool using and even rudimentary tool making has, or should have, altered our thinking about Dart's *Australopithecine osteodentokeratic* (bone, tooth, and horn) cultures. It would be belated acceptance because Koehler (1925) had demonstrated the chimpanzee's tool-making abilities and proclivities in the 1920's. This included the use of sticks to reach fruit and of straws to collect ants. He even uncovered one genius that could fit sticks into bamboo to make longer sticks, thus making the equivalent of a jointed fishing rod—appropriately, for fishing food into his cage from otherwise unobtainable positions. Seemingly only the lack of a system to transmit learning has prevented the chimpanzees from taking off on the cultural accumulation trail, the road to civilization complete with traffic lights, smog, and parking problems. It is hard to see how the significance of this tool making was missed. The total picture, old observations and new, supports a theme of the early use of wood and bone. Man may have sentenced himself to the rock pile only belatedly, having been a tool user and wood and bone worker long before he took up stone as his tool to make better tools.

There are problems, of course. The general name for the situation is the eolith problem. Eoliths, literally "dawn stones," are broken stones of such crudity that it is arguable whether man or nature broke them. W. J. Sollas in 1911 discussed the problem of identification rather sensibly. He noted that broken flints had been reported from the Upper Oligocene as early as 1867 and from the Upper Miocene somewhat later. Man most certainly was not around to break flints in those times. He then went on to note that in the Andaman Islands only the fact that we know that man broke the stones found there "ensures their artificiality." But he quickly added that this does not allow us to take all broken rock as man-made.

Some of his most interesting comparisons dealt with the Tasmanians. He considered these people to be good representatives of the Lower Paleolithic or at most of the Mousterian (Middle Paleolithic) culture. Their tool kit (figure 13) is startlingly like the Buchanan Canyon, Texas Street, and Calico assemblages. The making of chopping tools by unifacial flaking of huge flakes, the making of concave scrapers, the working of simple end and side scrapers, and the striking of true blades very closely duplicate the very early southern California work. Whether this resemblance is accidental, there being only a few ways to break rocks to make tools, or whether there is a possible historical connection will be discussed in the final chapters of the book.

Like many of those who followed him, Sollas made observations on the breaking of rock under varied conditions. He noted that cart wheels on flint made what appeared to be notched scrapers and did some fine edge flaking that simulated man's retouching of artifact edges to shape and sharpen them. My own observations, in this day when steel-rimmed cart wheels running over flint-gravelled roads are somewhat hard to find, have turned toward gravel pits, where flints are first washed clean and then piled and in the process run over by bulldozers, whose steel tracks and immense weights do flake flint. Sollas and many today would extend these findings to generally invalidate the use of mere broken rocks as evidence for man. It would seem wiser to limit interpretation of their significance to the situation to which they really apply: flints taken out of

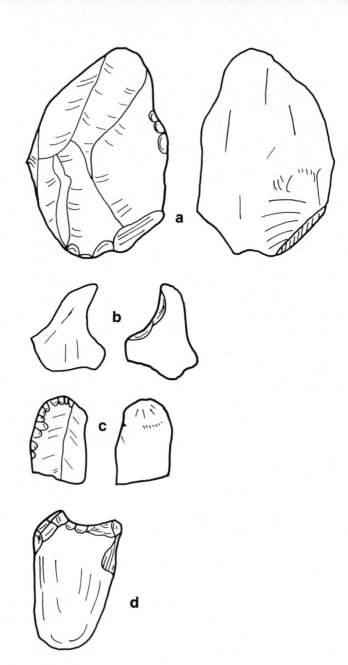

Figure 13. This Tasmanian tool kit duplicates the material found in America on the blade and core stage. Comparable material is found at Texas Street, Calico, the Yuha Desert, and similar sites. Compare British Mountain also. Item *a* is like a skreblo; *b* is a concave scraper; *c* is a section of a blade; *d* is a nosed cobble.

a natural matrix that would buffer them and exposed to heavy pressure from steel tires or treads. These are not natural forces, and their products are artifacts, items made by man. One should not extend these special circumstances to streams, glaciers, soil creep, fire, frost, and other natural actions that may or may not break rock.

Our interest here is in differentiating human work from natural work, assuming that nature at least occasionally breaks rocks percussively or by pressure. First, what would be the signature of natural work? If natural forces are breaking rock, the circumstances should be obvious and explainable by simple field observation of the forces at work on that particular rock in that region. These forces should operate with some uniformity in time and space and should be obvious and identifiable. The effects of such forces should be randomly distributed, or if they are associated with special events—mud flows, torrential situations, or landslides—these should be easily visible in any undisturbed geomorphic situation. Should the hypothesis be advanced that the evidence of the causative act (e.g., a mud flow) was later erased by the work of water, the objects created by the hypothetical mud flow must show wear, for even brief transportation, such as would be required in the reworking of a deposit, would initiate wear. Natural wear should be random.

Human breakage is the opposite: localized in time and space, patterned, not related to natural forces, having many breaks due to percussion or pressure, no overall wear when found "in place," but wear patterns on working edges exactly as on known used implements. Transported artifacts will show overall wear, but the wear will be superimposed on objects broken to patterns familiar from sites with material in place. Figures 14 and 15 show man-broken rocks that are typical of two tool-making traditions.

Steep edge work has short flakes along the edge of a cobble or a slab of rock. The work is clearly by percussion, and there is little regularity of tool form. Flaking is often bifacial but at times unifacial. Such work was done very early in human history and persisted for making unspecialized cutting tools in many later cultures. This makes it difficult to sort out in mixed sites. Our best knowledge of it comes from the desert where these tools lie on ancient land surfaces and are so weathered as to separate them from all later tools.

Unifacial work as used here describes the biscuit-shaped tools

FIGURE 14. These items from Buchanan Canyon, the important site discovered by Herb Minshall, illustrate the presence there of an early lithic industry. Notice the short, steep flakes. These artifacts are close to the steep edge stage of tool making (see figure 1, in the introduction). Also, compare the short, round flake scars here with the long, flat planes in figure 15. The two flaking traditions are totally different. While neither Buchanan Canyon nor Texas Street is a pure site, one industry is more prominent in one than the other.

with edge flaking done wholly or predominantly from one flat side. When this work is done on cobbles, the flat surface is often a flake surface of the cobble.

Elongate or ovate bifaces are pieces flaked alternately from one face and then the other. One form, elongate, is longer than wide and usually wider in the center than at the ends. Ovate bifaces may be nearly oval or be wider at one end than the other.

Blades are flakes that are two or more times as long as they are wide. They are made by striking cores on one end in such a way as to split off a long flake. An anvil may or may not be used but is more necessary with such difficult-to-flake rocks as quartzite and porphyry. The typical marks of blade making are long, flat flake scars often intersecting at obtuse angles.

Men rarely flaked according to one plan 100 percent of the

FIGURE 15. These tools from the Texas Street site are made by an entirely different plan than the tools from Buchanan Canyon shown in figure 14. The flaking here is done by placing a cobble on an anvil and striking the top of the cobble, so that long flakes, technically blades, are driven off the core. *A* is a core, which if flaked would produce a blade such as that at *D*. *B* and *C* are classic cores for striking blades. *E* and *F* are two views of a long, slim blade flake. *G* is a large flake, showing a definite bulb of percussion, eraillure, and all the marks typical of percussion flaking. (Photo from Carter, 1957, by permission of Johns Hopkins University Press)

time. Styles of flaking predominated in different periods, however. Later periods often had a dominant style while carrying some of the earlier types of flaking as a minority activity. I have used the dominant style and the type tool to designate the different stages. It is a bit like calling this the automobile age although there are still horses and buggies around, quite a few airplanes, and numerous bicycles.

The problems that arise in distinguishing man-made flaking from natural flaking are partly mythical, partly in the realm of the history of ideas, and partly parochial. The whole set of ideas is of course interrelated. There is the myth that nature frequently breaks rocks percussively or by pressure. If it were true, then given enough rocks to select from it would be possible to assemble a pseudo–lithic industry, but these would be geofacts, made by nature not man. It is claimed by many archeologists that this is the actual situation, and it is the common reason for dismissing early sites such as Texas Street at San Diego, Calico in the Mohave Desert, and the Timlin site in New York.

The odd notion that nature frequently breaks rocks in the way man does—that is, by percussion and pressure—and thus duplicates human work stems from about a hundred years ago in Europe, when the first Lower Paleolithic tools were being presented to the reluctant scholars of that day and rejected on the ground that nature had made them. Two sets of ideas met head-on. Tools were present in gravel deposits along with the bones of extinct animals. The stand-patters refused to acknowledge the existence of the Lower Paleolithic tools and the presence of man along with extinct animals. The overly enthusiastic began to find "tools" in impossibly early horizons, and this gave the standpatters the ammunition they needed to attack the proponents of what we now know as the Lower Paleolithic.

This is the old eolith problem mentioned earlier. In this case, the hand axes of the Lower Paleolithic of Europe won recognition as artifacts: eoliths became artifacts, or at least some of them did. Those that were admitted as artifacts had shaping by numerous blows to produce an implement, the hand axe, so obvious that one wonders that it could ever have been questioned; but it was. This case does not of course give one a license now to claim that all eoliths (geofacts, cartifacts, etc.) are artifacts, but it should put everyone on notice that the obvious can be and often is denied. The questions then become: are we now denying the obvious, and how are we to go about determining this?

The first discovery of early-man evidence in the Old World (Gruber, 1948) led to a controversy so like that in America today as to be worth a brief review. In 1897 John Frere reported finding flints obviously broken by man underlying the bones of extinct animals; he cautiously suggested that they might date to some very remote period. In 1858 Boucher de Perthes put forth his evidence for worked flints in the gravels of the Seine. For twelve years "the scepticism [was] pushed to an extreme," to use Sir Charles Lyell's words. S. J. Mackie in 1862 was even more blunt. He stated that the Abbevillean flints were accepted by no one, that everyone thought Boucher de Perthes mad. Even after Rigollet, Prestwich, Flower, Lyell, Evans, and other geologists went as so many doubting Thomases to look and returned believing, ". . . there were those in unbelief who hazarded wild theories of ocean-waves chipping out artificial forms, and of recent objects sinking down in the ground, and burying themselves, and other equally untenable notions . . ." (Gruber, 1948). The naturally chipped and self-burying stones are still with us a hundred years later in America. Prestwich in 1859, in a curious statement echoed nearly ninety years later by Kroeber, argued that, if the facts of the contemporaneity of man and the extinct animals were proved, it could just as well be taken as evidence of the late survival of the animals as of an early date for man. Gruber, in reviewing this controversy, refers to the rejection of evidence as a recurrent phenomenon in science and asks how many such distortions are present in today's science. He comments that "it is disconcerting to find the Cuviers, Mayers and Virchows—all as equally devoted to the methods and objectives of modern science as any of today's scientists—with intellects imprisoned and imaginations shackled by hypotheses of their own making, hypotheses purportedly based on fact and uninfluenced by metaphysical considerations" (p. 439). Gruber, in wondering how much of this dominates our thinking today, makes it clear that there must be a lot of it.

There is then a history of resistance to the idea that "broken stones" mean man, and this resistance, which the Europeans have fairly well outgrown, has had a belated heyday in America and only now slowly begins to crumble. It would hardly be worth discussing, except that it casts such interesting light on academic mental processes, which are shown to go on in pretty rigid straitjackets. The resistance to early-man evidence has led to ignoring the evidence and denying the evidence and casting doubts on the evidence and allowing the evidence to be destroyed even when amateurs tried to flag the professionals' attention. It is against the stonewalling by the professionals that amateurs have had to tilt. The fundamental question for the early lithic industries is: can we tell human breakage from natural breakage? If we could advance the degree of certainty in this area, we would have gone a long way to settling the question. So, let's break a few more lances on this question.

NATURE AT WORK: SERUTAN, NATURE'S IN REVERSE

The biggest myth in American archeology is that nature breaks rocks by percussion and pressure with considerable frequency and that this breakage reproduces human work. It is further assumed that this applies to all lithic materials. Few myths have less substance or greater persistence. To make it worse, some think that fire, frost, and chemical action also simulate human work. Most of this can be easily disproved by observing natural processes.

Many people are convinced that nature normally dashes rocks together so violently as to break them. I have repeatedly taken such believers to the nearest beach or stream and said: "Find some broken rocks and especially some that look like artifacts." Except for special cases to be discussed below, they cannot. Stream-worn pebbles are rounded and smoothed, and so are beach cobbles. Glacial gravels are a special case, but even they are not artifactlike. Glacial gravels are often subrounded, with planes ground on them by ice action. They are often striated and are not sharp edged. A collection of "most artifactlike" material laid alongside a collection of all broken rock from an early lithic site or a quarry shows extreme differences in form. The same is true of material from steep talus slopes. Rocks on such slopes often are angular and have sharp edges. Examination shows that the breaks have followed natural joint planes in the rock and that they neither show the marks of percussive flaking nor duplicate known artifact forms. Sheer vertical fall of rocks from cliffs will break rock percussively, but here too, artifact types are not produced, and certainly patterns of tool assemblages are not. Most of these assertions will be illustrated by description of specific sites, but a better beginning can be made by examining the general process of rock breakage by streams as geomorphologists have unraveled it.

The discussion here will begin with P. H. Kuenen's work, "Experimental Abrasion of Pebbles: 2. Rolling by Current" (1956).

Not only is this the best study I have found, but inquiry amongst geomorphologists suggests that no one has improved on it in the ensuing twenty years. It has some limitations for archeologists. Kuenen was interested in rounding and wear, and he used a non-archeological vocabulary, but these differences are easily adjusted for.

Kuenen reviewed the very large literature on pebble rounding, shaping, and weight loss from wear on beaches and in rivers. Although he credited his predecessors with adding much to our knowledge, he faulted their use of tumbling mills. In a tumbling mill rocks are lifted and dropped to fall on the mass of rocks below. There is nothing comparable in nature, for even in waterfalls rocks are sliding along a bottom and when they go over the fall they normally land in the deep water of the plunge-pool at the foot of the fall. They are then cushioned from impact with stones on the bottom.

For his work Kuenen used a large, concrete basin in which water, driven by paddles, in turn drove the stones along the bottom, much as a stream current would do in nature. Kuenen varied the bottom environment: bare concrete, sand added, cobbles cemented in the bottom. He used a wide range of materials, too, of which flint, quartzite, quartz porphyry, vein quartz, obsidian, and glass were the most significant for archeology. The stones were sawed into angular shapes: cubes, rectangular blocks, and polyhedral shapes. All stone entered the system unweathered, a significant difference from natural systems where most stone is weathered to some degree at the time it enters a stream or surf environment.

In a sandy environment such as would be normal in nature, wear was considerably less than when rocks traveled without any sand. The influence of velocity was slight, and wear on sharp edges was due to skidding. When the bed of the experimental tank was given a cemented-pebble bottom, wear increased. Kuenen carefully discussed his variables and concluded that the artificial pebble bed approximated the action in a mountain stream while the smooth cement and sand bottoms approximated a river bottom.

Of particular interest to archeologists was the finding that pebbles below fifty millimeters (two inches) show increasing loss of roundness with decreasing size. This indicates increasing breakage

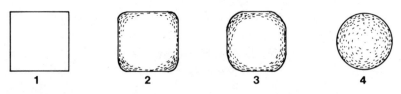

FIGURE 16. This shows the kind of rounding of a cube that Kuenen found. In nature such perfect rounding is rare, but, in homogeneous material rolled by surf up and down a cobble ramp, rocks round enough to serve as cannon balls are produced. Nature rounds rocks; man bashes and smashes and breaks and flakes to create sharp edges.

for pebble sizes below those normally used by man. The larger stones of interest to man become rounder, but they do not break (see figure 16). After reading this, I examined a set of beach gravels and found them exactly as Kuenen described them. The cobbles were rounded; the pebbles showed evidence of breakage, followed by rapid rounding. Most pebbles were split approximately in half and resembled no artifact form—not blades, blade cores, uniface work, or biface work (see figure 1, in the introduction). The platform angles, to be discussed below, were usually right angles.

The abrading processes consist of seven more or less distinct actions: (1) splitting, the breaking into two or three parts of roughly equal size, (2) crushing, pulverizing to produce particles of an entirely different size class, (3) chipping, "the loss of small flakes from sharp edges . . . the chips from pebbles becoming part of the sand" (Kuenen, p. 351), (4) superficial cracking to form cone-shaped concussion cracks, (5) grinding, (6) chemical attack, and (7) sand blasting. Of these actions, only splitting and chipping would produce anything artifactual, and I have quoted Kuenen exactly on chipping. He not only describes the chips as sand-grain size, but he also refers to the photographs of chipped cubes. These show no trace of anything resembling human flaking but only minute edge fracturing or shattering. Further, this breaking action ends as soon as protruding edges are rounded off. Wentworth, Krumbein, and others have also described this action; Wentworth called it spalling, according to Kuenen. It is important to note that the geomorphologist's vocabulary does not match the archeologist's. These chips and spalls are sand-grain size, not the fish-scale sizes of pressure flaking or the one-by-two-inch spalls of heavy percussive flaking done by man. The fissured and battered edges illustrated by Kuenen most closely resemble the battered edge of a hammer stone.

Kuenen differentiated cracking from chipping. His chipping, it must be kept clear, is what archeologists call battering. Cracking shatters the rock surface, actually forming a cone that penetrates the rock, but the cracks die out in a shallow surface layer. This action is found on the body of a rock and on rounded rocks is, or may be, found all over the surface of the stone. Large cobbles subjected to violent action often show these cones as overlapping rings on their surfaces. The fissured bits may hold together, with minute wedges falling out from between neighboring cracks. While chipping ends with the rounding of sharp edges, cracking continues as long as pebbles strike one another.

A pebble rolling on a sandy bottom makes countless contacts with sand grains, each of so little energy that cracks are not induced. Wear is then reduced to grinding. Examples of wear on artifacts from a sandy environment are shown in figure 17A and B. The absence of chipping even on edges is clear. Even the artifact, item A, from the rocky bed of the San Dieguito River near the Harris site shows far more evidence of grinding than of cracking. Item B is from the cobble ramp at Cape Colnett. Its very thick edges and enormously worn flake scars are orders of magnitude different from the artifacts from less violent environments than the surf-agitated cobbles that created and wore down this geofact.

Numerous experiments have shown that irregularly shaped stones rapidly round up and that 6 to 7 kilometers is the common point for achieving roundness; it can be as little as 2 or as much as 10 kilometers. In nature most material entering a stream is weathered, and this weathered crust is rapidly removed, yielding well-rounded rocks within 0.75 kilometers to 2.75 kilometers (0.5 to 1.5 miles).

Kuenen was particularly interested in the wide divergence between measures of attrition and rounding in streams and in his experimental work, for streams seemed to round materials several times as fast as the experimental apparatus did. Breakage in his experiments was rare, even though pebbles occasionally were hit by the steel paddles with a loud bang. Yet "only with flint and with other material that already showed cracks or joints did very occa-

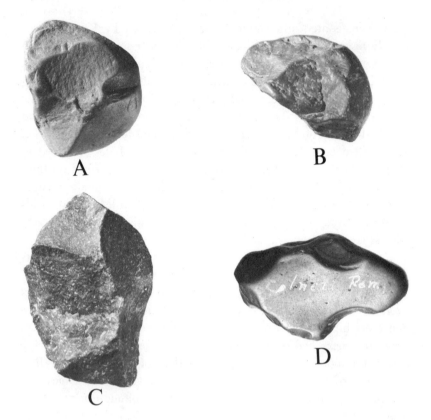

FIGURE 17. These worn stone tools illustrate the effects of natural wear on artifacts. Item *A* is a cobble tool from the sand and gravel bed of the San Dieguito River at the Harris site. It has been transported a short distance under torrential flood conditions. It shows overall wear but no flaking. Item *B* is a similar tool from the beach at the Scripps Institution of Oceanography, a sand and cobble environment. The wear is similar to that on *A*. Item *C* is from the torrential gravel bed of Buchanan Canyon. Transportation there has been so brief that wear is barely visible and sharp edges predominate. Item *D*, included for comparison, is a geofact from the cobble ramp at Cape Colnett. The wear is extreme, leaving thick, rounded edges and nearly obliterated flake scars. The wear is enormously greater than on the other examples, and detailed examination shows a sequence of flakes with differing degrees of wear.

sional flakes come off or a pebble split in half." It is significant that flint is listed as the most prone to flake. It was this quality that endeared it to man, and it is this quality that makes it perhaps the most difficult in which to differentiate human and natural work. Still, human work, even when buried in gravel deposits should show patterns of flaking, and these patterns should reoccur in known sites. The problem is not really all that difficult, though it is this tendency for flints to flake that underlies the eolith problem.

Kuenen also noted that if breakage were frequent in normal rivers, it should be dominant in torrents. Yet he cites Tricart and Shaeffer (1950), who found granites to be well rounded after 3 to 5 kilometers. Van Straaten told Kuenen that flint pebbles in the south of the Netherlands were well rounded by marine action during the Pleistocene and are unbroken in Pliocene river deposits. This is also true of the porphyries and quartzites at San Diego where the Eocene stream and Pliocene beach gravels are well rounded and not broken. Kuenen concluded that natural stream transport is not able to split unweathered hard rocks by impact. "If as this indicates, splitting is insignificant in a torrent, it can hardly be expected to occur in a lowland river. . . . For all these reasons, it is, therefore, considered highly improbable that the rigor in natural stream transport is sufficient for splitting by impact to play a significant part" (pp. 364–365).

Kuenen concluded by conducting a simple test. Pebbles of varied sizes of quartzite, quartz, and chert were dropped repeatedly into a bucket that had a floor of pebbles covered by five centimeters of water (two inches). Splitting never occurred. Heights of seven meters, giving an impact speed of twelve meters per second, produced only an occasional chip, and it must be recalled that Kuenen's chips are minute, not the archeologist's chip. Kuenen calculated the maximum velocity possible for pebbles striking each other in a stream as one-third of this (four meters per second), yielding only ten percent of the kinetic energy in his experiment. If ten times the maximum natural force can produce only a rare chip—a Kuenen chip, that is, a sand-grain-sized bit of rock—then the notion that streams break rock would seem best relegated to the archeological dust bin.

As often happens, a contradiction in data stimulates a tentative answer, and a fuller and better answer appears later. Theoretically, this repeated occurrence would teach us to treat our ideas lightly: hypotheses, not revealed truths. Kuenen's perfectly valid processes and his suggestion of weathering as the cause of the difference between tumbling barrels, flumes, and tubs—all of which gave measures of much slower wear than was observed in nature—can now be augmented by another process, one that vastly increases wear but does not lead to spalling or splitting.

Schumm and Stevens (1973) report that cobbles and boulders in streams can be rounded and reduced to size within a short distance from their source. This occurs because, while these rocks will not move downstream until a critical stream velocity is reached, the rock is constantly subject to a large lift factor (lift being the force generated by flow over a curved surface—the force that sustains airplanes and moves yachts upwind). Under varying current, rocks can vibrate in place and become subject to wear without downstream motion. A cobble was measured moving up and down 280 millimeters (10 inches) vertically in ten seconds with no downstream motion. This extrapolates to 600 meters of vertical movement in ten hours with no downstream movement. This rapid vibration does not cause splitting, spalling, or flaking, but it causes five to ten times as much wear in a stream as in an experimental apparatus. Quartz and chert in particular show this kind of discrepancy: much more rapid wear in nature than in tank, tub, and flume experiments.

In one torrential stream, Buchanan Canyon in San Diego with its gradient of 300 feet per mile, H. L. Minshall has waded into the floodwaters and found that the rocks moving along the stream bottom only gently bumped his legs. The flow was so rapid that the clatter of moving rocks could be heard for a quarter of a mile. Schumm and Stevens refer to a rattling roar being set up by their cobbles, which were vibrating but not travelling, and it may be that much of the noise attributed to rocks "bounding along" is simply due to the vibrating phenomenon noted in flume experiments. Despite the rapid flow down the steep canyon at Buchanan Canyon, the forces at work were far below the breaking point of the cobbles, as evidenced by the absence of freshly broken rock in the stream channel and by the wear pattern on the artifact material.

There is now general acceptance of the Buchanan Canyon material as artifact, and these obvious artifacts show wear within a hundred yards of their points of origin in the canyon floor. It is quite clear that even torrential stream action cannot break these tough porphyries and quartzites, and it is probably incapable of breaking even much more easily flaked rocks, though as we have seen above flints are so easily flaked as perhaps to fall into a special category.

The case remains: streams round rocks and do so very rapidly. Flume and tub experiments show about one-tenth of the actual wear that occurs in nature and demonstrate that splitting and cracking are the dominant forms of the breakage that does occur but that even this breakage is minor and not at all like human flaking. The gist of Kuenen's extensive review of the literature and his careful experiments is that nature does not exert forces in streams capable of breaking unweathered stones and in fact exerts only about 10 percent of the needed force.

My own attempts to find percussively broken rocks in streams or in beaches cover a wide range of environments. In the San Diego region I have observed the beaches for many years, with special attention to winter conditions when the sand cover tends to be swept off, leaving unsuspected (to the casual summer visitor) extensive berms of cobbles. These cobbles are porphyries and quartzites derived from the local geology and were the kind of stone extensively used by all the cultures that occupied the area. During winter storms they are subject to heavy surf action. With Malcolm Rogers in the 1930's, I spent hours on these berms. We could find no broken rock, much less artifactlike material. We used the berms for extensive flaking experiments, creating hundreds of flakes and many crude bifaced and unifaced core tools, none of which could be found on subsequent visits. Currently this beach carries a small amount of crushed rock derived from housing construction on the beachfront. This man-made gravel in the summer of 1976 showed an overall sheen or polish from the sand environment in which it lay. I doubt that it can even be detected in the cobble ramps that will appear in winter and in which rounding is extremely rapid. This is all completely in accord with Kuenen's observations.

Just north of the Scripps Institution of Oceanography pier, the erosion of the cliff has dumped occupational debris into the beach.

The surface source was a La Jollan midden dated by C-14 as 2,000 years old at the top and 7,000 years at the bottom. Beneath that, the alluvium has supplied dates up to 50,000 years on fireplaces and a Pleistocene horse skeleton, and these levels also contributed flaked stone that is now being worn in the beach. In all cases the material from the midden is being rounded—not broken and not flaked (see figure 17B). The dominant action is grinding and polishing.

Two hundred yards to the north of this site, there is a 300-foot high, vertical-faced cliff with a very high content of cobble strata. Rocks falling out of this cliff face fall onto a cobble berm. Since the cliff is being undercut by the sea, a fresh vertical face is maintained, out of which cobbles frequently fall. Falling from heights of 100 to 300 feet, they attain high velocities, and on hitting stones on the cobble ramp they frequently break. The result is a ramp with an unusual amount of broken rock. Collections of this material resemble quarry debris except that, as Barnes found, there is a very high amount of high-angle fracturing. There are no arti-factlike forms—no pattern of bifaces or unifaces or blades and cores, and of course no knife- or projectile-point-type material or even psuedo-preforms or blanks. In this unusual situation with everything favoring percussive breaking in nature, there is nothing artifactlike. The material in the ramp varies from fresh breaks to slightly worn breaks to heavily worn breaks. Series of breaks showing fresh, slightly worn, and heavily worn surfaces all on the same piece were not seen. This suggests that the breaks were created by the fall from the cliff, all at one blow, and that there is little breakage going on on the cobble ramp due to surf action.

The cobble ramps of Baja California present quite a different case. There are linear miles of such ramps with much fine-grained, quite brittle metabasalt cobbles. The ramps may stand up to twenty-five or more feet above sea level and are exposed to hurricane (*chubasco*) force winds and waves far exceeding the forces expectable at San Diego. Both in brittleness of rock and in the force of storms, the situation in Baja California leads one to expect greater probability of broken rock. Nevertheless, despite a deafening roar created by each wave's surge and retreat, which rolls rock up and down the ramp, freshly broken rock cannot be found in the active ramp. It is otherwise on the top of these ramps, for broken rocks, some freshly broken, can be found. Some of the rocks show multiple flake scars. Large flakes with bifacially flaked rims, which bear considerable resemblance to steep-edge flaked disc choppers, are one example of a near approach to artifact forms. The location of the material is significant: high up on the ramp. At the back of the ramps, stiff desert brush has caught and held some small cobbles. They were obviously thrown through the air and must represent a minute percentage of the storm-thrown rock. Clearly some rock is broken there by being thrown out of the surf and falling on the rock on the top of the ramp. This is percussive flaking and poses problems of differentiating the natural work from human flaking.

First a note on storm-thrown rock. Ting (1935, 1937) wrote that in Scotland storm-raised cobble ramps show signs of having been "beaten together," while true shore cobbles are well smoothed. I would translate "beaten together" as indicating the presence of battered and perhaps broken rocks. The magnitude of the storm forces is measured by boulders 10 feet long that are piled 50 feet above sea level and by cobbles that are piled 80 feet above sea level. Storm-thrown rocks have been known to break lighthouse glass at elevations of 150 feet above sea level. The enormous forces vastly exceed normal surf action, which in turn far exceeds stream action. Kuenen commented on the greater force in surf than in streams, and anyone wading into a cobble ramp with even modest surf will find the bruising impact of the wave-agitated stones unbearable. Nonetheless, rocks are smooth not broken.

Rock breakage certainly occurs during severe storm conditions on the cobble ramps that contain brittle rock, as do those in Baja California. Rock breakage does not occur on cobble ramps at San Diego under normal wave action (surf of sufficient height and force for both board and body surfing; three- to five-foot waves), and I have found no evidence of storm breakage (greater than six-foot waves) in these very tough local cobbles. The Baja California record is, then, of special interest. If it does not produce artifactlike material, other beaches are not likely to do so. And since surf action far exceeds stream action in violence, streams certainly would not create artifacts or break rocks.

The limitation of the broken rock to the tops of the storm

beaches and the clear evidence (rock caught in stiff brush) that rocks are thrown out of the surf provide clues as to the action that produces broken rock. Breakage is clearly due to extraordinary stress during storms, and some of the breakage goes on not in the water but on the ramp due to the impact of stones flying through the air.

Close examination of the broken rock from the storm-built ramps shows rare fresh flake surfaces and great numbers of worn flake surfaces. This is the exact opposite of human work. When a single piece from the ramps shows several flake scars, one at most will be fresh, and usually two or occasionally three generations of worn flakes can be determined. These fall in a series from lightly to heavily worn. On archeological sites and at quarries, generations of flaking can be found on cores and artifacts, but this is rare, not a regularity. And it is not accompanied by an overall wear pattern. The generations of flaking on artifacts are normally separated by evidences of weathering. On the coast at San Diego, the evidence is usually an oxidized rind on old artifacts that have been reused by later people whose flaking exposed fresh stone. In the desert reuse is usually shown by old surfaces' having a coating of iron and manganese and young surfaces' lacking these coatings or having them to lesser degrees. Even more telling is the kind of wear found on artifacts as compared with that found in beach-broken rock. On living sites, wear on flaked stone is limited to obvious working edges: in the concavity of concave scrapers, on the edges of used flakes and knives, on the tips and edges of drills, and so on. The use wear is limited and specific to the use that the artifact was manufactured for. Wear does not extend all over an artifact or into the hollows of the flake surfaces, except, rarely, on a long-used tool, on which it appears as very fine polish due to hands' grit, which has polished the hand-held surfaces. The contrast with the pseudo-artifacts from the cobble ramps could not be greater. Enormous degrees of wear are evident all over the beach rock except on the occasional fresh flake. Wear is universal. It is not confined to working edges or to ridges but extends into all depressions. This is due to impacts that have created what Kuenen called "surface cracking." Blows that were lighter than required to break the rock (split it or flake it) shattered a minute, often microscopic, bit of the surface.

In a surf or stream there is a random rain of such blows, and the surface is worn away by a pecking action. The action is exactly the same as that used in pecking stone tools into shape, except that the blows are much lighter and are delivered by a round surface rather than a sharp-edged instrument. The blows delivered by man in pecking a rock into a desired shape (e.g., an adze or ax) are vastly stronger and more concentrated on a point, as is shown by the deeper pock marks left by the blows and by the very rapid "wearing" of the stone into the desired shape. In nature, ridges and edges are more exposed than hollows and, being thinner, have less strength to resist blows. They wear, or are reduced, more rapidly than hollows, and as a consequence rounding occurs. As Kuenen and others found, rounding is very rapid, especially for material that has been exposed to weathering.

While some of the flaking on cobble ramps clearly is due to flying stone and probably all flaking of cobble-sized rocks goes on under storm conditions capable of throwing rocks out of the surf, there is the possibility that some flaking goes on in the ramp during storm conditions. A storm of hurricane force (100- to 200-mile-per-hour winds as compared to normal winds of 20 to 30 miles per hour) is of so large a magnitude of change that cobbles in balance with the normal environment might well be broken by the intense forces of the storm environment. Nevertheless, the uniform testimony of Kuenen and those he consulted and of others as well is that while storm ramps have rocks that are "beaten together," normal cobble ramps have smooth, unbroken cobbles. This must mean that if rocks are broken in ramps under storm conditions the evidence of the breakage is erased with great rapidity. Any stone broken and then edge-chipped in the surf would be subject to enormous wear in this environment. If it were thrown out of the storm environment and left on the storm ramp, it would retain the sequence of flakes, complete with the sequence of wear that these processes would call for. Only on the upper ramp out of the reach of the daily grind of the churning surf would this record of storm breakage be preserved.

Observations in Maine on cobble ramps exposed to north Atlantic storms show the same thing. The wear on bricks used for weights by lobstermen in their traps is of particular interest. When a lobster pot is thrown up on a beach and broken, the bricks become part of the beach gravel. Because they are soft, they wear rapidly, and because the material in them is uniform they wear evenly. The result is that bricks change from their familiar rectangular shapes into nearly perfect spheres, forming exact duplicates of Kuenen's experimental work. The hard, angular igneous rocks resulting from frost shattering of rocks on these same islands long retain their sharp-edged angular patterns determined by the joints in the country rock. They round very slowly, but all materials are obviously rounding. On one island a very uniform metabasalt rounds up into nearly perfect spheres, collectors' items called cannon balls. The rule of rounding rather than flaking seems general, even on the stormy coast of Maine.

The gist of all this is that nature does not percussively break rocks except under exceptional conditions, in one of the most violent geomorphic scenes that we know. Since stream forces are much less than surf forces and since Kuenen's figures indicate that only about 10 percent of the requisite force is available in stream environments, the indicated conclusion is the same that Kuenen reached. Streams do not break fresh rock percussively; nor does normal surf. And at this point I feel that I have worked the subject to death. But I am impelled to go to such length because of the seemingly unshakable opinion that one can go to the nearest stream or beach and pick up just lots of good old broken rocks: geofacts, cartifacts, naturifacts. The evidence is simply totally against this.

It has been a game played in the field with many to try to find broken rocks in natural settings: with Phil Orr of the Santa Barbara Museum of Natural History on the cobble ramps of Lake Lahontan and on the cobble ramps of Santa Rosa Island; with M. G. (Reds) Wolman of Johns Hopkins University and squads of graduate students on the river gravels of the Appalachians, which are subject to enormous floods on steep slopes when dying hurricanes stagnate there. Elsewhere with others the challenge often has been thrown down: "Find me some cartifacts!" Reds Wolman loved to hurl the challenge at a class of graduate students in geomorphology. The eager seekers, confident that remains of torrential stream action would be filled with broken rocks, always returned empty-handed.

There are ways to break rock other than by percussion, but

these leave utterly different marks. There is, or should be, no problem with breakage of rock by frost, chemical weathering, or fire, but it is necessary to mention these matters for those who have not looked into them. The characteristic of all such forms of weathering is that they produce a granular parting surface. How granular the surface will be depends on the rock. In general the more coarsely crystalline the rock, the more granular the parting surface. While this variable graininess applies to percussively flaked stone also, it need not be a source of confusion. Quartzites flaked by percussion have granular parting surfaces, but when they are broken by fire, frost, or chemical action the surface is still more granular.

The reason behind the granular nature of the weathering and fire fractures is that rocks are combinations of crystals. Each crystal has a different rate of expansion when it is heated or when it is oxidized or hydrated, the principle actions in weathering. This unequal response tends to pry the crystals apart, and when the resistance to these forces is overcome the rock becomes a fissured mass of cracks that tend to follow the crystal boundaries (see figure 18). Experimental work shows that until a critical temperature is reached no change occurs in the rock and that this temperature, although it varies with rock type, is far beyond any sun temperature, even that recorded on desert rocks. Freezing of water that has penetrated a rock acts in the same way. It penetrates along joint planes or follows crystal surfaces and pries the rock apart by expansion.

Breakage by percussion or pressure acts quite differently. A wave of force sent through the rock tends to sheer right across the crystals, tending to slice through them rather than run around them. They are not pried apart along the crystalline boundaries but are cleaved along the parting plane. The difference between breaking a stone by fire, frost, or chemical action and flaking it is equivalent to the difference between tearing a cloth in two and cutting it with scissors. One operation leaves a ragged edge; the other is vastly smoother. The degree to which this is true depends in part on the crystalline structure of the rock: a very coarsely crystalline rock has coarse parting planes even when it is broken by percussion. But it has even coarser parting surfaces when it is broken by fire, frost, or chemical action. In the fine-grained rocks preferred by man for tool making, the differences between flaking and other breakage

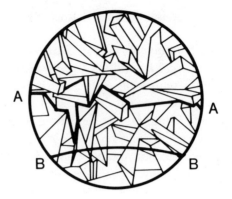

1

2

3

FIGURE 18. In this idealized picture of a piece of rock under high magnification to show the crystal structure, weathering breakage is compared with percussion or pressure breakage. The course of the fracture at *A* follows the crystal boundaries. This is the action that accompanies hydration, fire breakage, or frost breakage. As shown in 2, it produces a very rough surface. Percussion and pressure fracture tends to shear right through the crystals and to produce a smooth fracture face, as shown by the line at *B* and again in cross section at 3.

is less than in the coarse-grained rocks, but it is still there and is easily seen.

Even though it is clear that rocks are not commonly broken percussively by streams, some people will still mutter through clenched teeth, "But I still think nature breaks rocks percussively and by pressure sometimes." These Galileos in reverse (they are defending the dogma, not the observed facts) will still argue that streams break rocks. So let's look a bit more at the problem.

Nature has no plan in mind when she breaks rocks—if she does break rock percussively. A "broken round" or a clast, a cobble or pebble that breaks for whatever reason, a weathered rock entering an active stream environment with its resistance to even light blows destroyed by oxidation and hydration of its minerals, or, more confusing, a rock thrown by storm waves or broken by free-falling rocks from a cliff immediately becomes subject to random wear. This comes as grinding, sandblasting, cracking, and battering. Chipping, if any, will be comparable to that seen in hammer stones: a battered surface, not a chipped edge. These forces act on all surfaces: on all edges and ridges, on all faces, on convexities, and in concavities. Thin edges are battered back and rounded. Ridges are reduced more rapidly than hollows and, as all the geomorphic studies show or as anyone can confirm by visiting the nearest streambed, the angular object rapidly becomes a rounded object. Perhaps the extreme case is bottle glass in a rocky surf environment. Even this brittle material is rapidly reduced to rounded bits of colorful gravel. The only natural object likely to be confused with a man-made object would be one broken and then moved so small a distance that normal wear had not begun the rounding process. Conversely, of course, any humanly broken rock that had been acted upon by nature, especially in stream or surf, would rapidly become worn and presently unrecognizable as human work. So, how does man's work differ?

MAN AT WORK

Anything modified by man is an artifact. Broadly interpreted, this includes the flake debris produced in the manufacture of a tool such as an arrow or spear point, a hand axe, or a chipping tool. A great many simple flakes and many more complex items, such as concave scrapers, were the tools used to make the tools that mankind used in pursuit of food, shelter, and clothing. Sharp flakes are excellent for shaving down wooden shafts to make spears. Heavy, thick-edged cobble choppers function well to hollow out wooden bowls or to shape a digging stick or to peck the surface of metates and manos to make them grind wild seeds more effectively.

The debris from flaking stone to make tools is then itself artifactual: formed by man and often used. Even the unused flakes can tell a great deal, for the type of flaking is characteristic of the industry. For example, thick flakes with exaggerated bulbs of percussion are created when heavy chopping tools are made by striking stone with a stone hammer, and these are the products of utterly different activity from the thin flakes that come from making points and knives thin in cross section. The flakes produced in fluting a Clovis point are just as surely evidence that Clovis points were being produced as the finding of the Clovis point is. It is as if one found the fender off a Model T Ford; it is all the evidence one needs that Model T's were being made. A struck blade implies a fluted core and vice versa; and percussive flakes imply percussive flaking. These are hardly profound thoughts, but they do have a degree of scarcity.

We may well review the process of flaking stone, for much of the problem of recognition of man's work with stone stems from ignorance of the fundamentals. Flaking is breaking stone under control. Early man accomplished this by striking the stone and sending a shock wave along the desired path. This is percussive flaking, and even this requires sophisticated application of physics, which the pre-*sapiens* men learned by trial and error and passed on to their descendants. It is this kind of thing that indicates that we probably have been underestimating the intelligence of pre-*sapiens* man. Later man learned that he could produce the same effect with even greater control by the application of pressure. This was a problem in loading, that is, concentrating force on a tiny area until the strength of the stone at this point was overcome and a piece was forced off.

This sophisticated knowledge is many hundreds of thousands of years old and comes down to us in the nearly imperishable stone that man worked with. We are left to wonder about fibers,

cordage, basketry, wood and bone carving, and the manipulation of
vegetable materials, including the ability to extract bitter principals
and to use poisonous materials. What kind of record would we have
if these other materials were not perishable? The stonework remains, and, as poor a window as it is, it is for long ages the best
record that we have of the working not only of man's hand but of
his mind.

The earliest men used the stone locally available; later man
often ignored the local stone but went great distances to get superior
stone. A measure of the narrowness of the specialist's knowledge
was the attack, in a recent meeting, on the validity of early tools
because there was no imported material—"and it is known that the
Clovis people imported desirable stone over hundreds of miles."
Of course, but the early men were not the men of 10,000 years
ago but those of 50,000 and 100,000 years ago, and they did not
import stone for any appreciable distance. See for instance Robert
Begole's data (1974) for the Borrego Valley: there was no impor-
tation even of very fine stone from the Truckhaven site fifteen or
twenty miles away, a quarry certainly used from very early time on.
At Olduvai Gorge in East Africa there was no stone, so—even 1.75
million years ago—men went long distances to get material to make
tools. Where there were abundant local supplies, early men used
stone profligately; they threw away useful flakes, for they could
anywhere and any time make others. Those who imported their
stone tools, on the other hand, used them till they were sharpened
to exhaustion. Some laws of supply and demand are apparently
timeless and apply to all cultures.

Over most of the world, however, stone is available. There are
limitations: great deltas such as that of the Mississippi are virtually
stone free. Tropical regions, with their accelerated weathering and
ancient land surfaces, often lack in near-surface layers any hard stone
except of the most resistant sort, and even this is often available
only in streambeds. Among the most chemically stable and abrasion-
resistant rocks are quartzites, and it is the presence of quartzite
cobbles in streambeds over wide areas of the world that probably
made this one of the preferred stones for the earliest stone flakers.
It is difficult to see why man used quartzite so persistently in areas
where other stone was available unless he was carrying on a tradi-

tion. It may be that the tradition was to use stream cobbles of any material rather than a specific rock type and that the chemistry of rocks in streams determined that these would often be quartzite.

In the San Diego area, a considerable variety of stone is available: quartzite and porphyry in the stream gravels and far finer-grained and more easily worked volcanics in the adjacent mountains. For an immense length of time man concentrated on the quartzites, largely ignoring the finer stone except where it was available in the river gravels. In adjacent Baja California very fine-grained metabasalts are dominant in the gravels, and man used them. Man was quite clearly limited in his view of rock sources and turned to river gravels as his source area. Whatever was there he used, and it was a long time indeed before he learned to lift up his eyes unto the hills—the hills that could supply him far finer rock for his stone tools. He clung overly long to gathering smooth cobbles beside the not-so-still waters despite the fact that the local streams often provided relatively poor materials.

One would think that the selectivity in breaking rocks and the strong localization of human breakage would make it easy to identify human breakage, but few things have created more academic uproar. The fundamentals are simple, so that is where we start.

Once man knew how to break rock under control, he could fashion it pretty much as he liked, but he was limited to three fundamental patterns (see figure 1, in the introduction). He could strike blows in alternate directions: bifacial flaking. He could strike blows in one direction: unifacial flaking. He could set his stone up and strike blows designed to remove long, thin, sharp-edged flakes: blade making. Bifacial flaking makes hand axes and, with increasing control, leads to bifacial knives, spear points, and arrow heads. Unifacial flaking is a dead end. It is best for producing scrapers and adzes. Blade making is also limited. All three processes produce a vast abundance of sharp flakes, and early man was no dummy; he used them, too.

Man was also smart enough to combine two or even all three of these patterns, and this was especially true in later times. However, man was also subject to fashion, and over large areas and huge expanses of time, he tended to emphasize one method over another and to combine his stone tool making into distinctive patterns of usage of one, two, or three of these fundamental skills. Man's first work was with the cobbles found in streambeds, and his first stone tools were cobbles from which a flake or two were removed to give a sharp edge. These are the so-called pebble tools. Some men struck their flakes in alternate directions to create an ax-type edge. At first the flaking was steep, the flakes were thick, and the resulting edge was steep and sinuous. Progress consisted of learning to drive off flatter flakes, to make thinner working tools, and finally to make delicate points. In Eurafrica the pebble tools of one and two million years ago have steep edge angles, early hand axes of half a million years ago, less steep, and late Paleolithic hand axes of perhaps 100,000 years ago may have quite thin cross sections and thin edges. This is accompanied by shallower and flatter flakes, and on the core this is measured by shallower flake scars and more regular edges. Early, crude bifacially flaked objects have strongly sinuous edges; later ones, straighter edges.

Nature may under exceptional situations, as on cobble ramps, strike a strong percussive blow and remove a flake, but nothing in nature will strike in one sequence alternate blows from first one face and then the other with no intervening wear. Bifacially flaked objects with sequences of flakes with no intervening overall wear are then evidence of man at work. The flakes produced in this work are equally evidence of man. Nature occasionally produces a flake or two. Man regularly produces quantities of them (see figure 19).

Another approach to the problem of developing a good working edge was the uniface (see figure 1, in the introduction, and figure 17). A cobble or other irregular piece was split to create a plane surface, which served as a striking platform. All trimming blows were then struck from this surface. The product is technically an adze or chisel as opposed to an ax. It is a surprisingly efficient tool with varied utility. It can be used as a chopper, as a scraper, or as a plane and for cutting wood by chopping, for shaping wood, or for cleaning a hide by scraping. In addition, all the flakes produced are useful, and they were used. Since these flakes were produced by percussion, they differ little from those produced in bifacial percussive flaking.

A third way to flake stone was to place a cobble on a boulder and to strike the cobble on a surface opposite to the end resting on

FIGURE 19. Even simple flakes, such as *D*, indicate that percussive blows are being struck, and, as we have seen, nature would rapidly set to work to smooth up such a flake. When one finds clusters of such flakes, and when one sees on them the evidence of trimming or sharpening blows—as appears on *A*, *B*, and *C*—then one is surely looking at human work. One does not need a spear point to recognize the hand of man, and this kind of debris is about all one will find from the early period. Flakes *A*, *B*, and *D* are old, as shown by their dull color. Flake *C* is young, for it has the dark color of the unaltered basalt.

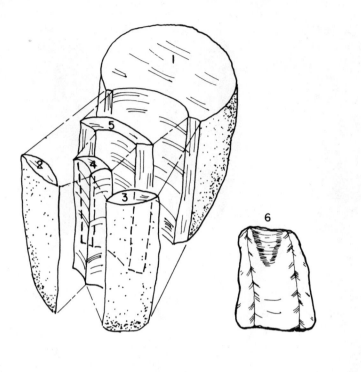

FIGURE 20. A classic section of a blade from the Calico site in the Mohave Desert is shown to one side (6). The steps required to produce such a blade are shown in the diagram: 1 creates a striking platform; 2, 3, and 4 are blows required to create a three-faceted surface; 5 is the blow to strike off a flake with three facets on its dorsal surface. All the flakes, as well as the core, can be used by man. Nature does not strike such series of purposeful blows, but man does.

the boulder (see figure 20). For good control, the part of the lower end of the core where the flake is to terminate must be free of the anvil. The tendency of such flaking is to drive off long, narrow flakes, which with skilled management and good flaking material run from end to end of the core (see figure 21). The flakes, technically blades, driven off in this manner have sharp edges and are excellent knives needing no further work unless it be to blunt one edge to minimize the possibility of the worker's cutting himself.

Development of skill in this work through time included preparation of striking platforms, control of the percussive blow's direction and force, and finally the application of pressure tech-

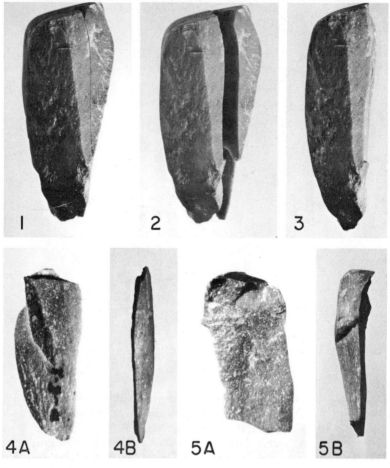

FIGURE 21. This series shows experimental work in blade making, starting with a core, *1*, that had been flaked in antiquity. The blunt end of a geologic pick served as a hammer and a large cobble as an anvil. The removal of flakes is shown in *2* and *3*. Flakes with flat ventral planes (shown in *4* and *5*) were driven off the core, leaving flat planes intersecting at obtuse angles on the core. Shattering occurred at both the anvil and the hammer ends of the flakes and the core. Bulbs of percussion were weak to absent. These are all marks typical of anvil flaking of blades, a very early lithic technology in America. (Photo from Carter, 1957, by permission of Johns Hopkins University Press)

niques and the production of tiny, razor-sharp blades, microblades. In this technology both the cores and the blades are distinctive. The cores show multiple flake scars running the length of the cores. The blades are more than twice as long as they are wide, and they

often show by long, parallel scars on their surface that they are one
of a series struck from one core. Any extensive collection, even
in quartzite, will provide some flakes with weak bulbs of percussion, and cores and blades may show anvil rebound scars and tip
shattering, neither of which appears in exfoliation due to fire action.
Long, narrow flakes with flat ventral planes and several, similar
flake scars on their dorsal surface testifying to repeated removal of
such flakes from a core are evidence of human work. Similarly,
cores with some combination of plural, long, parallel flake scars,
prepared platforms, anvil rebound marks, percussion marks at the
hammer end, and the absence of evidence of fire must be evidence
of man, not of nature.

If striking of blades is ancient in America, it should be widespread, and if it accompanied man from Asia there should be
evidence of it there. Simply as indications, here are two finds that
suggest how the winds blow. First, recall that blade making is
present at Choukoutien in north China as early as 350,000 years
ago.

Paul Tolstoy (1958) in reviewing Siberian data noted the presence of prismatic cores and blade tools. Any similarities of that
culture to one in America, Tolstoy noted, "would have to be to a
crude chopper using culture . . . [such as] has been postulated on an
early level in western North America." This is exactly what is now
widely reported—at Texas Street and adjacent sites in San Diego,
at the Calico site in the Mohave Desert, and at numerous sites in
the Colorado Desert. In the volume on lithic technology edited by
Earl Swanson (1975), one finds continued interest in blade and
core work. Kobayashi comments on blade and core work at Choukoutien and elsewhere in China and discusses his experimental work
with blade making. He reports that, of 300 flakes that he made
using heavy hammers and an anvil, the most common flaking angle
was from ninety to ninety-four degrees. By Barnes's platform-angles
method, to be discussed below, this would be evidence against their
being man-made. Barnes's method, however, while it works fine
on bifacial industries, is not as applicable to blade and core work.

In the same source (Swanson, 1975), Ranere reports on some
excavations in Panama that also produced such material. The site
has C-14 dates going back to only 4600 B.C., and this leads Ranere

to view it as an example of cultural lag. It may be another case of dating error, a suspicion enhanced by the high degree of weathering reported for this site. There are no advanced tools: no dart points, no bifacially flaked knives. The assemblage consists of cutting, scraping, and chopping tools. The technology is simple and changes little with time. While Ranere thinks this cultural lag is normal for tropical-forest tribes, I cannot refrain from pointing out that it is also characteristic of the southern California coast and desert people and of all the people of Australia, irrespective of the climate. It might also be recalled that the Mayan civilization was in a tropical forest. The tendency to reach for a physical-environmental explanation is too easy an out. There is abundant good stone, and so this is not a limiting cause. Flaking was done with hammers and anvils, and the work is described as a "fairly casual approach to flint knapping." Despite the use of a variety of lithic materials (chalcedony, quartz, and andesite), relatively few true blades (flakes whose length is twice their width) were produced. Illustrations of bipolar cores duplicate in detail those from southern California, and the "wedges" are suggestively like skreblos found in Siberia. What is interesting about all of this is that such assemblages are present and are easily recognizable as the work of man and that the technology used to produce such work is evident to almost any archeologist—just as long as the suggested antiquity is not beyond the accepted limits for man in America.

LITHIC TECHNOLOGY AND TECHNOLOGISTS

We have been making belated strides in the study of lithic technology—belated because the signposts were erected long ago, as Johnson (1978) has pointed out. The first paper on stone flaking that I read, and it was old when I read it in the late 1920's, was by a Frenchman who dealt with a cube of glass. Striking it just the right blow at dead center on one face would send a shock wave through the glass to remove curved flakes and leave a spherical core, he said. It was a beautiful hypothesis and not too far from reality. A more realistic example can be seen wherever small boys and BB guns get on the loose. The perfect cones punched out of window glass, and the much thicker and finer ones punched out of plate glass, show the cones of dispersion of force in classic form.

Master flakers like Don Crabtree (1972) can describe just how to control this dispersion of force in such a way as to give one as much control in flaking stone as a whittler has in shaping wood.

Malcolm Rogers and I taught ourselves lithic technology in the 1920's by reading what little there was and practicing percussion flaking to duplicate the Paleolithic-like stonework that we were finding in the Encinitas area and along the coast. We were not expert flakers, but we came to an appreciation of the degree of skill required to work the coastal cobbles. The difference between flaking those tough porphyries and fine cherts and flints is the difference between whittling sugar pine and cross-grained oak. With that and the handling of many thousands of pieces of flake debris and cores, as well as artifacts, we gained considerable insight into what man did, and hence we could recognize human work, even flake debris. We were nearly limited to Paleolithic work, for while there were late (Diegueño) villages with pottery and arrow points, there were vastly more sites lacking any such refined material. I grew up working on and collecting the kind of material that most archeologists had been throwing away as flake debris, cores, quarry discards, and so forth. Since the only artifacts these sites possessed was like the debitage and quarry discards of later sites, we concluded that this "debris" was the whole kit. Decades later, I put this material under the microscope and could demonstrate wear and thereby prove that these crude stones were well-used tools (Carter, 1957).

Southern California had square miles of occupation debris on the coast, and I was conditioned to view much of it as man's tools and all of it as man's work. A great many of my contemporaries focused instead on the fine flaking technology that produced arrow points and the wonderful flaking ability shown by the makers of the magnificent points of the Great Hunters, the Folsom and Clovis people. Unfortunately this prepares one poorly for working with pebble tools and the Lower Paleolithic. Since almost no one conceived of a Lower Paleolithic state (a cultural level, rather than a time level is meant here), this inadequacy did not disturb many scholars.

An early break from this disinterest stemmed from John Witthoft's work (1952). He not only studied and solved the problem of how men had first made a delicate point and then removed long flakes down each face, as was done by the Folsom and Clovis people, but he studied the wear pattern on tools and worked out the technology of blade and core work. It was at this time that it dawned on the eastern archeologists that the little conical flint objects they had called scrapers were cores and the little flakes they had thrown away by the thousands were the tools—microblades used in working bone and wood. Witthoft's work prepared him for the recognition of the blade and core work at Texas Street.

I first met John Witthoft at a dinner before he spoke to an archeological society in Maryland. I was asked if I would like to attend and meet Witthoft. My enthusiastic acceptance was greeted with such obvious reservation by my host that I asked why. "Well, I don't know what will happen. John certainly does not think much of you." We sat together at dinner, talked continuously, and were good friends thereafter. Witthoft agreed to look at the Texas Street material. "Sure, I will look at anyone's broken rocks," he said good-naturedly. I took him up on it by loading the car with material from Texas Street and driving up to Harrisburg, Pennsylvania, where John then held the position of state archeologist. I followed my usual custom of handing the material to the expert and withdrawing to let him look it over. I stood around for a while, listening to the rattling of rocks as John arranged them in groups. Finally I could stand it no longer and burst out with: "Well, are they artifacts or not?" "Oh, of course, they are artifacts," he replied. "I am just arranging them typologically, separating the Clactonian flaking from the bipolar work." He recognized the bipolar material at once because he had made a worldwide survey of this type of work. He was probably the only man in the Americas who had, and I learned as much about the Texas Street material in one day with John Witthoft as I had in the several years that I had been collecting this material in the field.

An early study of stone tools by Barnes (1939) emphasized study of the platform angles formed when men struck flakes to make tools. In essence this said that man strove to create a cutting edge and that cutting edges were more efficient if they were thinner. Man would strive therefore to strike flakes at such an angle as to thin the edge and thus sharpen the implement. Nature would have no such goal, and natural breaks would be at high angles, often ninety degrees or more. It is an interesting measure and generally, though not universally, applicable, for men deliberately made tools with steep cutting edges. Some human activity was designed to explore or prepare material; this led men to break rocks open by smashing them, and the products, though created by man, have many high-angle breaks.

Barnes's study covered flint, chalcedony, jasper, chert, "and other hard brittle material." He stated: (1) that natural forces are able to produce flaking similar to that on eoliths, (2) that the flaking on eoliths differs from that of human work, and (3) that "fortuitous concussions do not produce large numbers of tools with parallel flake scars." If eoliths are not artifacts and the flaking on them is different from that of human work, and if "fortuitous concussions" rarely produce items that look like tools, then it does not appear that the problem of distinguishing artifacts from geofacts should be a large one. Barnes's eoliths, the product of natural breaking, seem not to have been made by percussion but by some other force, perhaps pressure, but he was remarkably incurious about what in nature breaks rocks.

Barnes noted that beaches flake flint freely but failed to note the wear pattern that sets beach-fractured stones off from human manufacture. He cited foundering of limestones as producing huge pressures, but also called on solifluction, a very dubious cause. He also believed that noon heat and nocturnal frost had covered hundreds of square miles of Australia with conchoidal flakes, and this I most seriously doubt.

His illustrations make it clear that he is working solely with bifacial flaking in artifacts—the striking of blows from first one side and then the other. Even in this work, he had up to 25 percent right-angle blows. "The flaked tools of an industry made, or supposed to be made by percussion—may be considered to be of human origin if not more than 25 percent of the angles of platform-scar are obtuse (90° and over)." I have never seen any lithic industry in America that did not meet this test. This includes the steep edged unifacial work such as that seen in the La Jollan industry and repeated in the Kartan culture of Australia and the Soanian-Anya-

thian-Hoabinhian in Southeast Asia. The method is least applicable
to the cores of the blade industries, for the blades are often struck
from vertical faces. Kobayashi, mentioned earlier, struck 300 blades
using the anvil technique and reported that most of the platform
angles were around 100 degrees (Kobayashi, 1975). However, the
preferred platform angle is generally something less than a right
angle. The significant point is that in this industry the sharp edge
sought by man is not on the core but on the long flake or blade
detached from the core. Surprisingly, however, the obtuse angles
formed by the intersections of the flake scars left by the detach-
ment of blades are now described as extremely efficient edges for
shaping bone by scraping.

Barnes's method, then, in part states the obvious and in part
is directed to one type of stone flaking, and even then its applica-
tions as a test of human work would eliminate no controversial
material known to me: certainly not Calico, Texas Street, Yuha,
Farmington, or Lively, to mention a few.

It is startling to see in America the extent to which the clichés
influence the experts. Don Crabtree, as expert a stone flaker as we
have, gives a formidable list of natural forces that in his opinion
produce naturifacts. No evidence is advanced, and it is obvious that
he is simply listing the archeologists' clichés. For the record, they
are: soil movement, glaciation, wave (surf) action, high-velocity
water movement, gravity on steep inclines, rapid temperature change,
internal pressures (starch fractures and pot lids), exfoliation, tectonic movements, diastrophism, solifluction, and foot trampling. One
feels as if, as a final word, one should add "and acts of God."
By the way, solifluction and soil movement are the same thing,
expressed in Latin and English. Atmospheric temperature changes
cannot break rock, though freezing with water can, but frost breaks
do not resemble percussion breaks. High temperature in forest fires
can break rocks, but the fire breakage is readily detected. Internal
pressure is probably mythical, for pot lids are usually due to fire
or frost, and starch fracture is a cliché invoked as needed to account
for the very flat fracture planes normal to bipolar flaking. Starch
fracture does occur in some rocks and does create parallel planes
suggestive of blade and core work, but the surfaces are granular and
bulbs of percussion, lines of force, and so forth are lacking. Foot

trampling, also known as the elephants' toe-dance theory, if not entirely mythical, has little or no application to lived-on floors or most habitation locations. Water, surf, slopes, and so forth have been dealt with, perhaps by this time ad nauseum.

The evidence so far is: Kuenen and others have demonstrated experimentally that streams and surf do not break rock by percussion, they round them. Fire, frost, and chemical action break rock but leave distinctive evidence of their actions. Man's actions leave a whole galaxy of distinctive marks. So, why is there so much argument about the obvious? It is simply fixed ideas versus facts.

Repeatedly someone tells me of some special circumstance in nature that breaks rocks. Usually the descriptions are vague, without specification of rock type, breakage patterns, and forces at work. The few specific cases involve relatively weak rock or unusually readily flaked rock, as in the Brazos Valley flints, and none of these shows artifact patterns rather than random patterns. The earliest stonework known to me in southern California is in the extremely tough rocks that, according to Kuenen's experiments and my personal observation as well, are very rarely flaked by nature and that, even when they are flaked, yield nothing that fits a human artifact pattern. What we need are very specific cases, where the lithic material and the forces acting on it to produce special forms that might be mistaken for artifacts are reported in detail. We have virtually no such reporting.

Alan Bryan and I have carried on a long correspondence, one that began somewhat acrimoniously twenty years ago and that I broke off saying: "Perhaps we will meet some day and can settle down for a couple of beers, and I predict that the result will be mutual respect even if not total agreement." This has actually happened. Bryan has moved to the forefront of the early-man proponents and has included an article by me in a book on early man in America (Bryan, 1978). But he has plagued me with statements that he knows of locations where broken rock similar to that which I was showing him had obviously been broken by nature. I had the impression that he thought that nature was making blades and leaving fluted cores.

When he sent me material from such a location, it turned out to be in a relatively weakly cemented fine-grained stone, and the flaking was bifacial. The location was below a waterfall, and the assumption was that the high-energy situation of the fall broke the rock. The natural cleavage of the rock is so pronounced that tabular pieces with rounded edges were frequently created by natural forces. Some of the pieces have numerous percussive flakes removed from one or two edges. These flake surfaces are all of the same age and usually show no wear, and these are traits that, we have seen, are typical of human work.

I tried Barnes's platform-angles analysis, using a division of angles around ninety degrees, around sixty degrees, and around thirty degrees. According to Barnes, a predominance of ninety-degree fractures indicates nature at work; lower angles indicate that it is man that is at work. In this case the edges, the areas that were struck, had angles around thirty degrees in 90 percent of the cases measured. Only a few approached even sixty degrees. Two specimens, separately catalogued, could be put back together, and one piece had been broken into numerous pieces during shipping, having been subjected to random battering by the other pieces in the package. Ninety percent of the breaks resulting from this random battering were at ninety degrees or very close to it. The contrast between the two sets, those definitely broken without human purpose, and those for which there was a question of human purpose or random natural breakage, could hardly be more extreme.

As it stands, these broken rocks show all the marks of human action as opposed to natural breakage, and we even have a cross-check, since when we have some random breakage it conforms to the classic measure of nonhuman breakage. The differences, moreover, are not minor. There is almost no overlap of the known non-human breakage with the material of questioned breakage. My conclusion is that the riverbed at the waterfalls where this material was gathered has served as a source for easily flaked rock and that the area is littered with man's work—mostly quarry work. A fundamental difference between my outlook and that of the usual archeologist appears here. I do not have to have finished tools to recognize man's handiwork. If it isn't nature, it is man, and as this now-lengthy review shows the differences between the two are enormous.

Bryan's reaction has been to propose to take a further step. He will look upstream above the waterfall. If this same material is found there, then the waterfall surely did not break it, and the probability that man did will be further confirmed. It is a good step to take, and it is to Bryan's credit that he would ship me questionable rocks, enter into a dialogue as to their significance, and propose a near-final step in settling the question.

The cherts of the Brazos River valley are among the most easily flaked of any in the world. In past times the river has carried gravels composed of these cherts to the vicinity of Bryan, Texas, and these ancient gravels are now mined by open-pit excavations with a dragline. Repeated surveys of these gravel pits reveal a very low percentage of broken chert but nothing artifactlike. There is no pattern to the breakage, and no recognizable tool types appear. Equally interesting is the absence of artifactlike material in the very roughly handled processed material. The gravel is lifted in a dragline bucket, dumped into trucks, hauled to an endless belt and dumped, and run through sets of rotary screens. The large rock (of the sizes of interest to man) are carried by an endless belt and dumped ten to twenty feet onto a reject pile. A small percentage of breakage occurs in this violent operation, but still nothing artifactlike appears. When the reject pile becomes too large, it is bulldozed down and spread out. The immense weight of the steel treads pressing rock on rock now presses off long flakes, leaving multifaceted cores. These, at first glance, resemble blade cores. Most of them show no platform. Flakes usually are pressed off from points rather than from surfaces. Occasionally a natural plane surface has flakes pressed off, with the plane in the position of a striking platform. These pieces are deceptively like true blade cores. Still, I do not know of any situation like this in nature.

If an elephant were to walk over gravels in a stream bed, would he produce work like this? It would be interesting to have some experimental observations. Would the rubber tires of an automobile approximate the foot of an elephant? In driveways where the unmodified gravels of the Brazos River are used as road metal, flakes rarely are pressed off. These flakes differ from those produced by tractor work in that there is no evidence of excessive force as registered by platform crushing and by strongly developed waves of force. The flakes also tend to be feather edged at both ends. There is no platform on which the pressure or blow was delivered. In none of these cases is there any evidence of use wear or associated hearths. Nor are there other evidences of human activity.

I have examined glacial moraines, looking for artifactlike material. It should be noted that artifacts in Wisconsin moraines would not be too unexpected a find, though surely they would be rare unless one stumbled onto an occupation zone that had been over-ridden by the ice with little disturbance. This seems to be the case for the Sheguiandah site in Canada and for the Timlin site in the Catskills (see Cole and Godfrey, 1977, for a lively discussion of the problem there). In general, the rocks are less rounded than in stream deposits, and in some areas a fair number of the rocks are striated from having been ground along in the ice. I have found no evidence of flaking by percussion or pressure. One would expect at least some pressure flaking on flinty stones frozen in place and then moved against other rocks. Probably the glacial mill rather quickly erases traces of such work.

In the Sierra Nevadas between Tahoe and Reno, the principal rocks involved in the glacial mill were granites, useful for gauging weathering age but not useful for flaking. There was a fair amount of basalt that man used in adjacent campsites, but I could find no evidence of its being flaked by the glacial ice. In Maine the story is much the same. Subangular rock is frequent, but it is not flaked, and it resembles nothing in the realm of human work. Even in the Catskills in New York state, where the Onandaga flint supplies material that is very readily flaked, Dr. Raemsch and I could find no evidence of natural flaking of this stone by the glaciers. It seems to me, after decades of observation, that the natural breakage of rocks by percussion and pressure is exceedingly rare in nature. Only where free-fall of rocks from cliff faces occurs have I found anything like percussive fracture of rock. Even talus slopes fail to supply sufficient free-fall to produce flaking. Or I suppose the better statement is: after examining a few hundred talus slopes, including some with very fine-grained, easily flaked material, I have never found any evidence of flaking that resembled human work, and indeed I have found virtually no evidence of flaking from such tumbling down slope at all.

In Europe it is argued that solution of the limestone allows settling that cracks flint nodules in half and then moves one half against the other in such a way as to press off long series of flakes. The result resembles a unifacial tool with extensive edge retouch. The drawings are impressive. Although I have looked for similar evidence in the limestone regions of Texas, which have similar chert nodules, I have seen no trace of such action. Perhaps the semiarid climate of Texas versus the humid climate of Britain makes the difference, but if this is true then we should be very cautious about extending findings from one area to an unlike area.

I have examined the broken flint material from the Friesenhahn Cave in Texas, with its impressive list of Upper Pleistocene animals and much broken stone. I agree with Alex Krieger (1964) and E. J. Sellards (1952) that this material has been broken by man. A particularly impressive piece is a chert nodule five inches in diameter that has been struck three times on one end. The first blow split the nodule and ended in a hinge fracture. The second blow hinge-fractured midway down the face; the third, at one quarter of the way down the face. It is an extremely clear case of percussive fracturing—done in sequence, and certainly done by man. The dozens of other pieces of fractured flint are good examples of flake debris, with some showing good bulbs of percussion, and none showing more than slight evidence of retouch. The presence of charcoal and one freshwater mussel shell in the cave reinforces the evidence for man. At the moment it seems probable that weathering released some nodules of flint and man entered the cave in search of them, broke up the nodules, took the best material with him, and left masses of flake debris. The total picture, including clear evidence of percussive work, typical quarry debris, and the presence of many pieces with evidence of sequences of blows, is entirely different from that found in natural deposits, whether from stream, glacier, or talus.

I have also examined briefly some broken flint material from the Colorado River near Austin, Texas. This material shows by its weathering that it is of several ages, and some of it is very old. The opinion at the University of Texas is that, except for such obvious things as fragments of projectile points, this is natural breakage. Given the great ease of flaking of the cherts in this region, all material with no cultural context must be viewed with caution, but an interesting test would be to sort the material by degree of weathering and to see how the pattern of breakage changes with the degree of weathering. One end of the scale should clearly be nonhuman breakage, if nature breaks this chert frequently. The other end, it is obvious from the dart points of a few thousand years' antiquity, is clearly man. But what of the great middle class? Does it contain human or natural breakage patterns? The material is all there for a classic study, and one wonders why it has not been done.

At San Diego, where the argument has steadily been that nature breaks rocks percussively and by pressure, I have repeatedly taken those who say so to examples of the identical rock (quartzite and porphyry cobbles) exposed in the Eocene and Pliocene. Despite the evidence of violent water action—boulders up to eighteen inches in diameter moved—no percussively or pressure-broken rock can be found. There is weathered rock, but that poses no problem to any skilled observer. Weathering produces a granular parting plane and usually penetrates the rock along natural planes within the rock. The immense exposures available are very convincing.

CONCLUSION

The gist of all this is that nature rarely if ever breaks rocks percussively or by pressure and that the marks of human work—repetitive, patterned action without intervening overall wear—set artifacts apart from geofacts.

The great furor over geofacts versus artifacts is very largely a tempest in a teapot. It is manufactured and maintained by archeologists primarily as a rearguard action against the evidence for very early man in America. As this discussion makes clear and as will be made clearer in cases to be discussed below, it is maintained in spite of massive evidence to the contrary. On the other hand, there is a steady trickle of pseudoartifacts dribbled onto the harried archeologist's desk by amateurs who are unable to distinguish between natural parting planes and percussive fracture planes, and the archeologist gets so used to giving these people the double-0 brush-off that he too easily extends it to all uncomfortable situations. Any situation that challenges his fossilized beliefs in the recency of man in America is uncomfortable, and the easiest way to deny the evidence is to snort: geofact or naturifact or, the ultimate put-down, cartifact.

Of all people, the archeologist should know better. But then, the geophysicist should have known better than to say that continents cannot drift about or that the geometry of earth-sun relationships cannot cause glacial periods and—the list is endless. The experts are often wrong, and the more vociferous they are about it, the more probable it is that they are wrong. With artifacts, naturifacts, geofacts, cartifacts, and the associated folklore and numerology placed in proper perspective, we can move on to examine some of the controversial sites.

But first we need a few names and descriptions of tool types to be sure that the necessary vocabulary is present. As table 1, in the introduction, shows, there is, in my view, a long series of cultural stages marked by characteristic tools or patterns of tool making. Anticipating some of the discussion by supplying names and descriptions will help the understanding of the text.

The earliest tools show unskilled trimming that creates a steep edge, even in bifacial work. Men of this stage often used cobbles or pebbles, and this is sometimes called the pebble-tool stage. Where pebbles were not available, any piece of stone would do. The unifying thread is the steepness of the edge flaking. Such work may appear in later stages, but there is always some better work present. In the steep edge stage, only this clumsy flaking appears.

This is followed by a stage when men learned to split off long flakes, technically blades. This was an entirely different style of work, and the sites with the blades and their accompanying cores are distinctive indeed. Blades are ready-made knives, and this useful technology persisted very long, often into quite late cultures. At the time we are concerned with, the blades are heavy and thick, so this stage will be called the heavy blade stage.

Another lithic technology, or way of flaking rock, emphasized bifacial flaking, but with increased ability to drive flakes into the face of the rock to thin the edge more efficiently. This is the hand-ax stage in the Old World and the ovate biface stage in the New World. It is an improved pebble-tool technology.

This was followed in America by emphasis on unifacial flaking. Instead of striking blows in alternate directions, all blows were struck in one direction. The products are thick and often steep edged. They functioned as adzes, scrapers, skinning tools, and so forth with surprising efficiency, and many uniface tools continued in use in later cultures.

Beginning sometime before 12,000 years ago men began to make finely flaked thin points, perhaps first as knives but presently for projectile points. This marks the beginning of the late phase in American archeology: the Clovis and Folsom hunters of the late Pleistocene and the opening part of the Recent.

Chapter 5

Early Sites: I
The American Middle Paleolithic

To this point we have reviewed the history of ideas about the antiquity of man in America and our centuries-long struggle to calculate
time. We have looked at the geomorphological record of time—
and the changes in climate, sea level, and landform that time brings
—as well as the record in rock that man can be expected to leave,
including how man-broken rock differs from natural rock. We finally
come, then, to the examination of some of the key sites at San
Diego and elsewhere. It is the long, elliptical approach, but the
stage is set, the actors identified, and the show can now go on.

There are at San Diego several sets of sites to be discussed:
ancient concentrated sites that usually have much shell, traces of
human occupation in alluvial deposits over ancient beaches, evidence
for man beneath the present sea level, sites in the alluvium of
ancient valley fills, and ancient dispersed sites. For each of these
categories, one or two key sites will be discussed in some detail,
and others treated more briefly. Whatever the time of the first
appearance of man at San Diego, it was somewhat later than the
first entry at Bering Strait, somewhat earlier than the first appearance
at the Strait of Magellan, and near enough to the center of events to
be interesting. We will never know the actual year of the first man's
arrival in America, and we may be lucky to get within a few
thousand years of that epoc-making event. An early date at San
Diego will establish that man was in America at least at that time
and had gotten at least that far south from his entry point—and
to establish that is to do quite a bit.

I will limit myself primarily to sites at San Diego, with which
I have some personal familiarity, for I find it difficult to be sure of
the circumstances on sites I have not seen. Everyone has his own

criteria, not to mention his own vocabulary, and my archeological colleagues seldom report on soils and landforms, or, if they do, they often do so in terms incomprehensible to me, and equally often they do so with quite positive statements about postglacial pluvial or postglacial warm periods that seem pretty dubious to me. It is otherwise with sites that I have been on. Then not only have I made my own observations but I even know what it is that the other man was trying to tell me. It is all too true that the miracle is not that we sometimes misunderstand one another but that we ever understand each other at all. So I will discuss the sites at San Diego that I know very well, the sites in the Colorado Desert and the Mohave Desert that I know fairly well, the sites in the glacial deposits in Canada and New York State that I know less well, and a few others because of some special interest. We will start with San Diego, since that is the area I know best.

CULTURE SEQUENCE IN THE SAN DIEGO AREA

In the San Diego area three basic lithic traditions have been identified: blades struck from cores, bifaced core tools, and unifaced tools. That there is a still older lithic tradition is argued by Begole (1974), Childers (1977*b*), and Minshall, and they are probably correct. This is steep edge work or Malpais and is appearing in the Colorado Desert sites and elsewhere. The blade and core work is associated in the literature with the Texas Street site, for which an interglacial age has been proposed. The biface industry is best represented in the adjacent desert areas and will be described from the East Rim, a Mohave Desert site. The uniface work follows the blade and core work and the biface work in time. It is associated with the La Jollan culture at the La Jolla and Torrey Pines Mesa sites, but it continued to be used, with additions and modifications, right into the historic period.

The cultural sequence at San Diego has long been accepted as: San Dieguito, beginning about 8,000 or 9,000 years ago, followed by the La Jollan, beginning about 5,000 to 7,000 years ago, and then the historical Diegueño, the successor of the La Jollan. This sequence was established by the dating of the San Dieguito culture at a site in the San Dieguito Canyon. There was believed to be nothing earlier than that culture—not at San Diego, not anywhere else in America.

Most recent in the sequence were the Diegueño. The Digueño in contact times made pottery, used the bow, and tipped their arrows with finely flaked stone points. They cremated their dead, while all the previous people had buried theirs. Pottery and the custom of cremation had clearly come in from the east, from the Colorado River country, and presumably the bow and arrow had been introduced from that direction also. These traits came in quite late, a few centuries before the Spanish arrived. Prior to that the Diegueño tool kit would have been virtually indistinguishable from that of the preceding people, the late La Jollans. For the Diegueño we have a richer inventory of artifacts than for earlier people, in part because we know of their perishable material. They made basketry by coiling and sewing rather than by weaving. They had string and snares and digging sticks. They hunted rabbits with a curved throwing stick, functionally equivalent to the Australian boomerang, though not a returning type. They had puberty ceremonies for the induction of boys into manhood, and these were associated with sacred paintings, sometimes ground paintings (designs on the ground made with colored earths) and probably sometimes paintings on rocks. Some surely, and perhaps all, of these more perishable traits extended back far in time, though it is most difficult to prove such things. One of the key things suggesting continuity through the San Dieguito, La Jollan, and Diegueño sequence is the presence of unifacial scrapers. This is apparently a deep-seated, traditional way of tool making, and it ties these three local cultures together.

The La Jollan people, considered the Diegueño's predecessors, were thought of as coast-oriented people, but that misconception is now passed, for the occupation traces have been found far inland. Instead of hunters, they were foragers, gathering shellfish along the coast and getting seeds from grasses and acorns from the oaks. They ground their vegetable foods in platter-sized slabs of stone with small, hand-held stones. It is customary in some archeological circles to call these milling stones, but in my generation we called them by the old Spanish terms: *metate* for the grinding slab (from the Aztec name for these implements, *metlatl*) and *mano* for the hand-held

stone (*mano*, "hand" in Spanish). The change from the old usage
is due to a misunderstanding of how these implements were used.
Since the new term is based on a misconception, I prefer to use the
old term. All that is necessary to follow the discussion is to accept
that my terms, mano and metate, represent a broad usage encompas-
sing all tools used to reduce grain to a flour by rubbing the grain on
a large nether stone with a smaller, hand-held stone. For the archeologist who is trained to use some other term, such as milling stone,
saddle quern, muller, and so forth, it will be necessary to remember
my definition. At any rate, the La Jollans are marked by their persistent use of this implement and the custom of grinding their food.
Use of the metate persisted right into the twentieth century, despite
the fact that mortars were coming into use, apparently first introduced as basket-hoppered mortars more than 5,000 years ago and
developing into deep mortars later in time. From this pattern one
gets the feeling of great conservatism among the La Jollans, for
elsewhere in California and in the United States the metate was
often entirely replaced by the mortar.

The La Jollans were also conservative in their use of unifaced
tools. They made plano-convex scrapers and unifacially worked
flakes to serve as knives and scrapers, just as the Diegueño would
do and as the San Dieguito had done. Inexplicably, La Jollan work
is cruder than that of their alleged predecessors. Further, they
seldom used the fine-grained volcanic rocks that their precursors
had used.

The San Dieguito were essentially a hunting people who came
in out of the Great Basin. They had leaf-shaped, bifacially flaked
points, presumably used as dart points. They made finely worked
scrapers on a plano-convex plan. Some were thick with steep edges,
resembling little haystacks—the typical plano-convex scraper. Others
were made on flakes, with one or more edges trimmed unifacially
to create flake knives or side and end scrapers. San Dieguito work
is notable for its fine retouch and for the predominant use of fine-
grained volcanic rocks, which were quarried in the nearby Black
Mountain volcanic hills, an ancient range of mountains that parallels
the coast roughly ten miles inland. There has been little discussion of
what became of the San Dieguito people, and M. J. Rogers at times

toyed with the idea that at some point the area became depopulated
and that then the La Jollan people moved in.

My disagreement with numerous colleagues is on the cultural
sequence and the time depth for these cultures rather than with the
cultural content. The San Dieguito, La Jollan, and Diegueño have
been fairly well described, but it seems to me that their relationship
to one another is scrambled.

We have an odd situation, one that is allegedly true for most
of America. We start with a culture showing great skill in stone
flaking, possessed of points suggesting a hunting specialty, and with
the knowledge of how to go to special sources for the superior stone
to make their fine stonework. Then abruptly we drop to a lower
cultural level—to foragers who use local stone to make crude stone
tools. It could be true, but it does seem a bit odd. What happened
to the Great Hunters, locally represented by the San Dieguito? It is
rather casually assumed that they killed off all the great land mammals they had previously preyed on and, with the accompanying
climatic changes of the end of the Pleistocene, were compelled to
change their life and become foragers, inventing the metate and
substituting gruel for elephant steaks. But why would they abandon
their good stonework? Good points would still be useful for hunting
the not-too-lesser game of moose, bison, deer, and bear, the available
animals varying from region to region.

The idea has been repeatedly suggested that the Great Hunters
were not the first people, and that the cultural sequence is in part
wrong (Carter, 1950). The foragers had long been here, and whoever the Great Hunters were, the foragers both precede and succeed
them. But the evidence for this view is brushed aside as tenuous
and as manufactured out of whole cloth, and such corroborating
sites as Sheguiandah and Timlin as well as a host of others are not
even mentioned (Graham and Heizer, 1967). Perhaps I should be
grateful that the Texas Street complex of sites drew so much notice,
although it reminds me of the man tarred, feathered, and being
ridden out of town on a rail: "Except for the honour of the thing,
I'd rather do without."

There is a more logical way to arrange a culture sequence than
to start with the best, revert to a lower order, and rebuild. The

more sensible way would be to start simple and build up. It would be easier to view the La Jollans as earlier and simpler and less skilled people than to account for this cultural retrogression not only in skills but also in utilization of local resources. But logical as this might be, it need not be the way it was. To establish that, we need evidence. But by dismissing as merely controversial all reports that did not fit their notion of perfection, the accepted authorities established majority opinion, and all opposition was ridden out with raillery.

Into this seething controversy Jeff Bada thrust his protein racemization dates (Bada, Schroeder, and Carter, 1974). Of the first set of human skeletons that he examined, he reported: 48,000 years at Del Mar, 44,000 and 28,000 years at La Jolla. None of these skeletons was associated with cultural material, and so, while the data upset the time frame, it did not clarify the cultural sequence. The dating of subsequent materials did upset the chronology. The skeletons Rogers attributed to his early La Jollan culture did not date to 5,000 but to around 50,000 years. This led, naturally, to angry rejection of Bada's dating system and to labeling my accept· ance of it as "obvious, since it tended to support my ideas," or, as I would prefer, my data.

So we are faced with an important question. What is the age of the La Jollan culture? Is it, as the majority think, a 5,000- to 7,000-year phenomenon, a culture that follows the 10,000-year-old San Dieguito people? Or is it, as I have stated, a full Wisconsin-age phenomenon, something with an age of the magnitude of 40,000 or perhaps 60,000 years? The answer to that, as to so many other questions, lies in geomorphology; the considerations of land-sea relationships that determine the age of the blade and core industry will also go far toward dating the La Jollan culture. If it turns out to be as early as I have postulated—about 60,000 years for its inception—then it must precede the San Dieguito culture, for this is well dated at about 10,000 years, and the questions previously raised concerning the relationship between these two cultures will have to be carefully examined. Were the San Dieguito nearly pure hunters, lacking grinding tools? Or did they too have grinding tools and perhaps differ relatively little in lifeway from the La

Jollans? We can attack this problem by taking some typical sites
and examining the evidence that they provide.

TORREY PINES MESA SITES

The campsites on the Torrey Pines Mesa between Mount
Soledad and Torrey Pines, including the famous golf course and
the University of California at San Diego campus (site *1* in figure
22), had been excavated a little before nearly being entirely des-

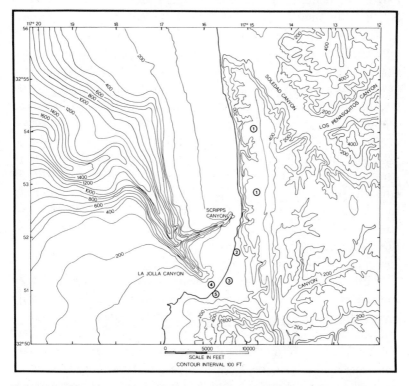

FIGURE 22. Sites from the La Jolla area discussed in the text are: (*1*) Torrey
Pines Mesa, extending between the two points numbered *1*; (*2*) Scripps campus site; (*3*) bay bar with skeletons 28,000 and 44,000 years old; (*4*) location of submarine mortars; and (*5*) Beach and Tennis Club sites.

The immense submarine canyons head just beyond the breaker line, and
behind the narrow beach at the head of the Scripps Canyon the cliffs rise
300 feet. A change from a glacial to an interglacial sea level here would
move the shoreline only 100 yards. There are few such spots in the world.

troyed by the army in World War II and by the real estate developers, the university, and the golfers thereafter. There are interesting
problems. What did man find so attractive on that high ridge—
300 feet above the beaches and bays from which he obtained the
shellfish—that he carried them clear up there? Why not eat them
at a handy spot near the beach? How old are these sites, and what
men with what equipment lived there?

The sites have been known for at last fifty years and probably
longer. M. J. Rogers put trenches through several of them in 1929
but, as with most of his trenching of coastal sites, with minimal
results. He got little cultural material compared with the wealth of
artifacts that littered the surface. He found no burials, no clear
stratigraphy, no sharp divisions between layers, with the upper ones
having arrow points, the middle ones dart points, and the bottom
ones lacking all points. Discouraged by this, he retreated to watching the sites, especially the eroding edges, and occasionally he found
a skeleton eroding out. Together we collected from these surfaces,
especially during the period when they were farmed by market
gardeners. The gardeners cleared the land, collecting the artifacts
from the surface and dumping them at the edge of the fields in neat,
rounded piles. The archeologists forty years later thought they had
struck a rich archeological zone when they found one of these, and
they were annoyed when I pointed out the origin of this artifact
concentration, by then flattened, scattered, and barely buried.

Bits of broken pottery and arrow points are rare, but they
indicate that even in near-historic times Indians had occasionally
lived here. At some places we could find nicely worked plano-convex
scrapers and fine side scrapers made of a greenish, fine-grained
volcanic rock, a felsite derived from the nearby Black Mountain
volcanoes. This material belonged to the classic San Dieguito period,
which Rogers then put at about 5,000 years old. This material is
now thought of as older than 5,000 years but younger than 10,000,
and perhaps it is still not correctly dated. It so interested Rogers
that he assiduously collected it, and it is greatly overrepresented in
the collections, especially from the site at the chancellor's house,
on the edge of the University of California campus.

The vast bulk of the material was not San Dieguito, but rather
was crude work in cobbles of porphyry and quartzite derived from

the local gravels. There were heavy bifaced choppers, thick plano-convex tools, multitudes of flakes, and quantities of manos, the hand stones used to grind wild seeds and other materials on a larger nether stone, the metate. These materials fit the concept of the La Jollan culture, and since they dominated the sites they were all attributed to that culture. When C-14 dates on shell began to be obtained for these sites, many of them fell around 5,000 to 7,000 years, and this became the date fixed not only for the La Jollan culture but for these sites in general—totally incorrectly, as we will see.

In the excavation in 1976 on one of the remaining bits of one of the once very extensive sites on the University of California's campus at La Jolla—actually in the chancellor's backyard—several burials were found, along with a fair amount of cultural material. The San Diego Museum of Man, of course, had quantities of cultural material and a number of burials from this and adjacent sites found in previous decades. About 1935 I had excavated a skeleton here that was buried in a cairn of La Jollan metates. That skeleton dates to around 8,300 years (Bada and Ike, 1979). Rose Tyson of the San Diego Museum of Man is reporting (1979) on skeletons with metates dated at 17,000 and 45,000 years. These dates extend the metate to times far earlier than the San Dieguito and quite in keeping with my geomorphic dates. As the review of Bada's protein-racemization dating showed, that method is probably fully as reliable as C-14, which is currently given biblical authority in the field.

For the Torrey Pines Mesa sites, there is an interesting check on age. The Dieguño over a period of a few centuries left a faint trace of occupational debris. The San Dieguito culture, which is assumed to have persisted for a few thousand years, left decidedly more, but still relatively little compared to the immense amounts of La Jollan material. If the sites are assumed to have had uniform attraction and no increase in population density, then the cultural remains suggest an immense length of La Jollan occupation, a short length for the San Dieguito occupation, and a very short length for the Dieguño period. The estimate is conservative, for with cultural enrichment the later occupation should have been more intense than the early. This is of course tenuous evidence if it stands by itself, but try it against hard dates: Dieguño a few centuries, San

Dieguito to 10,000, and La Jollan to about 30,000 by C-14, to 50,000 by protein racemization, and to about 85,000 by geomorphology. The proportions are the same orders of magnitude whether the evidence is time or materials: Dieguĕno little, San Dieguito some, La Jollan much.

Flies are forever getting in the academic ointment, however, and in this case the difficulty is the metate at so early a time. The metate has been confidently stated to be not more than 10,000 years old anywhere in the world (Krieger, 1959). The skeleton at La Jolla with metates carefully placed all around it to form a stone-lined grave pit has been dated to 8,300 years ago, but this is actually a modest figure. Further, so far as the data on that particular skeleton go, it could as well be that old metates lying around on the surface were used, so this is only a minimal date for the metate.

Without implying that the earliest American metates are this old, I will include here the comment that word now reaches me that the metate in Africa has been found to extend back 200,000 years, into the late Aurignacian.* This makes Krieger's "not more than 10,000 years anywhere in the world" a good example of how far off our guesses often are.

Nearby, skeletons were found that dated from 5,000 to 50,000 years. After I had returned to Texas the summer we found the La Jolla bones (1976), I was phoned to be told of the finding of two more skeletons. My callers described the skeletons as being in loose dirt, the bones rather orange in color, firm and strong, with all the small bones still in place. "What do you think?" they asked. I replied that it was time to look for the shirt buttons. They did not understand this at first, but I meant that the burials were obviously very late: historic or near-historic. They belong with arrow points and pot sherds, whose antiquity probably does not exceed 500 years. The interesting thing was that all of the burials came

---

*A letter from Peter Beaumont, August, 1979, cites: metates at Border Cave around 80,000 years; various specimens at Kalkbank, Transvaal, Middle Stone Age, around 100,000 to 120,000 years; metate at Florisbad, Orange Free State, around 200,000 years. This latter find is a single item underlying the Middle Stone Age and apparently associated with late Acheulean/Fauresmith. It is of interest that the site was reported as early as 1956, but apparently without any recognition of its great antiquity.

at about the same depth: 500- to 50,000-year-old remains all on
the same horizon. It is not very mysterious. The site has a very
thin layer, eighteen to twenty-four inches deep, of loose sand overlying an extremely hard, cemented sand—the sandy part of the
Sweitzer formation, an early Pleistocene formation. For all the immense length of time that man lived on this site and buried his dead,
grave pits stopped at that sandstone layer. Occupation was so scattered and probably so intermittent and thin that no deep layer of
debris ever built up, which would have made later burials be at suc-
cessively higher levels. This is the reason that Rogers got so little
stratigraphy from such sites.

A little geomorphology helps a lot. One is unlikely to get
much accumulation on a ridge top, unless the human occupation is
so dense as to bring in large amounts of material. That this was not
the case here indicates a thin, seasonal occupation spread over a long
time rather than dense and continuous occupation. This intermittent
occupation would take a vast amount of time to cover square miles
of land with even a thin coating of shell, charcoal, burned rock,
and percussively broken rock such as was found on the Torrey
Pines Mesa.

To get a deep record, one should look for areas where accumulation is going on. For the last 10,000 years, with the sea
levels rising and valley mouths all being drowned, there is splendid
alluvial accumulation in the valley mouths—two or three hundred
feet of it. The record is nicely stratified, and all one has to do is to
dig, and dig deep, in the right spots and have good pumps to keep
the water out. Further, these situations have been repeated every
time the sea level has risen. As we have seen, this cycle is about
40,000 years long, and thus there should be a repeated record if
man has been here for a long enough time to extend through a
cycle or two. The costliest part to research would be the last 10,000
years of deeply buried material. The earlier material is more available in the former valley fills, now left as valley-flank terraces.

What the work on the mesa-top sites reveals is that they are
poor places to develop a good stratified record. Everyone has lived
on this surface—at least the Diegueño, the La Jollans, and the
San Dieguito—and this record runs back for at least 50,000 years
(Bada, Schroeder, and Carter, 1974; Bada and Helfman, 1975) and

causes some embarrassment to those who think the record of man hereabouts is limited to 9,000 or 10,000 years. When "at least 50,000 years" is casually dropped in, it is with purpose. The earliest date we have at any time is just that: the earliest date at that moment. A new find tomorrow may be even earlier. We tend too quickly to cast the earliest date in bronze.

We can return now to some of the original questions asked: why did man ever live up here on these windy, arid, remote-from-shellfish-supply areas? When I was offering free advice, which "no one minded very much," during the 1976 excavations on the site at the chancellor's house, I tried to explain the situation to the excavators, but they listened with about half an ear. The area was originally (a few hundred thousand years ago) a series of roughly parallel sand ridges. Some of the intervening hollows collected water, and as the underlying sand became cemented they became good water-holding pockets and even held small lakes. In my youth, the last of these lakes was a favorite duck-hunting spot, but in World War II the use of the land for a large army encampment led to the filling of that last remnant of what was at one time a series of such lakes. On this dry coast, these lakes would have been attractive features and are the probable reason for these sites in this seemingly inhospitable area.

The steep canyons working back from the cliff front here tend to break through one ridge and then to erode at right angles to the ridge, cutting out the low area between the ridges. The erosion has now gone far, and little of the original low-lying area that held ponds at least seasonally is left. Rogers in his assessment of the area forty years ago noted that along the present cliff front there are relatively deep zones of sands, which apparently accumulated in a trough between the present ridge and a ridge that has now fallen into the sea. If there is any deep stratigraphy left on the old mesa top here, it must be in the remnants of these troughs. Since they have not been sought—and of course not dug—then we have to look elsewhere for the accumulation of alluvium that would bury a human record.

THE CONTINENTAL SHELF

We have just such a record nearby. When the sea level fell at the onset of the last glacial episode, 20,000 years ago, and before that at 60,000 years ago, a shelf was exposed at the foot of the sea cliffs that the sea had cut in the intervening high sea stands at 40,000 and 85,000 years. From the dating of the human skeletons back to 50,000 years and actually to 70,000 if we consider the skeleton from the San Francisco Bay area also dated by the protein-racemization method, we could expect men, obviously present in California, to have lived on these exposed shelves. They would be very attractive locations, for they bordered the sea, and where the sea and the land met man had the riches of both realms. For the earlier men, the sea offered an easy harvest in the intertidal zone. Shellfish were present and especially numerous on the rocky areas. Mussels, abalones, limpets, and crabs were there for the taking, and the myth that man only belatedly discovered that this was a food resource is simply contrary to man and his appetite and to the evidence.

At La Jolla there are added attractions. When the sea level was lowered, the heads of the great submarine canyons were exposed (see figure 22), and their rocky walls increased the amount of shore suitable for abalones and mussels. Furthermore, this lowering exposed springs that are known to be present at shallow depths off the beach at La Jolla. Fishermen who used to anchor regularly in the shelter near the La Jolla Cove knew where to lower a bucket over the side and get fresh water, testifying to the presence of large, flowing springs.

The evidence for the presence of shellfish resources and their use by man is abundant in the hearths and the large village sites in the area. The most striking site was (how sad to have to use the past tense for these sites) just south of the present Beach and Tennis Club (site 5 in figure 22). There was some good stratigraphy there. A late campsite with the usual black, "greasy" midden matter was underlain by a sterile layer of soil, and then there was a dense mass of mussel shells, with abundant charcoal and other evidence for man. The upper midden had pottery and arrow points in its upper few inches and below that the cobble tools characteristic of the La Jollan.

But who were the people of the mussel-shell midden? Their environment was entirely different from that of the upper midden. There are few mussels in the upper midden and few in the modern environment. There are masses of them in the lower midden. The easiest way to change the environment to make it suitable for this type of mussel would be to lower the sea level and expose a rocky cliff for the surf to beat on. If the dates that Bada supplied are correct, then men should have been living here when the sea level was down, but that is really so recent a date that even Heizer's date of 9,000 years will do, for the sea level was still a hundred feet below the present level as recently as 10,000 years ago.

We have good evidence that man did live out on the exposed shelf at that time. Around 1900, children swimming on the beach where the Beach and Tennis Club now stands found that by diving just beyond the breaker line they could find little stone bowls (see figure 22, site 4). In the 1940's the young oceanographers from the Scripps Institution of Oceanography, while diving for abalones, found more of these bowls, in somewhat deeper water. The divers soon had hundreds of the stone bowls, which they found out to the very edge of the continental shelf, here less than one-half mile offshore and in about a hundred feet of water, at which point the head of the submarine canyons are met and there are cliffs hundreds of feet high leading on down into the great ocean depths. This led to one of the continuing comic-opera episodes in the local archeology.

At a meeting of archeologists of southern California at the Scripps Institution of Oceanography, these finds came under heated discussion. I argued that they were evidence of man's living on the continental shelf while it was exposed by the lowering of the sea during the last glacial episode. I pointed to comparable evidence on land, in the deposits that had been laid down at the same time. Man was obviously present, but this was bitterly resisted. The archeologists came up with a number of ingenious alternative explanations. The "angry farmer" theme had it that collectors walking over his fields picking up stone bowls so annoyed some farmer that he threw the bowls into the sea. Some farmer! There were thousands of the bowls and some of them were half a mile out. The "Indian ritual" theme was that Indians made those bowls to use just once in some ceremonial and then took them out to sea and threw them away. When queried for evidence that there ever had been such a ritual, the archeologists smugly explained that it seemed more reasonable to them that there had been such a ritual than that man had lived out on the continental shelf during a period of low-ered sea level.

There are a modest number of other alternatives, a little less imaginative but perhaps a bit more realistic. Man may have been living on a relatively recent land surface that extended out into what is now sea, and the destruction of the land may have dumped the stone bowls onto the seafloor. This does not avoid implications of great antiquity, for even this process would involve a rising sea level and some considerable time. Or one could argue that the bowls were eroded out of relatively modern middens of about 5,000 years ago and swept out to greater depths by wave and current.

I tried checking on this by visiting the site in winter at the time of maximum tides. A minus-one-foot tide allowed me to ex-plore the rocky floor exposed near the Beach and Tennis Club. Artifacts and flake debris from the middens then eroding into the sea were trapped in the rocks and obviously had not moved far. In later years I was told that this material I had collected and put into the site drawers could not be found, and I have often wondered what became of it. In the summer of 1979 I looked myself, and, sure enough, that material had disappeared. It could easily be dupli-cated on any wintery day of maximum low tide, for no one pays attention to mere broken rock trapped on the shallow ocean floor.

Any explanation has to fit the fact that stone bowls of this sort are not found in the Dieguéño villages, are rare, if present at all, in the late La Jollan sites, and are certainly absent from the San Dieguito and earlier sites. In areas to the north of San Diego the sequence from early to late runs: metates, little stone bowls, mortars. At San Diego metates are early—just how early we will presently see—and mortars are late. If San Diego follows the pat-tern of the area to the north along the coast, then these stone bowls, actually bases for basket-hoppered mortars, should have some mod-est antiquity. An hypothesis that man used these bowls while living on the continental shelf is consistent with that age, since it does not require much time to remove the sea and expose the continental shelf for man to live on. Five or ten thousand years is ample.

At the Scripps Institution of Oceanography (site 2, figure 22), Hubbs, Shepard, and Moriarty pressed the divers to search closer, and they eventually came up with stone tools, including nicely flaked projectile points and organic matter, that allowed them to date one of the later campsites which the sea had overwhelmed. Moriarty and Marshall put the data together, and Moriarty's diagram of the distribution of the stone bowls is shown in figure 23.

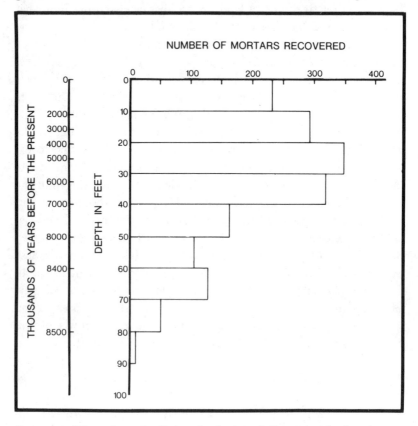

FIGURE 23. Divers from the Scripps Institution of Oceanography found stone bowls beneath the sea level—thousands of them. As this diagram shows, the majority were found between ten and forty feet beneath the sea level, and, as the time scale shows, this indicates that men using these bowls were living there about 2,000 to 7,000 years ago. If the bowls in the forty- to seventy-foot depth are a good indication of the presence of man at the time these depths were exposed, then the time reaches back beyond 8,000 years. Such stone bowls have generally been considered relatively late in the southern California sequence of cultures. (Redrawn from Marshall and Moriarty, 1964, p. 24)

The evidence quite clearly shows that there was a lot of occupation on the shelf here. There are hundreds of these stone bowls, which are rare finds in remaining middens, and the time seems quite clearly to reach back to around 8,000 years ago. This is the time that Heizer and many others would favor for the first people in America. But this is not evidence for early people, but for some relatively late people. The gist of this is that people of a relatively late cultural stage were living on the coast here well before the modern sea levels were established.

One always asks, if here, why not elsewhere? Of course, why not? The stone bowls at San Diego were hardly reported before word began to come in of similar finds along the southern California coast, first at one site and then at several. The finds were numerous—many stone bowls, literally thousands, indicating dense settlements or very long periods of time. Man was certainly in California, and specifically at La Jolla, while the sea level was down due to the glacial lockup of the waters of the sea.

If he was here for any length of time while these conditions existed, then he must have been present while the alluvial covers were accumulating over the beaches left exposed when the sea level fell. The protein racemization dates for skeletons on the nearby mesa top indicate the presence of man for at least 50,000 years. We can now take a look to see if this is supported by the record in the alluvium over the buried beaches. The mortars say that there should be at least an 8,000-year record in these covers, and the 50,000-year skeletons say that there should be a deeply buried record.

THE ALLUVIAL COVERS

I have looked at the alluvial covers over these buried beaches off and on for fifty years. The alluvium exposed in a long, vertical face about twenty feet high to the south of the Scripps Institution of Oceanography was one of Rogers' favorite hunting grounds (see picture of this cliff, figure 24). It had everything: archeology, a nice sand beach, good surf, and a western exposure with the cliffs to stop the wind, so that even in off-season times one could toast in comfort. We spent a lot of time on this little cliff.

It was cut by a steep-sided gully, and in the south bank of the mouth of that gully there was an obvious hearth—burned rock, burned earth, and a halo of chipping debris. Given Rogers' avoidance of excavation, we had the pleasant custom of visiting the site at least a few times a year to see what the erosion of wind, wave,

Figure 24. In this shot of the La Jolla Shores, made in 1936, the Scripps Institution of Oceanography is the little white building in the background. Rogers and Carter (in the hat) are preparing to photograph the alluvial cover over the Pleistocene beach. The differing strata, with their weathered surfaces, indicate periods of erosion and deposition during late glacial time. This is a winter scene, with the sand beaches eroded, gravels showing, and the cliff being undercut and collapsing. Traces of early man were to be found above the dark layer at the base of the cliff all the way to the surface.

and rain had brought out. At one time the University of Arizona anthropologists asked for a sample of this material, and Rogers took me out there, handed me a shovel, and put me to digging—not into his precious hearth, but at the foot of the cliff at a much lower level. I dug down through the beach sands and exposed the deepest alluvium available for examination at that spot, and we found a number of quartzite flakes. One would have thought that Rogers would have been interested in excavation if he could get such easy results, but he was not.

When I returned to San Diego to resume work on the study of early man, this was one of the sites I concentrated on. It had been watched with considerable interest by the Scripps Institution geologists, for it gave them a measure of the encroachment of the sea. Careful measurements over a long period of years showed that this cliff was retreating at a rate of one foot per year, primarily due to wave attack. This was a key fact for me. If a landform is being destroyed by present sea levels, then it cannot have been built at present sea level. If the land-sea relationship was different in the past, in such a way as to let this landform be built, then the sea either had to be lower or the land raised. Theoretically, one could choose even-handedly between the two, but not pragmatically, for one had not only to lower the land to cut a bench but then to raise the land to let the alluvium build up and then to lower the land again to let the sea attack the alluvium. And all of this had to be done in quite a short period of geologic time. As we have seen from the terrace evidence, there is little to show that this local region is that active geologically. On the other hand, we know with great certainty that the sea level is just that active. It goes up and down like a cork on the waves—in this case, like a cork responding to the glacial-interglacial climatic waves. So it was that I began to argue that it was sea-level changes not land-level changes that were more probably responsible for these cycles of erosion and alluviation. And cycles in the plural it most certainly was.

The more I studied this bit of micro-geomorphology, a low cliff only a quarter of a mile long, the more complex it became. There was the modern gully, obviously young, and adjusted to the present high and rising sea. It had a very young fill within it, and this contained hearths with abundant charcoal and shell. In the face of the cliff I could see two older gullies, each capped by a weathered soil horizon. This little landform had been repeatedly built up, gullied, built up, and gullied. Each episode was marked by rapid filling of the gullies, then slowing of the deposition as the alluvium was spread out over a wide expanse of the alluvial cone, followed by development of soils with strong profiles. That this was an alluvial cone was evident, for it was right at the mouth of a small canyon that headed back on the 300-foot mesa surface, and it had the convex slope in cross section characteristic of such deposits.

I found out the width of the shelf and the depth of the water at the edge of the shelf: one-half mile wide, and one hundred feet deep where it dropped off to the oceanic depths. Obviously, whenever the sea level dropped as much as a hundred feet, the shelf was exposed, and alluvium would accumulate. Then when the sea level rose significantly above that minus-hundred-foot mark, waves would attack the alluvium, cutting a cliff, and as a result a gully would rip through this little landform. It had happened several times, and I postulated a series of Wisconsin-glacial episodes of sea levels coming within a hundred feet of the present. This was out of step with the geologists' thinking, for they thought of all California as hopping around like a flea on a hot griddle rather than of the sea level's changing so rapidly and frequently. The glaciologists admitted much fluctuation in the Wisconsin, but I became disenchanted with using the work of the glaciologists, for they had so many minor advances and retreats based on their work in the Midwest that even the correlations within the region were suspect and their application to anything else in the world rather dubious. I began to talk of the oceans as the great totalizers. Minor advances and retreats of the ice could be going on all over the world depending on all kinds of local conditions—and this is actually happening today—but the oceans keep track of this confusion by gain or loss of water, a summation of the big picture. For the first fifty years of this century, the oceans were rising—more ice was melting than was accumulating on the land. Recently this has stopped, and the direction of climatic change has shifted. The tide gauges of the world record this quite accurately.

The sequence of gullies in the cliff would then represent a series of high sea levels that approached within a hundred feet of the present sea level, and the periods of alluviation would represent periods of sea level one hundred feet or more lower than the present. These should be records of alternately wet and dry climates also, for glacial periods in the north, which caused low sea levels around the world, were marked by humid conditions at San Diego.

In the cliff the soils were strongly developed, and I recorded their structure, clay content, pH, calcium carbonate movement, and depth of accumulation. I enlisted the U.S. Department of Agriculture soils scientists from the regional laboratory at Riverside in field and laboratory work on this and other sites. The soils in the upper part of the alluvium belonged to the Huerhuero series, but they were only moderately developed, indicating a modest age. A C-14 date from pismo clam shells from the base of the surface soil indicated about 5,000 years for that soil. The soil below it was at least twice as strongly developed, and there was another beneath that.

Further, each of these soil-forming episodes was separated from the other by cycles of erosion and deposition, with the soils forming when the landform stabilized again. The data from the soils themselves indicated that they recorded climates somewhat rainier than now. It was obvious that this little landform had a complex history and that it was moderately old and not the Recent alluvium that the geologists had considered it.

At that, it was only half the story, for at greater depth there were sticky brown soils that were mottled rusty and gray—indications of waterlogging and the formation of a gley soil. This soil records a marshy condition which would locally be called a *cienega.*

This gley soil could have two or more causes. The climate could have been wetter, or the flatter gradient at the time of first exposure of the former submarine shelf with its poorer drainage may have made possible the development of a *cienega*, a marshy area, at the mouth of this little canyon. Most probably the two causes coincided. The oncoming glacial lowered the sea level, and this was accompanied by an increase in rainfall. The relatively flat and poorly drained marine platform then supported a marshy area at the mouth of this canyon. Later, the accumulation of alluvium built an alluvial cone with a steep enough slope to assure good drainage. Man found this well-drained, sandy land good for camping, while the earlier boggy *cienega* had not been. The landform seemed to me to record at least all of the last glacial period.

It also contained an archeological record. Hearths were scattered on the surface of the whole area. These were marked by a sprinkling of shell, an occasional mano, a few flakes of quartzite, and very rarely a finished crude tool appropriate for a La Jollan site. In the face of the cliff, similar hearths could be seen exposed beneath the surface soil and beneath the first buried soil. At greater depths the shell was lacking, and only oval, basin-shaped areas of orange-colored earth suggested the presence of man. Admittedly it was meager evidence. But what in nature scoops out shallow basins and builds fires in them of sufficient intensity to bake the earth to a light orange? When I was doing my prospecting there, fires were permitted anywhere on the beach and were often built against the cliff face. I showed many visiting scientists that these modern fires burned the earth in just this way. Still, one would like to have a skeleton alongside one of these fireplaces, clutching a diagnostic stone artifact in one bony hand and in the other a bottle with a slip of paper in it giving the date of the interment—in the Gregorian calendar, of course.

This cliff is no longer available for study, for it is now wall-to-wall beach houses with seawalls in front. Despite Hubbs's and my hopes and years of watching, we never found that skeleton when the cliff was open to inspection and being sliced down by the wave attack. The best that I could do was to find a few percussively broken rocks and two manos. These came quite expectably from the sequence of soils associated with the cuts and fills and not with the gley soils at the base.

There was one bit of modest density of occupation remaining in the cliff front. Since another winter or two would clearly remove it, I undertook to excavate it and save what could be found. It was a hard and dirty job. The soil was very compact, and it was obvious that a soil profile had formed in a shallow midden. The surface layer was sandy and had very little shell. The next horizon was a tough clay loam and had more shell, and it overlay a sandy loam with better-preserved shell and with lime nodules marking the accumulation of the dissolved shell material from the upper levels. On the cliff edge the updraft threw all the dirt in my face, and I got as dirty as Carl Hubbs did when he was sifting the Indian village on Santa Rosa Island for shellfish. But his was the easier task, for his site was loose and fluffy. Mine was hard as baked clay. I saved every rock, throwing the whole ones in one pile, the burned ones in another, and the broken ones in another. I excavated one cubic yard of material, and I got not one definite artifact—not even a good flake with strong marks of percussion. As far as that kind of evidence went, I did not have a site. Yet the accumulation of marine shell in this terrestrial deposit, the presence of charcoal and fire-broken rocks, and the unnatural assemblage of shellfish made it perfectly clear that this was a habitation site of some intensity of occupation and of some duration. But if a moderately dense occupation produced not one definitive piece of lithic evidence for man, why the demand that casual hearths must have them? I have looked at thousands of scattered hearths. Perhaps one in a hundred has good lithic material with it. The point is important, for the alluvial

covers have thin records: scattered hearths, not thick middens. Artifacts should be rare, and they are, and the result is tenuous evidence
again.

If a site at a canyon mouth was too marshy for man at the
early part of the last glacial period, then what we should seek is
a site where the conditions would be drier and hence more attractive
to man. We have just such a site. Just to the north of the Scripps
Institution of Oceanography pier, on the campus itself, there is a
forty-foot thick alluvial mass standing in a vertical cliff. At the foot
of the steep cliff here and close to the head of the submarine
canyon, alluvium built up quickly, and drainage was good. There
was no period of swampy *cienega* conditions. Man could live here
as soon as the fall of sea level exposed the wave-cut platform.

At the base of the alluvium here a Pleistocene shell beach is
exposed, and on top of the alluvium there is a shell midden. In
between, there are soil horizons marking still stands (a pause, slow-
down, or cessation of deposition, allowing weathering to occur) in
the accumulation of the alluvium, and throughout the whole mass
there are lenses of burned earth, many of which have flecks of
charcoal. One land level has very extensive burned-earth areas, and
several archeologists have been up thirty-foot ladders to peer and
scratch at these (see figure 25). Alex Krieger was one of these
hardy souls—hardy, since clinging to a thirty-foot ladder leaned
against a sea cliff is not the best of all possible perches for trying
to examine an ancient hearth. Nevertheless, Krieger found, as I
did, that these burned-earth areas had all the marks of a hearth,
and Krieger is reported to have found some bits of bone in the one
he examined. He has consistently supported the view that these are
indeed evidence for man (Krieger, 1964), and he has been joined
in this by Luther Cressman, a man of vast experience in archeology,
who will be quoted on this below.

When C-14 dating arrived and with Hubbs taking a special
interest in the local archeology, dates were obtained from Hans
Suess's laboratory at Scripps for the midden on top of the cliff and
for some of the fire areas in the alluvial sequence. A date for the
surface of the midden was 2,000 years and for the bottom 7,000.
In degree of weathering this midden resembled very strongly the
one I excavated the last remnant of on the cliff top south of the

FIGURE 25. Archeology is no easy business. Here a thirty-foot ladder rests on the underlying Eocene rock. The Pleistocene beach is immediately above the exposed dipping stratum. The alluvium above that is filled with fireplaces, and a very prominent fire level is being pecked at by the man at the top of the ladder. Dates of 2,000 to 7,000 years came from an Indian shell midden at the top of the cliff. Dates of 20,000 to 30,000 years were obtained for fireplaces at, above, and below the figure on the ladder. An age of 50,000 years was determined for a Pleistocene horse skeleton at a level just below the feet of the man on the ladder. The underlying beach must date to nearly 80,000 years.

campus. The date seems to support a time of about 5,000 to 7,000 years ago for the last time the land surfaces on these low alluvial covers became stabilized enough that soils could form. Despite the clear evidence for man, there is a startling scarcity of stone tools from this site. Chipped stone is present, but flakes are about all that has been found. One might say that, while the site is clear evidence for man, its cultural association is tenuous. In general, by date and by its poverty of fine tools and its use of the local cobbles for tool material, it fits the La Jollan image. The sea level 7,000 years ago was forty feet below the present level, exposing much of the wave-cut platform, and its alluvial cover must then have been well developed.

This is the time when the people of the stone bowls were present. Why is there no evidence of them here? There is no good answer, though we can make some guesses. Perhaps the stone bowls were used at a permanent campsite near the springs that were then exposed near the Beach and Tennis Club. If the permanent camp was there and the Scripps Campus site was a temporary shellfishing camp where little was done except to build fires and eat the shellfish gathered from the nearby reefs, there would be a very slim archeological record at one, and a rich record at the other. Shellfish are heavy, and the weight of shell is high in comparison with the meat. It would be much more efficient to eat them near the source than to carry them a long and weary mile to a permanent camp. But if this line of reasoning is correct, then it would apply to many activities, and we should expect to find similar scattered evidences of man's activities with most incomplete records. Tenuous evidence again?

Dates for fire levels beneath the shell midden run from 20,000 to 35,000 years. Beneath this, there is a 50,000-year date on a Pleistocene horse skeleton, determined by protein racemization (see figure 26). Extrapolation of these dates to the base of the feature gives a figure of 80,000 years, and this fits the glacial time scale exactly, there being a high sea stand at that time.

Archeologists of the standing of Krieger (1964) and Cressman (1973) who have examined these fire areas consider them good evidence for man. Orr and Berger (1966), who have examined the natural-fire, man-made-fire arguments, have shown the dis-

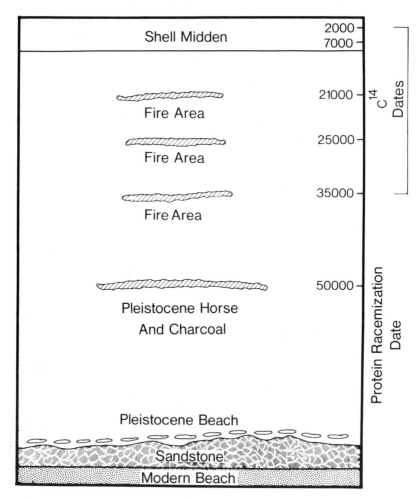

FIGURE 26. This sketch shows dates for the cliff north of the Scripps pier. The upper dates are C-14 dates determined in the laboratory at the Scripps Institution of Oceanography. The Pleistocene horse date is a protein-racemization date by Jeffry Bada. Note that it is in the correct stratigraphic position. These dates confirm the great age of these alluvial covers and the presence of man.

tinguishing marks of both kinds. These fire areas fit the distinguishing marks of man. Protein-racemization dates on human skeletons at San Diego indicate that man was present at these times. One has a choice: one can pick a flaw in each bit of evidence and stoutly maintain that these tenuous bits do not mean anything—and this is commonly done—or one can center one's critical faculties on how these various lines of evidence fit. If they fit, it is significant—to one but not to the other type of mind.

The story of this cliff is rapidly coming to an end. The university has built on the site and in the process destroyed most of the evidence, but by a fortunate accident it has produced some new evidence. I have mentioned that Hubbs found a hearth at the very base of this site about 1947 and that he later obtained C-14 dates for the hearths of the upper third of the site. The site then lapsed into a kind of limbo, and the little Scripps Institution that I had known where everyone knew everyone was replaced by a huge complex, with the usual loss of communication. Jeff Bada had no inkling that his own campus was the seat of a controversy in which his dating method was to play a sizeable role. He had never heard of the archeology in the cliff front. Why should he? He was a chemist. Why would a chemist in an oceanographic institution ask an ichthyologist if there was any interesting archeology around?

When I interested Bada in the local archeology, I took his graduate students into the field to show them some of the archeological sites, beginning with the site on their own campus. This alerted Jeff, and, when the construction of the building on the archeological site led to the collapse of part of the cliff, he noted the presence of bones in the talus and some bones left in place in the face of the cliff. Even this was a bit fortuitous: Bada runs a mile on the beach every day; his noonday run coincided with a collapse of the cliff front. He marshalled student labor and, at some risk because of the unstable condition of the cliff, took out as much bone as he could get. It proved to be the skeleton of a Pleistocene horse, strewn along on one level in the cliff, and to be associated with abundant charcoal, some of it large pieces indicating the burning of small logs (see figure 26). The protein-racemization date on the horse bones is 50,000 years. This is just what it ought to be in relation to the C-14 dates above it in the cliff. The question is: is this, too, the work of man. Did man kill and eat a horse here 50,000 years ago?

No stone tools were found, but then no excavation was carried out. Bones were snatched from the crumbling cliff. I pointed out the presence of the very strong fire level just above this horse skeleton. A professional archeologist, Jason Smith, was called in; he excavated a few cubic feet of material and, finding no artifacts, decided that it was not evidence for man. What it was evidence of he could not say, but that it could not be used as evidence for man was quite clear to him. The gist of the evidence presented here is quite to the contrary: the fire level most probably is evidence for man, but the horse skeleton is even more interesting.

Horses die of natural causes, and it is conceivable that a forest fire occurred about the same time, burying the horse skeleton and the charcoal together and making the whole thing just one of those natural accidents. Maybe the horse got caught in a forest fire and was burned to death. On the other hand, Orr and Berger's data (1966) show that most fires in the open burn to ash and do not produce scorched earth or leave large lumps of charcoal, the exception being stump burnouts, which are easily recognized by their pattern of jagged cavities following the root pattern. Hearths have smooth, rounded bottoms, not jagged ones. Man, by piling up firewood, commonly creates masses of charcoal, and this is most pronounced if he is cooking in a pit. It is a pity that the skeleton of the horse was not excavated to see if there was a fire pit or what pattern there was to the charred logs and especially to see if on the land surface that existed at that time there was any evidence of broken rocks that would have served as butchering tools. All that potential record is lost, and we must use other lines of thought. In none of this is Jeff Bada at fault. He saved what he could and tried to interest local archeologists in working on the find. He finally had to turn to Jason Smith in the Los Angeles area to get anyone even to scratch at the site.

Was man present in the region at that time? The protein-racemization studies say yes. The record in the alluvial covers—not only what we have already reviewed but what is to follow—says yes. If man was present and there was a horse in the landscape, dead or alive, would man eat it? The answer is an emphatic yes. Early man regularly ate horses—Frenchmen still do—and the California Indians ate dead whales when they washed ashore. A dead horse would be manna from heaven.

This is not the only evidence that suggests that men living here were harvesting large animals occasionally. I found a bit of a seal's skull at a much lower elevation in the cliff. The interest Hubbs and I showed in the cliff set one of the maintenance men to watching, and he found a horse tooth about seventy-five yards to the south of the 50,000-year-old horse skeleton and about ten feet above the Pleistocene beach. Bada and his group found another bit of bone a hundred yards to the north and much nearer the surface. This handful of bits of bones makes this the richest Pleistocene mammal bone location in the San Diego area. The yield of fifty years of searching had been pitifully small: one camel jaw from the alluvial cover on the west side of Point Loma and one elephant skeleton from the Tijuana River valley, for instance. The soils at San Diego are acid, and preservation of bone is poor. Even human skeletons are seldom preserved unless buried in the lime-accumulating level of a shell midden or, as at the site near the chancellor's house, buried on top of an impermeable stratum that decreased the rate of leaching of the bones. The total picture is impressive: human skeletons dated to 50,000 years, a Pleistocene horse with charcoal dating to that time, a sequence of hearths dating from 2,000 to 35,000 years, a most unusual set of Pleistocene animal bones. I choose to think that the protein-racemization method establishes man's presence and that he probably cooked and ate that horse about 50,000 years ago.

There is another set of skeletons found nearby with implications for this time period. These skeletons were the ones found by engineers excavating the old beach ridge or bay bar at the time that the marsh that once occupied the site of the Beach and Tennis Club was filled in (site 3 in figure 22). These were the ones that Edgar Lee Hewett, then director of the San Diego Museum of Man, was so uninterested in he would not even go and look, much less take advantage of the offer to let the museum conduct a salvage operation. However, some fragments were saved by M. J. Rogers. These were the skeletons that I thought should be tested by Jeff Bada's system and that dated at 28,000 and 44,000 years (Bada, Schroeder, and Carter, 1974). The 28,000-year-old skeletons fit with the C-14-dated hearths in the cliff on the Scripps campus. Cemented to the rib of one of these skeletons there was a whole olivella-shell bead.

The most interesting of the skeletal remains from this site is the fossil human frontal that came from the cross-bedded sands of this feature, and to understand this situation it is necessary to describe the landform and its origin (see sketch of the landform,

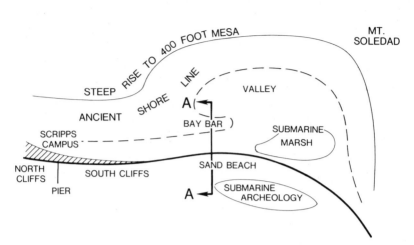

FIGURE 27. In this little valley along the La Jolla Shores, higher sea levels once created a bay, and a bay bar was built out into it. A human frontal was buried in the bay bar at this high–sea level time. Later, when the sea level was lower, men used the bay bar for a burial place, and still later other men camped on it.

Offshore, thousands of stone bowls and other archeological materials were found, showing that men had camped here when the sea level was lower than now. A–A shows where the cross section in figure 28 is drawn. The north cliffs and the south cliffs on either side of the pier at the Scripps campus are the locations of archeological finds described in the text.

figure 27, and location of the site, *3*, in figure 22). The landform itself was a ridge that had an elevation of about twenty-five feet. It projected southward into the embayment between Mount Soledad and the Torrey Pines Mesa. At times of high sea level this embayment must have been a bay, and the movement of currents along the shore would then sweep sands southward to build a bay bar into this body of water. If this process continued long, it would expectably close the bay off, with only a tidal inlet toward the southern end. The situation was duplicated in recent times. The sea level rose, a bay was formed, and a barrier beach was built across the bay. The modern beach is the barrier beach, and until the filling operation in the late 1920's the marsh that lay behind this beach was the last remnant of the little bay that was once there. In the past, with higher sea stands, the bay would have been larger, and the bay bar would have been higher. The twenty-five-foot height of land that extended into the dry-land embayment represented just such a sea stand. The presence of a human frontal in place in the cross-bedded sands of this feature meant that man was present when the sea stood at or near that height. The problem was to date that sea stand. As long as one insisted that the San Diego area jumped up and down with each earthquake that came along, there was no way to date it. Once one accepted that there was a stable coast and that sea-level changes were due to glacial controls, the sea stand became eminently datable, if one could pick the right sea level.

M. J. Rogers' original notes indicate that he considered land movement and sea-level movement and concluded nothing except that the frontal had the age of the landform, whatever that turned out to be. For many years the frontal was exhibited with a set of San Dieguito tools, thought by Rogers to be the work of the earliest men at San Diego and about 5,000 years old. When I published on the find, I placed it as in a twenty-five-foot-high feature and hence equated with a twenty-five-foot sea stand and thus in the early part of the last interglacial. When Bada's date for the frontal came out at about half the expected date, I was puzzled.

When the new concept of Pleistocene dating began to develop, indicating that Milankovitch (1930) was right and that we had many glaciations, not few, I reviewed the evidence as assembled by Evans (1971) and found his high sea stand at twelve feet at 40,000 years ago. This coincided neatly with Bada's date and supplied a high sea stand that could have built the landform in question, so I was compelled to go back and reassess the situation. The question was: is there any way that a twenty-five-foot high shore feature can be reconciled with a sea stand about twelve feet above sea level? It did not take long to see that the answer was yes.

When the sea rises against the land, it cuts an inclined plane, which terminates in the beach. It is this inclined plane that gets buried by the alluvial cover when the sea drops during a glacial period. During the succeeding sea-level rise, depending on how far the sea has cut into the old sea plane and its alluvial cover, one sees a beach exposed at some level lower than the maximum sea level stand. Most levels determined from buried beaches are therefore somewhat lower than the highest sea stand, and this makes it difficult to allocate these exposed beaches to the proper interglacial. It is the opposite with beach formations. They are normally built higher than the sea level, and how high will depend on the storminess of the coast, the exposure to waves, and numerous other factors.

As was reviewed earlier, in England storm-thrown rock may be piled up eighty feet above sea level, and the cobble beaches in Baja California that are exposed to hurricane-force winds are certainly piled twenty-five feet or more above the current sea level. So, in assessing the age of the twenty-five-foot beach at La Jolla, the factors that have to be taken into account are: it is a beach, and it was built to some level above the present sea level. The question then is which one of the many sea levels is represented here.

A fair starting point is to try the level that is appropriate to Bada's date, the 40,000-year-old sea level at plus-twelve feet. The tide range at San Diego reaches seven feet above mean sea level. The beaches are commonly as much as ten feet higher than that due not only to storm waves' piling sand up but even more to the building of low dunes along the back of the beach. The beach ridge at La Jolla had in addition at least two layers of occupation, according to the reports of the engineers at the time that the site was destroyed. If we allowed a modest eighteen inches for each of these, we would have twenty-five feet with some ease.

Sea level of 40,000 years ago	12 feet
Beach height	10 feet
Midden accumulation	3 feet
TOTAL	25 feet

It must be clear that there is no intention of attributing to these numbers any great accuracy. I intend only to show that a twenty-five-foot beach or bay bar is quite possible with a twelve-foot sea stand. The fossil frontal was well down in the feature and could easily have been within the reach of storm-laid deposits that would give the cross-bedded-sand phenomenon noted by the engineers.

In reexamining this question, I found my traced copy of the raised beach cross section that M. J. Rogers had prepared from the data supplied him by the engineers (see figure 28). My attention was caught by the notation that midway down in the feature there were marls. This indicated that there had been a lagoon at that level, over which a sand beach had been built. This would call for a sea level something like twelve feet above the present, and again the protein-racemization date on the fossil frontal seems to be verified, and the coastal phenomena at San Diego again are seen to fit into

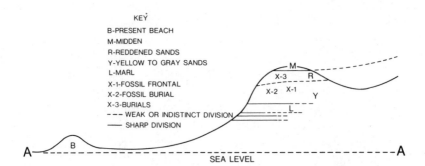

FIGURE 28. In this cross section of the bay bar at La Jolla Shores, the present beach, *B*, has a marsh with marly soils behind it. The marl, *L*, shows that this situation also existed at some past time, when the sea stood about twelve feet higher—about 40,000 years ago in Evans' system. Bada's 44,000 years for a fossil frontal, *X-1*, in the overlying beach sands is an excellent fit to this data. During glacial times, burials were made in this sandy soil—some as early as 28,000 years ago. The reddened sands, *R*, over the yellow sands, *Y*, indicate a long period of weathering before the Indians camped on this sandy ridge, leaving a black accumulation, *M*, composed of shell, ash, charcoal, and other camp debris.

Evans' worldwide findings. The whole picture is reinforced by the knowledge that the modern beach overlies old marly lagoon deposits. This shows that the process of building a sand-beach berm over old lagoon deposits is a regular feature of rising sea levels and advancing beaches, a mark of a deglacial period such as we are now living in.

Again, adding together tenuous data, the best fit seems to be that this is a valid 40,000-year-old fragment of a human skeleton. It most probably was eroded out of some landform built during the period of lowered sea level between 40,000 and 85,000 years ago. The 40,000-year date is then a minimal one, if the erosion of an old burial is correct. And again, the set of data fit: a Pleistocene horse with abundant charcoal at 50,000 years, skeletons at 50,000 at the Torrey Pines Mesa, fireplaces in alluvial covers of that date and greater. It seems rather extreme to insist on viewing this find in isolation from all of that other evidence.

The record of man's presence is scattered thinly through the alluvial covers over the twenty-five-foot beach all around the seaward face of Mount Soledad and Point Loma. The record is just like that at the Scripps Campus. There are hearths, percussively broken rocks, and rare manos and metates. Since the twenty-five-foot beach dates to 85,000 years, that probably is the maximum date for these traces. The set of artifacts, especially the presence of the mano and metate, and the exclusive use of local cobbles for making tools mark this as the remains of the La Jollan people, the makers of uniface tools and the grinders of seeds. This is a vastly earlier date than usually accepted and gives the La Jollan culture an age about eight times that usually suggested for the San Dieguito, who are the alleged first people at San Diego and who represent the Great Hunters, supposedly the first people in America.

CROWN POINT

Another site of great interest is Crown Point, in the Mission Bay area, on the south side of Mount Soledad. This feature too has a complex history (see figure 29). Crown Point is underlain by an old, strongly cemented shell reef. The species in it show that the main source of the shell was an open sand-beach environment, and this is quite in keeping with a bay bar. This reef was cemented and then highly eroded, leaving a very irregular topography. It was then buried by a sand deposit, at whose base there is another shell deposit, but a much thinner one. The sand deposit has two parts, an upper, loose brown sand several feet thick and a deeper one that is strongly cemented.

The sands are interesting for comparisons. The sands that Hubbs had dated in Baja California at 4,000 years are similar to those in the upper part of Crown Point. The hard, cemented sands of the lower part of Crown Point fit the description of the sands of the bay bar at La Jolla: old, hard, reddish yellow sands. These date to about 40,000 years.

The brown sands have a modest amount of archeology, which became best known in the period when Crown Point was a distant area that had no trash pickup or garbage service. The few residents dug deep holes and buried their garbage. In doing so, they repeatedly found stone tools, and a number of these finds were brought to the San Diego Museum of Man. This record is also exposed in the cliff faces all around the point. Unifacial tools and many flakes made from the local cobbles are frequent. I once found a metate at the base of the cliff and immediately climbed to see where it came from; I found a burial just beginning to be exposed by erosion. When I mentioned finding this, Heizer wrote to Gordon Ekholm, then president of the Society for American Archeology, complaining

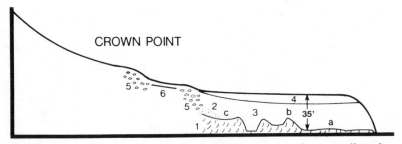

FIGURE 29. Crown Point is a good example of how complex a small geological feature may prove to be. The present little peninsula is just one of several that were built there in past times. Some of these features are indicated by the numbers: (*1*) the underlying strongly cemented shell deposit; (*2*) a younger shell beach; (*3*) cemented sands; (*4*) loose brown sands; (*5*) buried cobble ramps of old beaches; and (*6*) buried ancient soil. The archeological finds from this site include: (*a*) hearth, (*b*) mano, and (*c*) metates.

about my messing around with California archeology. I showed the burial to Clem Meighan of U.C.L.A. the time he came down to look at Texas Street, then I left it alone, not because of Heizer's objection, but because since I was a lone scholar investigating several fields at once there were limits on what I could accomplish, and working a burial out of a cliff face was just one more task, and one that I was unable to take on towards the end of a busy field season. As a result no one did anything, and the burial is now lost.

Of greater interest was the easily observed fact that the artifacts were also to be seen eroding out of the older sand, the hard, yellow, cemented sand. On one trip to Crown Point I found an obvious hearth at the very base of these older sands. This was a set of large cobbles set in a group and all strongly fire spalled. Except for their deep burial, they differed in no way from the set of rocks one might see about a picnic fire in those days on many of San Diego's beaches. These cobbles were totally out of place in these sands, for the nearest cobble source was nearly a mile away. Man would have good reason to be present, for at this time of rising sea level this would have been on the edge of a bay, with fish and shellfish resources readily available.

One-quarter mile away I found a very large granite mano sitting on a high point of the underlying shell reef. My attention was caught because the rock was out of place, and my interest was heightened when I noted that the exposed face, the one not cemented to the shell reef, was ground off in exactly the way a mano is.

This coarse granite had its quartz crystals ground off to a gently curving surface. The elapsed time since this grinding was so great that the less resistant minerals, the micas, feldspars, and hornblendes, had weathered away, leaving the quartz crystals standing in microrelief. It was notable that the edges of the stone showed no such smoothing or grinding. A cobble worn in a stream or surf is worn all over not just on one side, but a mano is worn on one or two faces but not on the sides. My conclusion was that this was a stone used for grinding, and I predicted that if the shell was removed from the covered side, it too would show grinding. It was many years before I cleaned the shell off to expose this face, and then there it was—a ground face, just as predicted. I had this stone on the doorstep in La Jolla the summer I found it, and a visiting archeologist, with whom I was sitting and talking, handled it absentmindedly and asked casually where I had found this huge mano. When I told him, he dropped it as if it were a hot potato.

At the Johns Hopkins University, I had a section sawed out for study, for the geologists were going to look to see how deeply the weathering had penetrated, expecting to find a shallow weathering rind. To their amazement it went all the way through. This would indicate something like 60,000 to 80,000 years of weathering, if we could be sure that man began with an absolutely fresh piece of granite but that is something we cannot be sure of. Half a mile from this find, engineers digging very deep sewer trenches struck this buried cemented shell horizon, and right on top of it they found two metates. Simpleminded folk, these engineering types. They promptly called the San Diego Museum of Man and were assured that there was no possibility of metates being in place beneath Crown Point, so they each took one and kept them as mementos. A metate is a large and very distinctive object. Its ground basin, the normal shape in the San Diego area, is diagnostic, and no one who has seen more than one would ever confuse a natural stone with them. These stones were in all probability just what the engineers said they were, but officialdom was too opinionated even to go and look at them.

After a while it begins to appear as if the San Diego Museum of Man were a target of my pique. It is not that. It is just that I know their failures. Other units' records, which I do not know, might well be worse. For instance, I was told of an Ohio museum to which a well driller brought a hammer stone. He laid it in front of the curator and asked, "Harry, what do you think that is?" The curator glanced at this most obvious artifact and said; "Bill, you know perfectly well that is a hammer stone. Where did you get it?" When told that it came from a gravel layer beneath a late-Wisconsin till sheet, he exclaimed: "Then you know darned well it is not a hammer stone." The well drillers had found such material more than once in their drilling for water into this well-known gravel sheet, but such facts were not sufficient to disturb the professional equanimity. And to make sure that someone does not leap to the conclusion that this is some peculiarly American phenomenon, I will include an anecdote from Africa reported by L. S. B. Leakey.

In *Adam's Ancestors* (1934), he discussed the finding of the Rhodesian Man skull, noting that it was an exceedingly important find, which could have been immensely more valuable if the world of archeology or paleontology or almost anybody had paid attention to what a geologist returning from Africa reported. The mine in Rhodesia was working out the contents of a cave that was filled with bones of extinct animals and that contained good stratigraphy. There were stone tools in these strata. No one reacted, and it was a near miracle that a couple of workers in the mine years later, when most of the material had been removed, finally recognized and saved a human skull. They saved no associated bones or tools, and Leakey did not fault them. He decried the neglect by the whole scientific world of this potentially rich site. This ignoring of riches is epidemic, and no field is immune to it. When I recite tales such as this to people in other fields, they chuckle and say, "You should see my field."

And so Crown Point, its neglect, and the loss of the two metates and an early-man skeleton are but a part of the ongoing circus of human error based on the very human trait of sticking to what is known and resisting any new ideas.

What is of interest now is an assessment of the age of this material buried by two fillings of the Mission Bay, apparently best interpreted as due to high sea stands. There are difficulties, as there always are. First, the most economical explanation is to place the two sands in the 5,000- and 40,000-year sequences of high sea stands.

The difficulty is that Crown Point is seemingly too high for this, and this is particularly true for the younger sand. If this sand is associated with an eight-foot sea stand, how did it get up on the point above thirty-five feet? The only explanation that comes to mind is that it may be dune sand, blown up there from the sand flats or from a nearby beach at the time the bay was filling. The exposures I saw did not have any water-laid structure to them. The underlying cemented yellow sands do have stratified characteristics and have marine shell at their base; these can quite certainly be allocated to a high sea stand, and the problem is to choose the right one. Is this feature a wave-built bay bar? If so, the twelve-foot sea stand, augmented here as at La Jolla by storm wave action to build a bay bar to something like a twenty-five-foot level, seems indicated, allowing then for dune action to complete the feature. Another alternative to consider would be an older and higher sea stand to create a bay fill, and this would call for a still earlier cycle, something like the twenty-five foot sea stand at 85,000 years. This gets exceedingly tenuous, and we will have to await some physical-chemical measures to tell us which alternative is the more likely correct.

SUMMARY ON THE GLACIAL-PLUVIAL UNIFACE STAGE AND AGE

This section could be expanded virtually endlessly to describe similar finds in the alluvial deposits around Point Loma or to go at great length into the indicated age of the metate over vast areas in which these implements are made of granite and where the oldest ones have rotted through—a clear indication of great age. Or one could make surveys of the distribution of the uniface tools that accompany the metate in these early levels and point to evidence that these too can be very old. Briefly, the metate has a virtually worldwide distribution that suggests great antiquity. It is in the Mousterian in Europe, suggesting an antiquity there of perhaps as much as 100,000 years. The uniface tools also have huge distributions in space and are very old in southeast Asia. Recent evidence from west Texas indicates that the uniface and metate stage is immensely old there and that the parallels to the San Diego sequence are very close.

The data for the San Diego area that once seemed so lonely now continue to gather support. The seed-gathering and grinding way of life is some tens of thousands of years old. On the coast of California it combined shellfish gathering to establish an even richer and longer-enduring lifeway. These are the people that M. J. Rogers originally called the La Jollans. Their stone tool kit was manufactured from the local cobbles available in the beaches and the local stream beds. They did not quarry stone of superior quality, even though it was readily available nearby. Their stone tools were made to a uniface pattern: all flaking came from one face, usually from a flat area created by splitting a cobble. They made great use of simple, unretouched flakes, and these were undoubtedly utilized to make a fair range of wooden tools. The stone kit is unquestionably like that of the people known as the La Jollans, and the geomorphic data now backed by geophysical dating simply extend their way of life back from 7,000 years to something like 70,000 years, give or take 10,000.

It amuses me to toss in that plus or minus. One can shudder at such ignorance: "Tsk, tsk, doesn't he even know within 10,000 years?" Or one could say: "What progress, we now know that the La Jollan way of life is not a mere 7,000 years but something like ten times as long." But that is a small item in comparison with the next step, for the La Jollan were not at all the earliest people at San Diego, and San Diego stands here for the Americas.

Chapter 6

Early Sites: II
The American Lower Paleolithic

THE confused La Jollan and San Dieguito situation was based on obvious evidence of the presence of man. The surface of the San Diego coastal area was covered with La Jollan sites, and M. J. Rogers had seen, but not fully understood, the extension of the La Jollan material deep into the alluvial covers. Lakes in the desert and coastal landforms requiring lowered sea levels had led me by the late 1930's to consider glacial times, perhaps 40,000 years, for the La Jollans—a thought so audacious in 1934 as to cost me my job at the San Diego Museum of Man.

This heresy, though, was a mere nothing compared to what my fieldwork beginning in 1947 was to lead me to. With the La Jollans and the San Dieguito, I was working with known and accepted cultures. Only my notions about their relations to one another and to absolute time were questioned by the mainstream of the field, and that questioning was fierce enough. However, I was about to step into deeper and hotter water, for I next stumbled onto evidence of previously unknown cultures of vastly greater age.

I returned to fieldwork in 1947 and began extensive field surveys of coastal terraces, their elevations, their sequence and extent, and their soils. Very shortly I was following the marine terraces inland, for they extended as valley-fill remnants far up the river valleys. In the Sweetwater River valley I found what appeared to be rolled and worn stone tools in an old valley fill, and at the south end of the San Diego Bay I found a huge core in a remnant of a fifty-foot terrace. I was obviously getting deeper and deeper into time and into unfamiliar stonework, too.

The most important site, however, was the Texas Street site. My 1947 notebooks have sketches of the huge pit dug to obtain dirt for landfills, with comments on the presence of burned earth areas that duplicated the hearths in the ocean-front terraces that

M. J. Rogers accepted as evidence of man. By 1950 I was noting the presence of artifacts in the Texas Street site, and by 1953 I had solved the problem of how the strange artifacts that character- ized this ancient deposit could have been produced. In retrospect, I can say that I did not set any speed records in concluding for evidence of man and a new lithic industry. But by 1950, the evidence had begun to indicate that the accepted cultural sequence and the accepted time frame for man in America were wrong. The La Jollans were an older people than believed, with a much longer history. And neither they nor the San Dieguito were even the first. My view of man in America as having at least a mid- Paleolithic history of some 40,000 years began to give way to evi- dence that indicated a lower-Paleolithic presence of man in America, something on the order of 100,000 years, perhaps more.

INTERGLACIAL MAN AT TEXAS STREET

The Texas Street site is a classic in perception. When I first saw it, it was a borrow pit, a source of dirt for landfills (see figure 30). The digging exposed the ancient landfill and its capping soils in classic manner, and that is what I entered the pit to examine. Only slowly did it become obvious to me that there was evidence of man present.

The glacial and interglacial sequence of cutting and filling is in broad outline fairly simple. Glacially lowered sea level will cause rivers that reach the sea to excavate their valleys near their mouths. When the glaciers melt, the sea levels rise, and the valley mouths fill with alluvium. With glaciations every 40,000 years or so, there should be many pieces of old valley fills left in most river valleys, for rivers rarely remove all of their former fills. As with marine terraces, the younger valley terraces will be lower and the older terraces higher, and there will be a weathering sequence parallel to this. Beyond that, things get complicated.

In downcutting, a river may leave a truncated-terrace remnant at any of several levels. There may be one valley fill superimposed on another or a remnant of a riverbed belonging to a period of downcutting left perched on a piece of older valley fill. Much of

FIGURE 30. This air photo shows the San Diego River Valley about 1930, prior to urban development. On the right side is the 300-foot-high mesa, part of the complex early Pleistocene series of broad terraces. The San Diego River has cut its valley through this surface and is now filling the lower valley to adjust to the high and rising sea levels of this (interglacial) time. Within the valley there are remnants of valley fills from previous times of high sea levels. The arrow points to the valley fill at the Texas Street site. (Photo by Erickson, courtesy of the San Diego Planning Commission)

this can be straightened out by study of the river sediments. The glacial times at San Diego were marked by greatly increased rainfall and by strongly flowing rivers, which carried coarse sediments. Interglacial times were marked, just as now, by weakly flowing rivers that carried fine sediments.

As a river valley fills with alluvium deposited by the main stream to meet the glacial rise in sea level, slope wash and debris from lateral canyons and from steep valley walls—if they are present, as they are at San Diego—will be laid down at the same time, giving rise toward the valley wall to an interfingering of valley wall and lateral canyon material with the river's alluvium. When the cycle reverses and the main valley cuts down, what happens along the valley wall depends on the width of the terrace the river leaves. If the terrace is broad and the lateral drainage weak, then lateral deposition will continue to accumulate on the terrace remnant. Usually any lateral stream will sooner or later cut a gully across the old valley-fill terrace, and its alluvium will then go on to the main stream, and the terrace surface will in a sense fossilize.

If this sounds a bit complicated, it is. It is the problem that I was stumbling into in this excavation into an old valley fill.

The back end of the borrow pit into the old valley fill at Texas Street already was perhaps fifty feet high, and it stood at a near-vertical angle (see figure 31). Climbing it was not exactly a mountaineering trick, but it required flattening oneself out against the steep face and being careful about finger and toe holds lest one find oneself sliding down with accelerating speed, leaving yards of skin behind. This flat position gives one perfect placement for minute scrutiny of the earth, for one's nose is not at some aristocratic five-plus feet away from mother earth but within a few inches of her ample bosom. I found myself facing piles of burned rock and alongside them lenses of burned earth. These burned-earth lenses were like the phenomenon I had been looking at in the cliffs for so long, but here there were masses of burned rock, in concentrated piles, all seen in familiar cross section. The trouble with looking at cliff fronts and borrow pits is that one is seeing everything in cross section and not in plan. It is a bit like Egyptian art, mostly profile.

I paused in my climb to look at these strange features and found some broken rock associated with them that was not broken by frost or fire or mineral decay. That left some force such as percussion or pressure, and this suggested man. But there was nothing in this broken rock that was anything like the broken rock on which I had been raised, and I was trained on La Jollan stonework that most archeologists in the 1930's and 1940's were studiously ignoring.

FIGURE 31. This picture shows the Texas Street site, circa 1950. The basal gravel at the car level is a culturally sterile zone, overlain by culturally sterile coarse sands. These levels contain dark areas, which are manganese rich. About a third of the way up the cut, the deposit changes texture to fine, silty sands, and evidence of human occupation begins. The greatest evidence for man is in the second bench, which contains alternate layers of rock and fine alluvium. The rock comes from Eocene gravel deposits in the lateral canyon this photo is looking up. The canyon built up an alluvial cone as the major valley filled. Most of the accumulation was slow, with long periods of stability. The hearths are on these old, stable surfaces. Intermittently, violent floods swept gravel sheets out onto the fan. Some hearths were destroyed and some artifacts moved down slope in these episodes, but many hearths with their associated artifacts were undisturbed.

I climbed on up and noted the soil profile, measured its thickness, recorded the clay content and the depth of migration of carbonate accumulation, and determined the pH. It was all quite as expected: an acid soil, with a well-developed clay B-horizon, with migration of calcium carbonate to depths not expectable in the present climate —a good record, then, of a past humid climate.

I paused in my cautious descent to look again at the evidence of fire and broken rock and to take one broken rock as a sample. At the foot of the slope, I sat down to make a few notes on the situation. In succeeding summers, I returned repeatedly to this exposure and made increasingly detailed notes and measurements. I carried an aneroid barometer about in those days; with its vernier scale, it could determine elevations within three feet. I used this

primarily on the terraces, to determine the elevation of the Pleistocene beaches, but here I used it to determine the elevation of this valley fill and of the levels of some of the fire areas within the fill. I also
collected more and more of the enigmatic broken rocks. The recollec-
tion of my puzzlement both gives me some sympathy with those who
have difficulty with "broken rocks" and makes me a bit impatient
with some of my critics. It is not easy to learn to recognize an
unfamiliar pattern of stone breakage. I did not leap to any sudden
conclusions but put a lot of time into the study of the material
and described it well enough that Gagliano, for one, found it to be
the key to his difficult lithic problems at Avery Island, Louisiana
(Gagliano, 1964, 1967).

One of the breakthrough finds in the identification of this
technology was not at this site but in the Sweetwater Valley south
of San Diego. In my study of terraces and their soils, I worked my
way steadily south to the Mexican border. In the process of examining some of the valley-fill deposits of the Sweetwater River, I found
a few rolled artifacts. The surface of the deposit had La Jollan–type
middens, typical scattered remains with some shell over a large extent and considerable amounts of broken rock with some artifacts.
The material in the valley fill was quite different: different stone,
different forms.

An even more important site lay on the the north side of the
valley. I chanced on it one day when I stopped to look at a highway
cut with a strongly developed soil profile: very reddish, with a
strong clay horizon. To my surprise the talus of the highway cut
was strewn with flaked stone, and I took along one bifacially flaked
piece that is the nearest thing to an ovate biface I have ever found
in the San Diego area (see figure 32). I marked the site in my
notebooks for intensive study the next summer, but when that summer came the "enemies of the Pleistocene" had removed the whole
thing in the process of widening and straightening a road.

At these sites there is no question of later slope wash confusing
the issue, for the sites were beyond the high valley walls of their
river valleys. The objects in the south side of the valley were in
the coarse sands of a strongly flowing river and showed clear evidence of having been transported some short distance. The ovate-
bifaced piece from the north side of the river shows by its sharpness

FIGURE 32. This is an ovate-biface piece from the valley fill in the Sweet-water River. The many flake surfaces show that this is the work of man, and the pattern of work is bifacial. The age of the deposit is interglacial.

that it had never been moved since being dropped by some ancient man. It was associated with a reddish soil and a strong clay forma-tion, guaranteeing that it too had considerable age.

Meanwhile at the Texas Street site, I found the fire-stained earth, fire-broken rock, and percussively broken rock more and more suggestive of the work of man. One day I picked up three cobbles in succession that had long, parallel flakes running down their sides from a flat platform at one end to a point at the other end. Two of the cobbles had not a bit of the original smooth and rounded surface that must once have characterized them. It was evident that force had been applied at one end of these rocks in such a way as to split long flakes off them lengthwise. In a moment of desperation, I put one of these split cobbles on a boulder, with its pointed end down, and hit it a lick at the opposite end with my geological pick. To my utter amazement a long flake came off, detaching not from the top, where I struck the stone, but from the bottom, where the stone rested on the boulder, which was serving as an anvil. I set the core up again and hit it another lick, and this time the blow took a similar flake off, but detaching this time from the top, at the point struck by the hammer. Again the flake was flat on its under-side, the side that detached from the core. On the core, the two flake scars intersected to give an obtuse angle. I had been looking at just such flake-scar intersections for five years.

As I looked in amazement at what I had done, the whole process came into focus (see figure 33). It was as if I had been looking at these stones unseeingly—seeing them of course, but not

FIGURE 33. This illustrates the blade-making technology I happened upon at Texas Street and which characterized the artifacts found there. The experimental flaking started with a cobble that had been flaked by man in interglacial time, item *1*. Two more flakes have been struck by me (*2*), using my geologic pick as a hammer and resting the stone on an anvil. The detached flakes are shown in plan (*4*) and profile (*5*). The larger flake would be most difficult to defend as the work of man if I had not struck it off myself.

understanding them at all, exactly as one looks at a page in an unknown language. Now suddenly I understood them, for I was looking at a well-known stone-flaking technique. In America it was supposedly limited to work in obsidian—in Mexico, by Aztecs— presumably a later and specialized kind of work. I knew that this kind of work was done in the fine flints of Europe and there too was moderately late, the work of the men of the Upper Paleolithic, about 20,000 to 30,000 years ago. But here I was in southern California, on a time level that I thought was 100,000 years ago, and with one of the more refractory stones one could work with—a quartzite, a stone that later men used only if nothing better was within fifty miles or so. And still there was no doubt about it: the strange pattern of rock breakage that had caught my attention and puzzled me for more than five years resulted unquestionably from someone's flaking tough, old cobbles in such a way that blades were produced and cores were marked by long, parallel flutes left by the scars of the detached flakes.

We know so much more about this kind of flaking now that it is embarrassing to look back on how crudely I understood the process. I struck straight down, holding the core at right angles to the anvil stone. This I then conceived of as bipolar flaking, and many people still do. Crabtree has correctly noted that this collapses the cone of percussion and produces flakes with very flat planes (Crabtree, 1972). Lee Patterson (Sollberger and Patterson, 1976a, 1976b) and Crabtree both insist that better control of the work results from striking at a forty-five-degree angle to the plane of the platform and that part of the far end of the core from which the flake is to detach should not rest on the anvil. Perhaps even more to the point, one does not even need to use an anvil, for the flint workers at Brandon, England, rested the core on a pad on their leg and struck off flakes with ease. Perhaps the quartzite is a tougher prospect, for we have had the best results using anvils. This often causes shattering of the tip of the core where it rests on the anvil. This shattering increases as the core is worked down toward the point of exhaustion. Many of the Texas Street cores show tip shattering, indicating that these people used anvils at least part of the time. At Texas Street this kind of heavy-handed flaking led to a great deal of compression stress, with hairline fractures across the blades' short axes.

The result is that there are relatively few complete blades but many short sections of blades.

At the time I withdrew from further archeological work at San Diego, I said that if I was wrong about these broken rocks' being artifacts no others would be found, but that if I was right other sites with such material should appear. It is interesting to see these types of artifacts showing up at more and more sites and at earlier and earlier times. First they were thought to be late—blades and cores in Mexico—then they were recognized for the Adena culture in the United States, around the time of Christ and earlier, and then for the Paleo-Indian level, or around 10,000 years ago. Most recently they have been reported for the Tlapacoya site in Mexico, age about 20,000 years. The stone used at Tlapacoya is andesite, a poor stone for flaking. The results duplicate the work at Texas Street. Most impressive is the presence of many short sections of very thick blades, nearly quadrilateral in cross section. These were frequently found on the living floors that we excavated at Texas Street. No one questions that these are evidence for man at Tlapacoya, and I fail to see why then they are not evidence for man at Texas Street.

I collected material from this site every summer that I returned to California. I did not see the site in its initial stages of excavation but only in its middle and late stages, and I had my best opportunity to study it after it ceased to be a borrow pit and was left with its back or valley wall standing in a set of three terraces: twenty, thirty, and twenty feet high respectively, with ten-foot-wide benches at the top of each section and with a bench sloped back so that runoff would not go down the face of the terrace. This also guaranteed that rock falls would be trapped on these terrace tops, thus preserving the lower faces from contamination by material from higher levels. The late B. E. McCown, city engineer and amateur archeologist, made a survey of the site for me, giving the original land level and the levels of the benches that the engineers left (see figure 34). He and his wife also collected on the site and found artifacts, hearths, marine shell, and in one hearth fragments of burned bone. It was the interesting commonplace: if you were not trained not to believe, then you could see the evidence.

Those steep back walls were to be the scene of many hours of

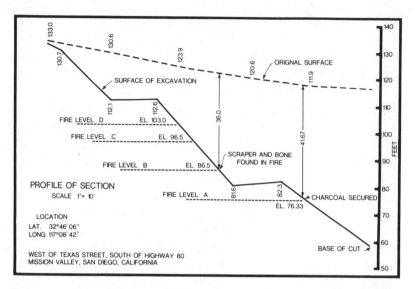

FIGURE 34. This is B. E. McCown's engineering survey of the Texas Street site, with his notes on fire lenses and artifacts. His observation of plural occupation zones buried in the alluvium is supported by the excavations by Carter, Minshall, and Moriarty. In fact, our excavation showed that there are even more occupation zones or floors than McCown mapped.

a human-fly performance on my part. The material was left at its maximum angle of repose, and that is very steep for conglomerates like these, with weathered soil profiles interspersed through them. I crawled along the faces looking for artifacts and for traces of fireplaces. Material that I found was recorded by the bench it came out of and by its position east or west of the gully that cut through the site. It was a crude method, but since there was no excavation or carefully surveyed control, it seemed sufficient for the state of the investigation. As it was, I only slipped occasionally, tobogganing down for twenty feet or so, always leaving a bit of hide among the boulders but managing to end up with my collecting bag and pick and all bones whole and unbroken at the foot of the slope.

The situation at Texas Street presents two major questions: is there evidence for man in the form of stone tools and fireplaces, and what is the age of the site.

The general sequence at Texas Street is quite clear. At some time the valley was filled with alluvium to a level far above the present. Thereafter it was cut out to levels far below the present, with a remnant of the old valley fill left in place. At present the valley is filling again. There are problems. Which glacial period caused the lowering, and which interglacial caused the filling? How much of the valley-fill remnant is due to the interglacial time, and how much is due to later accumulation from the little canyon that has been building its alluvial cone onto the old valley fill during post-interglacial time—or during how much of post-interglacial time and, again, which interglacial? These puzzles are not subject to easy or, at the moment, to absolute solution.

At the base of the excavation, coarse sands and gravels indicate the San Diego River was at work with a rate of flow far greater than its present rate. This would be a rainy condition and in southern California a glacial time. Above that, in the upper ten feet of the lowest bench, is a deposit of fine sands suggesting a slower-flowing stream, which would be appropriate for an interglacial stream. Evidence for man starts in these fine sands. The elevation here is eighty feet, and the present riverbed is at sixty feet. It would seem to require a twenty-foot rise of sea level to create this situation, and the indicated time would be about 85,000 years ago. This seems to be the absolute minimum age for the situation.

Above this eighty-foot level there is a fifty-foot-thick accumulation of sands, gravels, and cobbles swept out from the little canyon that reaches the stream at this point. The canyon must have deposited its load of coarse cobbles during floods throughout the period of valley filling. It probably also continued to deposit materials after the valley began to cut down. At some point the canyon cut a gully through the old fill, and thereafter deposition by this canyon onto the terrace surface ceased (the gully is very visible in figure 30). This was no short time ago, for the surface of the alluvial cone at the mouth of the canyon is strongly weathered. This still leaves us with no hard dates. We have a C-14 date for the upper part of the lowest bench, but it is not too helpful because it is one of these "more than" dates—more than 35,000 years. That leaves us not knowing whether that mass of charcoal was 36,000 or 136,000 years old. The surface soil is helpful, in that it is much more strongly developed than the 5,000-year-old soils at the Scripps Institution of Oceanography, but that leaves us wondering whether it is 10,000 years, 15,000, or what. Soils on the order of 5,000 or so years of age recur throughout the fifty feet of accumulation, but no one has had the agility, time, and inclination to count them. From a long acquaintance with the site, I would guess at fifteen or twenty or more soils, each of about 5,000 years, and this would suggest a pretty high age for that piece of alluvium.

A bit of unexpected archeological evidence has appeared. At the top of the second bench more than twenty feet beneath the original surface, two classic La Jollan pieces have been found, one by Herb Minshall and one by me. Minshall's appeared in a hearth zone just to the west of the gully, in the area we excavated in 1976. Mine was found alongside a hearth in an unpaved parking lot to the east of the church. With La Jollan material running clear through the alluvial covers over the twenty-five-foot beach on the sea front we have an age span of something like 80,000 years for such material, and nothing in the soil profiles or the geomorphology at Texas Street would be inconsistent with such an age. It amuses me to wonder about the reception of these two La Jollan pieces. Does their presence suddenly promote these burned-earth areas from evidence for forest fires to genuine hearths? If one accepts these, how does one reject the identical evidence at greater depth?

More than 90 percent of the material that I collected at the Texas Street site came from the face of the second bench (see picture of the site, figure 35). This is well below the two La Jollan pieces, and I found no La Jollan material in my years of collecting there. I did find much core and blade work, which is not found in the La Jollan culture, and there is a sprinkling of possible biface work. So we have some cultural sequence in the Texas Street site that surface collecting from those steep cuts simply did not bring out—but then the six five-foot squares that we excavated to a depth of thirty inches in the top of that second bench did not bring it out either.

It is hard to keep all of the parts of a puzzle like this in view, so let's review. Up to this time we have no blade-and-core material on any terrace surface beneath a hundred feet. Its absence implies a very great age, certainly something on the magnitude of 100,000 years, since that is the timing of the sea stands that must have erased the early record. There certainly is blade and core material in the midsection of the Texas Street site. In the upper section, it now appears, there is some La Jollan material, and as we have seen this

FIGURE 35. In this shot of the Texas Street site under excavation in 1973, Carter is upper left, Minshall lower right. The work shown here is at the top of the second bench, where most of the artifactual material—blade and core work—was found.

material can have a maximum age of 80,000 years. In addition there is some bifacial flaking mixed in the levels where the blade and core material is found, and from this material's position elsewhere we know it to be of glacial or even interglacial age. At the nearby Brown site, carefully excavated by Moriarty, although he has not published his findings, the sequence from early to late was: blade and core, ovate biface, La Jollan, San Dieguito, late La Jollan, Diegueño. Minshall's estimate for the maximum age of the site is 80,000 years. The cultures are not sharply separated but tend to overlap extensively. The culture sequence at the Texas Street site is blade and core, probably with some biface work, overlaid by La Jollan work. The site is glacial at base (no evidence for man), overlaid by interglacial sands with evidence for man, and the probable age for the sand deposit is minimally 85,000 years and possibly as high as 130,000. If the dating seems fuzzy, that is the state of the art. In a decade or two we should have some absolute dating.

But now let's look again at the controversy over the tools and the fireplaces.

The evidence for man was best seen when the site had been freshly worked over by the engineers, especially with the three terraces or benches cut across the face of the site to stabilize it. At that time the surfaces were clean, and fire areas could be seen both in plan and profile. On the top of the first bench, where the bulldozer blade had cut cleanly through the damp clays of a soil horizon that contained a hearth, one could see the fire-reddened center and the halo of charcoal stain around it. Fifteen years later when we excavated on the top of the second bench, we exposed the identical situation: hearths marked by fire areas and surrounded by dark, stained-earth areas, marking the living floors of these people. Broken quartzite was concentrated on these floors.

There were two kinds of hearths at Texas Street. Small ones of about thirty inches in diameter were simple, hollowed areas showing some signs of burned earth, charcoal, and ash (figure 36). Larger hearths were about four feet in diameter and often were lined with large fire-stained rocks. In one of our five-by-five squares we encountered a conical pile of burned rock, and in the adjacent square we found a pit where plural floors of burned earth and charcoal showed repeated use.

If one has two types of hearths—with living floors, with food bone and marine shell in a terrestrial deposit, and with an abundance of stone broken to a pattern—one wonders what more could be asked. Criticism of the site has centered on the artifacts and the fire areas, and these need some discussion.

The easier to dispose of is the fire-area criticism. Marie Wormington (1957), usually accurate in her descriptions of sites, slipped up on this one. She stated that the fire areas are several feet thick and one hundred feet long. This pattern she attributed to forest fires. Odd, for forest fires leave no such record. What I described as normal hearths are scattered along several hundred yards of outcrop and also scattered vertically through fifty feet of deposit. No one who has been on the site with me has questioned the accuracy of that description. That the black material in the areas with the burned rock and the burned earth is actually charcoal has been challenged by Alex Krieger. It is just manganese to him. He persists in this

FIGURE 36. This thirty-inch-diameter hearth exposed in cross section at Texas Street is typical of the smaller, non–rock lined hearths. The black zone is charcoal rich though, typically, structureless and powdery. Bits of this charcoal examined under the electron microscope show the characteristics of pine. This particular hearth was not in the bouldery deposit of the lateral canyon but in the very top of the fine sands of the interglacial river, right where they graded into fine alluvium.

error despite the fact that when he was on the site with me I showed him both manganese and charcoal and demonstrated how to distinguish the one from the other—and despite the fact that three separate laboratories have examined the charcoal and pronounced it charcoal and not manganese. Furthermore, some of the specks of charcoal have now been identified as coming from conifers. This is an interesting point, for the nearest conifers today are the few relict trees at Torrey Pines twenty miles away. To this evidence we can add Luther Cressman's statement. He visited the site with Carl Hubbs as a guide, found a fire zone, and excavated it. This is what he said of it.

> Hubbs found in an exposure a basin similar to those described by Carter and it contained what appeared to be charcoal. Hubbs later checked the material in the lab and found it to be true charcoal. I have excavated through forest fire debris, holes made by burned stumps with their distinctive patterns, hearths in the open, hearths in fire pits. The pattern of the basin shaped depression with its charcoal, now filled by slumped gravel and sand, and the true charcoal, when viewed in terms of my experience convinced me that the fire basin could be and most likely was what Carter thought it to be, that is a human artifact (Cressman, 1973, p. 8).

In this article Cressman also accepted the fire areas on the Scripps campus dated at 20,000 and 32,000 years as evidence of man.

Cressman's acceptance is interesting, for despite his long years of pioneering work in the Pacific Northwest he was still skeptical of the claims of very high antiquity for man in southern California. He said of his visit to Santa Rosa Island at Orr's invitation that he went as a skeptic but returned convinced of the evidence for early man there. While there, he aided in collecting charcoal from a site that dated more than 25,000 years old. He called attention to the sequence of dates—greater than 25,000, 29,700, greater than 37,000, all with fire areas—and to the association of the 29,700 date with a mammoth skeleton in a huge fire pit. Then he added: "The striking thing about these last three areas [Texas Street, Scripps Institution campus, Santa Rosa Island] is the similarity of the cultural evidence and the general conformity of the dates" (Cressman, 1973, p. 9). The dates are a bit deceptive, for when a date is designated "greater than" it is no real date. The dates at Santa

Rosa Island are in alluvial covers probably of Wisconsin age, Evans' cycles 1C, 20,000, and 2C, 60,000. The Texas Street site is a cycle or so older and has a probable age of 85,000 or 130,000 years.

For the fire areas, then, we can say that Krieger's manganese hypothesis has been disproved by repeated laboratory experiment and can be disregarded. Wormington's misrepresentation is simply a case of bad reporting. Cressman represents the archeologist who has had wide experience with field excavation of this sort of site and who has been on the Texas Street site and done his own first-hand excavation to test the data. One of the oddities of the situation has been the scarcity of scholars who have taken the trouble to look. When the excavations were underway in 1973 some of the people who came were astonished when, after hearing my explanation of what they were looking at—burned rock lining a fire pit, with ash, burned earth, and charcoal—I urged them to get into the excavation and look for themselves. I handed them trowel and whisk broom and asked if there was anything else they wanted. Apparently they were used to visiting sites where nothing could be touched. My outlook is quite different: "Here are pick, shovel, dental pick, and whisk broom. If you doubt my reports, you do it."

Another interesting comment came from an archeologist who had worked on the huge excavation under Melvin Fowler at the Modoc Rock Shelter in Missouri. He was the silent sort—said nothing, asked nothing, as I pointed out the fireplaces, the fire pits, the burned rock features. But as he left, he had just one comment: "Nothing you have shown us would have been out of place in the Modoc Rock Shelter." The ages of the two sites are vastly different, but to an unprejudiced eye both have similar evidence of man's presence.

The second criticism of the Texas Street site centered on the artifacts, which have been derisively called cartifacts, chimeras, mere broken rocks. We have reviewed the broken-rock situation in general, and the conclusion is that, while nature does break rock, it is usually by chemical action, frost, or fire and only rarely by percussion. In some special circumstances, as in the settling of limestones, which shear off flint nodules and then press off long series of flakes, there may be some rather convincing pseudoartifacts. I have never seen this—which is far from saying that it does not

FIGURE 37. This photograph from the Texas Street site shows a quartzite tool in place in the 1973 excavation. The worked edge is upward. In cross section this tool is triangular; it is the type of chopping tool that Minshall has noted to be like the *skreblos* of Siberia.

happen—but it certainly has no application to the San Diego region, where there are neither flints nor limestones. Some very brittle flints in streams subject to very turbulent flow in central Texas are broken, but the random breakage has no pattern to it, and nothing artifact-like results. In the central Texas case the most pertinent observation was that while a very low frequency of breaks occurred in the flint (technically, chert) there was no breakage of the quartzite. At the Texas Street site we are dealing with quartzite (see quartzite tool, figure 37).

The real test at San Diego has always been to take the skeptics to the Eocene and Pliocene deposits of gravels identical to those on our sites and challenge them to find breakage similar to that seen at Texas Street. No one has been able to do so. Nature did not break rock in this way in those periods, or in the early Pleistocene, either. But in the later Pleistocene, broken rock suddenly appears. The only thing that changes in that time level is a new creature: man.

There are numerous ways of determining that man did this breaking of stone. Perhaps most significant, there are many fractures that had to have been made by percussion, and in many cases the diagnostic marks of the percussive blow are well preserved: points of percussion with the mashed zone where the hammer struck, bulbs of percussion showing the dispersion of force typical of percussive flaking, lines of force, sheared-off crystals—every mark that is ever found in man's stonework is there. The work all started with stream-rounded cobbles. Some of the flaked pieces still have some of that surface—the cortex of the cobble—but many have been flaked so extensively that no trace of the original outer surface is left. Instead, one has a mass of flake scars. The most interesting of these cobbles found at Texas Street are the cores from which blades have been struck (see figure 38).

Blades, *sensu strictu*, are flakes whose length is more than twice their length. When a series of blades have been struck from a core, the later blades will have on their upper surfaces a series of long, parallel flake scars (see figures 39 and 40). Their under surface will be a single, relatively flat surface. At Texas Street the characteristic artifact is the core from which blades have been struck. Cores are marked by the long, parallel scars of the flakes struck from them, by their flat tops, which supplied the platform from which to strike the flakes, and by their tendency to develop pointed lower ends as the flaking process continued to thin them down and shape them (see figure 41).

As I related earlier, these cores are so diagnostic of man's work and so totally unnatural that Carl Hansen, a geomorphologist who has worked extensively in Africa on Lower Paleolithic problems, took one look at a series of these cores and went and sat down. He knew in two minutes' examination of such items that they were the work of man and not of nature.

Another implement of considerable interest in distinguishing artifacts from nature-broken rocks is the concave scraper. A blade or any fragment from the breaking of rock that had a useful edge was used for scraping, but occasionally a crescent-shaped hollow was deliberately flaked into a piece. These little crescents show battering along the concavity and under a microscope show wear on the bat-

FIGURE 38. This classic core from Texas Street was once a well-rounded quartzite cobble, but there is no trace of any of the orginal cobble surface left. All the surfaces are planes resulting from driving off long flakes from the upper end. The striking platform has been formed by striking two long, parallel flakes off the top of the core.

FIGURE 39. This artifact from Texas Street is a classic blade section. Maximum thickness is one-quarter inch. Such a blade has to be struck from a core from which at least two previous flat ventral-surfaced flakes have been struck. Identical pieces are known from well-accepted sites.

tered edge. Experimentally, it is evident that battering of such an edge increases its efficiency, for it converts the knife edge into a rasp or filelike edge. The only criticism I have heard of viewing this type of implement as an artifact comes from Haynes. He feels that this is the easiest pseudoimplement to account for by natural means. All one has to do is to have one stone resting with its edge on another and have any heavy weight applied, and a crescent-shaped piece will be pressed out. Voila, a concave scraper.

The question arises as to who is being obtuse here. Do the advocates of early man just run around picking up any rock with a chip out of it? Or do we have concave scrapers made on struck blades and on flakes? The latter is the case, as is illustrated in figure 42. Further, most of these concave scrapers are the result of many blows, not just one happenstance break. They have the battering

FIGURE 40. This complete quartzite blade from Texas Street is so delicate that such pieces are rarely recovered whole. Notice the long, parallel flake scars. Such a blade can only be produced from the type of cores illustrated in figures 38 and 41.

concentrated on their working edge, and there is wear on that edge. How now, brown cow? Nor do these items occur in environments suitable to the fortuitous pressure argument; they occur in sites along with other stone tools. They are not limited to any one kind of rock or to especially easily flaked rock.

The concave scrapers reappear at other sites of this blade and core stage, as they should if this is a stage with some uniformity to it. And since they do, in differing geomorphic settings, in different kinds of rock, but repeating a pattern of manufacture and bearing evidence of use, the evidence becomes all the more overwhelming, if your mind is open to consider it.

The third diagnostic or characteristic implement at Texas Street is a cleaverlike implement. It is obviously a chopping tool, but it

FIGURE 41. This artifact, shown in place in the gravels at the Texas Street site, is a core of quartzite, whose lower end is exposed. Five flake scars can be counted, one of which detached from this lower or pointed end. This suggests anvil flaking—positioning of the core on a rock with this pointed end down and striking a blow on the opposite end to detach long, roughly parallel-sided flakes, technically blades.

is not the familiar bifaced tool; many examples are instead unifacial. Yet the Texas Street tool is not like the La Jollan uniface chopper either. Any relatively thin piece of rock that resulted from the breaking up of some of the quartzite cobbles and that had at least

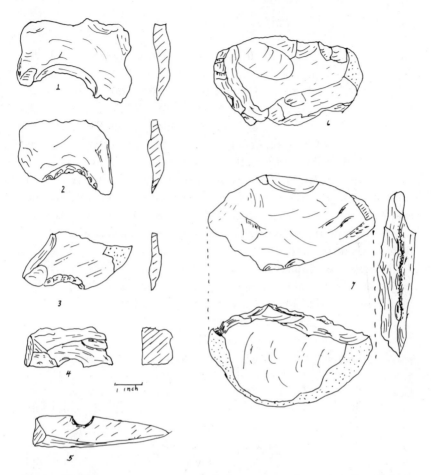

FIGURE 42. These concave scrapers and cleavers come from several early-man sites: (1) Central Texas; (2) Calico; (3) Buchanan Canyon; (4) Mount Soledad; and (5) Yuha Desert. The first three are made on flakes; 4 is made on a thick, blocky fragment; 5 is made on a heavy blade. The heavy, wedge-shaped, weakly retouched chopping tools at 6 and 7 are distinctly different from the bifaced choppers from Buchanan Canyon (see figure 44).

one thin edge was used for this chopping work. Sometimes these pieces are lightly retouched on the thin edge, but often not. The retouch may be unifacial or bifacial, but the resultant chopper is not at all like the ovate bifaces or other heavily flaked chopping tools common to other pre–Paleo Indian stages (see figure 42). Herb Minshall has called attention to the fact that they are similar in form and function to the implements called *skreblos* in Siberia. With the usual reservations that there may be no similarity in age, and possibly not even in cultural contact, the name can be used to designate this tool.

In 1976, while in La Jolla writing the first draft of this book, I had a very extensive exhibit of these artifacts laid out and took visiting scholars through the collection, pointing out the characteristic features and how one could tell that they represented man at work and describing the particular technology that was used to produce these items. With the younger men who had been trained in lithic technology, I had the pleasant experience of their taking the lead away from me. They would pick up the specimens and explain to me just how these different features were obtained. I was content to have them tell me.

There was similar material from the great quarry at Truckhaven, the Yuha desert, Texas Street, and Buchanan Canyon. This exhibit of cores and blades showed that these forms were created irrespective of the geomorphic environment (from inactive desert surfaces or extremely active torrential stream beds) and equally independent of material (quartzite, fine grained basalts, welded and silicified silts, and other fine-grained stone). Concave scrapers, skreblos, and single edge-flaked tools likewise ran the gamut of materials and locations. There was only one common denominator: man at work. In addition, material from the Truckhaven quarry was arranged by degree of weathering, and this could be seen to coincide with the lithic technologies. It was an impressive exhibit and won a number of converts.

That leaves the objections of Heizer, Krieger, Wormington, E. L. Davis, and a host of others to account for. Heizer never visited the Texas Street site and adamantly refused to look at the artifacts, even when I took them to Berkeley, as I have repeatedly done. Krieger visited the site with me and later on his own, so I am told. That he cannot or will not recognize the presence of artifacts but persists in the broken-rock thesis is most peculiar, particularly since he told me in a letter after he had visited the site with me that he saw evidence of man there. His devastating review of my book on early man, with its concentrated criticism of the Texas Street site, he said in his letter, was meant only to show that I had written a lousy site report and was designed to compel me to write a better one. No one but Krieger understood his review that way. Wormington has never visited the site that I know of. She has glanced at the artifacts that I have taken to meetings, but she has never sat down to a careful examination of them. Clem Meighan joins the band of "no seeums." He came, as I described, but was unconvinced. Most of the archeological profession have simply taken their lead from these few experts.

It is possible to construct rather elaborate classifications of tool types by sorting out differing shapes of broken rock from the immense amounts we are beginning to have available. I tend to resist doing this however, for it seems to me that there is a great deal of "just broken rock." There is no doubt that man used a great deal of it, but there is considerable doubt as to just how much of it was deliberately produced to a pattern. The items I have described above certainly were patterned products: cores, blades, concave scrapers, and cleavers or skreblos. Other types of implements may emerge as we have more material and can see patterns more clearly, but these four good, clear classes of artifacts are sufficient to identify this cultural stage.

One of the problems is that primitive man apparently did not read the flint knappers' manuals very carefully. In many days of working on quarry sites, often sitting in one spot and putting pieces of flaked stone back together I have seen that man could be pretty haphazard in his breaking of rock. It is not unusual on a quarry surface to find a piece of rock that was struck dead center. The blow broke the rock into pieces that are somewhat like the sections of an orange. Sometimes a section or two are missing, indicating that one of the shattered pieces offered some promise for working into an implement of some sort. Indians in the Pacific Northwest told enthnologists that sometimes they took a large boulder and, standing on a bank to give some elevation, simply threw the boulder down with maximum force on another boulder, shattering one or both, and then picked up one or two pieces that suited their needs and left the rest. At San Diego, John Alsozatai-Petheo broke a huge boulder all to pieces by holding it and slamming it against a larger boulder; in the process he produced a galaxy of useful, sharp-edged pieces. Much of the fried chicken eaten that night at the "Friends of the Pleistocene" banquet was carved with splinters of that rock.*

---

*The Friends of the Pleistocene is one of the least organized associations in existence. There are no officers and no dues. The only requirement is an interest in the Pleistocene, its plants, animals, soils, climates, landforms, and even man.

This particular stone was a very fine-grained, light-colored quartzite. This was the favored stone of the blade and core people at Texas Street. Although quartzite is a minor constituent of the gravel at Texas Street, most of the fractured rock is quartzite. Even more striking is the fact that it was the honey-colored quartzite that was preferred. As H. L. Minshall has found, it is at times hard to discover a piece that they have not used. To clinch the observation on selectivity, the choice reversed with the La Jollan people. Given a choice, they used the dark quartzites. These are cultural preferences and not at all what nature does. If nature were to go around smashing rocks percussively, it would not matter if the quartzite were light or dark. They both break much the same way. Note that this argument stays strictly with the quartzites, and so meets head on the great critics' "quartzites just naturally break that way." Why should light and dark quartzite break differently? And why should it break longitudinally to produce blades and cores in one period and then reverse and break in a unifacial manner in the succeeding period?

We have gone through a series of propositions that leads to a date for the site—including elevation in relation to past and present sea levels, climatic changes and the kinds of sediments expected, and also the kinds of soils expected—and have found that this complex all fitted but left us dangling somewhere between 80,000 and 130,000 years, more or less. For the evidence of man's presence, we went through fire, food bone, and shell, selectivity in use of stone and a highly distinctive pattern for breaking stone to make a distinctive set of tools. There were more details, but this should do for a review. We can then take the analysis one step further. If this site is actually a record of man's presence in America at this time with this technology, then there must be other sites. If there are not, then the analysis at Texas Street is weakened. If there are, it is confirmed. So, let's look at some other sites.

BUCHANAN CANYON AND RELATED SITES

It is a truism that you can only find what you are prepared to find; and you can only see what your mind, not your eye, is prepared to accept. In subtle shades and shapes the hunter sees his quarry crouching in the cover, but the neophyte does not, often even when the exact spot is pointed out to him. The eye reports faithfully, but the mind sorts, interprets, accepts, and rejects. Even the most obvious bit of stone flaking, obvious to the lithic expert, is just a bit of rock to the neophyte. Even to the general anthropologist, stonework is an only dimly understood process, better understood by the archeologist, and fully understood only by some lithic experts. Even of these experts, Vance Haynes once said to me, "George, did you ever know of two lithic experts who agreed?" Vance was being critical of some of the broken rock that I was advancing as evidence of man and equally critical of one lithic expert's acceptance. He had a point. Even the expert's knowledge is always limited and fallible and acutely subject to peer-group pressure. It is like the curator in Ohio who could look directly at a hammer stone and say, "It is no hammer stone." Lee Patterson after examining the Texas Street material and finding it to be obviously artifact asked a lithic expert why he had rejected it. "Well, when I see something new, different, and controversial, I always reject it" was the reply.

No archeologist with any thought of his future would in the past twenty-five years accept interglacial artifacts, no matter how obvious they were. The reverse of this is that if you have no preconceived notions, and no professional status to lose, and are inquisitive and alert, you are likely to discover something that the professional cannot. This is the story of Buchanan Canyon.

Herbert L. Minshall and I grew up together in San Diego, were Sea Scouts together, and shared an interest in Indians. Wars and their aftermaths spread us far apart, and we rarely saw one another for years. Herb became an artist and taught at San Diego, but his interests led him to read my book on *Pleistocene Man at San Diego*, and so his mind was alerted to the possible presence of a particular pattern of broken rock in the area and his artist's training tended to fix forms in his mind.

In 1970 a localized cloudburst hit his neighborhood, and the flood water raging down the deep canyon behind his home set up an immense roar. After the flood, he saw that a gully had been ripped through the canyon where there had previously been a smooth floor. Herb went down to examine this phenomenon and, in looking along the torrent's path, he saw among the bricks and bottles and cobbles some broken rock. One might not have interested him, but there were a lot of them (see figure 43). When he looked them over, it struck him that these were like the things that I had illustrated in *Pleistocene Man,* which he had read more than ten years before. Taking some of the most obvious examples, he visited the San Diego Museum of Man, only to be told condescendingly by E. L. Davis that streams break rocks. Artists of some sorts break rocks, and Herb had broken a few in his time, and he had looked at a lot of Indian artifacts and the debris that Indians left in the process of making stone tools. He had also read my book, and he simply rejected the experts.

The canyon-bottom gully became a virtual laboratory. Herb waded into it when it was in full flood, but only an occasional stone nuzzled his ankle, no more bruisingly than a fish bumping him. This fits, of course, with the geomorphologist's discovery that a huge amount of the motion going on and much of the noise is due to the rocks' moving vertically not laterally. Even in flood time in this steep canyon bottom's torrent, there was no motion going on at velocities that could flake these tough, old stones. Yet the canyon was filled with broken rock. Further, it was broken to a now-familiar pattern. Cobbles were split longitudinally, and flake scars ran down their long faces—cores from which blades had been struck. The blades were there in fair numbers. We also found concave scrapers, and this was the site where Minshall recognized the predominantly one-sided chopping tools that duplicated the Siberian skreblos. There were crude but effective bifaced pieces, Arnold's ovate bifaces. There was also an immense amount of debitage, the debris left by man in the process of breaking rock up to obtain useful pieces. We underestimate how easily this can be done. For men skilled in flaking rock, it was a simple matter to break up half a dozen cobbles, producing thirty to fifty flakes to get a good piece of stone or two.

Buchanan Canyon became a showplace where many visitors were taken. In answer to the objection that quartzite just breaks that way, we pointed to the high degree of selectivity: the light-colored quartzites were preferred. In answer to the objection that streams break rocks, we described Minshall's standing in the stream in flood with no damage to his shins. We also pointed to the

FIGURE 43. H. L. Minshall, shown in Buchanan Canyon, holds a huge, bi-faced cobble. His discovery of this site revived interest in the very ancient sites of the San Diego region, and he has gone on to show that there are many sites of this type in the area.

pattern of the stone breakage—its utter difference from the patterns of all the accepted cultures of the region and its strong overlap with the Texas Street material. There are differences between Texas Street and Buchanan Canyon. There is more bifacial work at Buchanan Canyon and a little bit of the later cultural material, both La Jollan uniface work and even a trace of San Dieguito work. But in the main it is a gold mine of blade and core work. It may be slightly younger than the Texas Street site, but we have no way of really dating it except by comparing the material with Texas Street work, which does have dating of a sort. Buchanan Canyon supplied the first really massive collection of blade and core artifacts, a collection so full of examples of cores and blades and concave scrapers and skreblos that when laid in series they were overwhelming evidence of man at work (see figure 44).

Another find resulted from another alert mind. Dick Gadler while a student worked on the excavation at Texas Street in 1973. The next year he found a site in Alvarado Canyon, near California State University at San Diego, about five miles farther up the San Diego River valley. This was like Buchanan Canyon except that there were only a few artifacts. They were again in place in the gravels in the base of the canyon. Dick's interest kept him looking, and presently he found the Brown site, mentioned earlier.

Minshall meanwhile decided that if one canyon had this material then perhaps others did also. He looked in one of the major nearby canyons, the Florida Canyon, and found that it duplicated Buchanan Canyon. It was full of debitage, cores and blades, and skreblos. Jack Davis, an amateur archeologist in the Poway area to the north of San Diego, was referred to Minshall and began to bring him broken rocks. They were just that—fire broken or chemically broken or just curiously shaped, not artifacts at all. Minshall had taught many years and had developed immense patience; he kept rejecting Jack's material and showing him samples of real artifacts and flake debris. In 1976 Herb called me and told me that Jack had now learned what to look for, and he thought that he really had something and that we had better go out and look. At Jack's house we found that he was filling the drawers of the sideboard with heavy pieces of broken quartzite, and it took only a

FIGURE 44. These "broken rocks" from Buchanan Canyon are so obviously the work of man and so obviously not part of any of the then-accepted cultures at San Diego that they assumed great importance in compelling the recognition that there were other and earlier cultures present. (Photo courtesy of H. L. Minshall, from *The Broken Stones,* 1976)

glance to see that he did not have Diegueño, La Jollan, or San Dieguito pieces but blade and core work and lots of it.

He took us to immense surface sites that covered acres. These lay on old land surfaces well out of the reach of modern stream action, though some of the material had been worked down into modern streams, where, as it was moved along the streambeds by the winter rains, it had rapidly begun to show wear—wear: smoothing, not flaking. What is striking about this is that no one had seen this material before. We had walked over it and kicked it out of the way but not seen it. Jack saw it only when Minshall sharpened his eyes, showed him what to look for. Then, with his mind unclouded by professorial injunctions concerning the absence of Paleolithic man in America, he simply went out and saw what littered large areas of his local landscape.

In 1973 while excavating at Texas Street and again in 1976 while starting this book, I rented houses on the top of Mount Soledad, the height of land that has La Jolla wrapped around it. For decades I had worked on the lower terraces of Mount Soledad, for they represented the late Pleistocene and Recent and carried a considerable archeological record. Except for a couple of excursions to look at the soils on the upper terraces, I had spent no time on the higher parts of Mount Soledad. In 1973 I used a shortcut over the top of the mountain to go to the Scripps Institution of Oceanography. En route I passed a spot where cars had destroyed the vegetation and started some erosion. In the eroded area I saw groups of rocks, scattered just as they always are about a hearth, and so I stopped to look at the material. To my surprise, it was not late material, but it was work in light-colored quartzite, and, although it was mostly flake debris of nondescript type, I presently began to find material that suggested the blade and core stage. I showed this material to a number of people and suggested that something should be done about the materials on these areas, which were obviously soon going to be built on. In 1976 I did some more looking and found that this material was widespread. There were square-mile areas with thousands of hearths with stone flaking scattered around them. They were being rapidly destroyed by the land developers, who undoubtedly had been given clearances by archeologists who certified that there was nothing of interest or value on these ancient land surfaces.

It struck me, belatedly, that it was odd that I had never seen this material on the lower terraces, where I had spent so many years studying the soils, landforms, and archeology. I spent a few hours on a couple of days trying to see how far down I could trace this material. I could find none below the 250-foot level. Below that lay the broad 100- 60- and 25-foot terraces, and it gradually dawned on me that these sea stands must have erased the record on those lower levels. I had books to write and classes to teach, and I returned to Texas.

Jason Smith had invited his former professor, B. O. K. Reeves of the University of Calgary, down to look at the sites that he was digging on in the Torrey Pines Mesa, and Reeves became interested in the area. His background was geology and archeology, with special interest in the question of when corridors were open to let man come south from the arctic into the warmer parts of America. He returned in the spring of 1977 to take a further look at the area. He read Herb Minshall's book *The Broken Stones*, which told the story of our work in the area, with special emphasis on the early sites and on my work. Herb took him into the field to see the sites, then showed him the collections of artifacts. Reeves then made a survey of his own and found further sites. His most interesting finding, recorded in an unpublished report he filed with the San Diego Museum of Man, was that, while there was an abundance of evidence of the blade-and-core material on the high land surfaces, he could find none beneath a hundred-foot elevation. He concluded that this meant that the lower record had been erased by some sea stand below the hundred-foot level, and he took the Nestor terrace at sixty feet, with its associated uranium-thorium-dated coral, at 130,000 years as the likely event. Actually, there was a sea stand at 170,000 that could also have served. How interesting. It is the man from outside, with less prejudice, who can come into an area and see what the people who have lived and worked in the area for a lifetime cannot see.

The point should now be abundantly clear. There is an overwhelming mass of evidence for the blade and core stage at San

Diego. It appears on ancient land surfaces but not on those younger
than something like 130,000 to 170,000 years. It is in the ancient
valley fills and in the basal cobble strata of the canyon bottoms.
It is everywhere except in the museum collections, and it is not
there because they, the experts, neither saw nor believed and, worse,
until very recently adamantly refused to look. Well, if you will not
look, you cannot see, and if you do not believe you cannot see, and
if you are not informed, you cannot see. It is no wonder that we
really see so little.

To follow the line of thought on probabilities, we can now ask
what the chances are that man lived only at San Diego at this time.
The conclusion has to be that this is most unlikely, but rather that
man probably lived widely over America and that we should find
evidence of his presence elsewhere. If we cannot, then the San
Diego evidence is weakened, but if we can the San Diego evidence
is supported. We can begin by looking at the adjacent area.

THE CALICO SITE

In driving into the Mohave Desert in the old, open Model T
Ford that Rogers gave the museum and that we used as our field
car, Rogers once drove off toward some ridges running out from the
Calico Mountains near Barstow, and we stopped at the foot of
them and walked across the sands and up onto the ridge. Rogers
explained that he wanted to show me an old river channel that
contained rock the Indians had used as a quarry. We found an
immense amount of broken rock littering the surface and showing
all the normal signs of percussive flaking and breakage. The material was of varied ages, as shown by the differences in weathering,
especially the accumulation of desert varnish and ground patina,
which are accumulations of iron, manganese, and clay minerals that
come in time to coat stones on old, stable land surfaces in the
desert. We were very familiar with this phenomenon. It marked
crude tools lying on ancient land surfaces—arrow points never,
dart points rarely, crude knives regularly but faintly, heavier and
still cruder tools, usually and often very heavily.

As I have said, I do not just argue from weathering to age or
from typology to age. My preference is to compound the lines of
evidence: an ancient landform, on which lie crude tools, which

show extreme weathering. I doubt that there is any way to read that sequence except: great age. An old landform could have a beer bottle on it. A broken rock could have been produced by man looking for material for an ovate biface or an arrow point or a mineral specimen, but the weathering would be utterly different: fresh on the last two, heavy on the first. Of course, the weathering could vary with the rock type, sandblasting, or even micro-position, that is, minute differences in the topography where two pieces of stone lie. And yet when one sees an ovate biface embedded in a desert pavement (an old-age feature of the desert) and having the same degree of weathering as the ancient rocks in the ancient pavement, then, I submit, the age of the artifact is great, as established geomorphologically, chemically, and typologically.

On this ancient surface most of the tools had heavy coats of desert varnish, a sign of great antiquity. Rogers dismissed the site as a quarry, a source of raw materials, and of course "all on the surface." He had a fixation on surface archeology and a phobia against digging. Ruth De Ette Simpson, "Dee" to her innumerable friends, fortunately was not so inhibited. She had been making a survey of the archeology of the southern Mohave Desert (Simpson, 1958), and her attention had been called to artifacts exposed in the face of a mine pit in this area. When she showed the site to L. S. B. Leakey, he warned her against that particular spot since it could be the result of the reworking of material into a talus. "Dig here," he said, and with a crew of amateurs, often with no funding, dig she did, straight down in the desert that M. J. Rogers declared had no buried materials.

The material that she dug down through is cemented approximately to the hardness of weak concrete. All work was done by hand, with small tools and brushes. Everything was photographed, recorded, and labeled with maximum care. I have never seen a dig conducted with such extreme attention to the tiniest detail or one on which more material was saved with minute recording of the circumstances. Even her critics admit all of these facts. Yet the site has been a center of controversy, and, as at Texas Street, the points at issue are how old it is and whether it is evidence for man.

Estimates of the age of the site have been an exercise in extremism. At the Calico Conference, convened in 1970 to let many experts from several fields look at the site and the materials, the time range suggested varied from one million years to a few tens of thousands. If one rounds the estimates off, it means that an assemblage of experts, including geologists, soils men, and geomorphologists, many of them with wide experience in the Pleistocene and some with very specific experience in the Mohave, varied in their estimates by a factor of one hundred. It does not give one much confidence in the experts.

The site is generally agreed to be an alluvial fan built out from the Calico Mountains. At some time a fault at the foot of the mountains uplifted the fan, cutting it off from the mountains. The fan then underwent erosion to the extent that little if any of the original surface was left intact, but only a set of fingers with deep, wide valleys in between. In the cycle of erosion described by W. M. Davis the landform was approaching maturity in its stage of erosion, but this tells us nothing except that it is not young. The weathering phenomena are more interesting. The material is cemented throughout. It has usually been assumed that this cementation is due to calcium carbonate, the usual desert cementing material. However, I have found that the materials react rather weakly to acid, indicating that there must be something else cementing the material in addition to calcium carbonate. In trying to clean some artifacts for finer examination, I tried an acid bath with no result. I then tried removing the film on the stone with a fine steel point and found that I could remove a skin of translucent material. It had an opalescent sheen, and this meant it was material that I was familiar with: amorphous silica, material released in the weathering of rocks rich in silicates. This has turned out to be a major clue in the conflict over the site's age.

Soils men have noted that on the two sides of the Sierra Nevada in this part of California the soils age at totally different rates. The granitic soils on the Pacific slope age slowly in comparison with the volcanic soils on the desert side. The Calico site has young volcanics in it, and these rocks have often weathered to the consistency of soft cheese. They can be cut with a trowel. In their weathering, they must have released quantities of amorphous silica, and in this dry environment this material would not move far before it was redeposited, cementing the material by locking the sand grains together into the cementlike material that was encountered in the excavation. The addition of calcium carbonate would simply increase the cementing action. The result was a precociously old soil: a soil old beyond its years, a case of premature senility or at least premature maturity. One would think that the assembled experts would have noted this, but not so.

How then are we to judge the age of this site? The degree of erosion indicates some relatively large age. The weathering phenomena also indicate very considerable age, though surely not the million or half-million figures so carelessly tossed about. The surface features with the full development of desert pavement and the strong development of desert varnish and ground patina are features typical of Pleistocene-age landforms. The surface artifacts are a mixture and hard to deal with. There is a little quite young flaking and much very old flaking. In the erosion of this alluvial fan, some of the material once in place within the fan must now be on that eroded surface. It poses a tough problem.

The major part of the surface of the fan's cultural debris belongs in the ovate biface stage. While the placement of this material is not precise, it very clearly precedes the dart-point cultures of 10,000 years ago, and from the evidence at San Diego I would estimate that it was younger than the Texas Street material but older than the La Jollan material. Here it is on the surface, while the material at depth, as will be shown presently, belongs to the blade and core stage, the kind of material represented at Texas Street. Suddenly then we have the blade and core material established as much older than the ovate biface material. But we have gained relatively little, for the age of the ovate biface material is uncertain.

Brigham Arnold in his work on Lake Chapala in Baja California (1957) placed the ovate biface tools in the early Wisconsin, an age of perhaps 60,000 years or more on Evans' scale. This has been challenged, but the challenge is typical of the logical positivists at work: a maze of nitpickings that do not really disprove Arnold's work though, as always, they raise doubts. In general, the ovate biface work, when found on land surfaces in the desert, occurs only on old landforms, never on young ones. In degrees of weathering, especially in desert varnish and ground patina, it is in the same

order of magnitude as the blade and core material and much older
than the uniface material.

We have no real date yet for the Calico site, but we have some
bits and pieces that we can fit together. It is older than the ovate
biface stage, and this is older than the uniface stage, and the uniface
stage runs through the Wisconsin. The Calico material is clearly
blade and core material, and at San Diego this may date somewhere between 85,000 and 130,000 years. If we were just casually
to pick a round number, the indicated age would be 100,000 years.

My first visit to the site after Simpson began excavation impressed me with the evidence for man not nature. The pieces that
most impressed Simpson at that time were large, lumpy things that
vaguely resembled exceedingly crude hand axes. I had no doubt that
they had been man-made, for they had plural flake scars and no
battering, such as occurs in nature. These are what Minshall calls
skreblos. I was much more impressed by the concave scrapers (see
figure 42, above). These neat little tools were made on flakes or
thick pieces of stone. They had a crescent worked into one edge and
were exactly right for working on a round shaft, as in a spear. I
made one and tried it on a piece of desert hardwood and found
that it became dull within two minutes. I sharpened it by chipping
the edge of the concavity, and it worked well for perhaps three
minutes. In resharpening it again, I battered the ever-steepening
edge and thought I had ruined it. Not so; it was much more
efficient. Reflection and examination showed that I had moved from
a single edge to plural edges, essentially from a knife to a rasp. I
then went back to the concave scrapers in the Calico collection and
found that they too had battered edges inside the curve, just the
edge that man would be using. In examination of similar concave
scrapers from other sites of this uniface stage, I found similar tools,
with similar sharpening, and under the microscope there was obvious
wear on just these areas. I know of nothing but man that does this
sort of thing, though I will deal below with the notion that this is
just nature's way.

I paid particular attention to evidence for or against natural
breakage in the region of the Calico site. I could find no evidence
of percussive or pressure chipping by nature on the surface. I followed the course of the dry beds of the torrents that descended with

extremely steep gradients from the tops of the ridges. Whole cobbles, artifacts with thin edges, and thin flakes were carried down these rocky chutes, but I could find no evidence that any of this material was being flaked. I followed the material from the foot of a talus, where blocky pieces of chert entered a desert wash, downstream and found that the material rounded, as is entirely normal in stream action. I visited the shores of the ancient lakes and found that the surf from the huge lake that existed here had produced normal, well-rounded gravel. Nowhere in the entire environment could I find any deviation from the normal action of rounding and smoothing. The only possible exception was an exposure of glassy material embedded in the old lake sediments underlying the site. This material had a natural fracture pattern that produced longish pieces with rectangular cross sections. They lacked bulbs of percussion, fissures, eraillures, and all the other marks beloved of the lithic technologist. This was material in place in the geology, and any movement of such material by a stream, even a desert wash, would rapidly round it. My conclusion was that there was nothing in that environment that would break that rock in the manner of the pieces Simpson and her crew were finding.

Over a period of years I visited the San Bernardino County Museum to look over the material from the site as it went through the museum mill: cleaning, complete cataloguing, sorting, classification, photography, microscopic study, and so forth. The evidence of percussive flaking of stone was overwhelming. There were bulbs of percussion, double flakes, nests of tiny trimming flakes, indicating that at one spot people had sat and sharpened their stone tools. One really needed nothing more. On one visit a tray laid out caught my eye. It had elongate pieces with long flake scars running down their length. I had not seen this type of material before, and I began to paw excitedly through the tray. There were small blades scattered in the set. I was looking at blade and core work, and now it was appearing in the fine chalcedony of the Calico site. Chalcedony is an infinitely finer recorder than quartzite or porphyry. I could see the whole process; anyone with half a training in blade and core work could read this as he would read the newspaper. Simpson shared my excitement, and the next time I visited the museum she had quantities of the material laid out.

This is the material now under study by Clay Singer, an advanced graduate student at U.C.L.A. Clay was trained in lithic technology at U.C.L.A. and then had several years of field experience, notably two years in France working with the French lithic technologists: some of the world's best. There he met the European Paleolithic, and especially the blade and core work of the upper Paleolithic. He was persuaded—by what means I do not know, since he knew for certain that Calico was one of those chimeras that Heizer was so adamant about—to look at the material from one five-foot-square column through the site.

I met Clay Singer at Mary Ella Green's house. Mary Ella is one of Dee's devoted volunteers and was working on the lithic analysis with a microscope and a book on lithic technology. Clay had been through the books, the laboratories, and the field, and it was a pleasure to watch him work. Everything went under the microscope, including bits and pieces that would normally have been discarded from anyone else's site. Clay noted that these tiny bladelets showed use. Sometimes the use was as a borer, sometimes as a graver, and the difference showed under the microscope by the direction in which microflakes were pressed off, the areas that were polished, and the kind of striation that resulted from use. As Clay worked, he muttered, "Most American archeologists are still throwing away 90 percent of the tools they excavate." I had stumbled onto this twenty years earlier when I had put a set of La Jollan flake debris under the microscope and found that 90 percent showed traces of use. I was trying to find a means of differentiating a quarry site from an occupation zone, and it was easy once I went to the microscope. At a quarry, little or none of the flake debris showed evidence of use. On an occupation site, 90 percent showed use.

At a conference on early man held at San Diego in the spring of 1977, Clay presented some of the results of his analysis. First, the artifacts were not randomly scattered as they would be if nature produced them. Instead they were concentrated laterally and vertically. He differentiated fifteen tool types with eight subdivisions of scrapers alone: thirty-two types counting his subdivisions. He listed the frequency of evidence of use: 100 percent for most scrapers and borers and for beaked gravers and burins (sharp-pointed tools used for carving wood and bone). These were artifacts, not geofacts, and they were made and used on the spot, hence this was a site, not even a mere quarry.

The first of many reports on Calico is now available in *Pleistocene Man at Calico* (Schuiling, 1979). In it one will find not only Clay Singer's analyses but important supporting statements by John Witthoft, Alex Krieger, Alan Bryan, Phillip Tobias, Thomas Lee, and other archeological notables.

A new challenge has arisen: that the rocks were broken in mudflows. Vance Haynes (1973) has produced this thesis to account for the broken rock at Calico. Actually he has done much more. He has dredged up every cliché in the field and added a few hypothetical considerations. Haynes, who tries to maintain a reasonable approach, claims that he is only raising some alternative hypotheses. However, he has reached so far for his hypotheses that the result gives a good example of the frantic opposition.

First, it should be noted that the rock at Calico is broken to patterns that are well known in human work. The most convincing and conspicuous pattern is that produced by striking blades from cores. This requires the positioning of a block of stone in such a way that a series of blows on one end can remove a sequence of flakes that run down the face of the stone. Second, the work at Calico is predominantly but not exclusively in the very fine amorphous silica—chalcedony—found there; the splitting has been attributed to starch fracture in this material due to dehydration. But this does not explain why the same pattern is found there in other stones, such as jasper. Neither does it explain why this same longitudinal splitting occurs in many stone types elsewhere in southern California—in quartzite at San Diego and in basalt, quartz, porphyry, and other stones in the Imperial Valley, notably in the Yuha Desert. The breakage cuts right across all the lithic boundaries and includes stones for which the starch fracture argument is inapplicable.

These stones, fractured in this pattern that is known to be a human pattern, also occur in all kinds of geomorphic situations. At San Diego they can be shown to be lying on occupation floors, undisturbed by natural events since the day that man abandoned his campsite. They also occur in gravels, where they then show wea due to stream transport. At San Diego rocks broken to this pattern are found in clays, gravel trains, and alluvial fans lacking any trace of mudflows, in fine-grained alluvium, and on ancient land surfaces, as on top of Mount Soledad, where no stream, surf, avalanche, or mudflow could have been active within a million years. Large areas of this work have recently been found in the Poway area of San Diego, again on ancient land surfaces not subject to stream action or mudflow or avalanche. When this material enters the seasonal creek beds, it promptly shows wear and begins to round.

In the southwest corner of the Colorado Desert in the United States, the Yuha Desert, stones of every kind of lithology have been broken to this pattern and can be found lying on ancient beaches, incorporated in the beach and stream gravels, in ancient gravel trains of alluvial fans, and on desert surfaces, where neither running water nor desert sandblast has been able to touch them, leaving their surfaces nearly as fresh as when they were first fractured.

Since this particular type of breaking of stone is found in many kinds of stone, it cannot be a peculiarity of one stone or even of one class of stones. Since it is found in many geomorphic environments, it cannot be the product of any single peculiar geomorphic situation, such as a mudflow. We have already seen that streams cannot do this type of work, and, while the mudflow thesis seems improbable, we should in deference to Haynes's status and his article in *Science* deal with it more directly.

One may ask where the field or experimental evidence of the competence of mudflows to break rocks is. As we have seen in stream action, the addition of sand decreases chipping and wear and splitting. Increasing the fine material to greater amounts should further decrease these actions. Increase of fine materials to make a plastic mudflow would make it impossible to develop the high-velocity blow necessary to create percussion fracture. Similarly, cushioning a rock in a jellolike matrix of mud would allow it to move under pressure long before reaching a level of stress leading to pressure flaking. Theoretically, a mudflow could press one rock against another, but in mud both rocks could slide away, or, if one were fixed in a matrix, the other could slide past in the ooze. I fail to see how rock-fracturing forces could be generated anywhere along this continuum from normal stream through increasingly muddy stream to a plastic mass of mud and rock. The proponents of rock fracture in mudflows are hypothesizing not observing, and their hypothesis is counter to the experimental work so carefully reported by Kuenen and others.

Haynes's review of the alleged artifacts at Calico acknowledges conchoidal fracture, bulbs of percussion, faceted striking platforms, many examples of concave-convex flakes showing positive and negative scars parallel to each other, some steeply worked edges suggesting scrapers, and a few bifacially flaked pieces. The list can be expanded greatly: hammer stones of two types, anvils, concave scrapers showing wear on the concavity, fluted cores with prepared platforms, struck blades, and a complete industry of tiny bladelets resembling a microblade industry with obvious wear on the working edges. The contrast with the expected fracture pattern as developed experimentally by Kuenen could not be greater. One can say with great confidence that this is not the result of stream action. But is it the result of mudflows?

If this material was produced by mudflows, then it was a frequent or usual product. Haynes mentions that there are hundreds of these broken pieces that may or may not be artifacts; actually there are thousands. Whatever force was breaking this rock, it was doing so with great frequency. Now, if this force was the mudflow, then it should have operated uniformly. Every mudflow, or at least many mudflows, should have broken some rock. There should then be a relatively uniform distribution of the broken rock through the deposit. This is strikingly far from true. The broken rock is strongly concentrated in a few levels. Haynes refers to the material as randomly distributed through eight to ten feet of gravel, as is required by his mudflow theory. Actually the material is concentrated in specific levels, as would occur with human occupation, and the depth of artifact material in the master pits exceeds twenty feet rather than Haynes's eight to ten feet.

Haynes leaves no stone unturned in his determination to discredit the Calico site and plows ahead with his alternative explanations, none of which are applicable when the material is carefully studied. Nevertheless Haynes's criticism brings together the usual objections in one concise package and is useful if only for this. The objections are enumerated under five headings. The first includes natural fracturing at outcrops by tectonic stress, weathering, freezing, solar heating, and so on to produce polyhedral fragments with sharp edges. Of these, breaking of rock by solar heating was long ago shown by experimental work to be nonexistent. The rest are acceptable, though none of them produces the gamut of evidence of flaking described by Haynes himself, and as Kuenen and others have reported even very short transportation promptly rounds such material. Weathering and freezing produce not bulbs of percussion but granular parting surfaces, not even faintly like percussion- or pressure-created surfaces.

Haynes's second series of processes is free fall, tumbling, sliding, and intergranular pressure. Free fall is restricted to cliffs and will break rock percussively, but there are no cliffs at any of the sites repeatedly referred to here: Calico and San Diego (Texas Street, Buchanan Canyon, Mount Soledad, the Yuha Desert, etc.). Tumbling down talus slopes has never been demonstrated to break rock to give artifactlike material, nor has a steep talus slope at Calico been demonstrated for this material to tumble down. The short talus exposed at the current chert outcrop contained nothing remotely artifactual ten years ago, though it is loaded with archeologists' practice flaking debris today. One would think that archeologists would be more sensitive to site pollution, but they frequently are not. To argue that the flaking requires a slope or a cliff and hence that cliffs must have existed would be to engage in circular reasoning. Intergranular pressure means rock pressing on rock, here in an assumed landslide—again, assumed as needed and, again, with no hard field data to show that any landslide anywhere produced artifactual material. Settling has occurred in the Calico site, and artifacts caught in this action are characteristically snapped at right angles. Using Barnes's platform-angle method would certify that these breaks are due to nonhuman forces; such breaks also lack bulbs of percussion and all other signs of human work.

Haynes's third group of processes—and on this he makes categorical statements—is that tumbling down slopes and transport by water and mudflows will cause abrasion, battering, and flaking. Abrasion and battering, yes. But, again, Kuenen and the direct observation and experimental literature show no evidence to support flaking, though one often finds flaking simply assumed.

Haynes's statement that "the pressure of a tough rounded rock against an edge of chert can produce a pressure flaked edge that can be indistinguishable from a man made pressure flaked edge" is true, as far as it goes, but it does not specify what situation in nature ever does this. Further, it cannot very well be used as evidence that man did not flake the edge. We know that man flakes stone with great frequency in this way, and if nature does it at all it is a very rare occurrence. At Calico the established phenomenon is a high frequency of breakage, and this indicates human work, not natural work. The argument runs: we know in absolute terms that man so flakes stone and that when he does so he does a lot of it. Hypothetically, but not demonstratedly, nature may occasionally do this, but if so it is random and rare, and the mechanism by which nature does this is obscure at best. Since the situation at Calico is that there is a lot of this flaking and this fits human tool-making patterns, it is much more likely the work of man than of nature. It is a bit unfair to belabor Haynes, a geologist, when the archeologists are equally confused.

Haynes is not the only target of this criticism. Alan Bryan, who at times can be a stout champion of the antiquity of man in America, looked over a lot of Calico material at the Friends of the Pleistocene meeting at San Diego in 1975 and said that a number of the pieces were probably the work of man. "Ah, then you accept it as a site," I said. "Ah no," he replied, "you have to have more than that." I was a while in finding out what lay behind his "that." A site, to the nitpickers, has to have a whole set of attributes: artifacts, food debris, living floors, and preferably some fingerprints on the nearest rock. I exaggerate, but then so do they. The battle long raged simply over the question of whether or not man had been present at this spot. Acceptance of the artifacts settles that question. But was this a living site, a campsite? The archeologist is asking us to go a step farther, and, fortunately, Simpson and her cohorts can do so. When it can be shown that the artifacts were not only made there but used there, then one is approaching proof of the existence of a site in the strictest sense. Clay Singer's work establishes that the tools were made at Calico and used there.

Near the bottom of the site, careful work has exposed a set of elongate stones arranged with their noses all pointing in, toward the center of a circle. It strongly suggests a hearth. A stone was taken out, sawed into cubes, and analyzed for magnetization. If the stone were heated more on one end than on the other, then there should be changes in the magnetic alignment of the iron in the stone. The changes were there, indicating that the stone had been heated at the inner end of the circle, just as it would be in a hearth. These stones also offer opportunities for thermoluminescence dating.

The picture is additive again. We have a set of tools of known pattern. They show all the distinctive marks of percussive flaking. They have marks that show they were not only made here but used here. There is even a group of rocks that have all the characteristics of a hearth. Near the hearth, there are some enigmatic stone alignments. Unfortunately, not enough of these can be seen at the bottom of the twenty-foot shafts so far excavated to know what the pattern is. Stone alignments are well known on the ancient surfaces of the desert, and they are often seemingly aimless lines of stones, just as these, so far as they can now be seen, appear to be. On the other hand, on those same ancient desert surfaces, there are stone circles, often called house circles, though there are other possibilities (Carter, 1964*b*). We need to remove about twenty feet of concrete-hard overburden over about a fifty-by-fifty-foot square. Dee has her workers at the job, working their way down with dental picks and whisk brooms, and in five or ten years we might know about these stone alignments. Since the museum already bulges with artifacts and the hillside is stacked with them, I have suggested that we have more than enough, and that it is time to call in the backhoe and get on down there and seek answers. For this, Dee has offered to toss me out of the Mohave. She is a purist.

L. S. B. Leakey got to the site about once a year, and in order to oversee what was being done he requested that all workable stone and all stone that showed any sign of breakage be stockpiled, so that he could see what they were throwing away as well as what they were saving. It sounded like a whimsical request, but seldom has a whim paid off so well. This was a most unfamiliar industry, and neither Dee nor her workers could recognize all of its parts. The result is that the stockpiles, as they are called, are gold mines. The heavy hammers, the large cores, and a host of other odd items are carefully saved and stored on the hillsides above the site in long, wormlike piles of stone—one line for each five-foot square, with the materials roughly placed by level. When I examined them in 1976, I was astounded to find enough definitive artifact material in the stockpiles to fill a museum. When I excitedly expostulated at this waste, Dee pointed out that the San Bernardino County Museum already was bursting at the seams with Calico material.

This triggered a curious argument at a conference on early man held at Vancouver during the Pacific Science Congress meeting in 1976. It was argued that since there was material in the stockpile that was as good as any in the museum—a vast exaggeration—then none of the material was artifactual. I have been on many sites where great piles of discarded artifactual material have been left behind. It is commonplace to leave more than one takes, but it is most unusual to leave material in such orderly assemblages that the information it bears can be redeemed. But that is the nature of the Calico dig; it is extraordinarily well done. Work continues at a slow pace. The site is a state park, open to visitors and well worth seeing. It is a classic site for early man in America, of comparable age to Texas Street, whatever that may prove to be when we have radiometric dates.

THE EAST RIM SITE

The ovate biface stage in America is anything but well established, despite the fact that these artifacts are much like the hand axes of Eurasia and are the kind of thing most likely to be recognized and accepted as artifacts by professionals and amateurs alike. A model report on an ovate-biface site has been done by John Alsozatai-Petheo, who, as will be seen, is hardly a madcap enthusiast for early man in America. He has made available a copy of his master's thesis, written for George Agogino at the University of Eastern New Mexico. I wrote George to say that he should have given John a Ph.D.

John A&P, as he is known to many of his friends, noted in his introduction that the majority opinion in 1975 still was that the big game hunters of about 12,000 years ago were the first entrants into America. From supposedly tenuous claims made in 1930, this stage has come to be widely accepted, while the claims for earlier levels are still described as tenuous. "Tenuousness" is an interesting concept. The finds in 1930 were of fluted points right in the skeletons of extinct buffalo. What is tenuous about that? Unexpected, hard to adjust to, difficult to swallow for men who believed America had only a 5,000- or 10,000-year history and thought that this evidence spelled 25,000 years—but hardly tenuous. John was right of course in describing the pre–fluted point stages as still tenuous in the eyes of the majority of the American archeologists. John's aim was to test a site of this alleged earlier stage in hopes of presenting less than tenuous evidence, and he selected the surface material at the East Rim Site, a duplicate of the Calico site's surface material.

This material was named the Lake Mannix lithic industry by Dee Simpson when she discovered these sites during her survey of the Mohave prior to beginning her work at Calico. Lake Mannix was a huge lake that occupied the area about Yermo in the Mohave desert. It was clearly a Pleistocene lake, and these sites were found around its highest, oldest shorelines. The lithic assemblage is quite distinctive, resembling in no way, form, function, weathering, or location the well-known later material that spans the last 12,000 years. The last of the lakes that once were sprinkled over the Great Basin have carbon-14 dates of 8,000 to 10,000 years, and it is on these lakeshores that fluted points are found—the traces of the Great Hunters, the alleged first Americans. If the distinctive traits of this clearly different culture point to a greater age, then a pre–big game hunter level in America would be established. Since all the features of the site (lithic work, weathering phenomena, location, and so forth) indicate greater age, the answer seems obvious. But if a person has been trained to see things one way, the obvious is most difficult to see. This truism applies to all. The Navy rejected submarines; the Army, automatic weapons (both invented in America); geology, Wegener's theory of drifting continents; biology, Mendel's genetics. The list could be expanded indefinitely. John A&P set himself the formidable task of presenting so overwhelming a case that by sheer overkill he would change the mind-set of his profession. Better that than to be exiled to Belgium as Browning, the inventor of automatic weapons, was.

John decided to do an intensive survey of an area selected for its lack of disturbance and its evidence of occupation, and the East Rim site provided him just that. It was in a remote area, and no one would bother or had bothered the primitive lithic industry on that surface. For a section about 50-by-30 yards (440 square meters) a grid was laid out, and every stone was charted as to its position, examined, and classified as artifact (modified by man) or natural stone. Extreme care was given to controls on collecting, labeling, mapping, and photographing. Tools and possible tools, flakes and debitage (4,862 pieces) were set aside, examined with a microscope for use wear, and classified by types, by weathering phenomena, and by location.

A review of the geology of the area led him to struggle with the relationship of the alluvial fan on whose surface this lithic material had accumulated. The history of Lake Mannix indicates a glacial-pluvial age for the two major stands and a Recent date (less than 10,000-year age) for a late minor stand. Direct linkage of any of these lakes to the East Rim site is tenuous (how often we have to use that word), though the probability seems high that the site was occupied when one of the early lake stands made this a shoreline area. There is no other reason for man to have lived in this area, and, as we will see, there is botanical evidence for the proximity of the lakeshore.

The surface soil is revealing. It is a strongly developed desert soil. Haynes says of a similar soil at the Calico site that it is more strongly developed than that of mid-Wisconsin soils elsewhere in the southwestern United States. I have examined the mid-Wisconsin and post-Wisconsin soils of the Lahontan Basin, both firmly dated, and both show slight development compared to such surface soils as those at the Calico site. If the East Rim site is comparable to the Calico site, then the soil is old indeed.

Advanced age for the soil is supported by the pollen analysis, for while the surface has modern pollen the subsurface has pine pollen, even some possible Abies (spruce) pollen. John obtained his pollen samples by lifting stones in the desert pavement and taking pinches of earth from beneath them, an imaginative procedure now being adopted by others with equally interesting results though usually with no credit to John. The pine-pollen count reaches the astonishing level of 75 percent of all pollen. Pines produce abundant pollen and send it forth on the wind. They do so today, and yet no pine pollen from the distant mountains now reaches the area. We must conclude that pine forests were nearby during this soil's lifetime. There is also pollen from lakeshore plants. This guarantees that some lake stage was high enough to bring shore features close to the site. This is very unlikely to have been one of the lower lake stands of Recent time and very likely was one of the high lake stands in full glacial time, which would here be a pluvial time. We have C-14 dates on the end of the high lake levels about 20,000 years ago, and these are the uttermost minimal dating for the lake plants and pine pollen. The probable date is older and possibly as much as two or three times as old, for, if the cold cycle that created the early lake stand is not the 20,000-year one, then the next falls at 60,000, and the next at 110,000. Comparison of degrees of weathering suggest a 60,000-year date at least.

This old desert pavement was already in existence during some phase of the lake's existence, and it cannot have been a late, minor Recent lake, for the pine pollen demands a full glacial cooling to bring any pine even within wind-dispersal range. Such pollen changes are well known as measures of a full glacial time in the Great Basin. Phil Orr reported them for the caves he excavated on the Lake Lahontan shorelines in Nevada. The age of the surface soil is then fixed as at least last-glacial age and probably older than the 20,000-year lake stand and hence more likely the 60,000-year pluvial.

The site is a desert pavement today. This results from the removal of fine material, leaving only a layer of stone to pave the surface. Once the surface is covered with stone, it is like a tile floor, and wind and the sheet wash of desert rains cannot touch it. It is an armored surface, paved, and will persist indefinitely until some condition changes, such as an arroyo's undercutting the landform. Scholars argue whether wind removal or water removal of soil concentrates the rocks at the surface, and it is probable that both work in concert to produce the removal of the finer materials, leaving the rocks. Heated argument surrounds the age of desert pavements. Cooke (1970) quoted E. L. Davis as dating artifacts with desert varnish on these old pavements as not more than 5,000 to 8,000 years old. Davis' thinking has changed, and she would probably add some years. I would add a cipher, and John A&P's data support a minimum of last-glacial age for some of these features, and not necessarily the oldest ones at that.

Alsozatai-Petheo also considered the desert varnish and ground patina. Varnish is the mahogany stain on the upper part of the rock lying in a desert pavement, and ground patina is the orange stain on the underside of the rock. This phenomenon has been known but little studied until recently (Laudermilk, 1931; Bard, 1979). Blackwelder (1931) hypothesized that it came from manganese from plants—lichens, pollen, and so forth—which was baked onto the stones. The hypothesis soon became fact by the interesting scientific method of repetition, with an added degree of certainty accompanying each repetition. The whole subject is under active investigation now, and it is found that the major part of the varnish is composed of clay minerals, which are added to the stone from the environment. Dorn (1980) has taken a huge step beyond Bard's work by showing that desert varnish is not confined to deserts but is a general phenomenon found in all climates. The concentration of manganese and iron, so evident in Bard's work, proves to be due to bacteria. We now know most of what we need to know about rock varnish, except for the cause of the long delay before varnish begins to appear. It is clear that, while there are variables in the rate of accumulation, there is no varnish on the late dart and arrow-point material. It is also exceedingly rare on the early dart points of 10,000-year age, but it marks the pre-10,000-year materials heavily whenever they are on old, stable landforms where the material can accumulate (see table 4). The material at the East Rim site is heavily coated, quite in keeping with a pre–Great Hunter age.

Of greatest importance at the East Rim site is the evidence that this was more than a quarry site; this material has usually been sluffed off as preforms, quarry debris, and other debitage. Analysis of the flakes, cores, and flaking debris showed that there were finished tools present and that under the microscope many showed use wear. Further, the finished tools were strongly concentrated in a cleared area. The desert pavement in this area was composed of small stones; the large stones had been removed. The desert stains and soil development in the feature were equal to those outside it. It is, then, a very old clearing. The lithic material, the rock broken by man, was produced by direct percussion. Block-on-block (slamming a large rock against an anvil rock) was commonly used for the initial breaks. The large flakes so produced were then usually

TABLE 4

Desert Varnish

Deposits on	Amount				Time (in thousands of years)
	None	Light	Moderate	Heavy	
Arrow points	x				2
Late dart points	x				5
Early dart points	x	x			10
Uniface		x	x		50
Biface			x	x	60
Blades			x	x	100
Steep edge work				x	?

NOTE: Desert varnish combines a film of clay minerals with the accumulation of iron and manganese and traces of other minerals. The manganese accumulation is due to bacteria. Some varnish may be 300,000 years old, and all varnish may be datable. If so, there will be a revolution in archeological dating in America. Here the first three dates are good approximations; the next three are open to question.

worked by hard hammers and only occasionally by soft hammers. The industry is described as a well-developed, highly integrated, and functional productive technique. This recalls John Witthoft's description of the Texas Street blade and core material as the most sophisticated blade and core material known to him in the world. Beauty lies in the eye of the beholder, and it takes a lithic expert to see these early lithic tools for what they are: the product of highly functional lithic technologies able to produce simple but effective stone tools. It is of particular interest that John Alsozatai-Petheo notes the presence of both natural and prepared platforms and successive double flakes. The appearance of these flakes in a stone pavement and in a very clear site further undermines the argument that nature makes them. Man surely produces them quite regularly. If nature perhaps does so, no one has demonstrated how or when or under what circumstance.

Tool types are described as bifacially flaked massive chopping tools, ovate bifaces, smaller bifacially flaked tools with straighter edges, wedge-shaped bifaces, bifacial cutting tools, scrapers (end, side, convex, concave) made on flakes and showing edge retouch and wear, small utilized flakes, and utilized cores showing edge wear. Hammer stones and pecking stones were present. An assemblage composed of ovate bifaces, chopping tools, end scrapers, and cutting tools form the single largest tool group at the site. They occurred in well-delineated areas isolated from the workshop areas and fit the requirements of butchering tools. Other tool groups represent finer cutting and working activities and are located separately, just as they would be in a camp where women worked here and men there. The striking thing is that the ovate-biface assemblage is precisely like material seen elsewhere. As Alsozatai-Petheo comments, the proliferation of ovate-biface shapes throughout various functional types of tools points to a stylistic preference. This is not only clear evidence of man at work, but it establishes a cultural marker. It is totally distinct from the La Jollans with their preference for unifacial work and from the Texas Street site where the preference was for striking blades from cores.

Alsozatai-Petheo found an attempt to relate this material to other sites difficult due to the lack of reporting comparable to his own. He found the attempts to set up cultural sequences impressionistic, and of M. J. Rogers' shifting terminology he commented: "Problems in terminology and definition . . . make this scheme fairly meaningless. . . ." This is a view with which I heartily concur. Of William Wallace's dictum (1962) that there is no early man, Alsozatai-Petheo snorts, "he sounds like Hrdlička." And at this point one begins to feel that a yeast is finally leavening the heavy dough of American archeology. Some of the youngsters are in revolt against the orthodoxy.

In a survey of the ideas of others (Daugherty, Davis, Brott, M. J. Rogers, Jennings), Alsozatai-Petheo makes abundantly clear without quite being blunt that their so-called early period of about 9000 B.C. with its lanceolate points and crescents is not what is present on the surface at the East Rim site. Further, he shows that there is a well-known sequence from Daugherty's "Intermontane Western Tradition" (1962), Jennings' "Desert Culture" (1964), and Davis and Brott's "Western Lithic Co-Tradition" (Davis, Brott, and Weide, 1969)—all of these are much the same thing, early phases of the dart-point stage in America about 12,000 years ago —to the historic cultures. The point is clear enough. There is no room in the last 12,000 years for the lithic industry of the East Rim site, but there it is—and older it not only has to be, but older is what all the evidence says it is.

John A&P notes the presence of other sites of this type in the same area, notably those found by Simpson in her survey of the Mohave Desert, but also those discovered by Glenman on a dissected fan 174 feet above and one and one-half miles away from the Lake Mohave shoreline. At the Lake Mohave site, the artifact assemblage includes bifaces, flake scrapers, plano-convex tools, and choppers. This seems either to be a mixed site or to mark a transitional site between the ovate-biface and the uniface stage. Comparing Lake Chapala, the site in Baja California dominated by ovate bifaces, with the East Rim, John Alsozatai-Petheo pronounces the resemblances superficial because details are not reported with the intensive care his study gives the East Rim. This is a bit like saying of two sites containing fluted points, one of which also had every flake examined and the other not, that there are superficial resemblances. The difference is in the reporting, not in the material there. Ovate bifaces appear as mixtures in later sites, but in pure sites they are a signature, the clear evidence of a cultural stage, and that is what Brigham Arnold reported for Lake Chapala.

When I was working with M. J. Rogers in the Mohave Desert, we saw many of these sites. The first that we found, as I recall, was near Clark Mountain in Nevada. An ancient alluvial fan had been dissected lightly, leaving the usual flat areas between the stream channels isolated from deposition, and these flat surfaces had undergone just enough erosion to leave a layer of rock on the surface, the familiar desert pavement. This had, as usual, accumulated a coating of desert varnish. Scattered on these surfaces were ovate bifaces made of a rock that, in weathering, lost much of its weight and took on the aspects of vast age. M. R. Harrington of the Southwest Museum in Los Angeles had also found these sites and showed some of the material to Rogers. I recall clearly Rogers' glee in being able to tell Harrington exactly where he had found them. It is not a minor point. The sites are there, several people have found them, the artifacts are in the museums, or at least in some museums. They are so characteristic with their oval plan and sinuous edges resulting from the heavy hammer flaking that they are recognizable as easily as a fluted point. They have been passed off all too often as preforms, something roughed out in preparation for making a finer tool, or as quarry rejects. But this is the hypothesis, treated

as fact, that John Alsozatai-Petheo shot stone dead by his meticu-
lous, time-consuming, detailed study of the East Rim site. He
showed that these are the characteristic implements of a people that
differed in their tool-making pattern from the several other early
cultures in the Americas. They are clearly later than the blade and
core stage, for their material overlies the material buried in the fan
at the Calico site, and they very probably are pre–La Jollan.

THE YUHA DESERT

With Rogers I spent many days in the Colorado Desert, the
low desert around the Imperial Valley of California, extending
from the lower reaches of the Colorado River on down into Mexico. It is a land of blazing hot summers and beautiful, mild winters,
which have made it a winter resort area in recent decades. We spent
hours on the terraces of the Colorado and days on the ancient alluvial
fans with their desert pavements and weeks on the beach lines of
the former lake that occupied the Imperial Valley. The lakeshore is
only about 500 years old, and it was strewn with pottery, arrow
points, shell beads, and the debris of the people of that time.

The ancient river terraces were enigmatic. They had stone
circles in their stone pavements, and we thought these to be house
sites. They were obviously very old, for the stones raked aside to
make the clearing were now as heavily varnished as the stones that
had never been disturbed. Usually we found no stone tools with
the circles, and this puzzled us. Since then it has appeared that
such circles can be made by man for several uses. They may be
ceremonial markings, they may be the mark of a former storage pit,
or they may be a clearing made for the drying and winnowing of
plants to obtain their seeds. None of these activities requires stone
tools.

The desert pavements also retain the trails of the ancient
people, and along these trails one finds a galaxy of debris. There
are trail shrines, heaps of stone to which each passerby added one.
There are broken pieces of pottery; careful collecting will yield
enough pieces to allow someone with infinite time and patience to
restore a whole pot. Occasionally one will see to one side of a trail
a block of stone that has been broken up to gain a supply of chips
suitable for making tools. Sometimes the stone sits there with its

fresh surfaces contrasting so sharply with the dark color of the desert pavement surrounding it that it is as obvious as a lighthouse. At other times it shines only dimly, for the passage of time has begun to varnish the fresh exterior and the flakes lying around it. And sometimes there is a whole range of flakes with differing degrees of varnish up to quite fresh, showing that men at various times visited this rock to test its tool-making quality and to get a flake or two to suit their needs.

Rogers never found the keys to this desert surface material. We mostly found just flakes, often with immense amounts of desert varnish, as much varnish as covered the geologically old surfaces on which the flakes lay. Since Rogers considered this a poor land if not a bad land, he used the term *Malpais* (from the Spanish) for it and so designated the crude, desert-varnished material that he collected from these surfaces. As the rocks cleared from stone circles showed, desert varnish can reform, and so it is possible that Rogers was lumping a rather wide range of material into one basket. When I examined his type specimens, the basis for his Malpais as published in *Ancient Hunters of the Southwest* (Rogers, 1966), it became obvious that he had done so. He had used desert varnish as his sole criterion, and he had a strange mixture of crude and fine tools lumped together.

The keys to the situation were to be found decades later by Morlin Childers of El Centro. Morlin is another of the bright amateurs, blessed with unending energy and a sharp eye and unhindered by an education that closed his mind to possibilities. He began by collecting fossils in the Borrego Badlands and has a number of new species named for him. He also has traveled widely in Baja California and is well known to and friendly with the remaining Indian bands there. He did so much work on the delta of the Colorado River, with its tidal bore, that he became an authority on that unusual area. Belatedly he turned his interest to archeology and especially to looking for early man. His was the naive view: he knew neither where to look nor where not to look. He was equally naive about broken rocks. He would look at anything that was out of the ordinary. Ah, the blessings of being unprejudiced by a narrow education but intelligently curious, and perceptive.

Years of work in the desert had equipped Morlin for traveling freely over it, and he knew a great deal of it well. Because of this familiarity, he was often asked to help geologists in their work in the Yuha Desert. The Yuha Desert is the southwesternmost corner of the Imperial Valley, a little rectangle of land with the Peninsular Range to the west, the cultivated Imperial Valley to the east, the Mexican border to the south, and highway 101 running through Plaster City to the north. In this work Childers became acquainted with the shorelines that were higher than those Rogers and I had worked on, which were a mere 500 years old. The ones we had studied ran around the Imperial Valley at an elevation of 40 feet above sea level and were as fresh as daisies and sprinkled with pottery, arrow points, shell beads, and other recent debris. Above them at 100 feet and 150 feet were more shorelines, and, to continue the daisy simile, they had wilted a bit in the desert sun and occasional downpours. But they are very definitely there and in some areas surprisingly well preserved. On these well-preserved areas, the remains of man's occupation are liberally strewn on their surfaces just as they are on the later beach line. These were very advantageous places to live. Man had water in the desert, fish, shell-fish, waterfowl, and the vegetation of the lake's edge, some useful for tools and some edible. And then there were all the resources of the land. But the tools on these lakeshores were utterly different from those of the well-known later Indians. There were no pottery, no arrowheads, not even dart points. Any observer was at once on notice that the ages of these features were beyond 10,000 years. Dates from these beaches now show that they are roughly 50,000 for the 150-foot beach and 28,000 years for the 100-foot beach. This poses interesting problems.

There is no way that lakes at such an elevation can be formed in the Imperial Valley today, for the height of land that separates the valley from the sea, the Gulf of Baja California, is only forty feet high, and that was what set the height of the lake that occupied the valley up to 500 years ago, a time so close to the historic that it is possible the first Spaniards saw the Imperial Valley not as desert mostly below sea level, but as a vast inland sea stretching to the northwest and leading them to believe that California was an island cut off from the mainland (Carter, 1964a).

How then are we to account for these shorelines so high above a possible lake? And lakes they were, for the shell in the shorelines is that of freshwater species. Attempts have been made to conjure up dams of sufficient height, but I have never seen any evidence for this, and we have a better mechanism at hand. The Imperial Valley is the result of action along the largest fault line in California, the San Andreas fault, which runs on the east side of the valley. There is an almost equally large one on the west side of the valley, the San Jacinto fault, and the floor of the valley undoubtedly is lined with parallel faults. All of this is due to the rifting away of Baja California and southwestern California from the continent. The earth's crust is splitting along the line of the Gulf of California and the Imperial Valley, and the split runs on up through California to go out to sea just north of San Francisco. Along this line earthquakes are frequent, and the earth jumps and slides along. In crustal activity this area is the exact opposite of the San Diego area one hundred miles to the east. The floor of the Imperial Valley is sinking rapidly, and its western margin is rising rapidly. The sinking of the valley floor is measured by its being 130 feet below sea level, and the rising of its western margin is measured by, among other things, the presence of lake shorelines at elevations impossible for the present valley conformation. As the Peninsular Range rose, it carried upward the evidence of old lakeshores that ran along its foot slopes in times past. The mountain range has risen about 100 feet since the lake existed on whose shores man lived.

The rates of sinking and uplift have been calculated by seismologists and geophysicists through gravity-anomaly measurements and by actual surveys that show the rate of change. Change in the Imperial Valley can be drastic. After an earthquake the highways may be offset several feet laterally and have to be realigned. On the valley margins there may be not only slippage but uplift or, in the valley, downthrow. It is an active region. When we were debating former dams or uplift, I calculated the amount of uplift that would happen in 50,000 years if the current rates of uplift were constant, and the figure came out about the right amount to account for the beach lines we were looking at. The rate probably has not been constant, and an exact fit is not expected, but the partial fit tends to support the idea that these features have been uplifted this much, about fifty to a hundred feet in 50,000 years. The dates seem reasonable, but that leaves other problems.

Where did all the water come from to form an immense freshwater lake in the desert trough known as the Imperial Valley or the Salton Sink? We know that the lake of 500 years ago was fed by the Colorado River, which spilled to the west into the Imperial Valley, filling it with fresh water—something that it started to do again in 1916 and that was stopped by heroic measures by the railroads. There would be times when the river could not spill into the Salton trough. One of these would be when the sea level was down during glacial times, for then the river would cut a deep valley to the lower sea level, about 300 feet lower than the present, and the river would then be running about 200 feet below even the bottom of the Imperial Valley. Only during interglacial times, when the seas rose due to the melting of the ice, would the river valley be filled and rise to a level where it could spill to the west, into the Imperial Valley. This is an event for which we now have some time estimates. The sea stood at its present elevation or higher about 5,000, 40,000, and 85,000 years ago, to pick a few of the later times, and freshwater lakes could be expected in the valley at those times. With the valley floor sinking and the western flanks rising, it is a little hazardous to make correlations over any great length of time. If the sea stood appreciably higher 5,000 years ago, there should have been a freshwater lake in the valley. Just such a lake may be recorded by the older tufa, the calcareous deposit made in desert lakes, for there are layers to the tufa and only the outer layers belong to the 500-year lake. Lakes would be expected about 40,000 and 80,000 years ago, and the dates from the 100- and the 150-foot beaches seem to be related to the 40,000-year episode. However, some of these stands are so high that one could expect not fresh water but salt water, and, not surprisingly, we do have marine shell appearing above the present 100-foot level. Unfortunately not all of the details of these episodes have been worked out. The gist of this is that, given some knowledge of the local geology and the relationships of sea level to the geomorphology, the beaches are expectable at about their given elevations at about the dates assigned to them (White, Carter, and Childers, 1979).

The beach lines near Plaster City dated at 50,000 years are strewn with blade-and-core material. The suggested date is much younger than that at either San Diego or Calico, and this raises some questions. Which dates are wrong? Or are they both right, and have we in the Yuha Desert a classic case of extreme cultural lag? There are abundant cases of this sort of thing. South Texas had people who both physically and culturally apparently represented some of the earliest people in America. They were isolated survivals from some very early time. The Yuha Desert could have served as just such a refuge. Or the dates could be wrong. Shell dates are notorious for being more variable than charcoal dates. Or the stone tools may have been reworked into the beaches. They often are enormously worn, but the marks that they bear today are those of wind erosion. These hard stones have been sandblasted until sometimes they are no longer recognizable as artifacts and only the concentration of imported stones onto these sandy beach ridges indicates that this was man's work. At other times, the outline of the tool remains, though all the signs of man's chipping are gone. Fortunately, some of this material was left on areas of desert pavement, where no sandblast touched it, and the artifacts are in nearly mint condition.

These show that a fully developed blade and core industry existed here. There are great numbers of cores and blades. In some areas the flakes struck from cores can be fitted back onto the core. Morlin Childers has many examples with several flakes restored but usually with one or two missing. These refitted flakes reveal the technology in fine detail. Either natural or prepared platforms were used for striking the blades. The preference was for striking behind the intersection of two planes, which was usually formed by the removal of bladelike flakes from the core. The result is that most of the blades are triangular in cross section (see figure 45). Most have two scars from earlier flakes on their upper surfaces, and a plane flake scar on their lower surface. The blades commonly run to a point, and the much-used cores also develop a characteristic pointed lower end. The blades and cores retain all the classic marks of percussion: eraillures, bulbs, fissure lines—everything that the lithic technology manuals call for. Equally interesting is the range of material used: porphyry, quartz, metabasalt with a texture almost as glassy as flint, coarser basalts, silicified sediments—every kind of

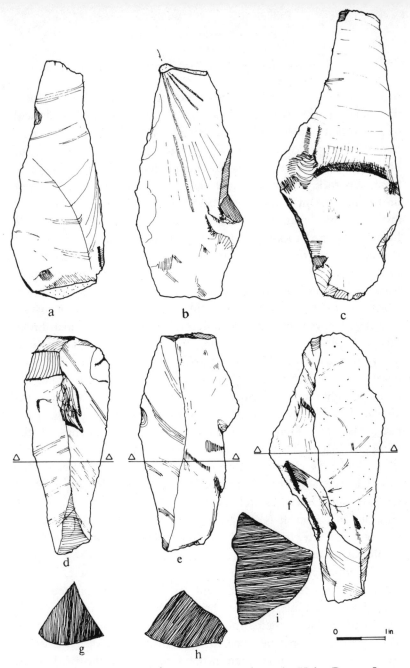

FIGURE 45. The heavy blades shown here are from the Yuha Desert, Imperial County, California. The ventral (*a*, *b*, and *c*) and dorsal (*d*, *e*, and *f*) views of these blades are shown so that the classic lines of force can be shown. As the cross sections (*g*, *h*, and *i*) show, these are thick, generally triangular blades. All three were struck from cores from which other blades had already been removed.

rock available and flakable. One cannot argue starch fracture for a phenomenon such as this. It is a case of man's impressing his will on the rock to create tools to a definite pattern, one that we now have seen on the coast and in the Mohave in a still wider range of lithic materials. Here on this low desert floor, there is no frost to break this rock, and there is not enough vegetation to create forest fires. And the myth that desert sun breaks rock is simply that—a myth. The breaks are not chemical. One can run through the whole litany of alleged rock-breaking factors and find that none of them will account for the phenomenon. Streams will not do it, as we have so clearly shown, and anyway, as at San Diego, much of this stone-work lies on surfaces where no more water could run than a heavy rainstorm could cause to flow in a thin sheet across the stony surface of a desert pavement. There is no escaping the fact that man broke this rock. And there is no escape in the familiar preforms-and-quarry-refuse excuse. This is a particular industry, often found in places that are not quarries but in places to which this stone has been brought, and the stone is broken to a pattern now well known. In addition the by-now-familiar concave scrapers again appear. They are often worked into the steep intersections of the triangular blades. They show the typical crescent shapes, the battered edges, and very clear examples of heavy wear concentrated in the battered edge. So there it is, the blade and core industry is present in the Colorado Desert, as well as in the Mohave Desert and on the coast at San Diego. It is at least a regional phenomenon, and, as we will see presently, it is actually continent wide and thus qualifies as a cultural stage in America.

La Jollan material is also present in the Yuha Desert, but it is surprisingly scarce. If the blade and core people held on here for a long period of time, they may have blocked the expansion of the La Jollan uniface people. In Australia just such things occurred. The metate-using people lived in the transition between the desert and the forest and used their metates to prepare the wild seeds. They thus gained a decided population-density advantage over their neighbors. One would expect their neighbors to take up the use of so valuable a tool, but they did not. On the contrary, they viewed the seed-eating people with contempt, calling them dirt eaters, an attitude about like an American watching a Frenchman eat a horse steak or a Chinese eat an ancient egg.

When I first asked Morlin Childers about metates and uniface tools on the early time levels, he shook his head in negation. There were plenty of metates in use by the later peoples, but there were none in the areas where the blade and core or ovate biface material was found. But then he reached deeper into his vast collection to show me two manos that he had brought in. They were about half gone, rotted away. The decay was most interesting for it had eaten into the interior, leaving most of the exterior of the rock as a shell. It is a familiar pattern of rock decay, seen particularly frequently in the granites in the desert. Granite weathering has been studied by the geologists, and they have found, all other things being equal, that such weathering as this requires at least all of Wisconsin time—say 60,000 years or more. Later we visited a site where a lava flow had dammed a little valley and a lake had existed so long that a deposit of diatomaceous earth had formed. The lava had weathered away, and the remnants of the former dam were now hard to see. Yet there was evidence for man in the lake deposits, and manos and metates were present. One very thick slab of granite that had been used as a metate was now weathered clear through. And again, the normal geologic conclusion would be that one was looking at all of the Wisconsin—and not just the 25,000-year Wisconsin but the early Wisconsin of 60,000 years or more time. All of this of course is in good agreement with the higher dates for metates and manos in the San Diego area, where geomorphic position and degrees of weathering also suggested all of Wisconsin time for the earliest ones. Some people are able to treat each case in utter isolation. The evidence is not conclusive, not provable on an absolute basis at any single point, and hence of no value. But time and time again, in different places and different environments, the answer comes out: all of Wisconsin time is probable for the mano and metate and the uniface material. To my mind many possibles make a probable, and many probables approach proof. It is heresy, I suppose, but that is the way it seems to me.

THE TRUCKHAVEN SITE

Each visit with Morlin Childers produces something new. One novelty was the Truckhaven site. This is an enormous quarry that appears to have been visited by every kind of man that ever lived in the vicinity, in order to obtain the extraordinarily fine rock available there. A fine Colorado River silt has been subjected to volcanic action that silicified and baked it. The result is a colorful stone with a fine texture, which is easily flaked. Where it outcrops, as at the site near Truckhaven on the west side of the Salton Sea, a huge area is strewn with the flake debris left by early and late men. The site covers at least a hundred acres, and one talus slope about one-quarter by one-eighth mile has an apparent depth of flake debris of ten feet or more. The flake debris lies in overlapping sheets like shingles on a roof. The oldest, deepest, and lowest shingles are black, the next brown, the next yellow. The fresh stone is light cream in color.

When I looked at this huge area and the evidence of the immense length of time man had been working on it, I thought of Vance Haynes's comment that there was not enough stonework strewn over the American landscape to be consistent with the vast antiquity advocated by some. This is but one of many immense quarries, and it is but a part of the even more enormous acreages covered with the camp debris of early man. One wonders how Vance Haynes has avoided exposure to such evidence.

Walking over the Truckhaven site is an experience. Your feet are crunching along on artifacts and debitage. You can find blocks of stone from which flakes have been struck and reassemble some of the flakes and so reconstruct the ancient man's technology. It is soon obvious that more than one technology is present. There are classic examples of unifacial work, of ovate bifaces, and of cores and blades. In addition there are unsuccessful bifacial points strewn around. I gathered a representative sample of each of these and laid them out by typology. This presented an interesting rainbow of colors, for the well-made bifacial points were creamy white, the unifacial tools were yellowed, the ovate bifaces and the blades and cores were orange verging on mahogany. And to my surprise there were huge slablike pieces and large round-in-plan flakes that were literally black with accumulation of desert varnish. This was all one stone, lying on one surface, and again it was showing a sequence of weathering phenomena that paralleled the lithic technology.

Morlin Childers has flakes that can be fitted back on a core, where the core and the flake have differing degrees of varnish. But neither he nor anyone else has an arrowhead with any desert varnish on it, and only the earliest dart points under special circumstances ever have any. Here the sequence was running true to the overall picture. Interestingly, while it distinguished neatly on the later end of the cultural scale, it distinguished poorly on the older end of the scale. It did not differentiate between the ovate biface and the blade and core work, which we know are different in time. But the big surprise was the clear evidence that there was something present that was older than either of these already ancient lithic traditions. Childers and Carter and Minshall have seen enough of this phenomenon to think that there is a still earlier lithic tradition to be recognized, defined, and dated, but for the present we can do no more than to indicate that we have more yet to learn and that the blade and core stage is still not the earliest evidence of man in America.

I was particularly interested in the granite cobbles used for hammers on this site. They are not in place in the quarry material but have been carried up from the desert wash below. Many of them were in such an advanced stage of decomposition that we could not flake any hard stone with them. No one would carry a rotten piece of granite up to use as a hammer, so the question intrigued me as to what kind of granite had been available to early users. All the granite in the wash was white, hard, unweathered, and relatively fine grained. This would be the kind of material that man would start with, and the geomorphology of the area showed that such material would in fact have been available then. For once, the condition of the granite that man used could be certified as "hard and fresh."

It has often been argued that the difficulty with trying to use the geologists' granite-weathering ratio is that granites vary too much and that one could not be sure man started with a fresh granite. It is true that granite is a catchall term for a great variety of rocks that are high in quartz, low in basic minerals, and generally of

rather coarse mineral structure. However, here we were dealing
with granites off one limited part of a mountain range, just those
granites that were in the drainage of this desert wash. Since the
wash has descended from the granitic ranges to the Salton Sink
through at least the latter half of the Pleistocene, we can assume
that the hard, fresh granites in the wash today are like those that
have always been available to man.

Observation of granite weathering in the mountains of southern
California shows that, although weathering penetrates very deeply,
within the weathered mass there are great round areas of finer-
grained rock that resists weathering. As the weathered rock wastes
away, these rounded masses emerge to form the immense boulders
that cover the hills and mountains of arid and semiarid southern
California. It is this fine-grained, resistant-to-decay granite that enters
the streams and is carried down onto the desert floor. Furthermore,
only hard fresh granite could withstand the forces of the torrential
desert washes. It is this granite that man picked up to use for his
hammer. He not only started with fresh granite, but he started with
the most resistant granite, which nature had weathered out through
chemical actions and then run through the ball mill of stream action.
It was the toughest and most resistant part of the granite spectrum.
Yet it is this granite that had weathered to a rotten stage that in a
lesser granite would spell pre-Wisconsin, more than 60,000 years.
It is the continuous finding of item after item like this that spells
great antiquity, and antiquity that makes the not-more-than-10,000-
or-12,000-year dictum look ridiculous and the presently daring
thought of 20,000 or 30,000 years look only slightly less so.

BLADE AND CORE STAGE: BEYOND THE SOUTHWEST

More than twenty years ago when looking through *American
Antiquity*, the archeologists' journal, I was struck by reports of blade
and core work in the Sheguiandah site in Canada (Lee, 1954, 1955,
1957). This has been as controversial a site as the Texas Street site
and for many of the same reasons. It was too old to suit the thinking
of the majority, and it had an industry that was impossible to place
in the accepted cultural sequences. It seemed to me that I had best
take a look at the original material, so I arranged with Tom Lee,

then in the national museum in Ottawa, to visit him and to look at the material.

At the museum we began pulling the heavy site drawers, starting with the surface material and working down. At some depth we began to find fine struck blades in quartzite, and I began to ask where the cores were. We presently found them in the lowest levels of the site. The quartzite at Sheguiandah on Manitoulin Island on the north side of Lake Huron, is some of the finest I have ever seen. The blades were as regular as those struck in the flints in northern Europe, and the cores were fine, fluted examples of this craft. The problem with the site is that the lower levels are clearly beneath glacial deposits. They are preglacial. This has been attested by Sanford (1957, 1971), a geologist who has made a special study of the site, but he is generally ignored. Lee's reports are clear enough and beautifully illustrated, but the opposition says that the site is just a Point Peninsula workshop. This is the old quarry and preform argument in a slightly new dress. If there is any Point Peninsula material at the site, it surely has nothing to do with the blade and core work.

THE CATSKILLS

In the Catskills Bruce Raemsch (1968, 1970; Raemsch and Timlin, 1971) has more material from within and beneath the glacial deposits. We have corresponded for years, and I finally had a chance in 1976 to visit him and to see the material. He has quantities of flake and core material, but the piece that most interested me was a fluted core, the obvious source of blade-type flakes. He has many cordiform flakes, heart-shaped flakes, normally with two long flake scars on the dorsal surface showing that the flakes were being struck off longitudinally from a core and that this flake had been preceded by two others. This is essentially a blade and core technique but with shorter and wider flakes than usual.

The opposition was present and prepared and highly vocal at the time of my visit, which coincided with a full-dress review of the findings (Cole and Godfrey, 1977). Against the claim that there was material under glacial deposits, the argument was made that the glaciers scraped everything clean, so this was impossible. I commented that one glacial deposit over another was a commonplace in geology, and that in Switzerland—we had been told in our geomorphology class at Berkeley by a Swiss glacial geomorphologist—there was a known case of a glacier's advancing across a meadow and retreating centuries later, leaving the sod unbroken. A geologist then raised perhaps a dozen hypothetical questions about the local geology of the site, but it turned out that although he had worked in the general area he had never worked in the actual area of the site. Generalities and hypothetical questions are just fine, but they often have the odd quality of not applying to specific situations. The statement was then made that glaciers regularly break flint and this produces quantities of broken rock out of which anyone could, with some patience and persistence, make a collection of artifactlike material. Raemsch and I spent some time looking in the local glacial deposits to check on this. Although we could find some Onandaga flint pebbles and small cobbles, we could find none that were broken and of course no artifactlike material. Even when we found a rock crusher that was breaking up the local rock, including the Onandaga flint, we could find no artifactlike material—no cordiform flakes, no fluted cores, indeed nothing that was artifactlike. I have looked in a number of glacial deposits, and I have never found any evidence of glacially broken rock that was at all artifactlike. I consider the glaciers-break-rock thesis to be just one more case of the streams-break-rocks, surf-breaks-rocks—anything apparently will do rather than face the fact that it is man that breaks rocks percussively and breaks them to patterns. So here we are again: rock broken to a familiar pattern, in a geologically old position, somewhere in the late glacial sequence, but that somewhere not well pegged at the present.

Blade and core work was once recognized only for the Mexican late cultures. Then it was recognized in the Adena culture, about the time of Christ. Then it was noted for the Paleo-Indian cultures of about 10,000 years ago. In all these cases the evidence had always been there; it was just belatedly recognized. So it is with the very early blade and core work. It has always been there, but it is only now being recognized in a few spots. It will undoubtedly be found widely over America once the barrier is broken and its characteristics recognized. The early examples of it will be found only when

people look in the early strata. You cannot find what you will not
look for and cannot or will not recognize when you stumble over it.

SOME RECENT DISCOVERIES

The Charles H. Brown site at San Diego gives the most recent
insight into the answers. It has been excavated by Jim Moriarty,
and Herb Minshall has sent me his preliminary analysis of the geology and stratigraphy and his notes on the cultural sequence. The
site is the classic layer cake—one culture stacked on top of another (see figure 46). Historic material overlies immediately prehistoric material, arrow points made of porcelain over arrow points
of obsidian and other materials, as well as pottery. Below that lies
late La Jollan material, with typical unifacial tools but no pottery.
Then comes the classic San Dieguito, with its finely made unifacial
tools, bifacially flaked points, and imported felsitic stone. Next is
found the early La Jollan, the continuation of unifacial tools with
the metate but no longer with bifacial points. Below that, there is
a mixture of materials like those found in Buchanan Canyon (both
biface and blade and core work), and finally there is a level of
only blade and core work.

What this means is that my combination of physical earth
science studies when applied to the archeology of the region, produced the correct ordering of the cultures. Minshall's analysis of the
complicated geomorphology yields a minimum age of 85,000 years
for the deepest materials. This is not far off from my estimate made
25 years ago: 100,000 years. We still do not know dates in any
absolute sense, and I suspect that Minshall's date is perhaps conservative, but there is need for patience. With the accumulation of
new dating methods, it is only a matter of time until we know
dates with much greater certainty.

In 1979, three years after I began this book, I participated in
a week's field work in the west Texas region with Antonio Andretta
of Alpine and Julian Hayden of Tucson, Arizona, and others. The
gist of that experience is this. The same culture sequence seen at
San Diego is present as far east as west Texas, and I suspect it is
valid for all of America. In the Alpine–Davis Mountain region of
west Texas, the Folsom-Clovis material of 10,000 to 12,000 years'

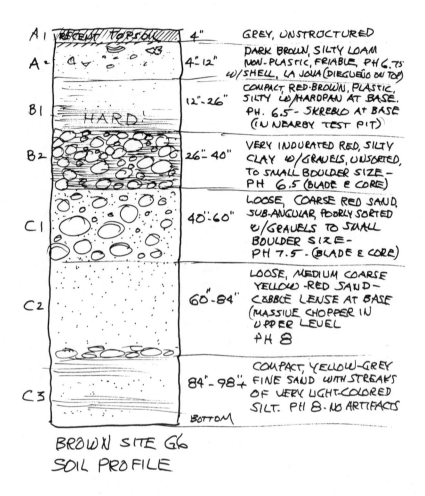

A 1 — RECENT TOPSOIL — 4" — GREY, UNSTRUCTURED

A 2 — 4"-12" — DARK BROWN, SILTY LOAM NON-PLASTIC, FRIABLE, PH 6.75 W/SHELL, LA JOLLA (DIEGUEÑO ON TOP)

B 1 — HARD! — 12"-26" — COMPACT RED-BROWN, PLASTIC, SILTY LD/HARDPAN AT BASE. PH. 6.5 - SKREBLO AT BASE (IN NEARBY TEST PIT)

B 2 — 26"-40" — VERY INDURATED RED, SILTY CLAY W/GRAVELS, UNSORTED, TO SMALL BOULDER SIZE - PH 6.5 (BLADE E CORE)

C 1 — 40"-60" — LOOSE, COARSE RED SAND, SUB-ANGULAR, POORLY SORTED W/GRAVELS TO SMALL BOULDER SIZE - PH 7.5 - (BLADE E CORE)

C 2 — 60-84" — LOOSE, MEDIUM COARSE YELLOW-RED SAND - COBBLE LENSE AT BASE (MASSIVE CHOPPER IN UPPER LEVEL PH 8

C 3 — 84"-98"+ — COMPACT, YELLOW-GREY FINE SAND WITH STREAKS OF VERY LIGHT-COLORED SILT. PH 8. NO ARTIFACTS

BOTTOM

BROWN SITE G6
SOIL PROFILE

FIGURE 46. Much of our knowledge exists in sketch form, like this, for publication of site reports is often delayed for years. This sketch of the geomorphology and stratigraphy of the Brown site was supplied by H. L. Minshall and is used with his permission and that of James Moriarty, the excavator. The lettering indicates what Minshall considers to be the natural units. A modest soil profile developed in midden material is indicated by *A1* and *A2*. *B1* and *B2* are parts of another soil profile, and the weathering is extreme, as indicated by both the heavy clay and the red coloration. The *C* units are still older deposits.

antiquity is on the surface. Deeply buried sites carry the familiar older cultures. Ancient landforms, especially the terraces of the Rio Grande River, carry steep edge work, and other old land surfaces have blade and core work. Still others have vast expanses of uniface work with manos and metates. The whole area—its geography and its cultures—repeats in detail the Mohave and Colorado deserts' records. As a group we had extensive discussions as to the significance of some of the evidence we were looking at, especially the significance of desert varnish. We had virtually no disagreement on the reality of the artifacts, the groupings that they fell into, or the fact that we were looking at a very long sequence and very high antiquities.

CONCLUSION

At this point we can summarize some of what we know about early man in America. The so-called Paleo-Indian period, the time of the Great Hunters with their magnificent points, is not the start of things in America but the beginning of the late period. Back of it lies the unifacial period with the mano and metate as the key artifacts. The age of that period is uncertain, but it probably begins about 60,000 years ago. It is preceded by the ovate biface period, whose age must be somewhere between 60,000 and 80,000 years if our guesses as to the age of the blade and core period are correct. Somewhere around 80,000 years ago seems to be the time for the blade and core or heavy blade stage, and back of that is the enigmatic steep edge stage. We are still guessing at the time placement of these cultural stages. The sequence is probably right, and the times are possibly minimal, but only further work will determine that.

When we are looking at an age of 100,000 years or so and the evidence of men with very simple cultures in America, we run into an icy problem at the Bering Strait, the probable gateway to America for early man. How did these ill-equipped folk ever pass that formidable barrier?

Chapter 7

The Bridge

SINCE man did not originate in America, he had to come here some-how. In 1590, Father Acosta, a Spanish priest, reasoned that man had walked in by some land connection at the northwest corner of America, and four hundred years later we still think this to be true, at least for the first man. It is at the Bering Strait that the New World of the Americas most closely approaches the Old World, the home of man. The gap is about seventy-five miles wide at the nar-rowest, and there are islands in the middle so that thirty miles is the maximum sea voyage required. A lowering of the sea by a little more than 100 feet would create a land bridge and a 300- to 500-foot lowering would expose a subcontinent-sized area, called Berin-gia. Since glacial lowering of the sea was somewhere between 300 and 500 feet and only 100 feet is required to form a bridge, it is obvious that a land bridge was created when only one-third of the ice for a glacial maximum had accumulated, assuming the geology of the past to be like that of the present. The bridge would persist until about two-thirds of the ice of a glaciation had melted off. Since sea level was 100 feet below the present level 10,000 years ago, we can take minus-100 feet at 10,000 years as the time when the land bridge was last breached. Even then for a few thousand years the gap must have been even narrower than it now is. All of this assumes that the Bering Strait region is tectonically stable, but this is far from certain.

"Land bridge" is somewhat of a misnomer. It is not a narrow bridge that emerges but a small continent: an hourglass-shaped landmass, its constriction at the present Bering Strait, 1,400 miles wide on its north-south axis and 1,000 miles along its maximum east-west extent, at both its northern and southern edge, is added onto unglaciated Alaska and Siberia (see figure 47). The two con-

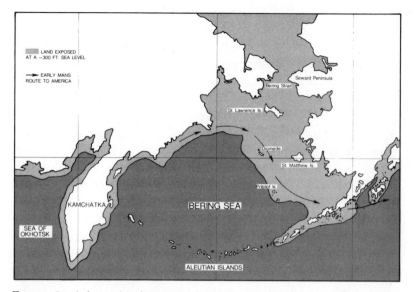

FIGURE 47. A large, barely submerged land mass separates, or, rather, connects America with Asia. It is often referred to as Beringia, but Amerasia would be a better term. During glacially lowered sea levels man could follow its southern edge to the base of the Aleutian Island chain. From there on into America a coastal route to the warmer south was open in glacial and interglacial times.

tinents are not really separated, but are connected by a broad platform with a number of hills that now stand out as islands: St. Lawrence, St. Matthew, the Pribilof, and the Diomede islands. A single mountain arc once straddled the continents, and its peaks are the present islands. We have been overly influenced by the present submergence, for there is evidence that this is geologically a fairly recent phenomenon and that through much of late geologic time the bridge, and not the present strait, was there. The problem is to relate these geological times to archeological time and to the problem of man's earliest entry into America.

In distant geologic time animals moved back and forth across this bridge: in early and late Eocene, early Oligocene, late Miocene, and middle to late Pliocene times. All of these precede man. Elephants of the mastodon type are an example of the animals that migrated at this earlier time.

A land bridge is dandy for land animals, but it is a barrier for marine organisms, and that the land bridge existed through most if not all of the Tertiary times—the last 60 million years—is shown by the fact that the marine animals of the arctic basin are related to the Atlantic species, not to the adjacent Pacific species. This is especially true of the molluscs, but even the pinnipeds, the seals and walruses, are Atlantic related. Sometime during the early Pleistocene the Bering-Chukchi platform was downwarped, and a narrow seaway broke through between the Chukotski Peninsula and the Seward Peninsula. The appearance of Pacific shellfish in the Arctic Sea indicates that this happened in earliest Pleistocene time. Thereafter, it is assumed, the existence of the bridge depended on lowering of sea levels during glacial times, but this idea may have been given too much credence.

There is evidence of considerable crustal movement at Bering Strait. On the American side the Seward Peninsula is described as having spectacular local deformation. The marine terraces there are warped—apparently a mid-Pleistocene action. At the major deltas loading is locally warping the crust downward, and the western Seward Peninsula is tectonically active.

An attempt at correlating data from the Siberian side of the strait with that from the American side indicated differential tectonic movement in the area, and this again raises the possibility of land bridges in interglacial time, which would be most significant for man's entry into America. In late Pleistocene time, then (glacial and interglacial), low and high sea stands may not have been the sole regulators of the existence of the bridge.

Archeologists have overemphasized the narrowest part of the strait—Cape Dezneva to Cape Prince of Wales—for a 100-foot lowering of the sea would connect Saint Lawrence Island broadly to Alaska and link it to Asia at Cape Chaplina. Saint Lawrence Island is 200 miles to the south of the narrow part of the Bering Strait and would be appreciably warmer, an important factor in early man's problem in entering America through this icy gate. With a 300-foot lowering of sea level, perhaps the last glacial maximum, the northernmost point for a crossing would be at a point in the mouth of the present Gulf of Anadyr, and there would be another 100 miles to the south. From that point the coastline would run southwest to Unimak Island in the Aleutians. This is over 700 miles to the south of the narrowest part of the Bering Strait and almost

200 miles more southerly in latitude than Sitka, Alaska. These will be key areas in the discussion of survival of primitive men in the Bering Strait region.

The relationships between sea level, glaciation, bridge formation, corridors, and culture are intricate. At the onset of the last glaciation, the falling sea level would soon expose the highest part of the Beringian platform and would thus connect America and Asia, as shown in figure 46. Following Evans for glacial time, the Bering Strait would be narrowing after 40,000 years, bridged at 35,000, and closed again at 10,000. Similar open periods would occur: between 90,000 and 50,000, 75,000 and 120,000, and 140,000 and 165,000 years. In each 40,000-year cycle a bridge would be in existence for at least 25,000 years, and Beringia would be an extensive area. If the corridors to either the east or the west of the Rockies, the interior route and the coastal route, were closed, it would only have been during times of glacial maxima. The key times for man's entry during a glacial time would be when the corridors were either opening or closing but still open and the expanding bridge had just come into existence or had not yet gone out of existence. These times would be more restricted than the bridge but one could very conservatively estimate that for 5,000 years on each side of a glacial maximum there would be both a bridge in being and open corridors to the south. These times would center about: 15,000 and 25,000, 55,000 and 65,000, 100,000 and 115,000, 145,000 and 155,000 years ago. The exact years are unimportant. It is the frequency and long duration of opportunity that is significant. Within the range of dates now before us, we have four pairs of opportunities reaching back about 150,000 years. Each of these should be viewed as time zones, not moments. There may have been a 5,000- or 10,000-year-long period when the glaciers were growing sufficiently to lower the sea level and create the land bridge but before the glacier growth closed either the coastal or interior routes to the south. Conversely, there would be periods when the ice melt was opening the corridors but the sea level rise had not yet drowned the bridge. In addition, it can be assumed that man's cultural equipment was increasing and that in each succeeding period, he would need less and less optimum conditions for passing the strait and penetrating southward. It is obvious that there were many, not few, opportunities for man to move across the Bering Strait.

The problem that Bering Strait presents is not at the 10,000- or even the 25,000-year level, when we can expect man to have tailored fur clothing, skin boats like the Eskimo umiak, and good arctic equipment that probably includes semisubterranean houses and oil lamps. All of these things were in existence in the Eurasian world in the 15,000- to 35,000-year period known as the Upper Paleolithic, if not earlier. Man was living in Siberia at this time, a far colder area than the Bering Strait. Recent finds at Old Crow in the Yukon show that man was living in that cold interior location 30,000 years ago (Harrington, Bonnichsen, and Morlan, 1975). Seldom have so many (the advocates of 12,000 years for man in America) had to eat so much crow, and Old Crow at that. The problem is how the icy gate at the Bering Strait was passed early, not how it was done late. How did the middle- and lower-Paleolithic people, the La Jollans and the Texas Street people of 60,000 to 120,000 years ago, survive in the immensely cold winters of the Siberian shore, the Beringian plain, and the Alaskan coast?

J. L. Giddings (1952, 1954, 1960, 1964) discussed this problem with unusual breadth. He particularly opposed the idea that man "migrated" across the straits. He favored saying "spread into America" during "an infinitude of time." "Spilled molasses does not 'migrate' across the table top." He insisted that man did not even follow the game herds, but awaited their seasonal movements: the game migrated; man waited expectantly. His point was that men entering America were drifting along, not seeking or searching. There was no mass migration but simply the establishment by new families of their own hunting and gathering range beyond their parents' ranges. Only with infinite slowness did these expanding familial ranges lead from one climate to another. The open territory for the first people lay to the east in Beringia and thereafter to the east and south in America. Behind them always lay inhabited territory, territory preempted by earlier generations. Ahead of them lay open land, unoccupied, unharvested, unclaimed. At Bering Strait Giddings assumed stable populations, no sequences of mass migrations. Ideas, however, he assumed, flowed freely through the area.

Giddings saw man and culture adapting to the arctic and then to subarctic and beyond. According to him, there were no migrations through Beringia of differing cultures that would account for the racial and cultural differences in the Americas, but there was time enough for differentiation once man got here. It is a thoughtful discussion, but one must examine his time scale. His infinitude of time reaches back to the Paleolithic, but his Paleolithic is the arctic microblade technology now seen as a late Paleolithic technology of at most a 10,000-year age. A quarter of a century later we have a greater "infinitude" in view. We do tend to reach too rapidly for superlatives, and "early" has the bad habit of becoming "earliest."

We need not discard Giddings' insights concerning spreads of man and the inflow of ideas, but we probably must modify his model to allow for successions of arrivals of men and ideas spreading into the Arctic over much longer time spans than he envisioned. In those longer time spans there is more likelihood of differing men and differing ideas, very much as the kinds of animals spreading back and forth across the straits changed with time.

Ice in the arctic was less a barrier than is often thought, for the Bering bridge has always been ice free, and most of the approach area in Siberia was also. Much of Alaska was ice free even at glacial maxima. If man could stand arctic glacial climates, he could have moved onto the Bering platform and on into Alaska.

A more immediate problem concerns the vegetation on the Bering platform during glacially lowered seas. Treeless tundra, alder scrub, and spruce forests are very different environments posing greater and lesser problems for primitive man's existence. Hopkins (1959a, 1959b), Colvinaux (1964a, 1964b), and others have concluded that the Siberian-American arctic forests have not been linked since earliest Pleistocene time and that there has not then been a continuous forest on the land bridge in that time. This conclusion, though, refers to linkage north of 65 degrees latitude and tells us nothing about the great extent of the Bering platform southwest to 55 degrees, nearly 700 miles to the south, including an area of expectable forest cover—the area most important to the survival of early man in the area. Further, during a glacially lowered sea the present Bering Strait would be a continental-interior location 700 miles from the seashore. Ocean-margin and continental-interior climates are greatly different, and they are especially so in high latitudes.

Colvinaux (1964*a*, 1964*b*) presented data from the Pribilof Islands near the southern edge of Beringia that showed enough spruce pollen to demonstrate the presence of a spruce forest during a glacial period. He considered it evidence only for scrubby spruce outliers on the flanks of the bridge, but this conclusion does not seem reasonable. The climate of the southeastern corner of the bridge even during a glacial period would not have been far different from that of modern Sitka, and spruce forest would have been quite expectable.

Much of this has important implications for the problem of the earliest entrants into America. What was the environment like? Did they have tundra, or was it a scrub brush–tree environment or dense spruce forest? Chard concluded that "the Bering Sea region may in fact have enjoyed a relatively mild climate whenever land bridges blocked off the arctic waters and allowed it to receive the full benefits of warm currents" (Chard, 1958, p. 24; see also Chard, 1963, 1960, 1956). It is notable that much of unglaciated Alaska had a flora 20,000 years ago that is similar to that of today, while Scandinavia was covered with ice. This suggests that more stable conditions have existed in Alaska than have prevailed in many other places. The review of Alaska's physiological climatology below will further substantiate the proposition that the Alaskan coast had a relatively mild winter in the past, just as it does today.

It should be obvious that there has been too much generalization concerning a huge area that must have varied enormously from north to south and east to west.

Vegetation is a good climatic recorder and is important for man's survival, so we may well work at this a bit. Colvinaux's map of the northern limit of spruce forest in Alaska today shows that it skirts the southern flanks of the Brooks Range, is absent in the mountains down to the Gulf of Alaska, skirts the cold sea margin of the Bering Sea, maintaining a respectful distance from the summer chill. The northern limit of tree growth is not set by winter cold but by the absence of summer warmth, for trees require at least one month above fifty degrees Fahrenheit. Near rctic coasts, summers are too cool. Arctic interiors, however, can be hot, if only briefly. Fairbanks, just below the Arctic Circle, can have 90-degree days, and a spruce forest thrives. One would expect that, when exposed, the broad Bering platform would have a Fairbanks-type temperature: continental warm summers and cold winters. The warmth would allow tree growth. The trees could even be expected to approach the coast, for the cold, arctic water was cut off by the land bridge, and the north Pacific must have been appreciably warmer. The spruce pollen at the Pribilofs should then indicate a spruce forest, not a scrubby fringe of distant spruce. The extension suggested is perhaps minimal, and it calls for a similar expansion on the Siberian side. This then makes questionable the total separation of the Siberian and American forests, a separation also questioned by entomologists, who find that forest insects crossed Beringia. If the forests were not linked, the gap was small enough for weak flyers to span it.

Spruce forest provides wood and shelter. Scrub alder, a more open plant formation, is better for berries and small game. An alder-fringed sea backed by spruce forest would be a tolerable environment for primitive man, one comparable to Tierra del Fuego, a land and people to be dealt with presently.

While the plant life is important for deciphering the history of the land bridge and the plants for our view of the habitability of Beringia, the warm-blooded animals, more like man, are even more informative. Eight species of mammals, mostly rodents, have spread across Beringia from Asia into America in very late Pleistocene time, as indicated by their wide range in Asia and very narrow ranges in America. Twelve species occupy wide ranges on both sides of Beringia and are thought to have spread in early last-glacial time.

In 1942 Raymond M. Gilmore anticipated much of what has been written since on the migration of animals across Beringia. As I have mentioned, he chided me for not citing his unpublished doctoral dissertation, "Review of Microtus Voles of the Subgenus Stenocranius (Mammalia: Rodentia: Muridae), with Special Discussion of the Bering Strait Region." The title is formidable, and the work was never published—not because of the title, but because his ideas were too advanced for that day. The gist of his argument is that voles migrated across Beringia when sea levels were down and were isolated on islands in Beringia when sea levels rose and that their length of isolation is in proportion to the depth of water around the islands. Their evolutionary divergence is thus proportional to the time of sea-level rise. It would have been a considerable contribution even if he had stopped there, but he had a flock of other ideas. The distribution of voles indicated that in America a corridor through the ice barrier opened up to the west of the Rocky Mountains, with melting proceeding from south to north, allowing the southern voles to occupy the newly ice-free territory before the northern voles had a chance to expand. Modern detailed mapping of the glacial meltback supports this. He noted the division of the Pacific and Arctic seals and read it as evidence of a long-continued land bridge at Bering—a reading fully supported today. His analysis of animal movements from Asia into Beringia and thence into America led him to hypothesize a sequence of: interglacial movement to the Siberian shore, movement onto expanding Beringia with the oncoming glacial that lowered sea level, survival in refugia in Beringia and unglaciated Alaska, and exit from Beringia and Alaska into America as the ice melted again. He viewed man as being involved in this same system and noted that this called for an interglacial entry for man in America. This was much too much for 1942, and his thesis was never published.

Gilmore lists the American moose and the American beaver among the late-Pleistocene migrants to Asia—actually as double migrants, from Asia to America, and later from America back to Asia. This is probably a good model for man also: to America and later some spreading back into Asia. It was not a one-way bridge. Furthermore, moose and beaver are forest dwellers rather than tundra dwellers, and this evidence supports some linkage of forest across Beringia in late-Pleistocene time.

Gilmore's work is supported by the 30,000-year-old finds at Old Crow, in the Yukon. This is the time of the last glacial period, and the location is in the deep interior of the continent, where the climate would be extremely cold in winter. The men who lived there at that time had to be well equipped: good housing, good clothing, and, from the sophisticated bone-working technology, they must also have had good stone tools. These are, in terms of the early entrants into America, late and sophisticated folk. They tell us that even as early as 30,000 years ago men had the equipment to withstand the severest climates outside Antarctica, but it tells us little about the simple folk who were in the San Diego area 50,000 and 100,000 years ago. For them we must look for the warmest route, not the coldest one.

There is more than one apparent entry to Beringia from Siberia, but one of the seemingly obvious routes, the chain of Aleutian Islands, is a false lead. The outer islands are separated from Asia by wide gaps, and in the icy and stormy seas of the Arctic they offer opportunities only for well-equipped seafarers. Along the coast of Siberia the mountains now reach the sea and make a coastal trip for foot travellers exceedingly difficult. The assumption is that early men did not have simple watercraft that would allow them to move easily along such a coast, but evidence from very primitive people such as the Tierra del Fuegians (discussed below) shows that assumption to be most insecure, for the Tierra del Fuegians moved freely along just such a coast using very simple watercraft.

During a period of glacially lowered sea level, a relatively level coastal shelf twenty to thirty or more miles wide is exposed on the Siberian coast. This change is so large (from great difficulty to great ease for pedestrians) that some are persuaded that the movement up the Siberian coast would be during glacial periods. Men with watercraft would pass through at any time, but this would be hard to prove since much of the evidence would now be beneath the sea. The same can be said of a northern route along the arctic seacoast from the mouth of the Lena River eastward. Along this vast plain, travel would be easy for those equipped for arctic conditions.

We may summarize as follows. We know the Bering Strait area to be tectonically unstable at its narrowest point, and this raises the possibility of bridges independent of glacially lowered sea levels. More than a possibility, however, glacially lowered sea levels are certain, and they will create not just a bridge but a broad continental linkage that makes unglaciated Alaska a part of Siberia.

We are uncertain about the total separation of Alaska from the rest of the Americas by ice during glacial maxima, but most of the evidence still favors such a separation. However, there were, as was pointed out earlier, opportunities at the beginning, in the middle, and toward the end of each glaciation, when men would have had both a bridge and a corridor. Southward two routes were possible: interior and coastal. A narrow corridor in the interior of North America between vast ice caps would be one of the most rigorous environments imaginable, for it would expectably be enormously windy as well as cold, and the windchill factor would freeze anyone without fully developed Eskimo clothing. Nevertheless, that men lived at Old Crow 30,000 years ago suggests some such equipment, and we will see that man lived in Europe under such conditions astonishingly early. But for truly primitive men a coastal route is far more feasible.

For the climate and vegetation of Beringia, we fluctuate between Chard's "perhaps as good or even better than today" to assumptions of greater cold. For vegetation we vary from all tundra to spruce forest, at least in the southeastern corner and more probably continuous across the southern one-third of Beringia. The evidence from San Diego states that man somehow managed to enter Beringia, to exist on it, and to spread on into America. Further, the evidence is that these were lower-Paleolithic-level people for whom we cannot assume Eskimo or upper-Paleolithic equipment in clothing and housing. Is it really feasible to bring ill-clothed, ill-housed, and ill-equipped men through such an environment?

DID SINANTHROPUS PEKINENSIS WEAR PANTS?

I posed the question of what if any clothing ancient man needed to my seminars in the early 1950's. Man lived near Peking, China, about 350,000 years ago. He used fire, made simple stone tools, and lived in caves. Did he need clothing? The climatic analog of Peking is Pittsburgh, Pennsylvania, and the probability is that man could not survive stark naked in so extreme a climate. Both J. R. Mather and Bernard Dethier, who came with M.A. degrees in meteorology and studied physiological climatology with Douglas H. K. Lee and then took Peking Man's problems for their own, wrote Ph.D. theses for me on the problem of primitive man's survival on the Bering bridge. The following discussion draws on their work (Dethier, 1958; Mather, 1951, 1954a, 1954b).

There are in a sense two climates. One is simple physical climatology: the actual temperature, humidity, and air movement taken over a period of time. There is also climate as it affects us:

"it isn't the heat; it's the humidity." This latter is physiological
climatology: the consideration of the reaction of warm-blooded
creatures to the physical climate. The first step in seeing what kind
of man could survive in a particular climate is of course to establish
the climate being considered. But at Beringia we do not know
whether the climate was better or worse than now. Mather has
shown that the movements of the great semipermanent high- and
low-pressure centers in the northern hemisphere determine airflow
and thereby temperature and precipitation. The results are not uniformly colder or warmer along a given latitude. During the period
of greater warmth in 1931–1940, taken as an approximation of
interglacial conditions, Alaska and northern Siberia were warmer and
wetter while central Asia became colder and dryer. If the reverse is
a glacial condition, central Asia would become warmer and wetter
while Alaska and Canada would become colder and dryer. The fact
is that the glacial and interglacial changes were complex, not
simple, geographically variable not uniform, and they are still not
well understood.

We can cut this Gordian knot by saying that the change was
probably not great in either direction and that the safest thing to
do is to take the present as an approximation of the past. The
changes were not of orders of magnitude: Fairbanks surely did not
go from its present near zero degrees Fahrenheit for January to
minus-fifty degrees, but, if colder at all, to perhaps minus-five degrees. The proportion of change is small compared to our many
other uncertainties.

Some of the evidence of great and sudden climatic change is
more romantic than real. The frozen elephants (hairy mammoths)
are good examples. They were not quick-frozen, for they show some
decay and their stomach contents show vegetation like that found in
those same regions today. Their preservation is more a matter of
the climate's having never been much warmer than it is evidence
for great cold. A Russian, Tolmachoff, who wrote about the car-
casses of mammoths and rhinoceroses in the Siberian frozen ground,
estimated that the four- to five-degree northward extension of Siberia due to glacially lowered sea levels caused a four- to five-degree
warming in Siberia. This would apply to the Canadian Arctic also
and may be the explanation for dry and grassy periods during the

Pleistocene. Faced with little agreement on the causes of the Pleistocene and conflicting evidence about whether glacial episodes were
colder or warmer, it is obviously simplest to assume the present
climate.

The problem for primitive man in the Arctic is cold, and the
critical temperatures would be winter temperatures. January temperatures in the Amerasia area (eastern Siberia and Alaska) show a
moderate thirty degrees Fahrenheit along the Aleutian Islands, and
zero degrees at the Bering Strait. The coldest temperature man
would meet in a trip from the Siberian coast along the coastline
exposed by glacially lowered seas is zero degrees Fahrenheit at the
northern end of the Kamchatka Peninsula. Beyond that, during a
glacially lowered sea level, he would find increasingly mild temperatures as he moved southeastward toward America, with a January
average of about thirty degrees Fahrenheit along the southern edge
of Beringia (see figure 48).

The contrast between coast and interior is enormous. Ver-
khoyansk, Siberia, has a January average temperature of minus-fifty-
eight degrees Fahrenheit, while Bering Strait, in the same latitude,
has a zero-degree January average. For warm-blooded creatures the
differences are life or death, and animals not highly adapted to
great cold move to the coast to survive. Thus in Alaska the deer
herd is limited not by summer grazing areas but by the grazing
area in the narrow coastal strip where they can find winter temperatures that they can survive. Early man must have responded in
somewhat similar fashion: wintering in warm, coastal refugia, preferably in dense vegetation cover that would reduce exposure to wind,
and foraging widely during the summer season.

If we were to get man to the Bering Strait area during an interglacial condition, actually just to Kamchatka, and then with the
onset of a glaciation allow man to spread across Beringia, clinging
to the warmer southern fringe where the resources of both the land
and the sea would be available, the warmest and hence best area for
survival would lie in Alaska at the inner end of the Aleutians.

The north Pacific may have been warmer than now in a glacial
period, for a bridge at Bering Strait would block off the cold, arctic
water. The Aleutian Islands were heavily glaciated in the past, and
this fits warmer temperatures, not colder, for it is the relatively

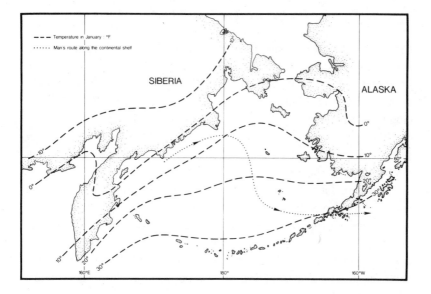

FIGURE 48. The winter temperature at Bering would be critical for early man. His route is shown by the dotted line with arrows. As is shown, his coldest weather was on the Siberian side, where he was exposed to about five degrees Fahrenheit for a January average. From there on into the Americas, conditions improved rapidly.

warm, moist sea air that brings snow to these subarctic regions.

Man's greatest problem would lie on the Siberian coast, for the winters there are dry and exceedingly cold due to the outpouring of cold, continental air masses. When the land temperature rises in summer, the winds reverse and bring summer moisture. The American side is the opposite. It has relatively dry summers, and the exposed land responds to the very long arctic days with a rapid warming—e.g., Fairbank's occasional ninety-degree temperatures. In the winter in the Gulf of Alaska the cool, wet, foggy conditions dominate the Aleutians and adjacent Alaska. The temperature at Unalaska in the Aleutians is a mild thirty-eight degrees Fahrenheit, and the sky is cloud covered. Siberia in winter is not only colder but less cloudy.

This difference is very important for man, for his radiant-heat exchange with the sky and clouds is as important as his exchange with the surrounding terrain. For radiant-heat loss in a snow-covered terrain, the air temperature measured in the standard instrument shelter gives the critical temperature. The loss of radiant heat to

the sky is difficult to measure, but when thick clouds are present
it is approximately the air temperature at the cloud level. The height
of the cloud cover in this part of Alaska (Aleutians and southwestern Alaska) is about 3,000 feet, and the temperature of the
clouds at that level is about sixteen degrees Fahrenheit. In Siberia
the ground temperature is far lower, and there are much longer
periods of cloudless skies, when radiation is being lost to an upper
atmosphere of enormously lower temperature.

Both surface temperatures and sky temperatures are much lower
on the Siberian side than on the American side. These conditions
would not change greatly from glacial to nonglacial times. The
question is: what kind of men with what kind of equipment could
pass through Siberia and survive in Beringia? Quite clearly the
problem area is not America. It is Siberia, and we need to know
how man's physiology reacts to cold.

Man must maintain a constant body temperature, and he does
so by balancing heat production and loss through complex physio-
logic processes on which later men have superimposed cultural
devices: clothing, housing, fire. Man produces heat in living and
working and loses heat by radiation, conduction, convection, and
evaporation.

Convection and conduction refer to the transfer of heat by
contact. In conduction, deep body heat is transferred to the skin and
then to any surface in contact with the skin. If there is air and the
air is in motion, convection carries heat away. Heat loss also goes
on in the lungs, as when we breathe in cold air and breathe out
warm air. The principal factors producing heat loss are low temperatures and high wind velocities. We also lose heat through evaporation: the less moisture in the air, the more rapid the evaporation.
We also lose heat by radiation, and the rate of loss depends principally on the temperature of the exposed surface and the temperature of the surroundings.

In latitudes north of fifty degrees, sunshine reaching the ground
during the critical winter months becomes negligible in comparison
with the other factors involved in the heat equation. A man standing
in the open is exchanging radiation with the land and the sky, and
they are extremely cold. So much for these processes, which in high
latitude in winter all lead to heat losses.

Man also produces heat, and in all conditions his heat production must equal his heat loss over any extended period or he freezes to death. We produce heat at a rate of forty kilogram calories per square meter per hour just in existing—breathing, pumping blood, and so forth. This is basal metabolism. In digestion we produce energy (heat) at a rate that utilizes approximately 10 to 17 percent of the ingested food. Table 5 shows the energy produced by digestion of a 1,000-calorie meal.

TABLE 5
Energy Produced by Digestion
(of a 1,000-calorie meal)

Hours Post-meal	Calories/Hour above Basal Metabolism	
	High Protein Meal	High Carbohydrate Meal
2	33.0	18.0
4	20.0	11.0
6	12.0	6.0
8	7.0	3.0
10	4.5	1.8
12	2.7	1.0

The Eskimos' high-protein diet has obvious advantages for their northern climate, and the tropical high-carbohydrate diet has equal advantages in hot climates where the goal is to reduce heat production.

We also produce energy when we work, and this varies from 90 kilogram calories per square meter per hour ($K cal/m^2/hr$) when strolling along, to 150 at a brisk walk and 500 when running at ten miles per hour. When we shiver, we produce up to 200 kilogram calories per square meter per hour. When we work, our muscles are only about 12 percent efficient. The rest of the energy appears as heat.

Man must maintain his heat balance, and if he lives in cold climates he has problems with heat loss. The Eskimos and probably the upper-Paleolithic man overcame this by clothing, housing, and fire. What did middle- and lower-Paleolithic man do?

The archeologic record is rather poor for such items as clothing, and it is even uncertain as to the use of fire. Man was using fire at Peking, China, about 350,000 years ago, and the expectation is that there was also early use of fire elsewhere at this time level. We can assume then that man approaching Bering Strait at any time within the last 200,000 or 300,000 years would have had fire. We are less certain about both clothing and housing. Clothing must have been skimpy, and we have little hope of recovering any from this time level. We have little reason to expect more than a grass-shack type of shelter at the very early times we are probably dealing with. Even the matter of caves for shelter is grossly misrepresented. There simply are not all that many caves available in habitable areas. Most men must always have lived in the open. The archeologist has a virtual fixation on caves since he often gets a long and well-preserved record there, and this has led to such stock phrases as the "cave dwellers of the Paleolithic." Probably men have always used caves when it was convenient, as some men still do. But most men for all of time must have had to live in the open to be near their sources of food and water.

One approach to this problem is to take the most primitive people we do know about, living in the coldest climate, and see what their heat balance is. We can then check that climate against that of Beringia to see if our primitive man could survive there. The most primitive men surviving for study in a severe cold climate are the people of Tierra del Fuego, living at fifty-five degrees south latitude, in a cold marine climate, and about as ill equipped culturally as any group in the world. Only Tasmanians and the people of southern Baja California could compete with them for lack of equipment, but the Tasmanians were living at only forty-five degrees south, the equivalent of the south of France, while the Tierra del Fuegians at fifty-five degrees south were living in a latitude comparable to Scotland, or, more pertinent to our interests, to the Aleutian Islands on the southern edge of Beringia, the gateway to America. A review of the climate occupied by these people will show what awesome problems they faced nearly barehanded and bareskinned.

THE CLIMATE OF TIERRA DEL FUEGO

Tierra del Fuego is at the end of the world, a thumb thrust

into the howling gales of the "roaring forties," the stormy, cold, cloudy, tempest-tossed belt surrounding Antarctica, where gale-force winds of forty miles per hour are normal. It is not a land that would be described by anyone as a desirable plum. It has been described by climatologists as probably the wildest region on earth.

Tierra del Fuego is an archipelago, a collection of islands 210 miles from north to south and 360 miles from east to west. The largest island, Tierra del Fuego, runs 140 miles in east-west extent. The area is forested on the west and grassy to the east due to decreasing rainfall eastward, for this mountainous southward extension of the Andes, 6,000 to 7,000 feet high, intercepts the stormy westerlies and concentrates the rainfall on the west side of the archipelago. The contrasts are 100 inches of precipitation on the western side and under 20 inches on the east half of the island of Tierra del Fuego. This is exactly comparable to the Alaskan panhandle.

The climate varies not only in rainfall but in temperature. The mean annual temperature for the region is forty-three degrees Fahrenheit. There is no great continental mass except Antarctica to supply cold polar air, and that from Antarctica reaches Tierra del Fuego only after crossing a wide sea, hence the immense cold of Siberia does not occur. Conversely, there is no continental mass to heat up the island, and summers remain cool—fifty degrees Fahrenheit for the summer mean. There are glaciers in the mountains and icebergs in the sea. It is a formidable challenge, even today and for a well-equipped man.

The people of greatest interest to us are the more primitive folk living in the harshest climate. These are the Alakaluf of the western islands, the Yahgan of the southwestern islands, and the Haush at the southeastern tip of Tierra del Fuego. For each of these, a nearby meteorological station gives us a climatic record: Evangelista Island for the Alakaluf, Ushuaia for the Yahgan, and Staten Island for the Haush. A review of their climates will illustrate the severity of the region in which people of little material culture survived for tens of millenia.

Ushuaia in the Yahgan territory has twenty-one inches of rainfall. Winter, the clearest season, has over 50 percent cloudiness, and relative humidity is high, averaging nearly 90 percent. It is a dark and damp time. Snowfalls of up to three feet with drifts twenty feet deep come with occasional great storms. The mean minimum winter temperature is twenty-one degrees Fahrenheit, and in 1950 the temperature during July never rose above twenty-five degrees Fahrenheit. In the 1820's, the winter was so severe that the sea ice in the channel between the islands froze, making the use of canoes impossible, and the solid ice on the beaches cut the natives off from their supplies of shellfish. Summer is only slightly better, for the frequency of storms increases then, cloudiness increases to 70 percent, and the temperature rises only to forty-eight degrees Fahrenheit. With the increase in storminess, wind increases in velocity and consistency and bedevils man and beast.

Ushuaia has thirty glaciers and permanent snowfields within a ninety-mile radius. The snow line is about 3,500 to 4,000 feet. Glaciers reach the sea and supply icebergs that at times choke the northwest arm of the Beagle Channel. It is a frigid land.

Staten Island, on the edge of the Haush territory, has sixty-seven inches of rainfall. It rains on 252 days of the year, snows on 67 days, and is cloudy 75 percent of the time. The average summer maximum temperature is fifty-nine degrees Fahrenheit, and the average winter minimum temperature is twenty-four degrees. The average wind is strong summer and winter, and calm is recorded only 16 percent of the time. The oceanic position causes milder temperature than at Ushuaia, but this is offset by increases in rainfall, cloudiness, and wind. This is no paradise.

Evangelista Island off the mountainous southwest coast of Chile is in the Alakaluf territory. Rainfall totals 117 inches per year, and periods of seventy-two consecutive rainy days have been recorded. The average wind velocity is 35 miles per hour—an extreme wind velocity of 151 miles per hour has been recorded— and calms are rare. The annual temperature range is only ten degrees Fahrenheit. Summer averages forty-seven degrees Fahrenheit, and winter averages thirty-seven degrees. Massive glaciers accumulate in the mountains and descend to the sea, and the summer snow line is only 2,500 feet above sea level. Notice here the relationship between precipitation, temperature, and snowfields. Evangelista Island is warmer than Ushuaia, but the snow line is 1,000 feet lower due to the heavy precipitation.

Anyone familiar with descriptions of the climate of the Aleutians and with the panhandle of Alaska, with their long, continuous spells of rain, fog, snow, and storm and with permanent icefields and glaciers reaching the sea will see the parallel. However, the Aleutians and the people of the northwest coast had snug houses, good clothing, excellent boats, and good hunting and fishing equipment. Their life in no way resembles that of the earliest man to enter America. They would best be characterized as upper-Paleolithic people at most, and some would place them as representatives of the Neolithic. The point is that they were certainly not lower-Paleolithic types, while the Tierra del Fuegians were, as the cultural survey that follows will show.

THE TIERRA DEL FUEGIAN AT HOME

The Alakalufs and Yahgans live on a mountainous coast with some of the rugged mountains sunk in the sea to form an island screen and others forming rocky-cliffed headlands, which seem to be nearly impassable on foot. Looking at such a coast leads the unwary to assume that it would have been untraversable by primitive man. This is commonly said of similar coastlines in Siberia and Alaska. However, the Alakaluf had canoes, and these enabled them to move freely and gain a livelihood in this forbidding area.

It is too easily assumed that canoes and other watercraft are late inventions. Technologically, it is hard to see why *Homo erectus* could not have made a log raft or a reed bundle boat. The Mousterian men of the middle Paleolithic, who could amputate an arm successfully, surely should have been able to do better than mere rafts: dugout canoes perhaps. The key area to watch with respect to this argument is Australia. Man has to pass water barriers at least twenty miles wide and, more reasonably, about forty miles to reach that isolated continent, and yet he was there by at least 40,000 years ago—and news accounts now suggest 100,000 years ago. The Tasmanians, by anyone's measure, were on a lower-Paleolithic stage, and yet they made that crossing and came to live in cool, mid-latitude climates. They used an extremely primitive raft to reach offshore islands to harvest sea birds, going as much as five miles to sea. Our scanty descriptions of their lifeway are strikingly like those of the Tierra del Fuegians given in the *Handbook of the South*

American Indians (Steward, 1946), and in Darwin's *Voyage of the Beagle* (1909).

The Yahgan and Alakaluf canoes were similar. Long strips of bark about one inch thick were taken from suitable trees in spring. Three strips were cut to cigar shapes and sewn together to form a canoe twelve to twenty feet long, two to three feet wide, and eighteen to twenty-four inches deep. The gunwales were lashed on, thin sticks bent in as ribs were laid side by side, and thwarts were placed about fifteen inches apart. The whole assemblage was strong and light but leaked badly where the bark sections were sewn together, making bailing a constant chore. The boat was in the women's charge. They paddled it, moored it, and tended the fire that was always kept burning in a hearth amidships. The women had to moor the boat to a kelp bed offshore and wade or swim ashore. Men are said not to have been swimmers, and they obviously were not concerned with equality of the sexes.

The Alakalufs, depending on their boats to get sea food, spent most of their waking time in them. Whole families with dogs, equipment, and fire traveled in canoes. Darwin marvelled at them. One canoe that came out to the Beagle in a sleet storm had a nearly naked family group. A mother nursed an infant while the sleet that caught in her hair melted and trickled ice water down her breasts and onto the baby. Darwin marvelled that any of them, but especially the baby, could survive such exposure.

The major food supply was shellfish, especially mussels. These were wedged into the end of a split stick, twisted loose from the bottom, and brought up to the canoe. When the supply in shallow water was exhausted, the women dived for the deeper ones in up to thirty feet of water. With the sea water close to freezing temperature, they could stand only about twenty minutes of exposure and then had to sit virtually on a fire to restore their body temperature. The men could not do even that, and this too is physiological climatology. Woman's body is thicker, hence better for retaining deep body heat, and women have a layer of fat beneath the skin that not only gives them their smooth roundness but insulates them. Lean and lanky men, well designed for running down game, are ill designed for arctic waters, but plump, well-rounded women are better suited to the frigid cold.

Birds, sea lions, otters, and coypus (*Myocastor coypus*) were hunted with dogs and spears and clubs. Fish were caught by driving them into shallow water where they were taken by hand or with dip nets. Hooks were not used in fishing, but bait on the end of a line sufficed to bring fish to the surface to be grabbed by hand. Plant food played a minor role in the Alakalufs' diet; some seeds and berries were about all they gathered. In terms of physiology, they needed a high-protein diet to survive, and that is what they concentrated on.

Home was a framework of saplings covered with seal skins, if these were available; if not, the saplings were thatched with bark or grass or ferns. Branches covered the floor, and branches or ferns closed the entrance well enough that in a good house the gale-force winds were slowed to a moderate breeze. A fire burned in the center of the hut, and a well-built hut with a good fire was described as warm and dry. Clothing consisted of a small cape of sea otter or fox skin plus a triangular pubic covering. Mussel-shell knives and adzes and a few other knickknacks made up their entire artifact inventory. A family's belongings could be laid on a kitchen tabletop without crowding, and only a little of their materials would survive long enough to be found by an inquiring archeologist.

The Yahgans, culturally like the Alakalufs, had no permanent villages and spent most of their waking hours in their boats. Despite a colder climate, they were no better clothed. For cold weather they wore a cape of two or more sea otter or fox skins with ties across their chests. Seal-skin moccasins with fur side out and stuffed with grass were worn, and occasionally leggings of guanaco skin were added. The Yahgans had fire with them constantly—in their huts and in their canoes. Canoes were so fragile that they were kept moored to the kelp beds offshore, and the women fetched the boats and moored them in all seasons and all types of weather. Then with the temperature in the twenties and the sea water just above freezing, the women hustled to get to the fire to get warm and dry. They were described as being short and fat. They had to be, for a lean and lanky woman could not have withstood the cold. All of the Yahgans had remarkable ability to withstand the cold and no ability to withstand heat. Darwin wrote of them that, while the British shivered around a bonfire "these naked savages, though far off were observed to our great surprise to be streaming with perspiration at such a roasting" (1909, p. 223). We now know that they have 150 percent of our basal metabolism, a striking physiological adaptation to cold.

The Haush were more like the Onas of the large island of Tierra del Fuego and represented a different lifeway in housing, dress, and economy. They were more hunters than shore-oriented gatherers. They built a windscreen of skin and in severe weather pulled the two ends together to form a crude tent. A fire burned either in the lee of the windscreen or in the center of the tent. They wore a long robe of guanaco skin, wide enough to be wrapped one and a half times around the body; it was held closed with one hand. Beneath this, men wore a loin cloth and women a small apron and a petticoat from just below the breast to the knees. All wore moccasins.

They could walk for hours in ice water without discomfort. At night they would wring the water out of their robes, put on dry moccasins, if these were available, wrap their still-damp robes about them, and sleep comfortably even when the temperature fell well below freezing. They clearly had an extensive physiological adaptation to cold, and it probably went far beyond their 150 percent of our basal metabolism, to include greater blood flow to extremities as in the Eskimo, peripheral reduction of blood flow to reduce heat loss as in the Australian natives, or some combination of these or other defenses against heat loss. Unfortunately, the investigation of the physiology of such people as these began only when they were on the verge of extinction. Civilization brought diseases to which these remote people had never been exposed and to which they had no resistance. Today only a handful of racially pure individuals remain to represent these people of Paleolithic technology living in a near-arctic climate.

When the heat balance formulas that apply to us are tried on the Tierra del Fuegians, we find that these people lose heat at such a rate that they cannot survive. However, there they are, and there they have been for thousands of years, and we are faced with evidence that they have heat-producing and heat-conserving mechanisms different from ours.

The Tierra del Fuegians pose a number of problems. Did they develop their physiological specializations there, or did they bring them with them? The same question arises for their way of life. How much was evolved there, and how much did they bring with them? If man had physiological adaptations that enabled him to pass through Beringia, it seems the more economical theory to assume that he kept them and because of them managed to fit into Tierra del Fuego. The alternative is, of course, that he redeveloped these mechanisms there.

If a cold-adapted man with a shore orientation entered America, he would have a cool coast and even cold water clear to the tip of Baja California. He would face a long, hot gap from there to northern Peru, where he would again find cold waters and a cold, foggy coast, which would in turn lead to Tierra del Fuego. Although not a lot of research has been done along this long coastal route, we know that there were crude cobble-using cultures, often showing indications of great age. In part they were surely boat- or raft-borne peoples, for these lithic traits extend to offshore islands: the Santa Barbara Channel Islands, the Coronado Islands off San Diego, and all the offshore islands of Baja California. Along all of this Pacific coast, the people were shellfish gatherers.

And here we face the peculiar myth in archeology that shellfish use by man is a late invention. This is surely not true. In southern California the skeletons dated by protein racemization to 50,000 years are from the well-known shell middens there. The occupants of the old land surfaces laid down over the Pleistocene beaches were shellfish users, and this suggests dates back to 60,000 years. There are traces of shellfish at the Texas Street site, and this may carry shellfish use back to the 100,000-year time level. We may assume that the earliest folk were gatherers of the products of the land and the seashore and that this at least included shellfish. Food was not the problem. How did they survive these severe climates with so little equipment?

Bernard Dethier's study (1958) proceeded as follows. He used average winter temperatures since the goal was not to find the ultimate limit of survival but the heat balance under normal conditions. It can be assumed that under extreme conditions primitive peoples sought shelter and endured. Their clothing can be evaluated as to its efficiency under normal conditions, and this gives a good starting point in a study of survival in extreme cold.

The clothing of these people was skimpy indeed, especially that of the Yahgans and the Alakalufs, and even the Onas' clothing was notable for its lack of tailoring. Clothing that is not properly fitted has a bellows action that pumps out the warmed air between the clothes and the body. U.S. Army clothing loses one-half of its insulating value due to such action. Eskimo clothing with its tight waistband and neck band and its hood with drawstrings is more efficient. Large openings further decrease efficiency, and Yahgan and Alakaluf clothing is mostly open. Ona cloaks are little better, for no active work can be done without relaxing one's grip on the cloak, and it then falls open, if not off. If necessity were the mother of invention, someone would have invented pants and jackets and parkas and boots, but despite apparent need for better clothing for comfort and efficiency none was invented. Their equipment was no better than the cloak and moccasin assemblage of the Paiute of Nevada or of most of the tribes in California. It was an ancient clothing style carried far toward its climatic limit, coupled in this case with the phenomenon, rare in man, of physiological change to meet an environmental challenge.

These people used animal skins for clothing, and these are about four times as efficient, measured in clo units, as is cotton. One clo unit is a measure of clothing with about the efficiency of a business suit. However, the Yahgans covered only ten percent of their bodies and did that with ill-fitting clothing; the end result was an average clo value of 0.2 clo, the equivalent perhaps of wearing a pair of cotton underpants. The Onas, when they could keep both arms inside their robes, were 90 percent covered, but activity would reduce the efficiency of their clothing at least 50 percent. Allowing a value up to 5.0 clo for fox and guanaco skins gives their clothing a rating of 2.5 clo.

If you use standard formulas and the usual figures for basal metabolism and heat gained from eating and working, then deduct heat losses by radiation, convection, and so forth, you get the interesting result that the Yahgans cannot exist. The Onas, due to their superior clothing, come out better, but they too still show a heat deficit. The whole exercise is intensely interesting. Physiologically unadapted and unacclimatized man could not survive in Tierra del Fuego, but the primitive inhabitants did. As it stands, we have evidence here of man on a lower-Paleolithic cultural level existing in a climate comparable to the southern edge of Beringia. It might be argued that all of this developed once man arrived in Tierra del Fuego, but we have evidence that suggests quite otherwise.

MARKKLEEBERG MAN

That man in Eurasia probably was at least as well adapted physiologically and culturally to great cold as man in Tierra del Fuego is illustrated by Neanderthal man's living in northern Europe even in glacial times, but an even more striking case is furnished by Markkleeberg.

The Markkleeberg site is five miles south of Leipzig and has been known since 1895. In 1955 Graham reported that the paleontologic and geologic evidence placed man there in the first part of the third glaciation. At that time there was an ice-free corridor between the Alpine ice and the Scandinavian ice.

One must hold some reservations about this date. In general, the Mousterians are thought to be the first truly cold-climate people and to date to about 100,000 years ago, and this may be a better time placement for the Markkleeberg site. Our interest is less in the specific culture and time and more in the ecological setting. With the changed glacial-dating systems, one is rather uncertain about what a third-glacial time means. In Evans' system, 3C would be 110,000 years ago. Time is indeed difficult. Markkleeberg is clearly at least middle Paleolithic and can serve as an ecological test area.

The world in which Markkleeberg man lived presented a situation of great cold and had little summer warmth, for trees could not survive. Steppe and tundra developed. Winters must have been very cold, with a snow cover, and a relatively windless situation is assumed. Spring was a time of snow melt and some precipitation, with westerly winds. Luxurious prairies held many grazing animals, including reindeer, muskox, wolverine, mammoth, wooly rhinoceros, cave bear, cave lion, horse, Irish deer, bison, and saiga antelope. If this was man's sustenance, then he was a big game hunter.

Summer temperatures are estimated to have been about fifty degrees Fahrenheit, and it must have been dry, for wind-blown silts (loess) were deposited.

There may be some misconceptions here. Summers above fifty degrees would allow tree growth, which is said to be absent. The deposit of loess is too often equated with drought. In Alaska, especially the Matanuska Valley, loess is related to meltwater flooding of glaciers due to warm days, followed by cold nights when the glacial streams are reduced to trickles. Strong winds descending from the glaciers then carry clouds of glacial flour from the now-dry riverbeds and spread them over the river banks to be trapped in the vegetation lining the rivers. This gives the familar loess lens: thick near the river and thinner away. The presence of loess may then be read as evidence of glacially fed streams with strong freeze and thaw phenomena. The parallel to the Matanuska Valley may be apt.

Autumn precipitation lays down a snow cover, and, with the oncoming of winter, high pressure spreads over the area blocking entry by moist winds and initiating the winter period of calm and cold. There is general agreement that this corridor was quite cold in winter, with a January average about three degrees Fahrenheit and with cold spells of perhaps minus-forty degrees. If man could seek shelter and had fire, then he could survive brief cold spells, and our interest is again on his ability to survive the average condition.

Wind is a liability for man—and as the temperature drops, wind's toll increases. Wind reduces the efficiency of clothing and by bringing increasing amounts of cold air into contact with exposed flesh it greatly increases heat loss. As a result, physiological climatologists speak of windchill. It is pleasant at 200 on the windchill scale, very cool at 600, very cold at 1,000, and exposed flesh freezes at 1,400, which is twenty-mile-an-hour wind at twenty degrees Fahrenheit or minus-ten degrees with a five-mile-per-hour wind. At three degrees Fahrenheit, the estimated average January temperature at Markkleeberg, the windchill factor places man in the area where exposed flesh freezes even at low wind velocities, so it must be assumed that man had considerable clothing as well as good shelter and fire.

Man would gain little from solar radiation at Markkleeberg due to the short days. Man would lose heat to the snow-covered terrain and to the sky. The cloudier the sky the less heat he would lose. Although winter is dry today at Markkleeberg, it is cloudy, and conditions during glacial times probably were little different.

Dethier worked with these variables and calculated that for man to live at Markkleeberg he would need a minimum of 1.2 clo units for 90 percent of his body. Since all of Dethier's assumptions are on the conservative side—less wind, more cloud, least possible time outside pursuing game, average temperatures rather than extremes—it would not be unreasonable to assume 2.5 clo units needed, something comparable to the Ona's clothing. With winter temperatures below the limit at which exposed flesh freezes, nearly complete coverage seems required. Markkleeberg man had available reindeer, one of the most efficient heat-conserving hides in the world, with a clo value of 6.5. If he made a robe comparable to that of the Ona, bootlike moccasins for his feet, and probably a headpiece of some sort, he could survive even the occasional temperatures of forty degrees below zero. Dethier calculates that under average conditions man could even have a heat surplus of 156 kilogram calories per square meter per hour. Awls and sinew are all that are needed for sewing, and awls were present. It is generally assumed that Markkleeberg man hunted, and this would provide reindeer skins. The objective evidence is that man lived there and that the physiology of man demands at least Ona-like clothing.

We have wandered far from Bering Strait, but all the data are applicable. The equation would seem to read: the Ona, and even more so the Yahgan and Alakaluf, were lower-Paleolithic survivals, culturally enriched later in time by such items as the bow and arrow, but otherwise having departed little from the Paleolithic lifeways. They could survive at Bering Strait today or on the southern edge of Beringia at any time. Furthermore, if Markkleeberg man could survive under the extreme conditions described, similar men should have been able to cross the Bering Strait any time, back for 100,000 years or so.

Francois Bordes states that men of the Acheulean period, about 200,000 years ago, lived on reindeer in the south of France when the climate there was steppelike—few if any trees. That is even earlier than Markkleeberg.

It is a long way from Europe to Bering Strait, but the evidence is pertinent nonetheless. Still, it would be even better to have an example of men of this time nearer to America, and we have just such a man living at Peking at just the right time. At Choukoutien, near Peking, man was living during the third glacial period, and for a longish time earlier—back 350,000 years.

PEKING MAN

This man was originally called *Sinanthropus pekinensis* but is now considered to belong to *Homo erectus*. There may be a major error in judgment of the site, for the human remains found there all suggest the possibility that Peking man was the prey of some more advanced man. The skeletal parts found in the cave are principally skulls that have been broken open as if to get the brain out for food. The tools are not really primitive, and the situation is reminiscent of Olduvai Gorge, where it was first thought that the *Zinjanthropus boisei* (an Australopithecine) made the stone tools. Now it appears more likely that *Homo habilis*, an early *Homo erectus*, made the tools and ate Australopithecines, at least on festal occasions. At any rate the evidence at Choukoutien is that some form of fire-making, tool-using, moderately good hunter lived in the Peking area about 350,000 years ago. Although it is a long jump from Peking to Bering, this is the time and cultural level of greatest interest for the peopling of America.

Again our interest is in winter conditions. Peking is south of the Shansi mountain range, which tends to divert the outflow of cold Siberian air. A low-pressure trough forms along the Philippine-Formosa-Japan island arc in winter, and the major zone of air-mass interaction, the zone of frontal activity, is along the China coast. Inland China and Manchuria are dominated in winter by the Siberian high-pressure cell. This brings dry, cold air of about thirty-two degrees Fahrenheit. The area is windy, and the low humidity is accompanied by much clear air. Solar radiation is high, but so is outgoing radiation, and this combination can cause extreme daily temperature ranges. Cold waves can drop the temperature to minus-four degrees, and this comes with clear skies and high, outgoing radiation. Such cold waves arrive three to five times during the normal midwinter period.

Temperature at Peking during the winter months ranges from

November's thirty-eight degrees Fahrenheit to January's twenty-three degrees. Daily minimums during the winter months are all below thirty-two degrees, and in January are fourteen degrees. Extreme lows are near minus-four degrees Fahrenheit. These figures are probably above those at Choukoutien, for they were recorded in the city, and city temperatures are usually about three to five degrees warmer than the countryside.

Rainfall at Peking comes in the summer, and little rain or snow comes in winter. A total of less than one inch of precipitation falls in the four winter months. While Peking is windy, it is not excessively so, as for instance Tierra del Fuego is. In short, Peking's winters, the critical time for man, are cold, dry, clear, and moderately windy.

During glacial times Peking would have been somewhat colder and perhaps drier. The loess of north China is always cited as evidence of drought, but again this may be a misapprehension. Loess, like sand, accumulates where wind has access to a supply of silt-sized particles not fixed by vegetation. The great dune fields of the world are not restricted to deserts, for some of the largest are associated with beaches in very rainy areas such as the Netherlands and at places on our American northwest coast, where strong oceanic winds and the constant sand supply on the beaches set the scene for immense sand accumulation. The Mississippi loess, like the Matanuska Valley loess, is a measure of glacially ground rock spread out on river flats alternately flooded and exposed to strong winds. Glacial winds in north China must have been strong, and some phenomenon supplied great quantities of silt. It is too facile to evoke aridity.

Inner Asia had no ice cap but only glaciation on mountains. Although one Russian scholar estimates that the greater continental mass exposed during glacially lowered seas might be as much as five degrees warmer in summers, the same increase in continentality would lead to an equal or greater increase in cold in winter. The outpouring cold air in winter would give Peking decreased precipitation, decreased relative humidity, decreased cloud cover, increased cold, and increased wind. All of these would increase the cold stress for man. It is thought that something like this created a steppe climate, though the presence of redbud and hackberry does not suggest great aridity. The fauna included deer, wooly rhinoceros, horse, gazelle, jerboa, and ostrich. Most of these animals are at home in the steppes, though deer are more common in woodlands than in grasslands.

Of the animal bone at the *Sinanthropus* site, 70 percent was deer bone; there was also some horse and gazelle bone. The man living there was obviously not only a hunter but a big game hunter. Hackberry fruits indicate that he was also using the plant resources. He used fire extensively and clearly had solved the problem of successfully coping with a severely cold winter area in higher mid-latitude, thirty-nine degrees north. Calculation of the heat balance for man in that area indicates survival was possible with only 0.13 clo, a value so small as to suggest the possibility of existing with no clothing. The lower latitude, longer days, and higher sun, together with clear skies assure much warming by the sun even in winter. The area is less stressful than Markkleeberg, Tierra del Fuego, or Bering Strait. Realistically, one could well imagine sandals and a robe, garb equivalent to the Paiute living in the Great Basin and subject to somewhat similar climatic stresses. Man, whoever he was, could do all of this 350,000 years ago. After these detours, we are now prepared to examine man's physiological problems at Bering Strait.

PHYSIOLOGICAL CLIMATOLOGY OF BERINGIA

Dethier calculated that during a glacial period nude man's heat loss at Bering would be 1,049 K cal/m²/hr for the Siberian side and 781 K cal/m²/hr for the Alaskan side.* Death, the icy reaper, would harvest such unfortunate nudes shortly. Since man did approach the strait from the Siberian side, cross it, and exit via the Alaskan side, he surely was clothed. From Markkleeberg and Peking we can get some measures of what he had to have. Peking man might have survived without clothing, but he probably had a minimal amount. Markkleeberg man had to have clothing of robe and moccasin and headgear type. Since he had bone awls and hides and survived, it can be assumed that he hid from the cold, probably in reindeer hides,

---

* Heat loss and gain, as reviewed earlier, are handled mathematically by the physiological climatologists and stated as an equation or balance between loss and gain. This is expressed in kilogram calories per square meter per hour (K cal/m²/hr).

and that was the kind of information we need to apply to Beringia.

Given an Ona-Markkleeberg-type equipment, man in northeast Siberia would have a plus-271 K cal/m²/hr heat balance, and with some care to get out of the wind and in by the fire, even in a crude hut, he could survive forty-below weather. In the southwest-Alaska section of Beringia he would have a comfortable 348 K cal/m²/hr surplus. Man need not have hustled through; he could have lived there for indefinite time. We can assume that the men who worked their way north in Asia to approach the Bering bridge had equipment at least as good as Peking man at 350,000 years and Markkleeberg man at plus or minus 100,000 or man on the Dordogne at 200,000. Perhaps a good guess would be that from some time around 200,000 years ago the arctic gate could be passed.

If man drifted into the Asiatic vicinity of Beringia during an interglacial time, then with the onset of a glacial period a great plain extending from Asia to America would emerge before him. It would be a millennium-long process, with the slowly emerging land welcoming a plant succession of beach species and then scrub alder and then spruce forest. The farther the sea retreated, the farther the land extended to the south and east, and the milder the climate and the woodier the vegetation cover. In the southeast corner of Beringia lay a refugium in the latitude of Sitka and with a climate much like Sitka's. Sitka's climate is less stormy than that of Tierra del Fuego, where not only the Ona but the even less-equipped Yahgan and Alakaluf survived.

The conclusion then is that from some time in the later lower Paleolithic, perhaps around 200,000 years ago, man had sufficient cultural equipment—fire, ability to get big game and warm skins, and sufficient housing and clothing—to reach Beringia, to cross it, survive on it, and, when routes afforded, to enter America. We must now examine the routes from Beringia into America.

THE WAY OUT

There are two routes: interior and coastal. The way to the interior route is either through exceedingly difficult mountainous terrain or over the roof of the world, skirting the arctic sea to follow the arctic coastal plain. East of the Rockies a corridor may have existed between eastern and western ice masses in later Wisconsin times. If this was not present during glacial maxima, it most probably was at glacial beginnings and endings. However, the high mountains and high latitudes of this route would seem to restrict this route to upper-Paleolithic man, such as the type of man that was living at Old Crow 30,000 years ago. For our lower-Paleolithic men it seems more likely that the milder coastal route was used. However, this route has long been considered impassable both because the mountains extend right into the sea and because it has been assumed that the shelf ice (continental glacial ice extending out into the sea) completely closed this pathway. But this conclusion has been challenged by K. R. Fladmark (1978).

The coast of the panhandle of Alaska and British Columbia is forbidding, but its ruggedness has been overgeneralized. It is 1,700 miles long, nearly 200 miles wide, and composed of three zones (see figure 49). An eastern mountainous zone, the inner coast, has inlets penetrating deep into the mountains. A coastal trough known as the inland passage has much lower relief, extensive areas of flat terrain, and long, broad strandflats. An outer mountain region, although mountainous, still possesses considerable areas of low-lying land and long strandflats. Thus the coastal trough and outer mountain zones make up a nearly continuous strip of low-relief terrain extending from the Columbia River to Prince William Sound at the base of the Aleutians. There are a few mountain fronts that extend right to the sea and present difficult barriers, and there are inlets that interrupt the continuous land connection. However, for a people of Tierra del Fuegian cultural level and equipped with even the most primitive watercraft, the region would be livable, traversable, and easily passable at any time it was not covered with ice. Fladmark addresses himself to this particular point by reviewing what has been thought and what is now known—two quite different things.

V. K. Prest of the Geological Survey of Canada made a map (1969) showing the retreat of the Wisconsin glaciers in North America. This map shows total ice coverage of the entire northwest coast at 15000 B.P. with the exception of a narrow coastal strip in southeastern Alaska. The map shows an unbroken mass of ice extending from the mountains of the inner coast into the sea at the edge of the continental shelf. Prest showed no ice-free areas and no

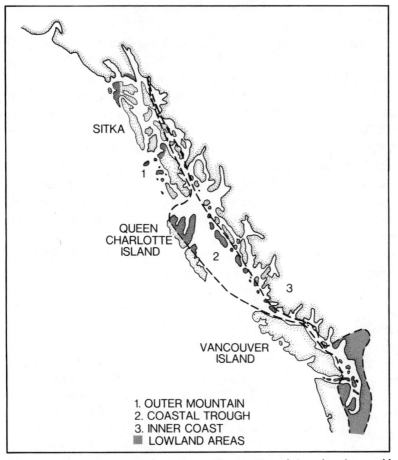

SITKA

1

QUEEN
CHARLOTTE
ISLAND

2

3

VANCOUVER
ISLAND

1. OUTER MOUNTAIN
2. COASTAL TROUGH
3. INNER COAST
■ LOWLAND AREAS

FIGURE 49. The three zones along the northwest coast of America that could have provided a road south are shown here, along with an indication of the extensive occurrence of lowland areas suitable for man's occupation. These routes into America would be no more difficult to survive in than the land now occupied by the Tierra del Fuegians.

topographic control but a great undifferentiated ice cover comparable to Antarctica's vast ice sheet that flows down into the sea and extends out as shelf ice. However, even Antarctica's ice has some ice-free areas and is subject to some topographic control. Fladmark noted that Prest considered his map speculative but that some archeologists, notably Vance Haynes, have treated it as "divine truth." Fladmark then reviewed the detailed geologic and ecological picture as revealed in the literature.

The late Wisconsin glaciation varied greatly depending on

ice sources. In some areas, for example the Strait of Georgia, ice did not appear until after 25000 B.P. and reached its peak expansion as late as 15000 B.P. Glaciers from the Cascade Range were not synchronous, for they had advanced over and retreated from Puget Sound by 17000 B.P. In general maximum glaciation on the southern coast was short-lived and fell around 15000 to 20000 B.P. This suggests that the southern parts of the central trough and outer mountains were largely ice free. They surely were covered not by a continuous ice cap during late Wisconsin but by brief and non-synchronous ice sheets. There were always ice-free areas. Indeed, recent evidence indicates that continental ice from the Fraser glaciation reached only Victoria, B.C., leaving Vancouver Island uncovered. On Vancouver Island there is clear evidence of limitation of glaciers to valleys, with ice-free areas between. The Queen Charlotte Islands present a similar picture: not under an ice cap but subject to glaciers following valleys. There is biological data to support this, for the Queen Charlotte Islands have endemic plants and animals that indicate long isolation during the Wisconsin glaciation. With lowered sea levels during glacial time, extensive shelves around these islands would have been exposed. Such areas would be suitable for forest growth, and the pollen profiles show the presence of a spruce forest. The oceanic gaps between the islands would be greatly reduced, facilitating human movement by boat from the mainland to islands or from island to island on a north-south route.

Most surprising is the fact that much of the coast southeast of the Alexander Archipelago was less glaciated during the Wisconsin time than during the Neoglacial about 1800 A.D. This surprising finding is attributed by the glaciologists and geologists to the rapid rise of the St. Elias range. Prior to its becoming a major snowshed, the area to the west had between 3,000 and 8,000 square kilometers of ice-free territory. There may have been further ice-free areas in Cook Inlet and Prince William Sound. The southwestern portion of Kodiak Island was an ice-free refugium, and there is little evidence for extensive Wisconsin ice on the continental shelf of the Gulf of Alaska.

The gist of this is that Prest's speculative continuous shelf ice has been proven wrong. Instead there was a string of ice-free areas that would have made possible the passage from the Beringian platform to the inner Aleutians to the Panhandle of Alaska to the coast of British Columbia and thence on into unglaciated America. If the way was open even during glacial times, it would have been a still easier route in interglacial time for people of the Tierra del Fuegian level of culture. It is an area rich in shellfish, the coastal foragers' prime target. The fish resources are great, and even the earliest people should have been able to harvest some of the fish that migrate in immense numbers up the freshwater streams, salmon and oulachon (a sardine-sized fish) in particular.

The question of watercraft recurs in many early-man problems. There are several sets of watercraft. The reed bundle boat requires only cordage for tying the bundles. It has an extraordinarily wide distribution in the world, is made to one pattern, and the suggestion is great antiquity and diffusion. This craft may well be a lower-Paleolithic invention. Its near relatives are the log raft and other "wash through" craft comparable to that used by the Tasmanians. These too are possibly lower Paleolithic in age, though it is unlikely that we will ever be able to prove that they are.

In terms of man's ability and tool using, the sequence could well be rafts and single-skin bark boats in the lower Paleolithic, dugouts of increasing complexity in the upper Paleolithic, and then ships in the Neolithic. This raises the possibility that the northwest coast of America was passable by coastal foragers with no more equipment than that of the Tierra del Fuegians from lower-Paleolithic times on. The fact that no such remains have been found along this route is negative evidence requiring only one chance find to offset it, and this area has had little archeological work. That done to date has focused overmuch on the spectacular late villages. Even so, lithic assemblages with no bifacially flaked points already are known. Some of these resemble work with cobbles so well known for the La Jollan culture of southern California, for which geomorphic dates of 60,000 years are suggested and for which we have protein racemization dates to the 50,000-year time level. Sites of glacial age will be difficult to find if man followed the now-submerged shorelines. Interglacial sites will have been subjected to some glaciation, will be in locations not related to either present- or last-glacial sea levels, and will probably first be found by accident. It will also be necessary that the finder be able to distinguish lower Paleolithic artifacts from geofacts.

These requirements may delay for a while the documenting of early man's passage through the coastal corridor into America. However, it should be clear by now that neither climate nor topography was a likely deterrent to man during the past 100,000 or 200,000 years. The bridge with its approaches and exits was available, and man was capable. We still must determine the actual times of entry, but we are free within that time limit to state at least that finds are not impossible. With man present in southern California, one must choose: man crossed the vast seas by boat by about 100,000 years ago, or he passed the icy gate of Beringia and exited by land or sea, inland or coastal. With European evidence now suggesting Acheulean boat crossings of the narrow parts of the Mediterranean (Bordes, 1978), we have the possibility of watercraft extending back as much as 200,000 years. People of no higher culture than Tierra del Fuegians could have entered America even through the arctic's icy gate on some such time level.

Chapter 8

Who Were They?

THE seemingly simple question of who the first Americans were quickly turns into a complex set of questions concerning who the first man at all was, when he developed, and from what prehuman form. Determining American man's identity presupposes knowledge of the time of origin of modern man—*Homo sapiens*—and of his development into most-modern man—*Homo sapiens sapiens*—and it requires some understanding of the relationship of this line of man to the beetling-browed Neanderthal man. Related to this problem is the question of when the races of mankind developed, and this in turn is complicated by the difficulty of distinguishing between races—a tricky task even among the living, not to mention in skeletons. These questions themselves are surrounded by controversies as lively as that concerning the antiquity of man in America, so we have a controversy within a controversy.

Thoroughly mixed into this are whole sets of clichés about man's inability to enter America via Bering Strait and floods of other pseudo-objections to evidence for the possibility of early man —man of say 100,000 years ago—and of particular kinds of men, such as Negroids, Negritoids, Australoids, and Europoids in America.

The view of early man in America has been confused by insistence on a single, late race of *Homo sapiens sapiens*—the Mongoloids. This view is wrong on two counts. First, the earliest arrivals most certainly were not Mongoloids, and perhaps neither were the second or third wave of arrivals. Second, the earliest arrivals may not even have been most-modern man (*Homo sapiens sapiens*), although, contrary to the popular view, that does not mean races had not appeared. We now have suggestions of very early *sapiens* types of men, something on the Neanderthal stage, as our first en-

trants, followed by Negritoids, then various Europoids, and belatedly the Mongoloids. This chronology is not mine alone but has been
suggested at times by such giants in physical anthropology as Ernest
Hooton and R. B. Dixon. It has not, however, been a popular notion. Let's begin by looking at some of the evidence in America
and then turn to an examination of the Eurasian situation that could
account for the American pattern.

THE EMERGENCE OF MAN

Our knowledge of man's emergence is in a ferment. We have
suddenly received so much new and revolutionary information from
East Africa that we will be decades in digesting it. The main thrust
of the new information is that relatively smooth-browed man, who
was a tool-making man, extends back to perhaps two to three million years instead of 200,000 or 300,000. We will obviously have
to change nearly all our time scales and many of our judgments
about man and his development through various stages and the appearance of races of mankind.

We have passed through a period in which each new find of
fossil man was given a separate genus and species name. This gave
rise to a forbidding jungle of *Pithecanthropus erectus* (Java man),
Sinanthropus pekinensis (Peking man), *Eoanthropus dawsoni* (Pilt-
down man), *Zinjanthropus boisei* (Leakey's first East Africa find).
Today the many fossil men are assembled in a few glades: pre-men,
early men (*Homo erectus*), early modern men (*Homo sapiens*),
and modern modern men (*Homo sapiens sapiens*). These are very
wide brackets. *Homo sapiens* includes both such primitive-looking,
very heavy-browed forms as Neanderthal man and the quite modern-
looking skulls of the upper-Paleolithic people of Europe. All living
men are placed in *Homo sapiens sapiens*.

While these grades of men are determined by cranial capacity,
skull form, and a formidable list of indexes, they also conform in
a rough way to a time sequence. *Homo sapiens sapiens* is thought of
as quite recent; only a few ten thousands of years at most. *Homo
sapiens* is thought of as dating from perhaps 20,000 or 30,000 years
ago to perhaps 100,000 years ago. Back of that are the truly primitive men of small cranial capacity, the *Homo erectus* men. How
much this chronology will change in the next decade is going to be

interesting to see. The smooth-browed skull from East Africa dating to nearly 2,000,000 years ago is one indicator of the great change needed. The redating of the beginning of the Middle Stone Age of Africa from around 30,000 to 200,000 years ago is also revolutionary, for it is characterized by *sapiens* men, as well as such "late" tools as the metate. Many of the clichés about the age of man in America are affected by all this.

Then there is the problem of races. Races are finer divisions than stages. If we had enough skeletal material for the stages of mankind, we would surely be able to distinguish racial subdivisions in all stages. We have traces of this. The Swanscombe skull is generally Europoid and the Peking skulls are generally Mongoloid. The stage is *Homo erectus*, and the time perhaps around 400,000 years. This raciation follows naturally from biological facts. Populations widely spread over the earth constantly diverge. This is because variation goes on constantly and unevenly, and, without perfect mixing of breeding populations, differences will arise between one population and another. This will occur whether there is an environmental pressure or not. But there are environmental pressures. Fair skins are selected for in cloudy areas and dark skins in zones of intense sun, and there are many more such selective actions. As a result, all living things diverge through time into myriad populations, each somewhat different from its nearest neighbors and increasingly different from its more distant neighbors. The elephants of Africa are certainly elephants, but any well-informed person can tell an African elephant from an Indian elephant. But for that matter, so can one easily detect the difference between the human inhabitants of India and those of tropical Africa. Man is no exception to the rule of variation.

Once man spread widely over the world, he developed varieties —or races, if you wish. Man certainly spread over much of the world while still in the *Homo erectus* stage, and a controversy exists in anthropology concerning how in the many parts of the world mankind progressed from the *erectus* stage to the *sapiens* stage, to the *sapiens sapiens* stage. Carleton Coon (1962) argues that he did so somewhat unevenly and that some living populations are still in the *sapiens* stage—an unpopular notion in this egalitarian age.

So if we look at man most broadly, we have all of living men in the *sapiens sapiens* stage, though some groups are perhaps more recent arrivals at this stage than others. Within this stage we have the broad breakdown of the black men, the white men, and the brown men: Negroid, Europoid, Mongoloid. The basic color is or was black (in Africa, India, southeast Asia, Australia, Tasmania, Melanesia). Two variants exist: the semi-albinos of northwest Europe and the yellow-brown people of inner Asia. Within these three groups we have races. In Europe, for example, there are Mediterranean, Alpine, and Nordic. There are similar divisions within the blacks and the browns, and there are enormous mixtures whenever one race touches the territory of another.

There is, contrary to this picture, a current theory that races emerged very late in time. Protsch, as discussed earlier, has decided that raciation in modern man cannot be detected prior to 40,000 years ago. There is also a tendency in some quarters to put the appearance of the classic Mongoloids as at least that recent. This seems to me to run counter to the simplest rules of biology. Variation is constant, and short of perfect mixing of genes differences will arise. Since man was widely distributed over the Old World by at least a million years ago, the beginning of racial differences goes back that far. By the time the peopling of the New World began, whether it was 10,000 or 100,000 years ago, raciation must have been far advanced. As can be plainly seen, one man could argue that if there are racial differences in America, the fact is insignificant as evidence of antiquity, for races arise quickly. Another could argue that races arise slowly and are ancient, and varied races in America means great antiquity. But the counter argument would be that races existed prior to man's entry into America and that the original entrants were already racially diverse. As we will see, it is probable that varied races entered America at differing times. So the argument from races has to be hedged rather carefully with all the usual disclaimers.

A word, too, on the use of *oid*, as in Negroid, Mongoloid, Europoid. If one says Mongol, one means a specific type of man, the classic inner Asian—a brown-skinned, roundheaded, tall, slant-eyed, straight black coarse–haired, nearly beardless type of man. Mongoloid would mean a type of man that approached but was not exactly like the classic type. The American Indians are said to be Mongoloid: like the Mongols, but somewhat different. We can similarly use Europoid, Negroid, Australoid. The problem is that these terms become awfully loose. The classic example is that of calling the American Indians Mongoloids.

THE MONGOLOID FIXATION

As I have said, the supreme fixation is that all of the American Indians are Mongoloid and that the earliest Americans were also. They may be classified narrowly as Mongoloids or, more broadly, as members of a great generalized race of "proto-mongols," but the latter is simply an escape hatch to let one include all kinds of men as Mongoloid. East Asia has Negritos, Negroes, Europeans, classic Mongols, and all possible mixtures of these. When these are lumped into the Mongoloid race, one has such a mixture of traits that one can prove anyone to be Mongoloid, and this is what has all too often been done. The peoples of America are themselves a hodgepodge of races labeled American Indian. Every race of mankind and almost every conceivable mixture is to be found among the American Indians. Lumping these variations together and then comparing them with an equally bizarre mixture in Asia can get us nowhere, and yet this is commonly done.

Opinions on how many races entered America vary from one to a few to several; and estimates of the time since entry, from 2,000 years to 100,000 plus. The epitome of the single-race and short-time-scale position is found in A. L. Kroeber's discussion, "The Present State of Americanist Problems" in *The Maya and Their Neighbors* (1973). This apparently represents Kroeber's thinking as of the late 1930's. There Kroeber acknowledges that some people, such as Carleton Coon, argue for the coming in waves of several races and rather great antiquity for man in America and that W. H. Howells believes there were a few races. However, Kroeber expresses a preference for a view of one pure race of men entering America about 2,000 years ago. He thinks that all the considerable variation in the American Indians came about thereafter, a truly incredible idea even in 1940. It may seem a bit unfair to hold the opinion of forty years ago against a man, but it is notable that there were alternative readings of the facts and that it was Kroeber who was wrong and Coon who was right.

The race problem in America is not simple; it is indeed extremely complex. Alexander von Wuthenau (1965, 1975) has assembled the portraits of the people of Mexico as seen by the prehistoric artists. Mongols, Negroes, and Europeans are clearly portrayed. Some of these probably are latecomers, a situation that has been suggested since Alexander von Humboldt's time by everyone from art historians to botanists. We now begin to see evidence from writing and even from linguistics of wholesale arrivals and colonization, and it is just this kind of sequence that would change the racial mix in America.

One of the early works pointing to plurality of races in America was done by Dixon of Harvard (1923). His book *The Racial History of Man* was an exercise in the use of a few key traits of the skull to designate certain combinations with racial tags: Australoid, Negroid, Europoid, Alpine, and so forth. He mapped the distribution of these clusters of traits for the whole world. The result in America should have been to destroy the Mongoloid American Indian myth. There were many races in America if one used the same criteria that one used in the Old World. Despite Dixon's high standing in his profession, he came under furious attack and is said in after years to have referred to his book as "my sin."

Hooton, in his examination of the skulls from Pecos Pueblo in New Mexico (1930), came up with similar findings. He detected Negrito, Mediterranean, and other race types there and considered the Mongoloid race to be late and to have left a smear of Mongoloid traits over a non-Mongoloid people. Aleš Hrdlička, to whom all Indians were Indians, studied the Pueblo Indians and found some surprising things (1935). They were not much like their neighbors to the north, west, or south, but they were like the eastern Indians. Even more startling, they were somewhat like the Old American Whites, the descendants of Europeans who had lived in America for several generations.

One can pursue such clues quite far. It happens that Europeans, Africans, and Mongols differ in their earwax. Europeans and Africans have sticky earwax, and Mongols have dry, flaky earwax. Everyone can do a little scientific digging in his own ear to test this one. If the Pueblos and the eastern Indians are Europoid, then they should have sticky earwax. We find that they do, to the extent that we have pure groups left to measure and that they have been measured.

The earwax relationship was found by Matsunaga (1962), and when he calculated the gene frequencies for peoples of many regions and races he found striking differences. The classic Mongols, such as the North Chinese, Koreans, Tungus, and Japanese, are at the high end of the scale for dry earwax. The farther south one goes, the lower the frequency of dry wax, and the expectation for the Negritos and Australoids is for very low frequencies. Europeans and American Negroes show very low percentages of dry earwax. Whole tribes of eastern United States Indians will score low on the Mongoloid, dry-wax scale. If Hooton and Dixon are right and the American Indians are basically Negroid, Australoid, and Europoid, to which belatedly some Mongoloid genes were added, then this is just what we might expect.

There are other such markers. For instance, there are many more blood groups than the familiar A, B, and O, and some of these are quite limited in their distribution in mankind. One interesting one is the Diego blood group; it is an exclusive Mongoloid marker. Just as in earwax type, the Eurafricans are sharply set off from the Mongols. The Diego factor is absent from the long-headed, marginal people of America, indicating that these first Americans were non-Mongoloid (Layrisse and Wilbert, 1964). In Middle America, where the Amerind civilizations are loaded with Asiatic arts, the round-headed races with the Diego blood group are present. They are Mongoloids.

Incidentally, the Ainu, those enigmatic little stocky, swarthy, bearded men of Japan, now relegated to the northern island of Hokkaido and long thought to represent a European race in the Far Orient, are in earwax clearly Europeans. Interesting, for that places Europeans on the doorstep to America.

It is now becoming increasingly evident that men began arriving from overseas, crossing both the Atlantic and the Pacific and colonizing various parts of America—the eastern United States, parts of Mexico, areas in the Andes, and elsewhere. In those areas, it is easy to point out either Europoid or Mongoloid traits. Since

up to now such racial additions have not been considered, by picking one's spot one could prove almost anything in the racial field
about early Americans.

The purpose of this brief excursion into a most complicated
problem is to indicate how immensely complex the racial history of
America is. It is pointless to look at the present population as a
simple input from Siberia. Similarly, the attempt to account for
racial sequences by distance from the Bering Strait is pointless if
colonization by sea across both the Atlantic and the Pacific occurred.
Only confusion can result, and confusion is what we have. Solemn
debate has been carried on as to how this admixture in America
could have resulted from a few inputs from Siberia. Was there a
single migration, and did all this differentiation take place in America in the short time available—a mere 10,000 years, or Kroeber's
2,000 years—from a single pure race? Or was the incoming population a mixture, which segregated out into these various types as
they spread over America. This explanation would help, but the
degree of difference must then have been very great, in spite of one
physical anthropologist's incredible statement that "when you have
seen one American Indian, you have seen them all." Consider that
the earliest explorers described some Indians as being as fair or
fairer than we are. Others are nearly black. Many have straight
hair, but some tribes have curly hair. Some are huge men, averaging
close to six feet, and others are nearly pygmies, with males averaging a mere five feet. There is every head shape: very long to very
round, very high to very low. There is not unity, there is immense
diversity. Only those hypnotized by the constant repetition of "they
are all Mongoloids" could possibly believe that the race situation
in America is simple or ignore the clear evidence of the presence
of all the races of mankind.

THE EARLY MEN

But our concern is not with this patchwork quilt of originals
and their hybrids as they were at A.D. 1500 or even with the increasing complexity that began with the arrival of populations by
sea, beginning perhaps some time around 3000 B.C. Rather, we are
concerned with what some of the much earlier people were like.
Here suddenly things become simpler. Every skeleton found under

conditions suggesting high antiquity has turned out to be long-headed. One of the classic examples where this was not the case was due to Hrdlička's faulty reconstruction of a skull to make it roundheaded. When correctly reconstructed, it proved to be a typical longheaded individual. I find it a little hard to view this episode in a kindly light, for Hrdlička laid about him with a heavy stick, berating those who committed lesser sins than this.

But longheadedness is indeed a strange finding, for the American Indians are supposed to be Mongols, and the striking thing about Mongols is that they are the classic roundheads of the world. Further, this is a dominant gene, and its travels into Europe, changing the Europeans from longheadedness to roundheadedness, are most apparent on the racial maps of Eurasia. The Mongoloid thrusts into central Europe are marked by roundheadedness, while the longheads persist on the northern and southern margins of this thrust line. Somewhat the same situation is found in America. The descriptions of the skulls that appear to be from early situations are startlingly similar; they all are described as beetling-browed, longheaded, slab-sided, pentagonal or roof-shaped skulls. They could hardly be less Mongoloid, and they characteristically survived in marginal areas.

It is of great interest to see Hrdlička at work on a skeleton that may not be a Neanderthal in America but surely is a bit odd for *Homo sapiens sapiens* (Bell and Hrdlička, 1935). The University of Nebraska excavated a skull fragment in Cedar County, Nebraska, that was unusual enough that they took special care with it and asked Hrdlička to look it over since it was a "low type skull," meaning a relatively primitive skull. The skull has a pronounced development of the brow ridges (see figure 50). In Hrdlička's words, it is "intermediate between that of a modern male and the Neanderthalers. . . . Such occurrences do not mean that Neanderthalers were at any time in America, but they do denote an ancestral connection with that type or phase of human development, somewhere outside of America" (Bell and Hrdlička, 1935, p. 8). That the mixture took place outside America is a pure assumption.

That there are in America's past beetling-browed longheads that would have been just the right men to give rise to such a hybrid as the Nebraska skull, if it is a hybrid, has long been evident

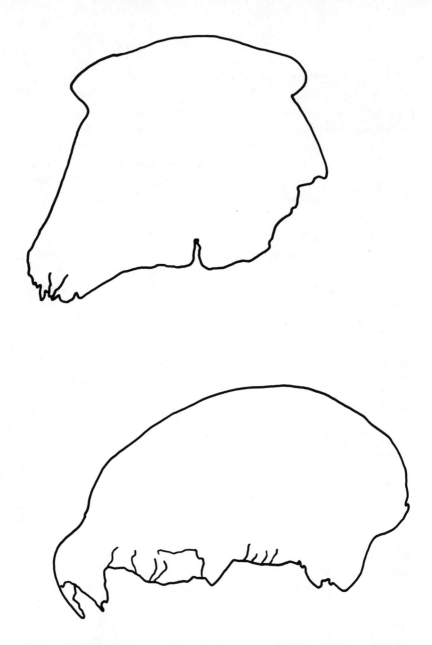

FIGURE 50. This type of skull—with huge brow bridges, constricted frontal, long vault with flat walls and a pitched roof—probably represents one of the earliest human types in America. This is not the most extreme type and may indeed be a cross between the even more extreme type known especially in Brazil and one of the later races to enter America. This particular skull was found in Cedar County, Nebraska, and was described by Aleš Hrdlička.

FIGURE 51. A skull fragment from Brazil illustrates the presence of Neanderthaloid men in America. The use of *oid* is to avoid saying that this is a true or classic, western European Neanderthal. It has distinctive features, such as a modest height to the skull vault and a very great interorbital distance. It is best described as the skull cap of a man on the Neanderthal grade and line of development. (Photo courtesy of Alan Bryan)

in America. Knowledge of an extreme type has been revived by a recent find reported by Alan Bryan (1978) and pictured in figure 51. Long ago a Swedish paleontologist named Lund worked in Brazil, where he found an abundance of fossils in the caves. His fossils were of all ages, from modern to highly fossilized bones of extinct animals. He found human skeletons showing the same thing: great range of age. He never reported on some of the human remains, though others who looked at his collections noted the presence of exceedingly primitive-looking skulls. Recently another skull has turned up in these caves, and Alan Bryan's illustrations of it show all the marks of a man on the Neanderthaloid stage of development (Bryan, 1978).

The Sauk Valley, Minnesota, skeleton is an example of what is certainly one of the earliest American types but probably not as primitive a type as the Brazilian skull illustrated by Bryan. The Minnesota skull has a pentagonal form, often described as house-like: flat floor, steep walls, pitched roof. The brow ridges are massive, and the frontal is sharply restricted. The maximum frontal diameter is 85 milimeters, compared with a world average today of 95 milimeters. The lowest racial mean reported is that of the tiny Vedda: 91 milimeters. The frontal-parietal index of 61.1 is lower than that of any racial mean. The fronto-biorbital index, 84.5, is a primitive index (Eskimo 89.8, Maon 91.0, Bavarian, 95.7, Ainu 96.2). Measure after measure is noted as primitive, and specific Neanderthaloid traits are noted: "occiput with a definitely downward and backward slope." This is clearly not a *Homo sapiens sapiens* but some earlier form of *Homo sapiens.*

I have taken a special interest in two early skulls, the Utah Lake skull and the Del Mar skull. The Del Mar skull, it will be recalled, was found by M. J. Rogers about fifty years ago, and when a dating method appeared that had promise for determining this skull's age I was the only man still alive who knew of the skull and the circumstances suggesting considerable age. The Utah Lake skull was found in the 1930's, washed out of lake sediments. It was given to Dr. Hansen, a paleontologist of the University of Utah. He did what any paleontologist would do with any bone. He measured it and then compared it with skulls of varied types. He presented his data in tabular form, very difficult for most people to visualize. I reduced the data to graphs and for years showed classes that the Utah Lake skull fell into the *Homo sapiens* range rather than into the *sapiens sapiens* range. When one uses the same indexes to plot the Del Mar skull (see figure 52), it falls still farther down the scale, on some dimensions falling below the average for Neanderthals. In table 6, I have simply grouped these skulls under the three types of *Homo* that they fall into.

By the usual measures these early American skulls are like the Middle Paleolithic men of the Old World, and if these standard measures are meaningful, then these men are *Homo sapiens* but not yet *Homo sapiens sapiens.* Physical anthropology in America is in a know-nothing stage, meaning that its practitioners refuse to pay much if any attention to such differences in skull types, and they especially wish to avoid any dating of skulls by their morphology.

At San Diego, then, the sequence is relatively simple, and it is tempting to guess at the racial affinities. We know what the La Jollans of about 50,000 years ago looked like. They were long-

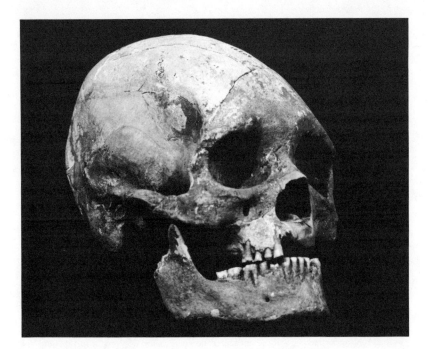

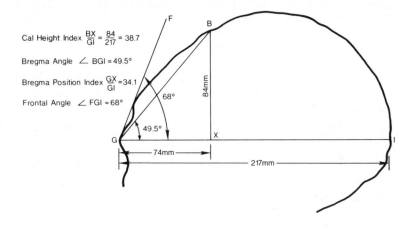

Cal Height Index $\frac{BX}{GI} = \frac{84}{217} = 38.7$

Bregma Angle $\angle$ BGI = 49.5°

Bregma Position Index $\frac{GX}{GI} = 34.1$

Frontal Angle $\angle$ FGI = 68°

FIGURE 52. The photograph of the Del Mar skull, dated by protein racemization at 48,000 years, is shown here with a diagram of its measurements and indices. By these measures this skull falls in the same grade of *Homo sapiens* as the Neanderthal men of 100,000 years ago. Yet as the photograph shows, in general appearance—especially in the lack of immense brow bridges—this appears to be a modern skull. (Photo, courtesy of the San Diego Museum of Man; measurements, courtesy of Spencer Rogers, San Diego Museum of Man)

TABLE 6
Ranking of Skulls

Genus	Skulls
Homo sapien sapiens	Modern man
Homo sapiens	Cro Magnon
	Tzu Yang
	Liu Chang
Homo sapiens	
	Utah Lake
	Neanderthal
	Del Mar
Homo erectus	Peking man

NOTE: Ranking of skulls by four indices: height index, bregma angle, bregma position, frontal angle. It is not implied that the Del Mar skull or the Utah Lake skull are Neanderthals. By these measures however, they do form a group, and the Del Mar skull falls lower on the scale than Neanderthal in three out of four measures. In bregma position it falls below Peking Man. The Nebraska, Sauk Valley, and Brazil skulls also probably belong in this early *Homo sapiens* grouping.

headed *sapiens* men and only dubiously placeable as *sapiens sapiens*. We know that there was more than one kind of these longheaded men with slab-sided skulls and that these types have been consistently labelled Australoid and Negritoid by leading physical anthropologists. We now have a glimpse of a still more primitive type of man, the beetling-browed men of truly Neanderthaloid status. With race tentatively established, it becomes tempting to try to put men and lithic industries together. If the La Jollans are Australoid and made unifaces—and that seems fairly reasonable—where are we to assign the others? Did the Negritoids make the blade and core work? Did the Europoids make the bifaces? These seem to fit with the Old World race and lithic correlations. That leaves the steep edge work to the Neanderthaloids.

Lithic Tradition, Race, and Time

| Heavy uniface | Australoid | 60,000 |
| Heavy biface | Europoid | 70,000 |

| Heavy blades | Negritoid | 80,000 |
| Steep edge | Neanderthaloid | 100,000 |

It may seem curious to say that we have made some progress when, while we can state such a problem and ask such questions, we have to end by saying that we are far from being sure of our answers. An informed guess as to these relationships between man, artifact, and time is given above. Professional archeologists are advised to take their heart pills before reading it. For my part, I view it lightly—as subject to change on the presentation of evidence to the contrary.

An era is ending, however, for we can now date the bones directly, and the primitive-appearing skulls turn out to be really old. Even the preliminary dating done so far yields dates out to 50,000 years and places these men in the middle Paleolithic in European terms. These are not modern men in terms of biology, culture, or time. It is becoming obvious that Dixon and Hooton were right. The race picture in America is complex, and such terms as Australoid, Negroid, and Europoid are more applicable to some groups than Mongoloid. It even appears highly probable that we must recognize a Neanderthaloid presence in America.

Hrdlička and many others have objected furiously to the use of such terms because they lead people to think in terms of identities and of present localities. No one argues that a group of Australians 50,000 years ago suddenly took off by land for America and ended up here pure in race and culture. On the other hand, everyone admits that man came from Asia to America. It is equally true that the men of Australia came from Asia. If at some distant time there were ancestral Australoids in Asia and some of them moved southeast to Australia and some of them north and east to America, then even if the movements covered thousands of years there might be some resemblances, and these might well appear both in physical and cultural traits. One would not expect identities, but one would expect resemblances. We can pursue this a bit to see if we do have such traces; these comparisons will be found farther on in this chapter, where the races of Asia are discussed.

It is hard to know which term annoys the American anthropologist more: Neanderthal, Australoid, Melanesoid, or Negritoid.

Negrito has a high-blood-pressure value in American anthropology. Yet responsible anthropologists such as Hooton and Coon have suggested that there were at least traces of such people in America. It really should not be so surprising when one reviews the history of the Negritos in Asia. They are widespread in refugia, indicating that they were one of the earliest people present. Or if one looks around in America, one finds that the Botocudo, one of the culturally primitive people of South America, are portrayed as pure Negrito: thick lipped, bushy haired, and very short in stature. The source for this description is the authoritative *Handbook of the South American Indians: Volume 1. The Marginal Tribes* (Steward, 1946), where the particular article is written by the well-known authority Alfred Metraux. No one can look at that picture and say anything but "Negrito." Nor can one consider the culture level of the Botocudo and say "late arrival." In Eurafrica traces of Negritos extend over 6,000 miles and at least 30,000 years, as will be discussed below, so it cannot be argued that such relationships are just impossible.

We can gain considerable insight into the effects of having waves of arrivals by considering the impact of the Europeans on the peoples of America that were here before A.D. 1500. In North America, especially in what is now the United States, the colonists flooded in in considerable numbers and occupied the land. They brought with them diseases for which the natives had no immunity, and as a result up to 90 percent of the native populations died very quickly. Into the emptied lands the settlers expanded, nearly totally replacing the native peoples. As a result of the continuing sweep of this type of contact in the United States, relatively few Indians survived. The original people are still here, however, though in greatly reduced numbers and located in a few spots, often out-of-the-way areas that were not particularly attractive to the newcomers.

The Spanish colonial lands felt a different impact. There newcomers were few, and they were oriented toward developed lands and settled people. They installed themselves as rulers in productive lands and intermarried with the local people and ignored good lands of little or no cultural development. Thus they explored and then ignored the eastern United States and California while they seized the civilized parts of America: central Mexico and Peru. They did not flood out and people the land, but intermarried with the native aristocracy. Their racial impact is to be understood in terms of the value system of the time: redheaded and blond enclaves in Spanish mining districts in northwest Mexico, strong influences in distant mineral-rich Peru on the "wrong side of the continent from Spain," or a distant outpost such as Santa Fe, New Mexico. These patterns are not explainable by mere proximity, and earlier men also may have made settlements distant from their points of entry. In Latin America the native people revived after the initial shock and racially are still there to an astonishing degree.

Thus the two cultural impacts were totally different. The Spanish conquistadors left islands of European mixtures in spots of special attraction. The English impact reduced the native peoples to islands in areas of least attraction. If the racial and cultural history of America is complex, then these types of racial influences may have occurred several times, and our failure to consider these possibilities surely has limited our understanding of the racial complex we call "the American Indian."

The evidence seems to me to suggest something like this. Initial occupation of America, via Bering Strait, was by longheaded people of at least three types, probably coming in separate waves. One was Neanderthaloid, one Negritoid, and the other Australoid. Later an Ainu-like group entered America, and last the Eskimo arrived. There may have been a Paleo-Siberian people who moved into the northern woodlands, or, equally likely, a northern woodland people who moved into Siberia. The first movements quite clearly were on the 100,000-year scale. It is too hazardous to guess at the time of the later movements, except to say that the Eskimo are late, and a Paleo-Siberian-Amerind movement somewhere between 10,000 and 30,000 years ago is a wild surmise. There seems to be no clear evidence of other people in northeast Asia in proximity to the Bering bridge, and it may be that all the rest are transoceanic arrivals at much later times. This could bring Oceanic and African Negroes, western Europeans of all sorts, eastern Asiatics of all kinds, including Negritoid people of Southeast Asia. Thereafter, innumerable mixtures with the classic Mongols, Oceanic Negroes, and Polynesians, whoever they are, would be expectable. There very probably was some late colonization of America, perhaps in the millenia just before and after A.D. 1. In short, the racial picture is probably enormously complex.

Some of this confusion will be overcome once the direct dating of skeletons by Bada's protein racemization is extended to some of the controversial skeletons lurking in museum closets. We can then expect to see race types set in chronological series. Advances in protein studies, and such minutia as earwax and Diego factors will also clarify race relationships. It is already clear that the earliest Americans, the longheaded, slab-sided, beetling-browed folk of at least two types—high vaulted and low vaulted—were not Mongoloid. They were members of the sticky earwax, non-Diego-blood-type people, and these are Australoid-Negroid-Europoid people. They are even now east Asiatic as to residence and surely precede the classic Mongols in southeast Asia, probably precede them in central east Asia (China), and possibly do so in northeast Asia (Siberia). We can well take a look at these potential first Americans' relatives who stayed home.

MEN FROM ASIA

Early man came to America from Asia, and in considering the peopling of America one should start with Siberia and discuss the cultural and racial sequences at this doorstep to America. But this is a forlorn hope at present, for we know almost nothing of that area. Archeologically it is an enormous space with occasional sparks of information, about like a match glowing in a football stadium. Chester Chard (1956, 1959, 1960, 1963) and others have repeatedly summarized the little known, but it is hopelessly too little and too late for the earliest Americans. If we are to gain insights into the men and lifeways of the earliest Americans, we must look beyond Siberia.

On the American side of Bering Strait we are only a little better off. We know that back of the Eskimo there is a microblade lithic tradition, and this can be related to developments in Siberia. Still earlier there are traces of projectile points suggestive of the Paleo Indian Hunters, but these traces of man in the high Arctic are relatively late. The oldest traces of man so far are the bone tools found at Old Crow in the Yukon, which date to about 30,000 years

ago (Harington, Bonnichsen, and Morlan, 1975; Bonnichsen, 1978).
They are highly significant, for not only do they date man in America at nearly three times the generally accepted dates but they show
that men could live in the high Arctic as early as that. Unfortunately,
our knowledge of these men is most fragmentary, being limited to
flaked bones of the Pleistocene megafauna—elephants and the like.
The one developed bone tool is a hide scraper no different from historic tools for this purpose, but this too is of great importance, for it
illustrates once again that fundamental tool types may continue in
use unchanged for 30,000 years, and perhaps longer.

We know even less about the Siberian side of Bering Strait.
Eskimo occupied its shores. The Eskimo show clear Mongoloid race
influences by having some B blood types and dry earwax, both good
Mongoloid markers. Inland the people were forest dwellers and
reindeer keepers, and among these people Hrdlicka found near
duplicates of North American Indians. The thought pattern of the
1930's assumed that this was the source of the American Indians,
but there are two obvious flaws in this hasty conclusion. First, these
could just as well be American Indians flowing back into Asia.
Second, given the great diversity of American Indians in time and
space and in races, these people could account for only some of the
North American Indians. The time depth now apparent—and
already strongly suggested in Hrdlicka's day—was simply ignored.
The variation in the American Indians was underplayed or attributed
to miraculously rapid divergence; one pure race entry and 2,000
years will do. Incredible remarks, and from the leaders in the
field—no wonder we got lost.

Our knowledge moves by leaps. Anatoli Derevianko (1978)
reports that recent discoveries in Siberia show man's presence not
only about 35,000 to 40,000 years ago, but between 100,000 and
150,000 years ago. While he thinks the first people in northern
Siberia date to only about 28,000 years ago, he notes that they had
chopper-chopping tools. These appear in America on something like
a 100,000-year time level. Men must have carried this technology
through the Bering Strait, and to do this they had to be in northern
Siberia. It seems clear that we have other discoveries to make in
Siberia.

Further south the Ainu of Japan signalled the presence in east Asia of Europoid people, but time, route, and the full meaning of this has escaped much discussion. One rarely sees any mention of the fact that there are strongly Europoid tribes on the Siberian mainland, along the lower Amur River, for instance. This is all the odder since Hooton and Dixon indicated the presence of Europoid people among the Indians. South of that one encounters the oft-reported but seldom noted presence of Negritos in China. Japanese history might be said to be that of Mongoloid people pushing the Europoid Ainu out of the islànds of Japan, mostly after the time of Christ.

Similarly, Chinese history is that of the Mongoloid people from the northwest of China pushing out the Negrito people of southeast Asia, who as late as the early centuries A.D. were still the dominant people of south China. Indeed in a real sense they are still there, for the short, dark south Chinese are pretty clearly the result of the mixture of the Mongols with the smaller, darker folk who had long been there. The Negrito folk survive in pure groups in the mountains of the Philippines, in Malaya, in isolated spots in New Guinea, and in the Andaman Islands, and they survived in Tasmania into the nineteenth century. We even have a bit of archeological data bearing on the antiquity of their presence, for in a cave in Borneo a skull typical of their race turned up at the 40,000-year time level. In terms of the antiquity of man, this is a very recent date, but when it is combined with the distribution of these Negrito people and their simple culture, one has the hint that these may be among the earliest, if not the earliest, *sapiens* men in Asia. It is not too adventurous to guess that they will prove to be the predecessors of the Ainu in Japan.

And that brings up one of those changing ideas that illustrate how knowledge advances by fits and starts and in spite of us professors. I learned in anthropology in the early 1930's that there was nothing in Japan earlier than the Neolithic, then thought to date to about 5,000 years ago. Now it appears that not only was there an upper Paleolithic in Japan, taking us back 20,000 or 30,000 years, but there was a lower Paleolithic, and that calls for something in the 100,000-year scale (Ikawa-Smith, 1978). If the Japanese are newcomers to Japan and the Ainu are either Neolithic or upper Paleolithic arrivals, then who were these earlier people? The most obvious candidates in the landscape are the Negritos, with some possibility of Australoids lurking in the vicinity, and if we have plenty of time maybe both were in Japan. This is all of immense interest to the peopling of America, for the sequence of race types that might have entered America via Bering Strait suggests: Negrito, Australoid, Caucasoid, and belatedly, the Mongoloid Eskimo.

The men of the Upper Cave at Choukoutien show that at that time, about 20,000 years ago, there was a mixture of races present in China. Skulls found there have been described as one Eskimo and a couple of types of slab-sided longheads, duplicating some of the early skull types in America. Back of the Upper Cave population, we leap to about 350,000 years—about, for figures range from 200,000 to 500,000 for Peking man. The skulls are long, low, beetling-browed, and all have apparently been broken into by hungry men. The stone tools in the site are surprisingly well made and include flaking to produce blades. Breuil, the noted French archeologist, said that many features of the tools at Choukoutien were not found in France until the upper Paleolithic (cited in Boule and Vallois, 1957, p. 145). He commented especially on the presence of true gravers and other tools of fine workmanship. The broken skulls, the good tools, the use of fire, all suggest that a more developed man was present and dining on *Homo erectus*, and something of just this sort now appears more likely, for Chang (1977) reports the finding of an advanced form of Peking man. The brows show reduced ridges; the skull vault is more vertical sided and thinner. This would be a good candidate for the earliest form of man to reach America.

Looking farther south in Asia, one finds masses of small dark folk indicated as the original inhabitants of the area. There are two sorts: Negritos and Australoids. We know the history of neither with any certainty. The Negritos seem to be the earlier people in southeast Asia. The Australoids may have a center of origin farther to the west, perhaps in India, and may be somewhat later arrivals in the Far East. It is not inconceivable that the Australoids are the result of racial mixing—some Europoid race's mixing with the Negritoids, then over vast periods of time segregating out as a relatively stable race type. Certainly the Australoids are dark skinned as are the Negritos, but they are beetling browed and hairy. These are not Negrito characteristics but would be natural traits to pick up from the Europoids.

The gist of this is that there are many races involved in Asia, and if man-in-America is man-out-of-Asia the expectation would be that there would be many races entering America. Late entries of mixed groups—or, more extreme, of one pure race, with divergence in America—is no longer a tenable view. We know that man is ancient in America and that a distinctive type or types entered first, to be followed later by other types of men. By the Bering Strait route alone, we can expect men close to the Neanderthal stage of development, Negritos, Australoids, Europoids, and Mongoloids, and just such sequences have been suggested on the basis of evidence in America. Colonization by other peoples who crossed both the Atlantic and the Pacific many millennia later further complicated this picture.

STONE TOOLS IN ASIA

When we turn from the race picture to the culture picture, with emphasis on stone tools, we find somewhat the same picture as for the races. The nearer one comes to the Bering Strait, the less one knows.

Most of the discussion of Siberian stonework has centered on a few sites in south-central Siberia, near Lake Baikal, for instance. This is nearly 3,000 miles from Bering. It is a bit like discussing Bering Strait in terms of the archeology of California. Most of the Siberian archeology known and reported is clearly upper Paleolithic in time and cultural level. It has bifacially flaked points, struck blades, microblades, and all the trappings well known in Europe and south Russia on the 20,000- and 30,000-year levels. It would not be surprising to find eventually that this represented the expansion to the north and east of the hunters of the great mammals of the north Eurasian forests and the northern grasslands. Perhaps it was a spillover of these people that brought the skills of hunting the huge mammals of the Pleistocene into America via Bering Strait. Or, as suggested earlier, maybe it was the reverse: American hunters entering Siberia. There certainly is a continuity of microblade work from Siberia through Alaska into America. Microblades are struck from prepared cores, and the relatively tiny flakes were often inset on bone to make harpoons or hafted for bone and woodworking tools. Often the blades were sharpened by special techniques, such as a blow on the edge that split off a vertical chip, very effectively renewing the cutting edge. This is the burin technique and is now well documented in America on the Paleo-Indian level of 10,000 years ago.

Also widespread in Siberia, often mixed in with the fine work of the Great Hunters, is a wide array of crude, heavy stonework. All people used some crude and heavy stonework for jobs that demanded just such implements. This makes it difficult to say, when looking at a mixed assemblage, whether what one sees is a mixture of new and old (mixed in the site from differing times), a mixture of two or more traditions intermingling in one people, or simply a functional mixture because even advanced people have some crude work to do. We lack good stratigraphy to test for the early pure sites of crude lithic materials. Since these crude lithic industries appear in America in pure sites, it seems expectable that such sites will eventually be found in Siberia. The mixed materials now being reported may then be either survivals or simple mixtures, and we will have to wait and see what the Soviet archeologists find. From Japan we already know that pure sites of lower Paleolithic–type implements are being found. China provides us with at least the Choukoutien site, a pure lower Paleolithic site. We can expect more.

If the time that we are looking at for man in America is nearer 100,000 years than 10,000 years, then we can and should look a good deal farther afield than we have looked. If we have men in America that look like Negritos and Australians—and some of the best anthropologists in America have had the temerity to say that such men are or were here—then perhaps we should look at the Negrito and Australian cultures to see if there are any parallels to America. The reasoning here is this. If there are racial resemblances and these are the result of men from Asia coming to America, then there should also be cultural resemblances, for these men must have brought their cultures with them. One may even invert this argument. If we find physical anthropological resemblances and cultural resemblances associated in both the Old World and the New World, we have greatly increased the probability that groups of men bearing specific cultures entered America as separate entities. The arguments then would shift to whether these could be preserved over such stretches of time.

Our view of races is infinitely too static and pure, and not just in America. It has been blithely ignored that there is evidence for a Negrito influence in Europe. Boule and Vallois reviewed this evidence briefly in 1957. They noted that there were Negroids of Bushman type in Europe at Grimaldi and spread widely in Italy, but also in the Rhone Valley. They concluded that this "must of necessity have been due to the fact that this race was formerly represented in our country by a whole group" (p. 292). They quote Verneau: "We must therefore admit that an almost Negro element lived in Southwestern Europe towards the Mid Quaternary Era, between the Spy race and the Cro Magnon race." I met this problem as a freshman when we were told that the skeletons at Grimaldi were thought by some to be Negroid, but that others disputed it. We were not told that in the Grimaldi Cave there were little figurines carved in the round that showed what these people were like in the flesh. They show the females to have had the classic Bushmanoid steatopygia. In layman's language, the women accumulated fat in the buttocks equivalent to a camel's hump; it was a built-in rumble seat for babies. It marks only one race: the Bushmen of south Africa.

As an interesting aside, the art of the south African is distinctive in that it features stick men usually shown in action. This distinctive art is found from south Africa right on up into Spain. It is totally different from the usual European cave art, where human figures are rare and where animal figures are featured and usually shown in static scenes. Thus for Eurafrica we have a race and cultural distribution traceable over a 30,000-year time span, with the survival of this complex being in south Africa almost 6,000 miles away from its northernmost extension in the past.

Can one point to Australian and American connections when the distance is so vast? Well, south Africa to Europe is no small distance, but the question is not whether such culture traces could persist, but whether they did. And the vast distances are meaningless if the cultures in question once had wider distributions. For the Australoid race and culture complex, the question is its distribution in the past. If it originated in Asia and became isolated and virtually fossilized in Australia, why could it not also have reached America and become fossilized in out-of-the-way places here? For the Negritoid people, we have already seen that they can be easily traced as far north as China and the Philippines, and they survived as far south as Tasmania, where they even retained their ancient lower Paleolithic culture. Faced with that kind of distributions, it is not difficult to envision men of central and southeast Asia being at one time or another in the vicinity of the Bering Strait. So, let's look at the cultures of these people.

When I graduated in anthropology at the University of California at Berkeley, we had to take senior examinations and write a senior essay. We had no advance notice on our essay topic but chose our topic from the set of possibilities we were presented after we entered the examination room. One question called for cultural comparisons, and I chose to compare the southern California Indians with the Australians. I pointed out that they not only had Australoid physical traits but they shared ceremonies, such as initiation of the boys at puberty with the exclusion of the women, with the women warned away with the use of a bull roarer. In these ceremonies ground paintings were used. That is already a considerable list of similiarities to contend with, but it can be extended. Both people used throwing spears and a curved throwing stick in hunting; the bow and arrow is very late in America and especially in southern Califronia and never reached Australia. Only a part of Australia had returning boomerangs; the rest used simpler, curved throwing sticks such as the Indian people of the Southwest were still using at the beginning of this century. Even the pattern of stone tool making was similar. In both Australia and southern California, stone was worked unifacially, and originally there were no bifaced points or knives, and stone tools were not hafted but hand held. It is a formidable list of comparisons to have "just happen." It is much more reasonable to expect a historical connection and, since the people of America and of Australia both came out of Asia, to look to Asia for the ancient common root for both the physical men and the culture. In this case we have the interesting connection of a race type and a culture type. This analysis suggests that it was the Australoids who bore the planoconvex lithic tradition.

The Australians have always fascinated me, and I should long ago have gone there to see the aborigines. Everything that I read of them struck responsive chords. I had seen just such people among the American Indians, and I was aware that many people had written of Australoids in America. I was also aware of the bitter resistance to such a notion, but, from work in southern California and in the desert, I was also aware of extensive cultural parallels. M. J. Rogers read widely about the Australians and was forever comparing the stone circles in the desert with Australian sleeping shelters. So, over the years I have read in desultory fashion on Australia. I have compiled a list of trait similarities for Australia and the southern California area.

American-Australian comparisons:
Physical: Australoid and Negritoid types present
    Early *sapiens* forms present: Gow Swamp in Australia
                            Nebraska man and others in America
    No direct comparison of these types is implied; only the presence in both areas of primitive *sapiens* men.
Cultural: Two (or more) Lower Paleolithic lithic traditions
        1. Unifacial work: Kartan culture in Australia, La Jollan in America
        2. Blade and core work: Small tool and, later, Pirrian in Australia
           Blade and core work in southern California
Ceremonial
    Stone alignments
    Stone circles
    Male puberty rites
        female exclusion
        bull roarer used to warn women away
    Ground paintings
Economic
    Spear thrower used; bow absent
    Curved throwing stick for hunting
        (returning boomerangs have limited distribution in Australia)
    Mano and metate for grinding wild seeds
        (limited distribution in Australia)

No domestic animal other than dog
Absence of pottery
Absence of boats except in areas of New Guinea contact
Use of reed and bark bundle rafts

The list could be extended, and not all elements in the list are of equal value, but the combination of these traits is extensive enough to be significant. Individual items could be expanded upon, and I will do so with one here.

Stone alignments in Australia can be grouped as fish traps, monoliths, heaps, and linear and elaborate arrangements (Gould, 1968; Gould and Gould, 1968; Rowlands and Rowlands, 1966; Campbell and Hossfeld, 1966). All of these are also found in the Colorado Desert of southern California. Perhaps the best reporting has been by Robert Begole for the Borrego State Park area (1979), but M. J. Rogers (1939) long ago reported on them, and Morlin Childers has recorded vast areas of all types listed for Australia, although he has not published his findings. In the Colorado and Mohave deserts it is obvious that the stone features are very old, for they occupy ancient landforms, have extreme weathering, and the pollen from beneath such weathered stones indicates that they were piled when the climate was vastly different from the present: a full glacial-pluvial climate. At the moment we lack any determination of just which glaciation.

In America as in Australia there has been little success in dating these stone alignments. In Australia they are still in use, and we gain immensely from reading the Australians' explanations. Stone circles in the desert have been a source of endless debate. Rogers thought them to be sleeping circles and cited Australian parallels. I have looked at the Australian campsite plans, and I do not find circles—clear areas, with windbreaks, but usually of elliptical or crescent form, not circles. Circular cleared areas in Australia were made as threshing floors. Wild plants were stacked on these cleared areas like little haystacks. When dried, they were threshed, and the seeds were gathered up and winnowed. This would account for a great many of the stone circles in the Colorado Desert area. Other stone circles in Australia had a pile of rocks or a single rock in the center, and just such circles are also found in America. In Australia these are known to be cult centers, and men will go long distances to bleed themselves onto the rocks in a life- and food-producing ceremony. There may be groups of these circles, with each one representing an individual clan.

Some of the Australian stone alignments are elaborate—virtual mazes—and mazelike stone alignments are well known in our deserts. Other stone alignments wander about seemingly aimlessly, both in Australia and in America. In Australia some of these stone lines are to warn the women of sacred areas that they are to avoid, and the probability is that this was their function in America also. The difficulty with these comparisons is that we know form and function in Australia but only form in America, for the use of these stone figures is lost here. The historic people denied building them, but rather attributed them to men of the past. Even if they stood alone as evidence, they would be impressive, but, when associated with similar wooden and stone tools and ceremonies and especially with such oddities as female exclusion compounded by the use of the bull roarer to warn the women away, the data become powerfully suggestive of some cultural connection.

To a southern California archeologist, one of the most striking things in Australian archeology is the stone tool kit of the Kartan culture. This work duplicates that of the La Jollan culture. The work is strongly unifacial. Cobbles were split to provide a flat striking surface, though at times a natural flat surface was used. All flakes were then struck off from that surface. The result is a core or core tool, with a haystack outline, or, as the Australians prefer, with the shape of a horse hoof. There were many uses for flakes without much sharpening of the edges or of shaping the flakes into definite, fixed tool types. Much use was made of scraper planes, some hand axes (bifacially flaked tools), and some deep concave notches on flakes to make spoke shaves for shaft working. The tools were used primarily, if not exclusively, as hand-held tools, and their principle use was for working wood to make spear shafts, wooden shields, wooden bowls, and digging sticks. This tool set was in use by at least 26,000 years ago.

There are problems with Australia. Just as in America, archeologists began with the expectation that there was no great antiquity for man on the continent. Tindale, their pioneer archeologist, storm-

ily argued against this notion of Recency and for a Pleistocence presence for man in Australia (1937, 1957, 1974). He thought of man
as being present as early as perhaps 100,000 years ago, whereas his
colleagues were thinking of 5,000 years. Dates are now out to about
30,000—six times his opposition's guess and one third of the way
to Tindale's estimate. Most recently, there are news releases of
100,000-year-old finds.

Meanwhile in the Gow Swamp in south Australia a whole set
of skeletons has appeared that was at first publicized as *Homo
erectus*. Now, though, the skeletons are being described as very
primitive *Homo sapiens*. Quite obviously we have a form of mankind somewhere in the transition zone, and it is hairsplitting to argue
about which side of the line he is placed on. Astonishingly, this
primitive form of modern man survived in Australia up to about
8,000 years ago. This is no small thing. The sea barriers between
Australia and the mainland have been very effective in preventing
any of the higher mammals except man—and the dog that he
brought with him—from reaching Australia. The first man to reach
Australia already had watercraft capable of crossing a water gap of
something like forty miles, and it now appears likely that this was
a type of man in the transition zone between *Homo erectus* and
Homo sapiens. The Australian archeologists acknowledge that the
presence of such people indicates that they have whole chapters of
Australian archeology yet to find.

Australia, like America, thus seems to have been peopled by
waves of humans that reached there at different times, bearing
different cultures, and representing different races. The Gow Swamp
people are an enigma at present. What culture did they bear? Who
were the bearers of the Kartan culture that parallels the La Jollan
culture? We do not yet know.

Oddly, we do know what race is represented in Tasmania.
These are Negritos, a type called Tasmanoid, and they were represented on Borneo 40,000 years ago. If they are not the first inhabitants, they may be second only to the Gow Swamp people. Most
unfortunately, they disappeared under the impact of the British,
leaving very little description of their way of life and relatively little
knowledge of their material culture. They had rafts made by tying
bundles of buoyant materials together, and with these they went

to offshore islands to get sea birds and their eggs. This is an excellent way to get blown away and, survival permitting, to begin to people adjacent islands. This may help explain their having reached Australia across formidable sea barriers.

India has a mixture of stone industries that are poorly understood as to time and external relationships. The earliest materials are said to be much like the early African stonework. The hand axe tradition of bifacial flaking of heavy tools is well represented, especially in western India, but it also appears far to the east, reaching even into Indonesia. One gets lost in discussions of Clactonian, Levallois, and other techniques. When one leaves the technical jargon and looks at the illustrations, one finds things a good deal simpler. Under the heading of clactonlike flakes are illustrated long, bladelike flakes that must have been struck from elongate cores. They are indistinguishable technologically from the blade and core work at such sites as Texas Street, Calico, and the Yuha Desert. When the lithic industries are arranged by terrace heights, the clactonlike flakes are earliest, followed by proto-Levallois, and finally by microliths. Elongated or bladelike flakes are illustrated in late Soan B, and about one half of these have facetted butts, showing that they were struck from cores with carefully prepared platforms. The early Soan material of northwest India, which was first reported by Movius, is strikingly like La Jollan material (see figure 53) and somewhat like the Kartan materials from Australia (Movius, 1949). It is characterized by unifacial work that produced typical thick cores, which were at the same time chopping tools. The flakes struck from them were very often used without retouch.

It seems rash to suggest connections between such extreme locations. However, the unifacial work is known to run northward in Asia at least as far as Manchuria. In America it appears from the Bering Strait area south to Tierra del Fuego, according to Junius Bird, who made the comment when he handled a set of southern California material in New York some twenty years ago. Concerning India and Asia in general, archeologists have repeatedly commented on the incredible survival over immense time periods of the early fundamental tool types. And it must not be forgotten that the parallels reach into race and culture. No one denies that man came to America out of Asia, but too many have looked only at northeast

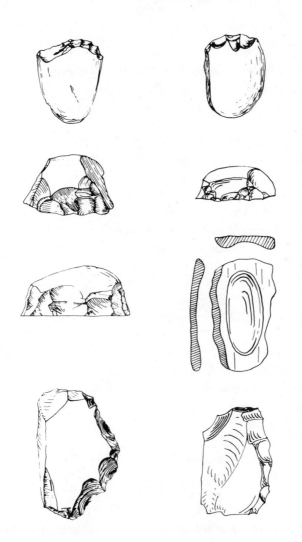

FIGURE 53. This sketch compares some early Soan tool types (*left*) with La Jollan tool types (*right*). The metate is present with these tools in America, and, given the miserable reporting of this implement, it may also be present in Asia. It surely is present in Australia, where this type of tool making is dominant. The top row shows unifacially flaked cobbles. On the next row are cobbles split in two and then flaked unifacially. Another tool of this kind (split cobble) is shown on the third row—from India—opposite a metate from America. Finally, the artifacts on the bottom row are large, slablike flakes that are unifacially retouched. These startling resemblances were not found by exhaustive seeking for pairs, but by comparison of illustrations of short sets of type tools.

Siberia, or at most at eastern Siberia. But if the time period under consideration is longer, then we are entitled to look farther, and that leads us to southeast Asia, to India, and to Australia. There we find both the races of mankind often suggested as the earliest entrants to America and the lithic traditions that are now appearing in America at the earliest levels. When one adds to that curved throwing sticks, spear throwers, ceremonial stone alignments, initiation ceremonies with such pecularities as exclusion of the females and warning them by use of the bull roarer, the evidence of ancient connection becomes too extensive to be lightly dismissed.

We know so little that any new report is likely to raise innumerable questions and have potentially far-reaching meaning. Karl Hutterer discussed some of the evidence appearing in Asia (1976). He noted that in the Pintu rock shelter in northeastern Luzon a most peculiar sequence was found. The lowest two soil layers had a blade tool assemblage with small scrapers and no pottery. The overlying strata had a totally different lithic industry— Hoabinhian—and had pottery. Early blade and core work should not seem too startling in an area where this manner of working stone was present as early as Choukoutien. It is even interesting to note that the Philippines is an area of ancient Negrito culture. Were they blade and core people?

Hutterer's article appeared in *Current Anthropology*, where many articles are subjected to extensive discussion. Chester Gorman in discussing it commented on the persistence of ancient lithic technologies in Asia. He noted that some pebble and flake tool types persisted for nearly a million years with little change. Hoabinhian tool assemblages that reach back into the Lower Paleolithic persisted as late as A.D. 1000. In Australia, D. R. Moore commented, the Hoabinhian flake and core industry gave way to a highly developed blade industry about 5000 B.P. Hoabinhian in Australia is also called the Kartan culture, and it is the look-alike of the American La Jollan culture. The gist of this is that in Asia and in America one gets similar sequences sometimes, with the blade and core work in early levels and with enormous persistence of ancient lithic technologies through time and space.

These are the lithic technologies that appear in America, and they were apparently available both early and late—how convenient.

There are huge gaps in the distributions of such lithic assemblages between Asia and America, but the gaps seem to be filling. The British Mountain, Canada, assemblage (see figure 54) would fit well into the southern California early blade and core assemblages. One could wish for better-dated sites, but at least this looks like a straw in the wind.

It would be possible to press the similarities further, but in terms of our present knowledge—with all the uncertainties of archeological dating, with the lack of detailed knowledge of specific lithic industries by sites, and especially with the enormous time and space gaps in our knowledge in Asia—it is futile to do so. The lithic industries that appear in America are all in Asia, and men in America came from Asia. It seems more probable to me that those men brought those lithic traditions with them than that they independently reinvented them in America.

And here again time obtrudes. When the age of man in America could be thought of, even if only philosophically, as a mere 2,000 years, then looking at the Lower Paleolithic of Asia could be thought of as a form of madness. When we progressed to thinking of the age of man in America as only 12,000 years, there was little point in looking beyond the Upper Paleolithic material of eastern Siberia. The microblade work there had parallels in America, and so the Asiatic source was accepted without many qualms. We now have moved to dates in America that touch 100,000 years, and this should move us to consider materials in Asia on that time level. It is by no means certain that we have the ultimate dates for America, for in the Colorado Desert and elsewhere in the West there are sets of steep-edge flaked artifacts that fit no known cultural pattern, and they are weathered beyond all other lithic tool types.

We have moved from a time when Soan–La Jollan comparisons could be brushed aside as too widely separated in time and space to possibly be related. Lower Paleolithic artifacts including unifacial core work now are known at least as far north as Manchuria, and they reappear in Alaska. The gap is in the area of our greatest ignorance. In time, the La Jollan has jumped back from 5,000 years to 50,000 years. With the time and space gap closing at that rate and with the prehistory of northeast Asia and northwest America still poorly known, it seems reckless indeed to discard the possibility

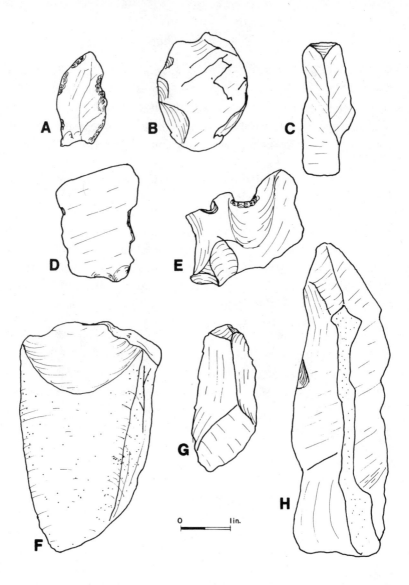

FIGURE 54. This assemblage from British Mountain in Canada duplicates the blade and core material from Texas Street, Buchanan Canyon, and the Yuha Desert (see figures 40, 44, and 45). It is thought that the British Mountain site is old, but no firm dates have been suggested. *A* and *B* are flakes with some edge retouch. *C* is a triangular, blade-type flake, while *D* is a large, flat flake. *E* is a flake with a concave scraper worked into one edge. *F*, itself a large flake, has another flake removed to make it a possible chopping tool. *G* appears to be a thick flake, and *H* is a very large, triangular, blade-type flake. Only typological comparison with American stonework is intended here.

of racial and cultural connections, especially when the cultures and the races are so similar on the two sides of the gap. Uncomfortable as it may be, we are forced to face comparisons across broad gaps in time and space. It is clear that all the races that appear early in America are present in Asia, and we can even begin to glimpse some race and cultural connections. That is a lot of progress.

Chapter 9

Past and Present

THIS has been a personalized and retrospective inquiry into the age of man in America, and, as has been very evident, it was not only ancient man that was being discussed but also the modern men who peer so selectively at the evidence before them. I am under no illusion that my gaze is any less selective than that of others. It is different, and the difference is between those who refuse to speculate and those who are willing to do so. It is the Kroeberian school, which could insist in the 1930's that our hard evidence reached to only 2,000 years or later to only 12,000 years, versus those of us who keep trying the tenuous bits of evidence to see how they fit.

I like the analogy of the jigsaw puzzle. No one piece of the puzzle tells you what the picture is. From each piece, or from a few pieces, one might make a tenuous guess. When enough pieces are fitted together, the nature of the picture can be seen, and progress in assembling the whole piece then moves faster. If one attempts to see the whole picture, one tends to reach this acceleration point more quickly. I find in working with students and struggling with colleagues that some try to see the whole picture and some shrink from it as nonscientific. Further, I find that, even when they try, individuals differ greatly in their ability to see the fit of tenuous bits of evidence. Some can see what the picture will be early on; others only much later. People differ even more in their comfort in trying to make out the pattern—some eagerly guessing, others insisting on assembling all or most of the bits before doing any guessing. I speak of "comfort" in making out patterns with all due deliberation, for I have seen men become acutely uncomfortable when forced into speculation about the meaning of the facts before them. They want to stick to the facts, just the facts—or so they say. I find that in actuality everyone speculates a bit, but people's speculation is determined by their cultural pattern, the particular school of thought in which they have been raised.

Furthermore, these differences probably have deep psychological roots. It has been noted that, if people are shown a pair of objects and asked to comment on them, a sharp difference appears. One type of person will tell you all the differences between them; the other will tell you all the similarities they share. This is the hallmark of two very different minds. The difference man sticks to facts; he loves to measure and plot and weigh and calculate, and he tends not to go one inch beyond his charts. The similarities man tends to look widely around him and to pick up tenuous bits of evidence, exclaiming with interest on how like this bit is to something that he has seen or read somewhere else. He tends to spin a web of connections. It is a spider's web to the difference man— insubstantial, unimpressive, unscientific. To the similarities man, it is symmetrical and beautiful and evidence of meaningful patterns, even if constructed of gossamer. There should be no doubt in anyone's mind where I stand. I am a classic similarities man.

But there is a further dimension to this. We do have schools of thought. Young men go to school and sit at the feet of the "great masters" and drink deeply not only of their learning but of their attitudes and prejudices. As a result it is usually possible to tell either from looking at a man's publications or from talking with him where he went to school and hence which mental track he is running on. This type of ongoing tradition sets the pattern of thought and directs fields down set paths. It is true of all fields, as was so well set out in Kuhn's *The Structure of Scientific Revolutions* (1970).

It is, then, sad to see the world of study concerned with the antiquity of man split into warring camps with anger and contempt boiling in the scholarly journals. Much of the problem is simply the conflict between men of differing psychological makeups, with the major source of misunderstanding flowing from the difference men, who simply cannot understand the similarities men and come not only to mistrust them but to dislike them thoroughly. The similarities man, on the other hand, often respects the difference man. It is to his finely honed, carefully measured facts that the similarities man turns for much of his constructions. The pity of it is that we really need both types.

It is hard to change the set of a field when minds are made

up and when nothing less than perfect evidence is accepted. But there is no perfect, no absolute knowledge. The so-called absolute dates churned out from the laboratories of the physical chemists all have cautionary flags, a plus or minus within which it is probable that the true date falls. But it is only probable that the true date does fall even there. The C-14 dating system that was embraced as the ultimate word in dating has proved to be subject not only to systematic error, which of course can be corrected for, but to random errors, for which there is no guard except more dates, preferably from dissimilar dating systems.

When a new idea is advanced, it necessarily challenges the previous idea. This disturbs the holders of the previous idea and threatens their security. The normal reaction is anger. The new idea is then attacked, and support of it is required to be of a high order of certainty. The greater the departure from the previous idea, the greater the degree of certainty required, so it is said. I have never been able to accept this. It assumes that the old order was established on high orders of proof, and on examination this is seldom found to be true. Some of what we believe in science is habitual: we have learned it in our academic infancy and repeated it *ad nauseum* and so believe it implicity and have never questioned its validity. I have referred before to the classic case of the latter part of this century: the drifting continents.

The evidence that the continents were all together in the not-too-great past in geologic terms is painfully obvious in biology and should long ago have been obvious in geology. Instead, the geologists lampooned the notion that continents drifted around until the geophysicists demonstrated that they were moving today and have been for tens of millions of years. The tenuous facts, and some very solid facts, were always there, but the established fields rejected them because they conflicted with their firmly held notions, which they mistook for facts, naturally. So why should Wegner and his supporters have been asked for inordinate levels of proof? They were right, and the entire fields of geology and geophysics were wrong.

The gist of this argument is that the case for the antiquity of man in America and its reception is no different from that of innumerable other cases of new ideas. Once the notion of the recency of man in America was established, all other ideas were treated as if they were the rantings of madmen or at least of men who did not understand that which archeology had established and from which it was not to be moved by anything less than a case of absolute evidence.

This is indeed curious when it is considered that the association of man with extinct animals in America was reported from Jefferson's day onward and that more than a hundred years ago such chemical tests as the fluorine method had shown that the ages of the human bones and those of the Pleistocene animals were the same. The fluorine method could not tell what the absolute age was, only that the animal bones and the human bones had the same age, but the extinct animals spoke of something on the ten-thousand-year scale at least. Further, stone tools were found in conditions suggesting great antiquity, and the form of the tools supported that suggestion. In the early days these finds were often made by amateurs and enthusiasts with no training in either archeology or geology, and a lot of foolish claims were made. But some finds were made by trained men, and they were also brushed aside. J. D. Whitney's finds of stone tools in the very latest Pliocene (read very latest Pleistocene in modern terminology) were and still are treated as some sort of idiocy. Read with some knowledge of the history of geology, they are rather modest claims for antiquity for man in the Sierras of California.

The men who did the most at the turn of the century to freeze the field of American archeology were W. H. Holmes and Aleš Hrdlička. Holmes examined and destroyed a great many claims for the antiquity of man and cast doubt on all the rest. There was always a flaw that he could pick in the evidence for antiquity. It is an unbeatable technique, for there is no absolute evidence, and there are always alternative explanations. It is to Holmes's credit that toward the end of his long and destructive life he called attention to the fact that, although he had shown the weakness of a great many claims for high antiquity for man in America, he had not disproved all the cases. He admitted that the fact that there were many situations that all indicated the possibility of very early man in America should not be ignored. Too few have noted this.

One of Holmes's investigations was of the stonework in the vicinity of the Great Falls of the Potomac. There are immense accumulations of flaking debris there, and the area undoubtedly was a camping and quarrying and tool-making zone. He identified it all as recent work, but he illustrated classic Paleo-Indian points. True, he had no way to know that decades later this type of point would be found with the extinct animals of the late Pleistocene, but he was supposed to have been a geologic expert, and, if he was, he should have seen some evidence of the presence of man at least 10,000 years ago, for that is no small amount of time. It is too often overlooked that Holmes entered the field as an artist and worked over into being the authority on the geologic field of archeology.

Why in the face of this kind of evidence should it be required that the proponents of high antiquity be required to present inordinately great amounts of evidence to prove that the early position was wrong? I do not mean this in any way to be an excuse for poor work or inadequate work. I simply mean to point out that the foundations of the recency-of-man-in-America school stand on quicksand.

Holmes's companion in arms—and they were indeed a militant pair—was Aleš Hrdlička. Hrdlička started out studying the insane, branched out into physical anthropology, and became the single most destructive individual in American archeology in the first half of this century. He reviewed physical anthropology and concluded for the recency of man, the very great recency of races, the great plasticity of man, and the certainty that any skeleton more than a few thousand years old would be markedly different from any living man. He showed, to his own satisfaction, that all the skeletons found to which great antiquity were attributed were just like some living Indian and often like some Indian group living in the same area where the skeleton was found. None of his assumptions were sound. Man is very ancient, *sapiens* man may be as old as 250,000 years, and races are probably in excess of 50,000 years old and may be far older. Note that the Tasmanian skull form was in existence as early as 40,000 years ago. Weidenreich, the great physical anthropologist, found a whole series of Mongoloid traits in *Sinanthropus*, the man of Choukoutien (1943). The skull of the Swanscombe lady in England is said to fall on the low end of the English woman's scale. Both date to about 300,000 years ago. If these tenuous notions, based on many measurements, are right, the modern races are foreshadowed by 300,000 years ago. Hrdlička was totally wrong.

His friends have often chided me for seeing only the harm that he did and have pointed to the immense amount of work he did in physical anthropology and the fact that he was virtually the founding father of physical anthropology in America. All true, I suppose, but he also falsified the evidence on the Florida skull, attacked Sellards on his Pleistocene skulls from Florida on specious grounds, and together with Holmes put those valuable skulls into limbo. They did so not only as scientists but with personal attack. We can do without that in science and scholarship. To which some readers may comment: look who is talking. The point of my argument is not to engage in personal attack, but to use these men as examples of how fields get set in a particular posture. It is often on weak evidence solidified by authority and usually by domineering types of personalities who use their position to destroy those with the temerity to come up with new and different ideas.

In the present archeological wars the position of Holmes and Hrdlička is held by such people as Heizer and Haynes and Griffin. Heizer was skilled at casting doubts on all sites that were counter to his dictum. True, he couched his criticism in the demand for better evidence and stated himself willing to change his ideas when hard evidence was presented, but it was pretty difficult to find evidence hard enough to change his hardened opinion. My book-length treatment of one small area in California, Heizer's domain, was crammed with measurements, statistics, and field observations that led inevitably to the conclusion that man was present in the last interglacial time. In 1977 Jason Smith, until recently of the Peabody Foundation, and B. O. K. Reeves, of the University of Calgary, were publishing weekly in the San Diego newspapers their triumphant discoveries of man of just this age. Reeves later filed an unpublished report with the San Diego Museum of Man (1977). Both are professional archeologists. Their reports all tend to verify my findings. So what Heizer, in his position as the leader of the California school of archeology for the twenty-five years between about 1940 and 1965, accomplished was to hold the field back for twenty years. Heizer is used here as a type. He had plenty of assistants, many of them trained by him.

We started with personalities, and here we are again. Science and scholarship are carried on not by bloodless automatons but by very real people, brimming with passions, psychologically patterned, and scholastically warped. Others might choose to use some other word than warped, but it seems appropriate to me. We do too much training, indoctrinating, and brainwashing in our schools, even in our graduate schools. There is far too little exploration and inquiry, the opening of minds by the asking of all kinds of seemingly outrageous questions. But enough of all this. It is important to seeing how we got into such a ridiculous posture, but it can be overdone. The real question is what is the antiquity of man in America. Who were these men, how did they get here, and what did they bring with them? After that come the questions of what they did in their splendid isolation in this New World before belatedly in time, though not so late as some think, men and ideas began to reach them from overseas.

Retrospectively, we have come a long way. We have moved in my lifetime from a view of man's antiquity in America as being 2,000 to 5,000 total years to a point at which we now are debating at San Diego whether my figure of 100,000 years was about right or was a bit conservative. We have moved from a view of man as entering America with an early Neolithic culture to the notion that the first arrivals were on an upper Paleolithic level. We are slowly coming to face the reality of a long and complex set of lower Paleolithic cultures in America, which not only must accompany the high dates now clearly about to be established but which are equally clearly indicated by the kinds of stone tools that long littered the American landscapes, trying in their mute way to signal the past presence of truly primitive men, the men of the lower Paleolithic.

There is much yet to do. We are moving rapidly on the dating of the very early remains, and with the multiple systems now being developed we will presently have cross-checking systems that should give us the nearest approach to hard dates that we have yet had. We have much to learn about the kinds of men, the physical anthropology of the first men, their contribution to the physical anthropology of the inhabitants the Europeans found when they "discovered" America in 1492. Now we know that it was a rediscovery and that we have whole chapters of cultural and racial additions to the American scene, roughly from the Bronze Age onward, to identify and to separate out from the races and accomplishments of the earlier Americans. What we have before us is a simultaneous great expansion of the time depth for the history of man in America and an equally great increase in the complexity of the whole picture of American prehistory.

It is a stimulating prospect, and scholars are going to be busy and excited for many decades to come working out the main outlines of the story. Thereafter will come the many decades of working out the details. I wish that it could be done without rancor and ill will, with open minds and hearts. But I know that it will not be. Schools of thought will be formed, and indefensible positions will be defended to the death. Nevertheless, in the long run the restless probing that characterizes scholarship will unearth the truth, and, despite all opposition, evidence will be compiled to overwhelming heights, to finally burst the dams of opposition. Thus it has always been, and thus it will always be. Man is ancient, and man is little changed. I do not know what our first Americans argued about, but I am sure that they held their opinions as firmly as any professor does today and with equal certainty that right was on their side. So be it. I have had the good fortune to live to see that my major themes—that the antiquity of man in America is lengthy, not short, and that the first entrants were on a Lower Paleolithic stage, not a Neolithic stage—win out. I hope for some more years so that I can see what we will learn now that the barriers of short chronologies are crumbling.

Glossary

ALLUVIUM. Sands and silts deposited by running water

ARTIFACT. A product of man; for example, a rock broken by man, usually for use as a tool or as waste in the making of tools

BLADE. A flake two or more times as long as it is wide, made by striking a core on one end in such a way as to split off a long flake

BLADE AND CORE. A lithic technology in which long, thin flakes (blades) are percussively separated from a rock (core), which may also be used as a tool

BERINGIA. A subcontinent-sized area in the Bering Strait that would be exposed by a 300- to 500-foot lowering of the sea

BIFACIAL FLAKING. A lithic technology in which tools are produced by striking blows off a rock's edge in alternate directions

CARTIFACTS. A term coined for broken rocks found by Carter in ancient formations

EOLITH. A broken rock over which there is controversy concerning whether man or nature is the manufacturer

FISSION TRACKING. Method for determining age of rocks by counting tracks left by high-energy particles released by the breakdown of radioactive minerals

FLAKE. A piece of rock driven off its parent rock, either to be used as a tool or as a byproduct of the making of a tool

GEOFACT. A rock broken by nature in such a way as to resemble human rock breakage

GEOMORPHOLOGY. The study of earth's surface phenomena

LOESS. Unstratified loamy silt deposits, believed to be deposited chiefly by wind

MANO. A hand-held stone for grinding seeds

METATE. A platter-sized slab of stone used for grinding seeds

MICROBLADE. A tiny, razor-sharp blade produced by percussive blows on a rock core

MIDDENS. The refuse heaps left by people on sites where they have lived; a valuable source of artifacts

NEOLITHIC. The most recent part of the Stone Age

OVATE BIFACE. A lithic technology in which tools are made by flaking rock alternately from one face and then the other

PALEO-INDIANS. Big game hunters of the American latest Pleistocene and early Recent geologic epochs

PALEOLITHIC. The earlier period of the Stone Age, characterized by cruder tools than the Neolithic

PEBBLE TOOL. A stream cobble from which man has removed a flake or two to give a sharp edge

PROTEIN RACEMIZATION. A method developed by Jeffrey Bada for dating material containing protein

SKREBLO. A chopping tool made of relatively thin rock fragment with the edge retouched only lightly if at all

STEEP EDGE. A lithic technology in which tools are formed by striking short flakes from the edge of a cobble or a slab of rock, leaving a steep edge rather than a thin, "sharp" edge

TALUS. A slope formed by rock debris, often at the base of a cliff

THERMOLUMINESCENCE. A method for dating rocks by measuring the electron output produced when they are heated to high temperatures

TUFA. Porous rock formed by deposits from springs or streams or, in arid-region lakes, through the work of algae

UNIFACIAL FLAKING. A lithic technology characterized by biscuit-shaped tools, with edge flaking done wholly or predominantly from one flat side of a rock

WEATHERING. The action of the elements on materials, such as rock, at or near the earth's surface, or the signs of that action

Bibliography

Allen, C. R., P. St. Amand, C. F. Richter, and J. M. Nordquist. 1965. Relationship between seismicity and geologic structure in the Southern California region. *Bulletin of the Seismological Society of America* 55:753–797.

Allen, C. R., L. T. Silver, and F. G. Stehli. 1960. Agua Blanca Fault: A major transverse structure of northern Baja California, Mexico. *Bulletin of the Geological Society of America* 71:457–482.

Alsozatai-Petheo, J. 1975. The East Rim site. Master's thesis, Eastern New Mexico State College, Portales, New Mexico.

Antevs, E. 1935. The spread of aboriginal man to North America. *Geographical Review* 25:302–309.

Arnold, B. A. 1957. Late Pleistocene and Recent changes in land forms, climate, and archaeology in central Baja California. *University of California Publications in Geography* (Berkeley) 10:201–318.

Bada, J. L., and P. M. Helfman. 1975. Amino acid racemization dating of fossil bones. *World Archaeology* 7:160–173.

Bada, J. L., R. A. Schroeder, and G. F. Carter. 1974. New evidence for the antiquity of man in North America deduced from aspartic acid racemization. *Science* 184:791–793.

Bard, J. 1979. The development of a patination dating technique for Great Basin petroglyphs utilizing neutron activation and X-ray fluorescence. Ph.D. diss., University of California, Berkeley.

Barnes, A. S. 1939. The difference between natural and human flaking in prehistoric flint implements. *American Anthropologist* 41:99–112.

Bass, E. J., and J. F. Jackson. 1977. Cerumen types in Eskimos. *American Journal of Physical Anthropology* 47:209–210.

Beals, R. 1957. Father Acosta on the first peopling of the New World. *American Antiquity* 23:182–183.

Begole, R. 1974. Archaeological phenomena in the California deserts. *Pacific Coast Archaeological Quarterly* 10:51–69.

Bell, E. H., and A. Hrdlička. 1935. A recent Indian skull of apparently low type from Nebraska. *American Journal of Physical Anthropology* 20:5–11.

Birkeland, P. W. 1972. Late Quaternary eustatic sea-level changes along the Malibu Coast, Los Angeles County, California. *Journal of Geology* 80:432–448.

Bischoff, J. L., R. Merriam, W. M. Childers, and R. Protsch. 1976. Antiquity of man in America indicated by radiometric dates on the Yuha burial site. *Nature* 261:128–129.

Black, D., ed. 1933. Fossil man in China. Peking: Memoirs of the Geological Survey of China.

Blackwelder, E. 1931. Pleistocene glaciation in the Sierra Nevada and Basin ranges. *Bulletin of the Geological Society of America.* 42:865–922.

Bonnichsen, R. 1978. Critical arguments for Pleistocene artifacts from the Old Crow Basin, Yukon: A preliminary statement. In *Early man in America from a circum-Pacific perspective*, ed. A. L. Bryan. Occasional Papers, no. 1. Edmonton, Canada: Department of Anthropology, University of Alberta.

Bordes, F. 1978. Preface. In *Early man in America from a circum-Pacific perspective*, ed. A. L. Bryan. Occasional Papers, no. 1. Edmonton, Canada: Department of Anthropology, University of Alberta.

Boule, M., and H. V. Vallois. 1957. *Fossil men.* New York: Dryden Press.

Breuil, H. 1931. Le feu et l'industrie lithique et osseuse à Choukoutien. *Bulletin of the Geological Society of China* 11:147–154.

Broecker, W. S., and P. K. Orr. 1958. Radiocarbon chronology of Lake Lahontan and Lake Bonneville. *Bulletin of the Geological Society of America* 69:1009–1032.

Broecker, W. S., D. L. Thurber, J. Goddard, T. Ku, R. K. Mathews, and K. L. Mesolella. 1968. Milankovitch hypothesis supported by precise dating of coral reefs and deep-sea sediments. *Science* 159:297–300.

Bryan, A. L., ed. 1978. *Early man in America from a circum-Pacific perspective.* Occasional Papers, no. 1. Edmonton, Canada: Department of Anthropology, University of Alberta.

Campbell, E. W., and W. H. Campbell. 1935. *The Pinto Basin site.* Southwest Museum Papers, no. 9. Los Angeles: Southwest Museum.

Campbell, E. W., E. Antevs, C. A. Amsden, J. Barbieri, and F. Bode. 1937. *The archeology of Pleistocene Lake Mohave.* Southwest Museum Papers, no. 11. Los Angeles: Southwest Museum.

Campbell, T. D., and P. S. Hossfeld. 1966. Australian aboriginal stone arrangements in north-west South Australia. *Transactions of the Royal Society of Australia* 90:171–178.

Carter, G. F. 1978a. An American Lower Paleolithic. *Anthropological Journal of Canada* 16:2–38.

———. 1978b. The American Paleolithic. In *Early Man in America from a circum-Pacific perspective*, ed. A. L. Bryan. Occasional Papers, no. 1. Edmonton, Canada: Department of Anthropology, University of Alberta.

———. 1977a. Hibiscus rosa sinensis. *Anthropological Journal of Canada* 15:26–27.

———. 1977b. The metate: An early grain-grinding implement in the New World. In *Origins of Agriculture*, ed. C. Reed. The Hague: Mouton.

———. 1977c. On the antiquity of man in America. *Anthropological Journal of Canada* 15:2–19.

———. 1976a. Chinese discoveries of America, Fusang again. *Anthropological Journal of Canada* 14:10–24.

———. 1976b. Voting in science: Early man in the New World. *Anthropological Journal of Canada* 14:28–30.

———. 1973. Some comments on Calico. *Anthropological Journal of Canada* 11:25–26.

———. 1971. Pre-Columbian chickens in America. In *Man Across the Sea*, ed. C. L. Riley, J. C. Kelley, C. W. Pennington, and R. L. Rands. Austin: University of Texas Press.

———. 1966. On pebble tools and their relatives in North America. *Anthropological Journal of Canada* 4:10–19.

———. 1964a. California as an island. *Masterkey* 38(2):74–78.

———. 1964b. Stone circles in the deserts. *Anthropological Journal of Canada* 2:2–6.

———. 1959. Man, time and change in the far Southwest. *Annals of the Association of American Geographers* 49:8–33.

———. 1958a. Archaeology in the Reno area in relation to the age of man and the culture sequence in America. *Proceedings of the American Philosophical Society* 102:174–192.

———. 1958b. Is there an American Lower Paleolithic? In *Miscellanea Paul Rivet, Octogenario Dicata*, vol. I. Mexico D.F.: Universidad Nacional Autónoma de México, XXXI Congreso Internacional de Americanistas.

———. 1957. *Pleistocene man at San Diego*. Baltimore: John Hopkins Press.

———. 1956. On soil color and time. *Southwestern Journal of Anthropology* 12:295–324.

————. 1954. Disharmony between Asiatic flower-birds and American bird-flowers. *American Antiquity* 20:176–177.

————. 1952. Interglacial artifacts from the San Diego area. *Southwestern Journal of Anthropology* 8:444–456.

————. 1951. Man in America: A criticism of scientific thought. *Scientific Monthly* 73:297–307.

————. 1950. Evidence for Pleistocene man in southern California. *Geographical Review* 40:84–102.

————. 1941. Archaeological notes on a midden at Point Sal. *American Antiquity* 6:214–226.

————. 1938. Lima bean farming and soil erosion in the Encinitas area. *Pacific Coast Geographer* 4:15–20.

Chang, K. C. 1977. Chinese paleoanthropology. *Annual Review of Anthropology* 6:137–159.

Chard, C. S. 1963. The Old World roots: Review and speculations, early man in the western American Arctic. *Anthropological Papers of the University of Alaska* 10:115–121.

————. 1960. Routes to Bering Strait. *American Antiquity* 26:283–285.

————. 1959. New World origins: A reappraisal. *Antiquity* 33:44–49.

————. 1958. New World migration routes. *Anthropological Papers of the University of Alaska* 7:23–27.

————. 1956. The oldest sites of northeast Siberia. *American Antiquity* 21:405–409.

Childers, W. M. 1977*a*. Archaeological survey of the Yuha Basin, Imperial County, ed. J. von Werlhof and S. von Werlhof. El Centro, California: Imperial Valley College Museum.

————. 1977*b*. New evidence for early man in the Yuha Desert: A preliminary report. El Centro, California: Imperial Valley College Museum.

————. 1977*c*. Ridge-back tools of the Colorado Desert. *American Antiquity* 42:242–248.

————. 1974. Preliminary report on the Yuha burial, California. *Anthropological Journal of Canada* 12:2–9.

Cole, J. R., and L. R. Godfrey. 1977. *Archaeology and geochronology of the Susquehanna and Schoharie regions.* Oneonta, New York: Hartwick College.

Colvinaux, P. A. 1964*a*. The environment of the Bering land bridge. *Ecological Monographs* 34:297–329.

————. 1964*b*. Pollen evidence from Arctic Alaska. *Science* 145:707–708.

Cooke, R. U. 1970. Stone pavements in deserts. *Annals of the Association of American Geographers* 60:560–577.

Coon, C. S. 1962. *The origin of races.* New York: Alfred A. Knopf.

Covarrubias, M. 1955. *The eagle, the jaguar, and the serpent.* New York: Alfred Knopf.

Crabtree, D. E. 1972. *An introduction to flint working.* Occasional Papers, no. 28. Pocatello, Idaho: Idaho State University Museum.

Cressman, L. S. 1977. *Prehistory of the Far West, home of vanished people.* Salt Lake City: University of Utah Press.

————. 1973. *An approach to the study of far western North American prehistory: Early man.* Bulletin no. 20. Eugene: University of Oregon Museum of Natural History.

Dart, R. A. 1971. On the osteodontokeratic culture of the australopithecinae. *Current Anthropology* 12:233–236.

————. 1960. The bone tool-manufacturing ability of Australopithecus. *American Anthropologist* 62:134–143.

Darwin, C. 1909. *The Voyage of the Beagle.* Harvard Classic edition. New York: P. F. Collier and Son. First published in 1890.

Daugherty, R. D. 1962. The intermontane western tradition. *American Antiquity* 28:144–150.

Davis, E. L. 1966. How did they live and how long ago? In *Ancient hunters of the Far West,* ed. M. J. Rogers. San Diego: Copley Press.

————, C. W. Brott, and D. L. Weide. 1969. The western lithic co-tradition. San Diego Museum Papers, no. 6.

Day, M. 1965. *Guide to fossil man.* London: Cassel.

Derevianko, A. P. 1978. On the migrations of ancient man from Asia to America in the Pleistocene Epoch. In *Early man in America from a circum-Pacific perspective,* ed. A. L. Bryan. Occasional Papers, no. 1. Edmonton, Canada: Department of Anthropology, University of Alberta.

Dethier, B. E. 1958. The problem of man's entry into the New World. Ph.D. diss., Johns Hopkins University, Baltimore.

Dixon, R. B. 1923. *The racial history of man.* New York: Charles Scribner's Sons.

Dorn, R. I. 1980. Characteristics and origin of rock varnish. B.A. honors thesis, University of California, Berkeley.

Evans, P. 1971. Towards a Pleistocene time-scale. In *The Phanerozoic time-scale, a supplement.* Part 2. London: Geological Society of London.

Evernden, J. F., and G. H. Curtis. 1964. The potassium-argon dating of

Late Cenozoic rocks in East Africa and Italy. *Current Anthropology* 6:343–385.

Fenollosa, E. F. 1912. *Epochs of Chinese and Japanese art*, 2 vols. Reprint. New York: Dover Publications, 1963.

Fladmark, K. 1978. The feasibility of the northwest coast as a migration route for early man. In *Early Man in America from a circum-Pacific perspective*, ed. A. L. Bryan. Occasional Papers, no. 1. Edmonton, Canada: Department of Anthropology, University of Alberta.

Funk, R. E. 1977. "On 'some paleolithic tools from northeast North America.' " *Current Anthropology* 18:543–544.

Gagliano, S. M. 1967. *Occupation sequence at Avery Island.* Coastal Studies Series, no. 22. Baton Rouge: University of Louisiana Press.

———. 1964. *An archeological survey of Avery Island.* Baton Rouge: Coastal Studies Institute, Louisiana State University.

Giddings, J. L. 1964. *The archeology of Cape Denbigh.* Providence, Rhode Island: Brown University Press.

———. 1960. The archeology of Bering Strait. *Current Anthropology* 1:121–130.

———. 1954. Early man in the Arctic. *Scientific American* 190:82–89.

———. 1952. Ancient Bering Strait and population spread. In *Science in Alaska: Selected papers of the Alaskan Science Conference*, ed. H. Collins. Arctic Institute of North America, Special Publication No. 1.

Gilmore, R. M. 1942. Review of microtus voles of the subgenus stenocranius (Mammalia: Rodentia: Muridae), with special discussion of the Bering Strait region. Ph.D. diss., Cornell University.

Gould, R. A. 1973. Australian archaeology in ecological and ethnographic perspective. Warner Modular Publications, module 7.

———. 1971. The archaeologist as ethnographer: a case from the Western Desert of Australia. *World Anthropology* 3:143–177.

———. 1968. Living archaeology: The Ngatatjara of western Australia. *Southwestern Journal of Anthropology* 24:101–122.

———., and E. B. Gould. 1968. Kunturu, an aboriginal sacred site on Lake Moore, western Australia. *American Museum Novitataes*, no. 2327.

Graham, J. A., and R. F. Heizer. 1967. Man's antiquity in North America: Views and facts. *Quaternaria* (Rome) 9:225–235.

Grahmann, R. 1955. The Lower Palaeolithic site of Markkleeberg and other comparable localities near Leipzig. *Transactions of the American Philosophical Society* n.s. 45(6).

Grootes, P. M. 1978. Carbon-14 time scale extended: Comparison of chronologies. *Science* 200:11–15.

Gruber, J. 1948. The Neanderthal controversy: Nineteenth century version. *Scientific Monthly* 67:435–439.

Hansen, G. H. 1934. Utah Lake skull cap. *American Anthropologist* 36:431–433.

Harington, C. R., R. Bonnichsen, and R. E. Morlan. 1975. Bones say man lived in Yukon 27,000 years ago. *Canadian Geographical Journal* 91:42–48.

Harland, W. B., and E. H. Francis, eds. 1971. *The Phanerozoic time scale. Part I.* Special Publication No. 5. London: Geological Society of London.

Haynes, C. V. 1973. The Calico site: Artifacts or geofacts? *Science* 181:305–310.

Heizer, R. F. 1964. The western coast of North America. In *Prehistoric man in the New World*, ed. J. D. Jennings and E. Norbeck. Chicago: University of Chicago Press.

———. 1940. The archaeology of central California: I. The early horizon. *Anthropological Records* 12:1–84. University of California Press.

———, and R. A. Brooks. 1965. Lewisville—ancient campsite or wood rat houses? *Southwestern Journal of Anthropology* 21:155–165.

———, and S. F. Cook. 1952. Fluorine and other chemical tests of some North American human and fossil bones. *American Journal of Physical Anthropology* n.s. 10:289–304.

Hooton, E. A. 1933. Racial types in America and their relation to Old World types. In *The American aborigines*, ed. D. Jeness. Toronto: 5th Pacific Science Congress.

———. 1930. *The Indians of Pecos Pueblo.* New Haven: Yale University Press.

Hopkins, D. M. 1959a. Cenozoic history of the Bering land bridge. *Science* 129:1519–1528.

———. 1959b. History of Imurak Lake, Seward Peninsula, Alaska. *Bulletin of the Geological Society of America* 70:1030–1046.

———. 1959c. Some characteristics of the climate in forest and tundra regions in Alaska. *Arctic* 12:215–220.

Howells, W. W. 1960. *The distribution of man.* Scientific American Reprint Series. San Francisco: W. H. Freeman & Company.

Hrdlička, A. 1935. The Pueblos, with comparative data on the bulk of the tribes of the Southwest and northern Mexico. *American Journal of Physical Anthropology* 20:235–460.

————. 1917. Preliminary report on finds of supposedly ancient human remains at Vero, Florida. *Journal of Geology* 25:43–51.

Hutterer, K. L. 1976. An evolutionary approach to the southeast Asian cultural sequence. *Current Anthropology* 17:221–227, 237–242.

Ikawa-Smith, F. 1978. Lithic assemblages from the early and middle Upper Pleistocene formations in Japan. In *Early man in America from a circum-Pacific perspective*, ed. A. L. Bryan. Occasional Papers, no. 1. Edmonton, Canada: Anthropology Department, University of Alberta.

Jenks, A. E. 1936. *Pleistocene man in Minnesota: A fossil* Homo Sapiens. Minneapolis: University of Minnesota Press.

————, and L. A. Wilford. 1938. The Sauk Valley skeleton. *Bulletin of the Texas Archaeological and Paleontological Society* 10:136–139.

Jennings, J. D. 1964. The desert West. In *Prehistoric man in the New World*, ed. J. D. Jennings and E. Norbeck. Chicago: University of Chicago Press.

Johnson, L. L. 1978. A history of flint-knapping experimentation, 1838–1976. *Current Anthropology* 19:337–372.

Kobayashi, H. 1975. The experimental study of bipolar flakes. In *Lithic Technology*, ed. E. Swanson. The Hague: Mouton.

Koehler, W. 1925. *The mentality of apes.* New York: Harcourt Brace.

Kraybill, N. 1977. Pre-agricultural tools for the preparation of foods in the Old World. In *The Origins of Agriculture*, ed. C. Reed. The Hague: Mouton.

Krieger, A. D. 1964. Early man in the New World. In *Prehistoric man in the New World*, ed. J. Jennings and E. Norbeck. Chicago: University of Chicago Press.

————. 1959. Comment on George F. Carter, man, time and change in the far Southwest. *Annals of the Association of American Geographers* 49:31–33.

Kroeber, A. L. 1973. The present state of Americanist problems. In *The Maya and their neighbors*, ed. W. W. Howells. New York: Cooper Square Publishers. First published in 1940 by D. Appleton-Century Co.

————. 1948. *Anthropology.* 2nd ed. New York: Harcourt Brace and Company. First published in 1923.

Ku, T.-L., and J. P. Kern. 1974. Uranium-series age of the Upper Pleistocene Nestor Terrace, San Diego, California. *Bulletin of the Geological Society of America* 185:1713–1716.

Kuenen, P. H. 1956. Experimental abrasion of pebbles: 2. Rolling by current. *Journal of Geology* 64:336–368.

Kuhn, T. S. 1970. *The structure of scientific revolutions.* Chicago: University of Chicago Press.

Laudermilk, J. D. 1931. On the origin of desert varnish. *American Journal of Science* 21:51–66.

Layrisse, M., and J. Wilbert. 1964. Absence of the Diego antigen, a genetic characteristic of early immigrants to South America. *Science* 188:1077–1078.

Leakey, L. S. B. 1934. *Adam's ancestors.* London: Methuen and Co.

——, R. D. Simpson, and T. Clements. 1978. Archeological excavations in the Calico Mountains, California: Preliminary report. *Science* 192:1022–1023.

Lee, T. 1961. The question of Indian origins. *Science of Man* 1:159–167.

——. 1957. The antiquity of the Sheguiandah site. *Canadian Field-Naturalist* 71:117–137.

——. 1955. The second Sheguiandah expedition, Manitoulin Island, Ontario. *American Antiquity* 21:63–71.

——. 1954. The first Sheguiandah expedition, Manitoulin Island, Ontario. *American Antiquity* 20:101–111.

Macdougall, J. D. 1976. Fission-track dating. *Scientific American* 235(6): 114–122.

McHenry, H. 1975. Fossils and the mosaic of human evolution. *Science* 190:425–431.

Martin, L. M., and J. F. Jackson. 1969. Cerumen types in Cherokee Indians. *Science* 163:677–678.

Mather, J. R. 1954a. The effect of climate on the New World migration of primitive man. *Southwestern Journal of Anthropology* 10:304–321.

——. 1954b. The present climatic fluctuation and its bearing on a reconstruction of Pleistocene climatic conditions. *Tellus* 6:287–301.

——. 1951. Pleistocene climates and their effect on the New World migration of ancient man. Ph.D. diss., Johns Hopkins University, Baltimore.

Matsunaga, E. 1962. The dimorphism in human normal cerumen. *Annual of Human Genetics* 25:227–286.

Meighan, C. W., and C. V. Haynes. 1970. The Borax Lake site revisited. *Science* 167:1213–1220.

Menghin, O. 1931. *Weltgeschichte der Steinzeit,* Vienna.

Milankovitch, M. 1936. Mathematische Klimalehre and astronomische Theorie der Klimaschwankungen. In *Handbuch der Klimatologie,* vol. 1. Berlin: Verlag von Gebrüder Borntraeger.

Minshall, H. L. 1976. *Broken stones.* San Diego: Copley Press.

——. 1975. A Lower Paleolithic bipolar flaking complex in the San

Diego region: Technological implications of recent finds. *Pacific Coast Archaeological Society Quarterly* 11:45–56.

———. 1974. Early man sites at Texas Street and Buchanan Canyon in San Diego, California. *Anthropological Journal of Canada* 12:18.

Mirambell, L. 1978. Tlapacoya: A Late Pleistocene site in central Mexico. In *Early man in America from a circum-Pacific perspective*, ed. A. L. Bryan. Occasional Papers, no. 1. Edmonton, Canada: Department of Anthropology, University of Alberta.

Montagu, M. F. A. 1955. The Natchez innominate bone. *American Journal of Physical Anthropology*, n.s. 13:395–396.

Moriarty, J. R. 1969. The San Dieguito complex. *Anthropological Journal of Canada* 7:1–18.

———. 1966. Culture phase divisions suggested by typological change coordinated with stratigraphically controlled radiocarbon dating at San Diego. *Anthropological Journal of Canada* 4:20–30.

———, and N. F. Marshall. 1964. Principles of submarine archaeology. *Pacific Discovery* 17(5):18–25.

Moriarty, J. R., and H. L. Minshall. 1972. A new pre-desert site discovered near Texas Street. *Anthropological Journal of Canada* 10:10–13.

Morlan, R. E. 1978. Early man in northern Yukon Territory: Perspectives as of 1977. In *Early man in America from a circum-Pacific perspective*, ed. A. L. Bryan. Occasional Papers, no. 1. Edmonton, Canada: Department of Anthropology, University of Alberta.

Movius, H. L. 1949. The Lower Palaeolithic cultures of southern and eastern Asia. *Transactions of the American Philosophical Society*, n.s. 38:330–422.

Muller, R. A. 1977. Radioisotope dating with a cyclotron. *Science* 196:489–493.

Nelson, R. L. 1953. Glacial geology of the Frying Pan River. *Journal of Geology* 62:325–343.

Orr, P. C. 1968. *Prehistory of Santa Rosa Island, California*. Santa Barbara: Santa Barbara Museum of Natural History.

———. 1967. Geochronology of Santa Rosa Island, California. In *Proceedings of the Symposium on the Biology of the California Islands*. Santa Barbara: Santa Barbara Botanic Gardens.

———. 1964. Pleistocene chipped stone tool on Santa Rosa Island, California. *Science* 143:243–244.

———, and R. Berger. 1966. The fire areas on Santa Rosa Island, California: Part I. *Proceedings of the National Academy of Science*, 56(5):1409–1416; Part II. 56(6):1678–1682.

Patterson, L. W. 1976. Blade technology in the Texas Archaic. In *The Texas Archaic: A symposium*, ed. T. R. Hester. Special report no. 2. San Antonio: Center for Archaeological Research, University of Texas at San Antonio.

————. Evidence of Asiatic influence on Texas Pleistocene technology. Manuscript in possession of L. W. Patterson, Houston, Texas.

Powers, W. R. 1973. Palaeolithic man in northeast Asia. *Arctic Anthropology* 10:1–111.

Prest, V. K. 1969. Retreat of Wisconsin and Recent ice in North America. *Geological Survey of Canada Map*, no. 1257A.

Raemsch, B. 1970. Preliminary report on Adequentaga. *Yager Museum Publications in Anthropology Bulletin* 2. Oneonta, New York: Hartwick College.

————. 1968. Artifacts from Mid-Wisconsin gravels near Oneonta, New York. *Yager Museum Publications in Anthropology Bulletin* 1. Oneonta, New York: Hartwick College.

————, and J. P. Timlin. 1971. Pleistocene tools from the northeast of North America: The Timlin site. *Yager Museum Publications in Anthropology Bulletin* 3. Oneonta, New York: Hartwick College.

Ranere, A. J. 1975. Toolmaking and tool use among the preceramic people of Panama. In *Lithic Technology*, ed. E. Swanson. The Hague: Mouton.

Reeves, B. O. K. 1977. Mission Valley–Mt. Soledad early man: Geological-archaeological sites and sections, descriptive listings. Manuscript on file with San Diego Museum of Man.

Rogers, M. J. 1966. *Ancient hunters of the Far West*. San Diego: Copley Press.

————. 1939. Early lithic industries of the Lower Basin of the Colorado River and adjacent desert areas. *San Diego Museum Papers*, no. 3.

————. 1929. The stone art of the San Dieguito Plateau. *American Anthropology* 31:454–467.

Rowlands, R. J., and J. M. Rowlands. 1966. Aboriginal stone arrangements in the Western Desert of Australia. *Mankind* 6:355–358.

Sanford, J. T. 1971. Sheguiandah reviewed. *Anthropological Journal of Canada* 9:1–15.

————. 1957. Geologic observations at the Sheguiandah site. *Canadian Field-Naturalist* 71:138–148.

Schuiling, W. C., ed. 1979. *Pleistocene man at Calico: A report on the Calico Mountains excavations*. Redlands, California: San Bernardino County Museum Association.

Schumm, S. A., and M. A. Stevens. 1973. Abrasion in place: A mechanism for rounding and size reduction of coarse sediments in rivers. *Geology* 1:37–40.

Sellards, E. H. 1960. Some early stone artifact developments in North America. *Southwestern Journal of Anthropology* 16:160–173.

————. 1952. *Early man in America: A study in prehistory.* Austin: University of Texas Press.

————. 1916. On the discovery of fossil human remains in Florida in association with extinct vertebrates. *American Journal of Science* 42(4):1–18.

Simpson, R. D. 1958. The Lake Manix archaeological survey. *Masterkey* 32:4–10.

————, and W. C. Schuiling. 1970. *Pleistocene man at Calico.* Redlands, California: San Bernardino County Museum Association.

Singer, C. 1979. Lithic study of Calico. In *Pleistocene Man at Calico*, ed. W. C. Schuiling. Redlands, California: San Bernardino County Museum Association.

Sollas, W. J. 1911. *Ancient hunters.* New York: Macmillan.

Sollberger, J. B., and L. W. Patterson. 1976a. The myth of bipolar flaking industries. *Newsletter of Lithic Technology* 5:40–41.

————, and ————. 1976b. Prismatic blade replication. *American Antiquity* 41:518–531.

Steward, J. H., ed. 1946. *Handbook of South American Indians: Vol. 1. The marginal tribes.* Smithsonian Institution, Bureau of American Ethnology, Bulletin 143. Washington, D.C.: United States Government Printing Office.

Stuiver, M., C. J. Heuser, and I. Yang. 1978. North American glacial history extended to 75,000 years ago. *Science* 200:16–21.

Swanson, E., ed. 1975. *Lithic technology: Making and using stone tools.* The Hague: Mouton.

Tindale, N. B. 1974. *Aboriginal tribes of Australia.* Berkeley: University of California Press.

————. 1957. Culture succession in south-eastern Australia from Late Pleistocene to the Present. *Records of the South Australian Museum* 13:1–49.

————. 1937. Relationship in the extinct Kangaroo Island culture of Australia, Tasmania, and Malaya. *Records of the South Australian Museum* 15:131–164.

Ting, S. 1937. Storm waves and shore-forms of south-western Scotland. *Geological Magazine* 74:132–141.

————. 1936. Beach ridges and other shore deposits in south-west Jura. *Scottish Geographical Magazine* 52:182–187.

Tolstoy, P. 1958. The archaeology of the Lena Basin and its New World relationships (part 1). *American Antiquity* 23:397–418.

Treganza, A. E. 1952. Archaeological investigations in the Farmington Reservoir area, Stanislaus County, California. Reports of the University of California Archaeological Survey, no. 14. Department of Anthropology, University of California, Berkeley.

Tricart, J., and R. Schaeffer. 1950. L'indice d'émousé des galets, moyen d'étude des systèmes d'érosion. *Revue Géomorphologie Dynamique* 4:151–179.

Tyson, R. A. 1979. Early aboriginal burial practices of southernmost California. Paper presented at the 43rd International Congress of Americanists (Vancouver).

von Wuthenau, A. 1975. *Unexpected faces in North America.* New York: Crown Publishers.

———. 1965. *Altamerikanische tonplastic, Das Menschenbild der Neuen Welt.* Baden Baden: Holle Verlage. Also published as: *The art of terracotta pottery in pre-Columbian Central and South America.* 1970. New York: Crown Publishers.

Wallace, W. J. 1962. Prehistoric cultural developments in Southern California deserts. *American Antiquity* 28:172–177.

Weidenreich, F. 1943. The skull of *Sinanthropus pekinensis*: a comparative study on a primitive hominid skull. *Palaeontologia Sinica* n.s. D 10. Peking: Geological Survey of China.

———. 1935. The Sinanthropus population of Chou Kou Tien. *Bulletin of the Geological Society of China* 14:427–461.

Wendorf, F. 1966. Early man in the New World: Problems of migration. *American Naturalist* 100:253–269.

———, R. L. Laury, R. Schield, C. V. Haynes, and P. E. Damon. 1975. Dates for the Middle Stone Age of East Africa. *Science* 187:740–742.

White, K., G. F. Carter, and M. Childers. 1979. Geomorphology and Time. *Anthropological Journal of Canada* 17.

Witthoft, J. 1955. Texas Street artifacts. Part I. *New World Antiquity* 2(9):132–134; Part II. 2(12):179–184.

———. 1952 A Paleo-Indian site in eastern Pennsylvania. *Proceedings of the American Philosophical Society* 96:464–495.

Wormington, H. M. 1944. *Ancient man in North America.* Denver: Denver Museum of Natural History. Fourth edition (revised) published in 1957.

Index

(A page number in bold-face type indicates an illustration.)